Books

FRENCH POLICY TOWARDS THE BAKUFU AND MEIJI JAPAN 1854–95

Léon Roches, photographed in Nagasaki, 1866

FRENCH POLICY
TOWARDS
THE BAKUFU
AND MEIJI JAPAN
1854–95

Richard Sims

JAPAN
LIBRARY

MEIJI JAPAN SERIES: 3

FRENCH POLICY TOWARDS THE BAKUFU
AND MEIJI JAPAN, 1854–95

First published 1998 by JAPAN LIBRARY

Japan Library is an imprint of Curzon Press Ltd
15 The Quadrant, Richmond, Surrey TW9 1BP

© Richard Sims 1998

British Library Cataloguing in Publication Data
A CIP catalogue entry for this book is
available from the British Library

ISBN 1–873410–61–1

Set in Garamond 11 on 12 point by LaserScript Ltd, Mitcham, Surrey
Printed and bound in England by Bookcraft, Midsomer Norton, Avon

CONTENTS

Introduction   *1*

1 The Establishment of Treaty Relations Between
   France and Japan   5
2 The Struggle to Enforce the Treaties, 1859–64   23
3 Léon Roches and French Support of the Bakufu,
   1864–68   48
4 France and the Consolidation of the Meiji Government,
   1868–80   73
5 France and the Emergence of Japanese Foreign Policy,
   1870–85   110
6 France and the Revision of the 'Unequal Treaties'   143
7 The Decline of French Influence, 1885–95   177
8 French Trade and Its Influence on French Policy   219
9 The Broader Picture: Modernization and Culture   235
Conclusions   296

Notes   *304*
Abbreviations   *368*
Glossary   *369*
Appendices   *370*
Bibliography   *373*
Index   *386*

INTRODUCTION

SINCE THE OPENING of Japan by the 1854 Treaty of Kanagawa
with Commodore Perry and the 1858 Treaties of Edo with
Townsend Harris and Lord Elgin foreign influence on Japanese
history has been enormous. For some historians the foreign
intrusion was the main cause of the Meiji Restoration, but even
if it was no more than the catalyst which allowed internal
pressures and forces to combine in a successful movement
against the Tokugawa régime, the presence of the Western
powers in Japan had a crucial effect on Japan's development; and
after 1868 the image of the West, the example of particular
Western countries and the role of individual Westerners were all
of great importance to Japan's modernization and emergence as
a modern state.

In view of the significance of the part played by Western
countries in Japan's development it is surprising that the
relations with Japan of some of them have been explored only
to a limited extent. Such neglect was never true of American-
Japanese relations, and in recent years a considerable amount of
attention has been paid to British involvement with modern
Japan. Other countries, however, have continued to be ignored,
at least to the extent that no overall studies of their relations
with Japan have been published,even if various aspects have
been examined, at different levels of detail and sophistication,
over the course of time.

Among the countries which have been relatively disregarded,
the most obvious, apart from Germany, is France. There is, for
instance, still no general survey of Franco-Japanese relations in
any language. A number of historians (most notably Takahashi

1

Kunitaro) have, it is true, written (generally in Japanese) about the contributions of Frenchmen to Japanese modernization; and the remarkable activities and personality of Léon Roches, who as French minister to Japan between 1864 and 1868 played a crucial role in the events which led to the downfall of the Tokugawa Bakufu (and who alone among French diplomats receives a mention in general histories of modern Japan), have drawn several scholars to study Franco-Japanese relations in the *Bakumatsu* period, that is to say the years preceding the Meiji Restoration of 1868. A good deal of this research has remained unpublished, however, and the only thesis which has appeared in book form, Meron Medzini's *French Policy in Japan during the Closing Years of the Tokugawa Régime*, is not wholly satisfactory because it accepted too readily the view of French policy which was put forward by the pioneering Japanese scholars, Otsuka Takematsu and Ishii Takashi, on the basis of both preconceived ideas about Western imperialism and limited access to French diplomatic records.

In this book I have put forward an interpretation of French policy in the *Bakumatsu* period which differs from Medzini's in placing more emphasis on differences of approach between French diplomatic representatives in Japan and the French Foreign Ministry. In particular, I argue that Roches was following his own *'politique personnelle'* rather than the policy laid down by the Quai d'Orsay in Paris. Because French policy in the late Tokugawa period has been studied relatively intensively, however, especially by Ishii, whose *magnum opus* on *Bakumatsu* diplomacy (*Zotei Meiji Ishin no Kokusaiteki Kankyo*) runs to a thousand pages, I have devoted proportionally less space to the pre-1868 years than to French relations with Japan in the decades following the Meiji Restoration.

In one respect a more detailed coverage of the post-1868 period is regrettable, since French policy towards Meiji Japan was, in sharp contrast to Roches' dynamic and imaginative approach, mostly cautious, negative and short-sighted. Nevertheless, in terms of understanding the nature of the diplomatic environment in which the Meiji government operated, a close scrutiny of the policies and activities of the main Western powers is necessary. Without, for example, examining closely the attitudes, and changes of tack, of Western diplomats (among whom the French were arguably the most consistently obstreperous), it is impossible to understand fully the difficulties which Japan faced in striving to secure the revision of the so-called unequal treaties imposed in the 1850s. Other aspects of Meiji foreign policy also need to be seen in the light of a detailed study of Western policies and attitudes. Japanese diplomacy at the time of the 1894–5 war with China, and especially in its immediate aftermath, is one obvious case. Even more light, however, is thrown on Japanese diplomacy by examining in depth, as I have tried to do, French policy towards Japan between 1883 and 1885. At that time France was encountering stiff Chinese opposition to the completion of its takeover of control of Vietnam, and its unanticipated military difficulties led it to seek Japanese cooperation against the Ch'ing government. The fact that the Meiji leadership resisted the very considerable temptation which the French government was eventually induced to hold out is a fact which students of Japanese foreign policy need to take into account.

The justification for exploring French diplomacy in Japan after 1868 at some length is also that it allows a better reflection of historical reality and reveals the superficiality of some of the assumptions and generalizations about Western policies towards nineteenth-century Japan. France was far less 'imperialistic' than is often implied in Japanese writing, for instance, and to apply that label to Roches without major qualification is a gross oversimplification. Moreover, although most French diplomats shared similar perceptions of Japan, they did sometimes differ in ways which are concealed by generalizations. Only a detailed treatment can bring out the extent to which French policy would be affected by the contrasting personalities and approaches of the diplomats whom the Quai d'Orsay sent to Japan. Although the focus of this book is on French policy, and the major source of information was the French Foreign Ministry archive at the Quai d'Orsay, I have tried to provide a picture of Franco-Japanese relations which goes beyond the normal confines of diplomatic history. Apart from surveying the development of trade between the two countries, and investigating the influence of economic factors on French policy, I have, for example, given significant attention to French diplomatic views of Japanese internal (especially political) development. This is partly because such views may have influenced policy but also because, as Japanese historians have come to appreciate, diplomats sometimes gained important insights through their contacts with Japanese leaders.

The final chapter, which deals largely with individual Frenchmen, such as the dedicated legal expert, Gustave-Émile Boissonade, surveys French contributions to Japanese modernization, French and Japanese knowledge and images of each other's country, and Franco-Japanese cultural interaction. This chapter partly reinforces the impression, which can hardly be avoided in a history of Franco-Japanese diplomatic relations, that France mattered far more to Japan than Japan did to France. In part, however, it shows that the relationship was not wholly one-sided, since it deals also with the phenomenon of *Japonisme*, the fascination with things Japanese, and especially woodblock prints, which affected many Frenchmen and had a significant influence on many innovative artists. In a balance-sheet of what each country owed to the other, it is important that the Japanese impact on Western, and especially French, painting and decorative arts is taken into account.

It remains for me to acknowledge my debts. They begin with my long-standing one to Professor Bill Beasley, since this book, although now substantially rewritten, has its origins in a thesis which he suggested and supervised. I wish also to acknowledge the guidance of Professor Mitani Taichiro and the late Professor Oka Yoshitake, both of whom gave me invaluable help when I was a research student at Tokyo University. I must further thank Paul Norbury for encouraging me to revise and expand my thesis for publication and allowing me sufficient time to delve into the substantial number of relevant books and articles which have appeared in recent years. Above all, however, I want to express my gratitude to my wife, Denise, who has, not for the first time, willingly taken the chore of typing and retyping off my hands, however busy she may have been with other commitments.

R. SIMS
SOAS, Autumn 1997

1

THE ESTABLISHMENT OF TREATY RELATIONS BETWEEN FRANCE AND JAPAN

THE HISTORICAL BACKGROUND OF FRENCH ACTIVITY IN THE FAR EAST[1]

WHEN FRANCE signed its first treaty with Japan on 9 October 1858 in Edo (Tokyo), it was playing its part in a process the significance of which no Frenchman at that time could imagine. That treaty was one of a number which the Bakufu (as the administration of the Tokugawa shogun, the feudal overlord of Japan, was known) concluded in the latter part of that year with several Western powers (the others being the United States, Britain, Russia and Holland). Marking, as they did, the end of more than two centuries of almost complete national seclusion, they came as a huge psychological shock to many Japanese, sparking off intense political debate and leading to a complex internal conflict which within ten years would bring about the resignation of the seventeenth shogun and the overthrow of the Bakufu. From 1868 Japan was to be controlled by a coalition of samurai reformers who acquired legitimacy by acting in the name of the imperial dynasty – once the ultimate power in Japan and now the only real claimant to sovereignty. Under the auspices of the young Meiji Emperor, and under the pressure of the Western threat to Japan's independence, the new Japanese government was to abolish the still substantial remnants of feudalism in the 1870s and embark on a modernizing path which led to successful war with China in 1894 and Russia in 1904, and ultimately to a titanic struggle with America and Britain between 1941 and 1945.

If one seeks to understand how it came about that France was among the powers which led the way in the opening of Japan, it is logical first to examine the record of French activities in Eastern Asia before the middle of the nineteenth century, and in particular to look for elements of continuity which might have determined, or at any rate influenced, the French role in the region in the 1850s. One such element was French concern with the propagation of Catholicism. This can be traced back to 1625, when it was decided to send a number of French Capuchins into India, China, Japan and Persia, in order to 'establish a series of missionary stations whereby land communications with the seats of Oriental trade might be rendered permanent'.[2] French missionaries did not actually gain access to Japan at this time, but in 1663 the *Société des Missions Etrangères* was founded in Paris, and some of the priests belonging to this important organization either penetrated into hostile regions where they suffered persecution, or (though here the Jesuits were more prominent) acquired positions of influence at Eastern courts. They provided a possible means of political penetration in their wake, and there were notable examples of this happening in Siam (Thailand) in the seventeenth century and in Annam at the turn of the nineteenth. In Annam, especially, the military and administrative ability of Pigneau de Béhaine was a significant factor in the acquisition of power by Gia Long,[3] but France was too occupied with the Napoleonic Wars to take advantage of the situation, and when, in 1821, it sought a treaty of commerce, it was refused by the new ruler, Minh Mang. In the 1830s Minh Mang instituted a policy of persecution against the missionaries and it was this which in the 1850s provoked Napoleon III, who was not insensitive to the value of religious support, to serious military action on the Church's behalf. His willingness to adopt a forceful policy opened up the prospect of similar French behaviour elsewhere in East Asia, even though intervention in South East Asia at times absorbed French attention and in 1858 made it more difficult to match American and British efforts to secure a treaty with Japan.

It was not only in Siam and Annam that French missionaries created opportunities for intervention which France was unable or unwilling to take up until the Second Empire. Persecution in Korea from the 1830s onwards inspired no determined effort to intervene until 1866,[4] while in China, where a notorious dispute between Jesuits and other missionaries had brought about the proscription of missionary activities, occasional executions of French priests went virtually unheeded until 1844. In that year, the diplomatic missions sent out by the then French king, Louis-Philippe, were fortunate in that China's concern with the more demanding 'barbarians' from Britain led it to make a few religious concessions. Not until the murder of Father Chapdelaine in 1856 did France use persecution as a pretext for taking up arms on behalf of missionary interests, and then only because Britain also had a claim to press against the Ch'ing empire.

The other strand of traditional French activity in East Asia was trade. In the seventeenth and eighteenth centuries, this was mainly a monopoly of state-backed companies. Cardinal Richelieu provided the first impetus, but it was Louis XIV's minister, Colbert, who made them important. One of his creations was the French East India Company of 1664, which, among other things, had control of France's China trade. The Company made no use of its privilege, however, and France's backwardness in the area was confirmed rather than reversed. In 1719 its China trade finally passed into the hands of the *Compagnie des Indes* and there was some activity, with 92 French ships entering Canton between 1720 and 1770, but with the French Revolution the Company disappeared and in 1791 the right to trade was opened up to private merchants. Under the new conditions commerce expanded with three or four French ships per year on average visiting Canton in the first quarter of the nineteenth century. Nevertheless, figures such as these were small for the new industrial age, and according to Cady, 'commercial considerations played a very minor part in the nineteenth century revival of French interest in the Far East'.[5] This view finds some support in the assertion of Dunham that 'most French manufacturers had no interest in foreign trade, knew little or nothing about foreign markets or the needs and wishes of foreigners, and sold goods for export only when they could not sell them at home'.[6] Change was on its way in the 1850s with Napoleon III's establishment of credit institutions such as the Comptoir d'Escompte which 'not only performed well the services of a commercial bank, but by engaging actively in colonial and Far Eastern affairs, became a valuable economic instrument of penetration',[7] but no appreciable results were seen before the 1860s.

It should be clear from the foregoing outline that France's involvement in the opening of Japan cannot be explained simply as a continuation of traditional French activities in East Asia, for until the mid-nineteenth century these were quite limited and only marginally related to Japan. More important was the fact that by the mid-nineteenth century technological development had changed the balance of power between Asia and the West fundamentally. By the 1840s, and especially after Britain's acquisition of Hong Kong in 1842, Western warships in Eastern waters were able to exert a more intimidating pressure. In this situation direct relations between Western and Eastern governments became possible, and unofficial activities tended to assume a subsidiary role.

The second reason for not emphasising the earlier historical record too strongly is that after two centuries France had achieved little in the way of tangible gains, and in particular no base which would serve as a ready launching point for an expedition to Japan. Nor was there anything in its Far Eastern tradition that bore directly on that country. French missionaries had played no part in Japan's 'Christian century', nor had French ships, in the early nineteenth century, visited Japan. In any case, Japan's stubbornly-maintained traditional policy of isolation made it a somewhat different proposition from other Far Eastern countries. As later events were to reveal, what happened in the rest of Asia was not necessarily repeated in Japan.

THE MOTIVATION BEHIND THE TREATY

Justification for considering the pre-1850 record as of limited relevance is to be found in the testimony of the French documents relating to the opening of Japan.[8] In fact, neither of the two main traditional elements in French Far Eastern activity played a decisive part in the establishment of treaty relations between France and Japan. Missionaries, it is true, were among the most ardent advocates of such a policy, which was hardly surprising, since the memory of the century when Japan had been open to Christianity and when conversions had take place on a scale which seemed astonishing to the nineteenth century had not been allowed to die.[9] France, too, as the only maritime Catholic country which remained in the first rank among the Powers was now the obvious and recognized protector to whom they looked. But though Japan's opening was one of the prizes most desired by French religious interests, the complete success of Japan's exclusion policy meant that the missionaries could not provide the French navy with any pretext for intervention or intimidation.

Only in 1844 was a slight breach made in that policy. In that year French missionary and naval needs came together when Captain Fornier-Duplan brought to the Ryukyu islands (which vaguely acknowledged both Japanese and Chinese suzerainty) a priest from the *Missions Étrangères*, M. Forcade, who intended to learn Japanese there in anticipation of the country's opening.[10] Two more French missionaries were left in 1846 but by 1848 one had died and the other was returned to Hong Kong on Admiral Cécille's instructions after Chinese protests at his presence. In the meantime, Forcade now promoted (as bishop of Samos) to vicar apostolic of Japan, had briefly returned to Europe in 1847. In Paris he was granted interviews not only with ministers, but also with Louis-Philippe. His pleas for greater help for French missionaries in the East Asia, however, met with little sympathy except from prime minister Guizot, and he was sent away empty-handed. In 1855 several more missionaries were sent to the Ryukyus, but no-one ever came near to setting a foot in Japan proper. This failure to penetrate the country helps to explain why the missionaries played a negligible part in the opening of Japan and makes less surprising the fact that relatively little attention was paid to their interests in the instructions given to Baron Gros, when he was chosen to head the French expedition to China and Japan in 1857.[11] Missionary wishes notwithstanding, he was ordered not to press the religious question, save to obtain permission for Frenchmen to practise their religion in the ports opened by

Japan, a concession which had already been obtained by other Powers by the time France signed its treaty.

That France, whose primacy in Far Eastern missionary operations had been recognized by the Pope in 1839 and whose new ruler was still eager to ensure religious support for the Second Empire, should go no further to advance missionary interests than Britain or the United States requires some further explanation. One factor was that French naval power was inadequate to compel Japan to concede more than it had to the other Powers, especially when Annam and China were making simultaneous demands on that power. Moreover, Britain and the United States might possibly have withheld support, had such a demand led to a renewal of open Japanese hostility to foreigners.

Nevertheless, reports from China had occasionally suggested during the previous few years that the Japanese had become less hostile towards Christianity, and for some time it did look as if a special religious demand would be made. In 1854 the Quai d'Orsay indicated to the French minister in China that a treaty with Japan 'should as far as possible assure to our missionaries the freedom to penetrate and establish themselves in the country'.[12] Furthermore, in the draft instructions concerning Japan drawn up for Baron Gros on 16 May 1857 the same demand was listed in almost identical words and was supported by the statement that 'it is of general interest that the illumination and the benefits of Christianity have the means of opening Japan and of modifying in time the religious prejudices which contributed in so large a measure to the closing of that Empire to foreigners'.[13] Gros was admittedly warned that he must proceed with caution in order to avoid awakening the distrust of the Japanese government, but the fact remains that it was at this point intended to seek for missionaries the right of access to the interior of Japan.

In the event, the issue of the right to proselytize did not feature in the 1858 negotiations. Before Gros' instructions were finally approved, the passage concerning religion was crossed out because, a note in the margin explains, it would be dangerous to raise the question.[14] Exactly why the Quai d'Orsay changed its mind so speedily is not apparent from the documents of the main Correspondance Politique series, but is explained by a memorandum for the foreign minister, dated

May 1857, which appears in the supplementary series of *Mémoires et Documents, Japon*. This document begins by asserting that missionaries abused their position in Japan in the seventeenth century and continues: 'The prejudices and the hatred of the Japanese government in this respect have remained the same; a Frenchman who has lived for four years in Japan as a licensee (*fermier*) of the Dutch trade told me recently that if one entered into negotiations with this country it would be necessary above all, lest one excite a deep distrust and compromise everything, to avoid raising the religious question. It might therefore be preferable to suppress in the instructions given to Baron Gros that which relates to the right of missionaries to establish themselves in Japan.'[15]

This alteration of Gros' instructions has two interesting aspects. In the first place, it seems to have been done without any regard for or consultation with the missionaries who had spent years waiting eagerly for the opening of Japan. Secondly, and somewhat ironically, the Frenchman, Charles Delprat,[16] whose views were given so much weight, may well have been an anti-clerical who objected to missionary penetration of Japan on principle. The very fact that he was allowed to live in Nagasaki suggests that he was not a Catholic, but more substantial evidence can be found in the tone of an earlier memorandum which he supplied to the Quai d'Orsay.[17] In this he praised Japanese civilization, asserted that there were worse examples of persecution by Christians in Europe than of persecution of Christians in Japan, and implied that they could not really complain about their exclusion. An article written by him for the *Revue des Deux Mondes* in 1856 also conveyed an impression of anti-clericalism. Unlike other Frenchmen, he did not speak of the benefits which the Christian religion could bring to a re-opened Japan. Rather his conclusion suggested the opposite: 'In studying closely the customs, the institutions, the laws of the Japanese, one concludes by asking oneself if their civlization, entirely appropriate to their country, has anything to envy in ours, or that of the United States'. He claimed for Japan 'the impossibility of scarcity, the absence of taxes, freedom for the people . . . these are for the Japanese elements of happiness and well-being which their would-be civilizers would have difficulty in improving on'.[18]

One can only speculate about the significance of the alteration inspired by Delprat's warning, but it seems certain that if France had gone ahead with its original demand, this would have been rejected by the Tokugawa Bakufu. In all probability such a rejection would have been accepted by the French emissary, but it is not impossible that, in certain circumstances – such as negotiation with strong naval support – the French might have persisted in their demand, leaving Bakufu leaders uncertain whether they could risk standing their ground. What the outcome might have been in such a case must be an open question, but if there had been either an armed collision or a Japanese concession, the repercussions on Japanese domestic politics could have been far reaching.

If religion was not the key factor in deciding the French government to establish relations with Japan, neither was commercial pressure. Admittedly, the Ministry of Agriculture, Commerce and Public Works was interested in opening Japan to trade and on more than one occasion made its wishes known to the Foreign Ministry.[19] Moreover, some Frenchmen may have shared Anglo-Saxon hopes of a lucrative commerce once Japan was opened.[20] But against this must be weighed the absence of any indication of pressure for trade with Japan by French chambers of commerce and the slowness of French merchants to arrive in Japan after the ratification of the treaty. Surprising as it may seem, Frenchmen were still unaware of the export potential of Japanese silk and silkworms, later the main item of trade between the two countries. Even Delprat seems to have shared this ignorance, for in his article in the *Revue des Deux Mondes* he noted only that raw silk was imported into Japan from China; and this, as well as other information he had gathered at Nagasaki, underlay his 'doubt that Japan can ever furnish what is necessary for a large trade'.[21] Delprat's pessimism may not entirely have been accepted by the Quai d'Orsay, but if even Britain, with its greater commercial expectations, was willing to wait for the United States to open Japan, it is hard to believe that for France trade was the most significant immediate factor. No doubt its commercial interests would have led it to seek a treaty once trade with Japan was firmly established, but they do not in themselves explain why the French government began to make efforts to establish relations with Japan as early as the mid-1850s.

Even though neither missionaries nor commercial interests propelled France inexorably towards Japan, there was always a possibility that a French naval officer might seize his opportunity and secure an agreement, as Admiral Stirling did for Britain and Admiral Putiatin for Russia, on passing visits during the Crimean War. There was, however, no French counterpart to either of these men and certainly no equivalent of Commodore Perry, who as head of an official American mission in 1853–4 cajoled and threatened the Bakufu into signing Japan's first treaty with a Western power at Kanagawa. This was partly because, before 1855, the French flag seems to have appeared in a Japanese port (if one excludes the outlying Ryukyu islands) on only one occasion – in 1846.[22] Nevertheless, when, in May 1855 Captain Tardy de Montravel appeared at Nagasaki with four ships an excellent opportunity seems to have arisen, for he is said to have been offered a treaty identical to that which the Bakufu had signed in 1854 with Stirling. Instead of seeking to negotiate, however, he rejected the proposal outright on the ground that he did not possess the necessary powers.[23]

Tardy de Montravel's refusal was presumably motivated by his awareness that neither the Stirling convention nor Perry's 1854 treaty was regarded as satisfactory in Europe, principally because they contained no provision for regular trade.[24] Nevertheless, there does seem to have been a lack of enterprise and interest in his unwillingness to try to secure something better. A similar failure to pursue a possible opportunity had earlier occurred in 1848 when the officer who removed the French missionary from the Ryukyus made no attempt to use the attack by the populace in the previous year as an excuse for putting pressure on the local ruler. Admittedly, both Captain Fornier-Duplan in 1844 and Admiral Cécille in 1846 had both been rebuffed when they had sought commercial treaties with the Ryukyus, but it does seem that for the French navy Japan itself was not regarded as of major strategic significance.

What else, then, can explain why the French government sought and obtained a treaty with Japan in the 1850s? An answer is suggested by Delprat's article. 'France', he wrote, 'is disposed to join its efforts with those which other nations have just made; it cannot, whatever happens, remain outside the present movement towards this distant part of the world'.[25] In view of the fact that Delprat saw no bright future for trade, it is hard to account for his desire to see France emulate the other Powers in securing a treaty except by some invocation of the motive of prestige.[26] Nor should he be considered untypical in his concern with this factor. That it was prestige that prompted France – the feeling that it would lower France's standing in the world if it were not to show itself interested in East Asia – is a view for which there is a good deal of evidence in the correspondance between the Quai d'Orsay and the French representative in China, Bourboulon, the man first entrusted with the powers to negotiate a treaty. The instructions given by the Quai d'Orsay to Baron Gros also bear striking witness to it. In this important document the reason for his mission to Japan is stated thus: 'The Emperor's government has been for a long time convinced that France cannot continue to remain in the rear of those nations who have already been looking to assure for their trade access to a rich and populous country and that the moment has come to put itself in this respect on an equal footing with the Powers who have already gone ahead on this path'. [27] While commercial considerations are certainly mentioned, the language used makes it difficult not to feel that the chief preoccupation was with France's status as a leading Power. Similar indications of the influence of prestige are found in the course of France's attempts to secure a treaty.

THE ATTEMPTS TO SECURE A TREATY (1854–58)

The idea of a treaty with Japan can be traced back to the age of Colbert, for according to one nineteenth – century writer, Louis XIV's indefatigable minister lured into the services of France an ex-Dutch factor at Hirado, François Caron, with the intention of establishing trade relations with Japan, among other Oriental countries.[28] He appears to have had a plan to obviate Japanese religious objections by sending only Protestants, but the scheme ended with his death. Precisely when it was revived is unclear . It may have been in 1841, when, it has been alleged, two French warships were sent 'to occupy if possible some island to the south of Japan, which would be valuable for strategic and commercial purposes, and to make treaties of trade and friendship with Japan, and especially with Korea'.[29] Whether there was such an intention is doubtful, however, and Japan did not in fact see the French flag until 1846,[30] when Admiral Cécille appeared at Nagasaki on his own initiative with three ships and the double purpose of securing a promise of good treatment for any French sailors who might be shipwrecked on the Japanese coast and of displaying France's naval strength. He left empty-handed after three days, but his visit is said by Delprat to have made a favourable impression on the Japanese.[31]

Meanwhile, the French had been showing some interest in the Ryukyus. French warships called there occasionally from 1844 onwards, and there may possibly have been some trade in arms through the islands with Satsuma, the Japanese feudal domain which controlled them.[32] In the 1850s the French Navy Ministry became concerned about rumoured American designs on the Ryukyus, and a treaty allowing the French, like the Americans before them, to establish a coaling-station there was secured with local officials by Rear-Admiral Guérin in December 1855.[33] The fact that it was never ratified, however, suggests that it was not regarded as of much importance, and it certainly did not prove to be a stepping-stone towards a treaty with Japan.

The first real step towards a treaty with Japan proper had already been taken the previous year. In March 1854 the Quai d'Orsay informed the French minister in China, Bourboulon, that, as Commodore Perry's expedition looked like being successful, he was being sent the full powers necessary to negotiate in his turn.[34] When he received this dispatch, however, Bourboulon did not feel able to act on it directly. Not only was he uncertain about the extent of Perry's success, but he was fully engaged in trying to revise the treaty of Nanking. Above all, there was no French ship available. He had been offered passage by the British envoy, Sir John Bowring, who had similar instructions to secure an agreement with Japan, but had declined. 'What in fact would be the position,' he wrote back, 'of a French plenipotentiary presenting himself in a country like Japan to negotiate a treaty without being accompanied by a single ship of his own nation, and as the humble protégé of a great foreign Power?'[35] This was reasonable enough, but Bourboulon's concern for French prestige went a good deal further. Although the Quai d'Orsay advised him that 'the intention of Bowring's government, like that of the Emperor's government, is that you will give each other mutual support',[36] Bourboulon maintained that action in common presented grave objections.[37] It might well give rise to embarrassing difficulties over precedence, and it would highlight France's comparative naval weakness. His suggestion that the Japanese might in such circumstances be led to regard France as a British satellite, coupled with the further plea that the British were regarded by Japan with extreme suspicion and that it would be unwise to appear in association with them, induced the Quai d'Orsay to modify its instructions. 'Mutual support' was no longer to be interpreted as enjoining simultaneous action.[38]

By the time he received this communication Bourboulon had decided that 'an expedition to Japan would now be forced to be adjourned, because of the advanced state of the season, until the beginning of the next year'.[39] He was by no means displeased by his enforced inaction, nor by the effect of the Crimean War in preventing both Britain and France from negotiating a treaty so far, for he had learned that Admiral Laguerre, the French naval commander in the Far East, was to receive considerable reinforcements which would enable him to visit Japan in style in 1855. The belief that an impressive display was necessary when dealing with Japan was as much a feature of French thinking as it was of British, or indeed American.

The Navy Ministry had indeed decided in June to send out several more ships and these would have been sufficient for Bourboulon's purpose.[40] By 1855, however, the awareness that Perry's gains had been very limited and the unfavourable reception of Stirling's convention in Europe had made the whole question of treaties with Japan uncertain, and the Quai d'Orsay was unwilling to make arrangements with the Navy Ministry until it knew Britain's plans.[41] Clearly, France did not feel itself capable of isolated effort. In any case, in the Far East itself, Bourboulon would have suffered from the same difficulties which beset Bowring, in that while opportunities arose for both French and British squadrons to visit Japan during the course of the Crimean War, the very nature of war rendered any precise prediction of the time of these visits, and hence the planning of a diplomatic mission, next to impossible.[42] Furthermore, the war with Russia diverted British interest from the opening of Japan, and France, too, lost the relative eagerness which it had begun to display at the time of the Perry expedition.

In 1856, however, the coincidence of the *Arrow* incident and the murder of Father Chapdelaine led to the sending of imposing British and French expeditionary forces to Chinese waters. It was obvious that this could give France the opportunity to press for the opening of Japan to French trade, and given that this second Western war with China reinforced Japanese fears (which the Opium War had stimulated) that Japan might suffer the same fate as China, there were now only two things which could prevent the signing of France's treaty with Japan: a failure to bring the war with China to a speedy end or a refusal of the naval commander to regard the diplomatic mission to Japan as a high priority. In fact, while the first of these possibilities was more or less excluded by mid-1858, the second nearly proved a serious impediment. When, in July 1858 Baron Gros sought from Admiral Rigault de Genouilly the means to carry out the part of his instructions relating to Japan, he found that the Navy Ministry's plans differed somewhat from those of the Quai d'Orsay. All that the Admiral was prepared to spare from his expedition to Cochin-China were three unprepossessing vessels, one of which was not even a warship.[43]

It was this mediocre naval support which was responsible for the British and French treaties with Japan being negotiated separately. When Gros was given his instructions in May 1857, action in common was no longer regarded as inappropriate, and Paris's attitude was now that 'it could only be advantageous in our opinion and that of the Cabinet in London to associate ourselves with it during the negotiations which will soon be initiated in Japan'.[44] Gros did not protest this. Nevertheless, because of the inferiority of his force he decided not to accompany Lord Elgin when the British envoy set sail on 31 July for Nagasaki in order, supposedly, to make a preliminary reconnaissance. He understood that Elgin would shortly be back to settle Chinese tariff problems and would then return to Japan with a smaller force which the French could accompany without too great a feeling of inferiority.[45] In the event Elgin came back on 2 September with a treaty already signed, and

Gros had no alternative but to sail for Japan alone. His unimpressive showing may well have lost him the chance to secure some of the special concessions which he sought and which cooperation with Britain might have made possible.

THE 1858 TREATY

Despite the upset to his plans Baron Gros did achieve a Franco-Japanese treaty of friendship and commerce in Edo on 9 October.[46] In content it differed very little from the American, Dutch, and British treaties and like these it contained a most-favoured-nation clause, which guaranteed that France should enjoy any rights than Japan might grant to other Powers in the future. The most important concession secured was the right of foreigners to reside and trade at Nagasaki, Hakodate, and Kanagawa immediately after the ratification of the treaties, and at Niigata and Hyogo from 1860 and 1863 respectively. They were also to have the right to trade at Edo from 1862 and Osaka from 1863. In another important clause the Bakufu promised that no internal obstacles to trade would be imposed. Import and export duties were established at an average level of between 10% and 20%, though for some luxuries in which France specialized they were as high as 35%. The French treaty also contained, in common with the others, some jurisdictional clauses which, though not without ambiguity, ensured that Frenchmen could not be prosecuted in Japanese courts of law and could therefore under no circumstances be forced to suffer the rigours of the Japanese penal system. The religious provisions in the treaty were limited to the right of Frenchmen to worship within the foreign settlements; missionaries were given no special position. The right to travel within the interior of Japan was granted in theory to diplomatic representatives, as was the right to establish legations in Edo, but the details of such matters were left to be arranged in collaboration with the Japanese authorities. Finally, it was stated that revision of those parts of the treaty which had proved inconvenient could be demanded by either contracting party, one year's notice having been given to the other, but not until fourteen years had elapsed.

The negotiations which preceded the signing of the treaty require little comment. Apart from some initial Japanese attempts at prevarication over Gros' insistence on conducting diplomatic business in Edo rather than the outlying coastal settlement at Kanagawa, the Japanese officials whom the mission encountered were pleasant and courteous and made an excellent impression: Gros found them 'a race superior in everything to that which we had just left in China'.[47] Despite the existence of serious opposition in Japan to treaties with Western powers, an opposition which was no less significant because much of it was politically motivated, most Bakufu leaders were already reconciled to the idea that sacrifices were unavoidable, and had no intention of provoking hostilities by refusing to Gros the rights to trade and reside which they had granted to other countries. To some extent their fear of the West may have been unjustified, for Japan was in no immediate danger of attack in 1858. Indeed, as far as France was concerned, Gros' instructions emphasized the friendly character which Napoleon III desired to give the negotiations and concluded with the explicit acknowledgement that 'we have no valid grievances which can be used against Japan at all, we therefore cannot think of employing force against it to constrain it to negotiate with us or to accede to our proposals if it believed them to be prejudicial to its interests'.[48]

Such a self-limitation, together with the weakness of the French naval force and, Gros maintained, the lack of gifts for Japanese officials, inevitably restricted the French negotiating position in the five sessions that were held between 27 September and 9 October. Gros did his best to overcome these limitations by dropping hints of menace into his assurances of French goodwill. In the first session, for instance, he referred to France's 'entirely friendly and peaceful' attitude towards Japan, but then used language which was rather more double-edged: 'He [Gros] has not come here to impose a treaty by cannon fire, as he has been forced to do in China, whose government had insulted France; he comes as a friend to negotiate a treaty of peace and commerce. If the Japanese Government does not understand this situation, and the honourableness of the French Government's intentions, the Ambassador will immediately depart, but with the reservation that he will give an account to his court of the reception which has been given to him'.[49] The French plenipotentiary also attempted to off-set the disadvantage of not being able to bestow lavish presents by implying that these would follow upon the exchange of ratifications. 'From this moment a genuine and cordial intimacy was established between us', he wrote.[50] Despite this claim, Gros was not conspicuously successful in improving upon the American and British treaties for the benefit of a special French interest. He found it impossible to secure a reduction in the 35% duty on wines, whereas Elgin had been able to get the duty on cotton and woollen fabrics cut to 5%. Nevertheless, the French envoy left Edo on 10 October well satisfied and with a good opinion of the Japanese. The treaty was received by the Emperor with 'a lively satisfaction'.[51]

CONCLUSIONS

The main conclusion that emerges from the story of France's relations with Japan before the signing of the treaty in 1858 and of its attempts to secure that treaty is that Japan did not rank very high on France's list of priorities. The missionaries, it is true, were passionately concerned but their views on the concessions to be sought from Japan were not taken into account. Trading interests, which might have exerted greater influence, showed no apparent enthusiasm. This was hardly surprising considering that even the opening of China had brought few French merchants to the East. The Ministry of Agriculture, Commerce and Public Works displayed greater concern, but this was not exclusively commercial, as is evident from the note that the Ministry sent to the Quai d'Orsay when it first heard of the treaty signed by Commodore Perry at Kanagawa. It enclosed a report from East Asia by one of its representatives, Auguste Heurtier, who had been informed that the Americans had secured trade concessions from Japan which might be shared de facto by other nations. 'This situation', he declared, 'would subordinate in Japan the interests, as well as the influence, of other maritime countries to those of the American nation, and I do not think that such a position would be willingly accepted by them, especially by France'.[52] The Ministry therefore requested the Quai d'Orsay and the Navy Ministry to take appropriate steps. In effect, it was rejecting any trade which did not result from France's own action and was not based upon an independent treaty which confirmed France's status.

This desire for respect and prestige owed something, no doubt, to the belief that success abroad would bolster up the régime at home, but at a deeper level it sprang from the conviction that France must show that it remained a great power.[53] Since, as a trading nation, France clearly could not compare with Britain, Frenchmen tended, in order to prove France's greatness, to emphasise other attributes and qualities. Among its naval officers, Rear-Admiral Guérin provides an illustration of this. In August 1855 he visited Hakodate and, reporting his impressions, made the following remarks on Japan's attitude to foreign countries:

> Of all the European nations, the one which ought to show itself the most disinterested and the most honourable in their eyes is France, whose history they know, whose position in the current struggle they understand, and whom they fear only because it represents the catholic principle in the world. But this entirely moral danger must frighten them less than the invasive spirit of the English and the American merchants and the persistent ambition of Russia. Hence that benevolent attitude of which I spoke to you, and that extreme desire to see a treaty concluded between our two Empires.[54]

A still more striking expression of this belief that France's greatness was fundamentally different from that of other nations, and would be recognized as such, was that of Dubois de Jancigny, whom Louis-Philippe's government employed as a diplomatic observer in China in 1841–3, and who, in his unofficial negotiations then, sought to impress the Chinese with France's independence of Britain and its willingness to help China practically. In 1850, in a book on East Asia, he attacked Britain's desire to force Japan open to its manufactures and asked: 'Will the disinterested voice of intelligent humanity not be able to triumph over this greedy clamour? Will France, a noble and far-sighted mediator, dare to place itself between the thirst for conquest, the intemperate love of gain, the abuse of force on the one side, and on the other the murderous resistance of a nation which is heroic as much as egoistic in the dream of perpetual exclusion which its ignorance and its pride embrace?'.[55] His optimistic conclusion was that '. . . the voice of France will be heard here when it is raised to defend the relative independence of the Asiatic peoples, and we have proved for China what we do not hesitate to predict for Japan, namely, that our intervention, in such cases where events will come to proclaim its appropriateness in the eyes of liberal Europe, will be welcomed to the limits of the East by the trust of the populations there, threatened with subjugation to the yoke of British speculation'.[56]

Dubois' views can be discounted in part; they were extreme even for a Frenchman. Moreover, the French Foreign Ministry had a proper respect, in practice, for the facts of international power and national interest, and for the sake of European politics was careful to follow a policy close to Britain's. Nevertheless, such sentiments often found an echo. They can, for instance, be seen in the reflections by the Marquis de Moges, Gros' secretary, after the signing of the 1858 treaty. 'The Japanese government', he proclaimed, 'had . . . obtained ample proof that it was neither the lust of conquest nor commercial gain which had brought the representatives of France to those seas, but the necessity of protecting the political influence of the empire and the honour of the national flag in the extreme East'.[57] The existence of such thinking helps to explain some significant aspects of French policy towards Japan in later years.

From the foregoing evidence it should be clear that French concern with prestige and influence was extremely strong. Without that factor, the French government might have been content, like the Prussian and Austrian, to leave until the 1860s the signing of a treaty with Japan. At the same time the somewhat contradictory impression emerges from the French archives that, despite French pretensions to independence, French action was contingent upon the opportunity provided by the efforts of other Powers. Only after the groundwork had been prepared by the United States, Russia, Holland and Britain, and after cooperation had been arranged with the latter, did France seriously envisage sending an envoy to Japan. Had France alone been concerned, Japan would have remained in seclusion for many years to come.

2

THE STRUGGLE TO ENFORCE THE TREATIES, 1859–64

THE IMPLEMENTATION OF THE TREATIES

THE BAKUFU'S signing of trade treaties in 1858 broke a long tradition. Only with considerable doubts and trepidation was the decision to establish relations with Western powers taken, and the Tokugawa leaders' fears soon proved to be justified. Among Japanese generally, or at least among the samurai class and those commoners who were politically conscious, seclusionist feeling, already strong, was intensified by the Bakufu's peremptory action. The fact that the dominant figure within the Bakufu, the great councillor (*tairo*) Ii Naosuke, had ignored the expressed wishes of the Emperor by entering into such far-reaching agreements after only limited and inconclusive consultation with the daimyo (lords of semi-autonomous domains) meant that the rallying-cry of *joi* ('expel the barbarian') became closely linked with another old, but now more fashionable, phrase – *sonno* ('revere the Emperor'); and under the banner of *sonno-joi* a wave of intense hostility rose both towards foreigners and towards those who had allowed them to pollute by their presence the sacred or divine country (*shinkoku*) of Japan.

This upsurge of xenophobia characterized Japanese political life in the first half of the 1860s; and for Western diplomats in Japan especially it became the most fundamental cause of concern. To begin with, it put them in almost constant physical danger, since enraged samurai (some of whom had left their*han* (domain) to pursue their self-proclaimed mission not infrequently assaulted foreigners and sometimes killed them. On occasion they even attacked legations. This was only the most immediate consequence of the *sonno-joi* movement, however, for its rise and unexpected strength forced the Bakufu to seek to revise or even nullify the treaties which had created this problem and which had stimulated, for the first time since the early seventeenth century, open opposition to Tokugawa rule. As a result, the first French representative in Japan, Duchesne de Bellecourt,[1] found himself engaged, together with his British, American and Dutch colleagues, in a seemingly unending struggle to cling on to the concessions which had been secured with relative ease only a short time before.

Their difficulties were not made less by the fact that they often lacked adequate military and naval backing. Even more seriously, they sometimes had to contend with lack of understanding and support from their own governments. Part of their problem was that European governments knew, and cared, little about Japan; but the fact that dispatches took almost two months to reach Paris from Edo (while telegrams were not much quicker because there was no direct telegraphic link before 1871 – and they were in any case discouraged because of the expense) was also a cause of uncertainty and confusion. So bad did the situation appear that on occasion doubts were expressed as to whether the Western nations would be able to retain a significant foothold in Japan.

The possibility that the Western presence in the newly-opened Japan was not yet secure did not enter the mind of the French foreign minister in May–June 1859, when the instructions which were to be given to Bellecourt were drawn up. Admittedly, the statement that his main duty would be to ensure that the treaty was properly and fully implemented hinted at an expectation that some difficulties might arise, but there was no perception that a major crisis was looming. What principally concerned the Quai d'Orsay was that Frenchmen should possess all the privileges enjoyed by other nationalities and that, if possible, the French representative should secure further concessions such as a reduction in the duty on wine.

A similar combination of naïve assumptions and limited aims was revealed by the expectation that Bellecourt would not be involved in any political activity: 'For the rest, not having any action to take in regard to the court of Yedo [the shogun's government in Edo] outside the sphere of the interests naturally placed under the protection of the consulate-general, you have to fill in Japan from the political point of view, only a role of observation'.[2] Almost immediately upon his arrival on 6 September 1859, however, Bellecourt found that the situation would not be as straightforward or easy as the Quai d'Orsay imagined. His very first report from Edo struck a warning note: '. . . it is evident . . . that the Japanese Government is at this moment belaboured by a party essentially hostile to Foreigners and very discontented by the Treaties concluded with them'.[3] In his next dispatch he anticipated the central issue of the next four years: 'The Treaties have been concluded, but it is evident that their execution will meet, on the part of the Japanese Princes [daimyo], either a latent or an open opposition which the Foreign Representatives will overcome only by being firm and energetic in attitude, by acting in accord, and especially by the continual presence in Japan of forces which are sufficient to secure respect for their authority, perhaps even, one day, their persons'.[4]

The fact that the shogunate ratified the French treaty on 30 September did nothing to allay Bellecourt's concern. In November he had to report on successive days the murder of a Chinese servant of the French consular agent and an attack on the British minister, Rutherford Alcock.[5] In addition, he voiced, not for the first time, the suspicion that the Japanese authorities were trying to prevent the diplomats from leaving their residences or being visited in them. More worrying, perhaps, from his government's point of view was his comment on 10 December on the Japanese attitude towards the implementation of the commercial provisions of the treaties: 'The innumerable restrictions which the local Authorities arbitrarily impose on indigenous commerce are paralysing all transactions, and the traders are already thinking of leaving the country if the Japanese Government does not decide to change policy'. In somewhat alarmist fashion he concluded: 'To speak the truth, the Treaties no longer exist – they are played with using promises and words'. Worse still, there was no prospect of a change other than by drastic measures:

> The Foreign Representatives have no authority, no influence against this reaction which has risen to become a menace. Only the fear of forceful action by the foreign Powers can now halt the Japanese Government on this fatal descent. It is the last card to play and, however circumscribed the role which I have to play here may be, I must say that my attitude cannot be simply one of observation. I shall be prudent, but I cannot separate myself completely from my colleagues, because, it must be said, no distinction of nationality is made in Japan; all Foreigners, to whatever country they belong, are the object of the same repugnance and the same inconvenient, not to say injurious, behaviour.[6]

Bellecourt's hint that a forceful intervention was desirable ran counter to the more patient approach of the American minister, Townsend Harris, who had been in Japan since 1856 and who consistently argued that the problems which foreigners were experiencing were understandable in view of the newness of Japan's opening and could be settled eventually by peaceful reasoning. The French representative was not alone in favouring strong measures, however. Indeed, he may have been disposed towards them partly because they were already being advocated by Alcock, who had arrived earlier than Bellecourt and whose lead he often tended to follow. At this stage, however, there was no likelihood that either the British or the French government, both of which had pressing problems and commitments elsewhere, would accept that their interests were sufficiently substantial to justify military intervention.

As time passed, some of the difficulties which had caused foreigners to complain turned out to be less serious than at first thought. The problem of the introduction of new Japanese coins for foreign trade at an unrealistic rate of exchange proved not to be intractable,[7] and the decision by the Bakufu to transfer the proposed Western trading settlement at Kanagawa to nearby Yokohama, which was undeveloped, was readily accepted by most merchants even though it was initially opposed by Bellecourt and other diplomats as a breach of the treaties and a possible attempt to isolate Western traders in the way that the Dutch had been confined to the island of Deshima for two centuries.[8]

Other difficulties, however, became more serious. The night attack by samurai swordsmen on the British legation in 1861, the ruthless cutting down of the British merchant, Richardson, by samurai from the great south-western *han* of Satsuma in 1862, and the firing on Western ships in the Shimonoseki straits between Honshu and Kyushu during 1863–4 by the other major south-western *han* of Choshu, were only the most dramatic examples of a long series of anti-Western incidents which also included the killing in 1863 of a French lieutenant named Camus (although Frenchmen, being less numerous than Britons, were also less frequently the objects of attack). Substantial reparations were sought from the Bakufu and usually secured after persistent pressure, but this proved no more effective as a means of stopping the attacks than the withdrawal of the legations (which Bellecourt fully supported though Harris did not) from Edo to Yokohama for several weeks when the American interpreter, Heusken, was murdered in 1861.[9]

The other problem which became more difficult was the Bakufu's attempt to postpone the implementation of some of the provisions of the treaties. The first such case occurred in 1859, when a request to defer the opening to trade of the small port of Niigata was accepted by Western representatives in Japan without much discussion. When this was followed in September 1860, however, by a much more far-reaching demand that all the other ports and cities which were due to be opened by 1863 should remain closed until 1868, the response was quite different. Indeed, if things had been left to the diplomats in Japan alone, a clash between Japan and some of the powers, with unpredictable consequences for the former, would have been hard to avoid.

The question of the postponement of the opening of Japanese ports was to be the focal point of diplomacy for two years, but it also deserves attention because it throws light on how much importance France attached to cooperation with Britain. When he first received the Japanese request, Bellecourt's reaction was: 'For my part, it seems to me that to yield to the demands of this government would be to compromise Western influence in Japan still further', and he commented bitterly: 'After having annihilated one by one, in the space of an entire year, all the clauses of the Treaty, at this moment they have reached the

27

point of asking openly for its non-execution!'[10] The Quai d'Orsay, however, recognizing that the power which France could bring to bear upon Japan was limited, preferred to sound out London before making its decision, and it learned that although the British Government did not feel the demand to be reasonable, budgetary considerations made insistence on strict enforcement of the treaty unlikely. At the end of January, 1861, therefore, foreign minister Thouvenel wrote to Bellecourt informing him that if both London and Washington were to accept the Bakufu demand, 'I do not think that we ought alone to risk embarrassment by asserting a contrary attitude'.[11]

This indication of Paris's preference did not prevent Bellecourt from objecting in July (a few days after the serious attack on the British legation) to the length of the delay for which the Bakufu was asking: 'In Japan, this benevolent concession may be misrepresented as consented to under the threat of intimidation, and we would give, perhaps, to our enemies the time to prepare for a resistance which would later be difficult to overcome'.[12] Only in the case of Edo, he implied, should postponement be accepted. The Quai d'Orsay took this advice seriously enough to raise the issue again with London in October, this time letting it be known that it now had serious doubts about a policy of concession.[13] No sign that Britain intended to change to a more uncompromising position was forthcoming, however, and in November Thouvenel informed Bellecourt that he would not oppose postponement. He claimed that the Japanese had recently been showing signs of good will, but expediency was clearly a factor also, for the foreign minister observed that there was 'less inconvenience for us in making certain concessions to the difficulties of the Japanese Government's situation than in putting forward to it demands which would further increase its difficulties'.[14] Even more important, however, was his understanding that Britain would adopt the same attitude; and this was confirmed by a further dispatch which revealed that London had decided to accept postponement, although only in return for compensation, such as the opening of ports on the island of Tsushima and the Korean coast (where the Japanese government was believed to exercise authority) and the extension of foreign rights in Yokohama and Edo.[15] These conditions Bellecourt was to discuss and agree with Alcock.

Diplomats in Edo were less inclined towards concession than their governments were in Europe. In February 1862 another dispatch from Bellecourt reported that he, Alcock and the Dutch minister, de Wit, had decided that they should insist on the opening of Osaka and Hyogo after all: 'We have all three arrived at the same conclusion on the little faith that should be placed on these evasive promises of improvements which probably have no other motive than to lead the Western Powers, by concession to concession, to consent to the withdrawal of the most important clauses of the Treaty'. The Japanese government would, they knew, be unhappy with their stance and would resist the claims for indemnities for victims of attacks which they were making, as well as their demands for commercial concessions, such as the lowering of wine duties. 'But we have had to decide here', Bellecourt wrote in self-justification, 'according to our conscience, and to place ourselves above all on the standpoint of the maintenance of Western prestige, in a country where the sharpest duplicity continually submits this prestige to tests . . .'[16]

The question of postponement was now, however, taken out of Bellecourt's hands completely by a move for which he, ironically, was partly responsible: the sending of Japan's first diplomatic mission to Europe. By a further irony, the (identical) decisions which were taken in Paris and London were effectively made not by the French and British foreign ministers but by Alcock, who arrived home on leave in the early summer. When the Japanese envoys reached Europe in April 1862, Thouvenel's opinion was still that postponement must be conditional on compensation.[17] His attitude was slightly more moderate than Bellecourt's, but for the Japanese it presented much the same objection in that it demanded an immediate and inopportune extension by the Bakufu of relations with foreigners.

One month later, however, after a visit from Alcock, Thouvenel had moved further away from his own representative's way of thinking. As the British minister explained to Bellecourt before leaving Japan, he had become convinced that the Western powers were faced with a stark choice: either to accept the Bakufu demand in toto or to prepare for war. His doubts that there existed the will for the latter course led him to recommend the former, and this was well received. As Alcock recounted to Edmund Hammond, the permanent under-secretary at the Foreign Office, in a private letter of 29 May: 'I saw M. Thouvenel on Wednesday, and the Emperor yesterday, and a perfect understanding has been come to. They listened with much attention to all I had to say or suggest as to the best line of policy and each in turn said the French Government would cordially join in it if Lord Russell was prepared to adopt the line indicated'.[18]

Alcock's assessment of the French foreign minister's reaction was accurate, for on the day of their meeting Thouvenel wrote to the French ambassador in London: 'I am more than ever inclined to think, after all Mr Alcock has told me, that we cannot think of requiring of Japan the *strict and immediate* carrying out of the treaties without running the risk of political rupture with its Government, that is to say without exposing ourselves to the risk of being plunged into all the embarrassment and all the expense of a distant expedition the usefulness of which would, perhaps, in the last analysis be very doubtful'.[19] The British foreign secretary, Lord Russell, also accepted Alcock's advice. In consequence, all thought of opening alternative ports as compensation was dropped, and the only condition which was attached to acceptance of the continued closure of Niigata, Hyogo, Edo and Osaka until 1868 was that the other provisions of the treaties should be executed in better faith, especially as regards the restriction placed on the commercial operations of foreigners.[20]

The laying down of such a condition was essentially intended to save British and French face. There could be little hope that it would achieve anything except to buy time, for a mere postponement of the implementation of some treaty provisions was hardly likely to give the Bakufu more than a momentary respite from the internal political pressures which were building up. Alcock might have accepted that the anti-foreign movement in Japan could not yet be confronted, but Bellecourt, and to a lesser extent Colonel Neale, the British chargé d'affaires, became increasingly concerned, especially during the early months of 1863, that the Bakufu was giving in to its opponents. In May 1863, unwilling to accept any longer the policy of patience which they had been enjoined to follow, they took the surprising step of offering, without their governments' sanction, military aid to the shogun in the hope of re-establishing his authority and arresting what they considered a potentially disastrous development.[21] To understand how this remarkable proposal came to be made, however, it is necessary to examine in more detail Bellecourt's understanding of, and attitude towards, the political situation from the time of his arrival in Japan.

BELLECOURT AND JAPANESE POLITICS

Bellecourt's attitude to Japanese politics could not be objective. The government with which France had signed its treaty was that of the shogun. The shogunal administration, the Bakufu, was, therefore, the only authority in Japan which had under-taken a legal obligation to the Western powers, and in view of the evident hostility of Japanese towards relations with foreigners, it was important that it should continue in power.[22] The fact that Edo, the seat of the Bakufu, could be intimidated from the sea, where the foreign powers' strength lay, only reinforced this basic assumption.[23] Western diplomats in Japan were also in the position, especially in the first two years, of receiving their information about the internal political situation almost exclusively from Bakufu officials; and, not unnaturally, the latter invariably portrayed their own enemies as being violently hostile to foreigners, implying that it was solely due to the treaties that the Bakufu itself was resented by the various *han.* In addition, despite Bellecourt's valiant efforts to clarify the political background by drawing up a statistical list of the revenues of the Bakufu and the daimyo,[24] his view of Japan, like that of his colleagues, was distorted by an over-riding concern with trade and the treaties.[25] Moreover, although occasional pieces of useful information were gleaned by the legations in Edo through such men as Blekman, Bellecourt's Dutch interpreter, or Mermet de Cachon, who later served as his Japanese interpreter, it was not until they produced men like Satow and Siebold, whose talents and temperaments enabled them to make close contacts with a wider range of Japanese political activists, that it became possible for the foreign representatives to gain a deeper insight into Japanese politics and a fuller awareness of its ramifications. It is tempting, too, to suggest that the authoritarian nature of their own political tradition may have preconditioned both Bellecourt and his successor, Léon Roches, to be suspicious of the suggestion that the Bakufu should share its power with the powerful *han*. The idea of some kind of baronial council was one in which both Alcock and his successor, Sir Harry Parkes, found merit, but their two French counterparts tended to assume that any reduction in the Bakfufu's power was more likely to lead to conflict and prolonged instability than to harmony.

In his first reports on Japanese politics Bellecourt was content to reproduce the views of Alcock. As these early dispatches portrayed the situation, the central government of the 'Taikoun' or Temporal Emperor (i.e. the Tokugawa shogun) ruled over the reactionary vassal 'Princes of the Empire' (i.e. daimyo) some of whom were friendly to him while others were, on account of the admission of foreigners, hostile. These hostile Princes maintained numerous cohorts of warriors in Edo and looked to the 'Mikado' or 'Spiritual Emperor' in his capacity as guardian of the laws to express his disapproval of the Bakufu actions on the grounds that they threatened the political health of Japan.[26] The ambiguity regarding the location of sovereignty somewhat troubled Bellecourt and he raised with Alcock his doubts 'on the question of parity between the Sovereigns of Europe and the perhaps improperly named Temporal Emperor of Japan'; but he was soon persuaded by the British minister that 'since the Mikado never revealed his existence, no more to Foreigners than to the Japanese people, we can pretend to be unaware of him and can recognise in the Tycoon the prerogatives of sovereignty since he exercises it in reality, not absolutely, but by a delegation which the laws of the country have sanctioned for nearly eight centuries'.[27] This practical acceptance of the shogun's sovereignty was to be criticized by later arrivals, but in terms both of foreign knowledge of Japan in 1859 and of Japanese tradition, it was not without justification.

The Western diplomats' understanding of Japan gradually became less simple as additional information filtered through or slipped past the Bakufu. In its essentials, however, their original view persisted for a considerable time. The main modification was a growing realization that the Bakufu's power, and therefore its ability to respond to Western demands, was more limited than they had at first imagined. This led to some ominous reflections in Bellecourt's mind in September 1860. Having already reached the conviction that 'the Japanese cannot accept the thought that the treaties can modify their old ways and that their independence is only guaranteed on condition that they scrupulously observe the terms of their pact with Western civilization', he went on to draw the conclusion that to rectify this state of affairs it would not be sufficient simply to make the Bakufu again recognise its obligations towards the Powers:

'I am convinced', he wrote. 'that it is not only by an action uniquely directed against Edo that Japan can be obliged to keep its undertakings, but also that, if the time should come, it will be necessary also to act in particular against several of the Princes of this country, as much against the coastal provinces as the centre, which would be easy to attack by sea towards Osaka, in order to interrupt the communications between the north and the south of the Empire. Thus, following this hypothesis, it seems to me that one could easily bring about another way of thinking among the various members of this feudal body which is in agitation at Edo, but which would probably change its attitude if they felt that they might be reached in their own possessions.'[28]

As yet, these were just ideas. Within four years, however they were to be put into practice, with results not unlike those which Bellecourt had predicted.

In the meantime, Bellecourt's political dispatches mostly recorded the weakness of the shogun's government. The decline of the Tokugawa authority had become very marked since early 1860 when Ii Naosuke's assassination had opened the way to the much weaker leadership of Ando Nobumasa and Kuze Hirochika, and although both these *roju* (members of the highest Bakufu council) were anxious to avoid conflict with the Western powers, this anxiety was, unfortunately from the foreign representatives' viewpoint, matched by a need which seemed equally imperative – to placate the Imperial Court in Kyoto (where many xenophobic samurai were stirring up feeling) and the powerful *han*.[29] In April 1861, Bellecourt was sufficiently struck by the effect of this to write: 'One can therefore ask oneself if the Western Powers would not have had more certainty in their relations with this Empire by concluding separate treaties with the great feudal Princes rather than with the present government, which seems to keep its strength only from what is supplied to it by the Great Princes who can justly be considered as genuine kings'.[30]

The recognition that the daimyo possessed real power was accompanied by an embryonic awareness that their power had grown as a result of the opening of Japan to foreigners and by a realization that the Bakufu's perceived culpability in this respect might be used to weaken it still further. In June 1862, for instance, Bellecourt referred to 'several great Daimyo who are supposed to have gone to Miako [Kyoto] with the intention of seeking from the Mikado both the deposition of the present Tycoon and the reversion to the old Laws of exclusion. Among these Daimyo are mentioned the Prince of Satsuma, who, in league with two or three other great Daimyo, is supposed to have sworn the downfall of the present dynasty under the pretext of the national hatred inspired by foreigners'. What this and the current rumours of a rise in anti-foreign feeling among *ronin* around both Edo and Osaka signified he could not be sure: 'Does this state of things indicate a serious crisis or a calculated plan of intimidation similar to those which have been tried so many times? For my part I am inclined to believe in a great internal movement, but I can at this moment only seek to sound the depth of these agitations without being able to indicate exactly their real cause and importance'.[31]

Bellecourt's perplexity was not dispelled by the somewhat conflicting information which he received in mid-1862. First he learned of an unusual and important mission to Edo headed by a Court noble (but organized by Satsuma) which he mistakenly understood to be primarily concerned with the acceptance or expulsion of foreigners (although it was actually intended to induce the Bakufu to accept internal reforms).[32] Then he was shown a document which Mermet de Cachon had translated and from which it appeared that 'the Daimyo who are turning away from the Tycoon are much less opposed to relations with foreigners than has been supposed'.[33] In the following month he deduced from further news that 'it is becoming more and more evident that little by little the supreme power of the Mikado is being revived, with a view, probably, to bringing to bear in opposition to the foreign Powers an influence which is very worthy of consideration in that it comes from the traditional religious teaching of a country attached to its old customs'.[34] Bellecourt's apprehension about anti-foreign moves was not diminished by enquiries about French artillery inventions and improvements from Bakufu officials. Their motive, he suspected, was 'to permit them, at a given moment, to repulse what they call the pretensions of the West against their empire, their institutions, and their customs . . . In a word, the Japanese wish to utilise the presence of foreigners to extract from them everything which can protect their special policy and work to their own advantage and not that which can contribute to fusion and good understanding with other nations of the world'.[35]

Against this background of rumours, threats and chronic uncertainty, the Western diplomats in Edo were presented at the end of 1862 with yet another warning – this time that an attack by *ronin* on Kanagawa and Yokohama was possible. At first Bellecourt did not take this threat particularly seriously. 'I think', he wrote, 'that this news must again be seen as a game in this system of intimidation with the aid of which they count on making foreigners abandon the port of Kanagawa [meaning Yokohama], and that in order to prove to the Japanese Government that this task will be difficult we have good reason not to show concern'.[36] Moreover, when the Western representatives were advised in January 1863 that influential daimyo had persuaded the Emperor to insist on the closure of Yokohama and that the shogun was going to Kyoto to try to dissuade him, he was not unduly alarmed, since he felt that it was by deceit that what he termed 'the party of reaction' planned to drive the foreigners back to Nagasaki and that 'everything that has happened in the last six months seems skillfully prepared to arrive at this result'.[37] Nevertheless, the French minister was worried that Harris's successor, Pruyn, was considering recommending concessions to Japan, and in April there was a notable increase in tension when the British chargé d'affaires, Colonel Neale, presented the Bakufu with an ultimatum demanding an indemnity of £100,000 for the death of the British merchant, Richardson, the previous year, at the hands of Satsuma samurai. Since Neale had instructions to blockade ports if he were refused and also to require of Satsuma both an additional indemnity and the punishment of the murderers, it was plain that a collision was more than possible. Indeed, there was a widespread anticipation that there would be an attack on the foreign community, and urgent defensive measures were taken by the British and French admirals which were soon to culminate in the regular stationing of troops in Yokohama.

It was at this critical point that Bellecourt and Neale put forward their unauthorized proposal for helping the Bakufu. The French minister may well have been influenced by the fact that, with substantial French forces at hand for the first time, he was in a position 'to have in the counsels of our allies a voice with a certain authority'.[38] The deciding factor, however, was the disclosure of a letter in which the shogun promised the Emperor that he would work for the expulsion of foreigners. To Bellecourt this proved that 'the Japanese government had been drawn onto a fatal path and that there was reason to act without delay in a common entente, with the object of turning aside the storm which threatened at the same time the existence of our nationals and even that of the Treaties'.[39] He and Neale decided that

> ... to safeguard the rights and dignity of the Western nations there were only two ways – either to reject new delaying tactics on the part of the Tycoon's government and to enter immediately into hostilities against all, Tycoon and Daimyo, or to compel the Tycoon's government to state its position clearly on the foreign question by offering it immediate and complete support against the opponents, whoever they may be, who are inducing it to break its commitments. If the government of the Tycoon is loyal, if it wishes to maintain the peace with the outside world, it will accept this proposal and it will, by its decision, carry with it three-quarters of the daimyo against the audacious minority which is now stirring up the country against foreigners.[40]

This was an extraordinary choice of options, and it is hard to believe that the first alternative – of taking on the whole Japanese feudal regime – was put forward seriously; it must surely only have been mentioned to give the French and British governments some idea of the seriousness with which their representatives viewed the situation and to make it appear that the second policy – the one they proposed to follow – was relatively moderate. Exactly what they had in mind is unclear, because it was not spelled out more precisely and was not put into effect. A leading Japanese historian, Ishii Takashi, has assumed that it was to send a joint fleet, first to the Inland Sea, to support action by the Bakufu in Kyoto, then to the territories of the various hostile daimyo.[41] Such action would have been in accord with the views which Bellecourt had inclined towards since his arrival, as well as with the policies which were to be adopted by most Western representatives in the following two-and-a-half years. In May 1863, however, the plan was premature. The Bakufu official to whom they proposed it, Takemoto Masao, raised the diplomats' hopes by replying that 'at present the Edo government does not need it: later, if it was necessary, the Taikoun would ask for that support', and, by asking them to wait for an answer until the Bakufu leaders in Kyoto had been consulted.[42] When at the end of the month the answer came, however, it was a definite refusal: '. . . the Taikoun has been very sensible of the contracting Powers' friendly proposal: but amity being reestablished between him and the Mikado, he would soon return to the capital (Edo) to deal with matters pending there and set on course a policy entirely favourable to the extension of commercial relations with the foreigners'.[43]

A refusal couched in such terms, and promising what they had chiefly sought – the positive acceptance of the treaties – obviously deprived the foreign representatives of any pretext for implementing their plan of armed action. However, though abortive, the incident did more than merely foreshadow the recourse to force or intimidation which was to be tried later. According to Ishii Takashi, 'the important proposal of the English and French ministers gave great encouragement to the Bakufu faction which favoured the extension of Bakufu power and friendship with foreigners'.[44] It thus undermined the policy of compromise and cooperation often referred to by historians as *kobugattai* ('union of Court and military'), which Satsuma and other powerful *han* had been working for since 1862 in conjunction with elements within the Bakufu which accepted the need for change in Japan's political system.

It is questionable whether, even if the shogun's government had accepted the offer of aid, Neale and Bellecourt could have brought their plan to fruition, for the reaction in Europe to such intervention was unfavourable, to say the least. When the French foreign minister, Drouyn de Lhuys, read in Bellecourt's 3 May dispatch that the two representatives intended to send for reinforcements from China, he could not forebear writing in the margin a blunt 'no'. His disapproval was promptly expressed at somewhat greater length, but without dissimulation, in a dispatch to Bellecourt:

> I cannot moreover approve the offer that you have made to the Japanese government to give your assistance to overcome the opposition of the daimyo. The simplest reflection suffices to show that we would throw ourselves thus unthinkingly into the risks of a most compromising and unwarranted involvement in the internal affairs of Japan. Now, in the present state of affairs when, in so many other parts of the globe, questions of a capital importance claim our attention or already absorb us, it would be difficult to find a single reason which could justify an enterprise where the sacrifices of the Emperor's government would be so disproportionate to the hypothetical advantages which might result.[45]

In his (and the navy minister's) view, Bellecourt and Admiral Jaurès might have recklessly jeopardized French interests in Cochin-China. In his own defence Bellecourt claimed that he had had no intention of acting before receiving approval from Paris,[46] but it seems by no means certain that he would have exercised such restraint. If he had indeed been disposed in May 1863 to take independent action, however, the unusually clear show of displeasure by the foreign minister ensured that the French representative would thereafter adhere closely to a cautious policy. It is worth noting that the Quai d'Orsay doctrine of avoiding entanglement in Japanese politics remained official policy, save, ironically, for a brief moment in 1864, when the arrival in Paris of a Japanese mission allowed the foreign minister to take full control himself.

Bellecourt was to be left in Japan for considerably less than a year after his reprimand, his successor being nominated in October.[47] The remainder of his stay was mainly taken up by renewed efforts to secure Bakufu confirmation of the provisions of the 1858 treaties, for it was soon found that not only was the shogun's undertaking to take strong measures against hostile daimyo not being put into effect but that once more the Bakufu was being drawn into the position of promising the Court that it would expel the foreigners. At first this did not provoke great concern, since a curious episode which occurred in June 1863 seemed to prove that the Bakufu had again come to fear foreign warships more than it did its internal opponents. At that time, Bakufu leaders in Edo, led by Ogasawara Nagamichi, informed Bellecourt that they had again received orders to demand the evacuation of Yokohama but instead of pleading for diplomatic acceptance of foreign withdrawal on the well-established ground of domestic political necessity, they asked the French minister to reject the demand outright. He and his colleagues were requested to 'reply to this notification in terms of the most lively indignation because it was desirable that these responses, which would be shown to Edo and Kyoto, produce a deep impression on the mind of the most recalcitrant'. The foreign representatives readily complied. In reporting what had happened, Bellecourt commented with pardonable exaggeration that 'the action which has just been taken certainly has no precedent in history' and that it was 'indeed incomprehensible'.[48]

The French representative's bemusement indicates that he had little idea of what was going on below the surface of Bakufu politics. It also suggests that, even after his and Neale's offer of help, he was taken into the confidence of the Bakufu faction which wished to reestablish strong control to only a very limited extent, if at all.[49] Admittedly, Bellecourt's relations with the Bakufu improved sufficiently in 1863 for him to be able to write of 'the marked preference which the Japanese affect to give to the French authorities at this moment', but this should probably be attributed to the Bakufu's growing awareness of France's political value as a powerful friend and intermediary.[50] It certainly did not result from any development of particular sympathy for the Tokugawa regime on Bellecourt's part, notwithstanding the fact that, when in early 1864 his departure from Japan was imminent, the Bakufu requested that he be retained.[51] That Bellecourt – unlike his successor – did not seek a special relationship is clearly indicated by the warning with which he accompanied his observation about the Bakufu's show of favour: 'We must also avoid ever giving them reason to think that they can separate us from our allies, a thought which has perhaps suggested itself to them'.[52]

Bellecourt's basically negative response to indications of Japanese favour was a natural consequence of his distrust of the Bakufu. Not without reason he suspected that the Bakufu still nurtured some hope of easing its position by forcing foreigners to accept much more restrictive conditions. Beyond this, however, he alleged that the Bakufu was playing 'a sort of double game which would consist of putting forward a thousand pretexts to keep a crisis at a distance while leaving the most determined Princes to begin hostilities which it will be able to disavow if they they fail and enlist in aid if they have some chance of success',[53] and he warned a Bakufu official that 'the independence of Japan would be affected by this state of affairs much more acutely than by the loyal execution of treaties concluded for our mutual advantage'.[54] Such vaguely threatening language was discarded after the arrival of Drouyn's 18 July reprimand, and even though his sentiments remained essentially the same, the chastened Bellecourt did not presume to suggest the use of force when the murder of Lieutenant Camus in October was followed by rumours that big Japanese merchants trading with foreigners were being attacked. Rather he concluded, resignedly, that 'it will soon be preferable to give up and leave rather than see continue a state of affairs which offers little hope of stability';[55] and when, a few days later, he warned the Quai d'Orsay that the Bakufu seemed about to demand the closing of Yokohama again, this time in earnest, he indicated that he had limited himself to declining to discuss the issue with Japanese officials and informing them that any decision to alter the Treaties must be made in Europe.[56] A postscript announced that the Japanese government was considering a new embassy to Europe for that purpose.

THE 1864 EMBASSY TO FRANCE AND THE SHIMONOSEKI EXPEDITION

The decision to send a second Japanese embassy to Europe was announced to Bellecourt as definite in December 1863. He had encouraged the idea , as he thought that such a step would give the Bakufu a breathing space and also relieve the pressure on foreigners, at least temporarily.[57] Drouyn de Lhuys, however, initially did not welcome what he considered to be an unnecessary and inconvenient distraction.[58] At a distance of thousands of miles, he could not feel the tensions or sense the difficulties of the Japanese political situation as a diplomat on the spot could. The reports from Bellecourt that Satsuma and some other *han* were now known to be in favour of foreign trade, even if they could not avow it publicly, appear to have convinced the foreign minister that it was safe to refuse outright the demand for the closure of Yokohama; and he did not appreciate, as Bellecourt vaguely did, that if Satsuma was not an advocate of seclusion, as had previously been thought, neither was it a supporter of the traditional Bakufu monopoly of national power. Even if he had been aware of the forcible expulsion of xenophobic samurai from Kyoto in September 1863, he would not have understood that although this had weakened the *joi* opposition to the Bakufu, the fact that the action had been carried out not by the Bakufu but by Satsuma introduced additional strains into Bakufu-Satsuma relations. As these strains came to the fore, Hitotsubashi Keiki, who as the young shogun's guardian since 1862 held a prominent position in Tokugawa councils, became concerned that the policy of *kobu-gattai* seemed to be working in Satsuma's favour, and in early 1864 he effectively repudiated it.[59] While this restored the Bakufu's freedom of action, it also meant that there was no immediate prospect of persuading the Imperial Court to withdraw its opposition to the treaties (as Satsuma had been seeking to manoeuvre it into doing). In consequence, the shogun's government was almost as weak and isolated as before, and the sending of an embassy to Europe was necessary in order to forestall the criticizm that it was doing nothing to put into effect the expulsion order which the Court had issued in 1863.

Some Bakufu leaders, with the 1862 mission in mind may really have hoped to achieve the closure of Yokohama. Others may only have expected to gain time. In either case, the new embassy proved a grave disappointment. Having left Japan at the end of January 1864, it returned before the end of August.[60] It had visited only one country – France – and the shortness of the embassy's stay was clearly not unconnected with the nature of its reception by the French foreign minister, whose attitude to the Japanese envoys showed nothing of the caution he had enjoined on Bellecourt. On the contrary, Drouyn de Lhuys displayed an intransigence which came close to belligerence. For once the fear that France might be compelled to enforce its demands, should they be refused appeared to have been set aside.

Why this should have been so is by no means clear. It has been suggested that the evasive tactics of the mission leader, Ikeda, may have enabled Drouyn de Lhuys to see what Bellecourt had had to put up with for four years, but this seems implausible, especially since he subsequently reverted to his previous attitude.[61] A more persuasive explanation is that direct personal contact with the Japanese emissaries meant that the French foreign minister was no longer forced to rely on assessments by Bellecourt which might be out of date by the time they reached Paris or affected by the French representative's predilections or prejudices. In particular, it meant that he did not have to worry that he might be drawn by Bellecourt's miscalculation into any risky and costly undertaking. For the first time he was in a position of full control, and this even allowed him the option of engaging in pretence and bluff. He may not have been dissembling when he offered to aid the shogun, should the latter require it to overcome his internal difficulties;[62] but when, in the second of six conferences held between 7 May and 10 June, he threatened to insist on the immediate opening of Osaka and Edo if Yokohama, Nagasaki and Hakodate were not made free ports, he cannot have meant what he said. When the envoys said such a concession would provoke fresh hostility within Japan, the foreign minister's extraordinary reply was: 'Then France must use force.' Upon this the envoys hastened to say that they were not refusing, merely making an observation. In their fifth conference with Drouyn de Lhuys they proposed making Nagasaki and Hakodate free ports in return for the closing of Yokohama, pleading that 'the fate of Japan depends on the decision which will be taken on this matter by France and its allies'. Again, the foreign minister's response was blunt and uncompromising.

Drouyn de Lhuys did not, it should be noted, insist on opening new ports or making existing ones free in the convention which was signed on 20 June, but this agreement did contain a remarkable (and questionable) provision whereby France pledged itself to aid the Bakufu in opening the Shimonoseki straits (barred to foreign ships since June 1863 by the coastal batteries of Choshu, which remained a stronghold of anti-foreign feeling) if they were still closed in three months' time.[63] France also undertook to allow Japanese students to study in Paris and to facilitate the purchase of arms and warships by the Bakufu; and in return it secured the promise of reductions in import duties, plus an indemnity of 140,000 dollars for Choshu's bombardment of a French ship.[64] None of this had been anticipated in Japan, either by the Bakufu or by Western diplomats, and it is possible that Ikeda and his colleagues signed the convention only because they hope to preempt any further demands or surprises by the French Foreign Minister. At the final conference the envoys stated that they no longer intended to visit any of the other European capitals. In view of Drouyn de Lhuys' attitude, they may have felt that it was less dangerous to negotiate in Japan than in Europe.[65]

The 1864 Japanese embassy conspicuously failed to secure the significant breathing-space which was its most realistic aim. No less seriously, Ikeda's acceptance, albeit conditional, of French help against Choshu rendered the Bakufu even more open to *joi* attack. It is consequently not surprising that the new French minister, Léon Roches, was secretly very relieved at the Bakufu's refusal to ratify the convention, although he naturally put on a show of indignation.[66] To appreciate his position fully, however, it is necessary to see it in the context of diplomatic developments in Japan during the first half of 1864.

The most significant of these developments was the return of Alcock from leave in March 1864, determined never again to submit himself to the uncertainties of Japanese politics. By the time Roches arrived to take up his post as minister on 27 April, Alcock was already planning to make use of the strong British fleet which was currently in Japanese waters. On 19 May, Roches reported that he had received a letter from the British minister proposing punitive action by the treaty powers against Choshu in the hope not only of opening the Shimonoseki Straits but also of weakening the chief bastion of anti-foreignism and thus, it was hoped, strengthening the cooperative elements within the Bakufu.[67] Since both the American and Dutch Ministers were in complete agreement with this scheme, Roches was faced with a dilemma. On the one hand, he could not have been ignorant of the fact that Bellecourt had been severely rebuked for his 1863 proposal to support the shogun by a similar use of force. On the other hand, it was customary for France to act in common with Britain in Japanese affairs. At first Roches maintained an equivocal attitude, but his natural inclination towards bold measures, backed by his conviction that the situation would deteriorate if the Powers did not counteract the internal pressure on the Bakufu by a show of Western strength, made it likely that he would sooner or later find a way of collaborating with Britain.

Already before the receipt of Alcock's letter, Roches had reported that the prospect facing foreigners was eventual expulsion, once the Japanese had bought Western arms in sufficient quantities.[68] A week later he added that, in his very first interview with the *roju,* he had been surprised to receive a demand for the closure of Yokohama and even more taken aback when this was followed by the declaration that the Bakufu would soon be unable to protect foreigners there, thus making trade impossible. This, he claimed, was a threat to the treaty which he had been instructed to observe religiously, and in the light of this danger he had re-read the instructions sent to Bellecourt and concluded that he would be justified in according his moral support to his colleagues' scheme if the Japanese government persisted in its attitude. He had also promised his material support in protecting the persons and goods of their nationals.[69]

When this dispatch reached Paris at the start of August, Drouyn de Lhuys was somewhat disconcerted, though not as much as he would have been had he known what Roches had been doing since it had been sent. The foreign minister invited Roches to disregard any resolutions by his colleagues and 'to avoid engaging our flag beyond what is required for the security of your Mission and that of the foreign residents'. He asserted that the British government was correct in believing that there were enlightened Japanese in positions of influence, and that 'it would not be wise . . . to make war in order to prevent war', and he expressed the hope that the convention which he had just signed would help to get the Bakufu back to a wiser line of policy.[70] Less than a week later he followed this up, most unusually, with a telegram stating that London was persisting in its peaceful approach and had recalled Alcock.[71]

Both these communications were fated to arrive too late to affect events, but in any case it seems likely, from the fact that he sent no further reports until 17 August, that Roches had resolved to disregard Drouyn's views and present him with a *fait accompli*. When he did write again, he informed his foreign minister that he had requested Admiral Jaurès to participate in the expedition, should the Bakufu fail to act against Choshu.[72] His dispatch significantly revealed little of his sustained campaign to overcome the resistance to which Jaurès' own reports to the Navy Ministry between 15 June and 25 July bear ample witness.[73] The latter also show that Roches was less than honest in explaining his decision to cooperate with Alcock. Conscious that he might be accused of agreeing to a line of action which ran the risk of leading to war, the French representative sought to exculpate himself by informing Paris that the Bakufu had given tacit consent to the Powers' action, but it is clear from Jaurès' reports that Roches was prepared to engage French ships even before he received this assurance.[74]

Having decided to ignore his instructions and having expended a great deal of effort in persuading Jaurès to do the same, Roches could not have been much less displeased than the Bakufu when the Ikeda mission returned unexpectedly early on 19 August with the Paris Convention. Neither the provision in the convention for the Bakufu to open the Shimonoseki Straits, nor the French pledge to act if the Bakufu failed, was realistic; but as long as both signatories were bound by their commitment, it was impossible for the allied expedition to carry out the task for which it was now geared. As Alcock a little later expressed it in a dispatch to London: 'The result of this convention was to undo the work of so many months, to break up the combined action of the Four Powers, and to isolate France from the other three'.[75] If the naval action was delayed, instructions prohibiting such an operation would have time to arrive from the Western capitals and the opportunity to strike a decisive blow might be lost altogether. It was for these reasons that Roches reported the Bakufu's refusal to ratify the Paris

Convention with scarcely concealed satisfaction.[76] The expedition went ahead, and on 23 September, Roches was able to report that not only had the Choshu batteries been disarmed, but that the allied forces had been able to occupy Shimonoseki and impose terms on the defeated *han*. A month later the Bakufu, anxious to prevent further Western contact with Choshu, agreed to pay a three million dollar indemnity for the damage done to foreign ships and for the allies' consideration in not burning the town of Shimonoseki.[77]

The indisputable success of the expedition meant that the foreign representatives ultimately had no need to fear for their careers on account of their independent action; nevertheless before its results were known in Europe, Roches in particular was condemned for his breach of orders. 'I do not admit, sir', wrote Drouyn de Lhuys, 'that distance authorizes agents, as you seem to believe, to thus depart from the line of conduct which has been formally prescribed and, in reiterating my previous directions, I must remind you that you cannot depart from their strict observation without incurring the gravest responsibility'.[78] Even when he learned of the favourable outcome he remained obdurate. After a delay of over a month he informed Roches rather pointedly that the information sent back by Alcock, and passed from London to Paris, had enabled him to appreciate the motives for the expedition. He praised the admirals for not allowing the fighting to turn into a war and insisted that his own pacific policy was not wrong and must be maintained. For Roches there was no commendation.[79]

However reluctant Drouyn de Lhuys was to acknowledge that the Western representatives had been justified in taking naval action, it was very quickly evident that the Shimonoseki expedition had had a decisive impact on both politics and diplomacy in Japan. Neither the Bakufu nor any of its rivals could henceforth risk pressing for the withdrawal of foreigners, and although the Bakufu could still be attacked for its past and current weakness towards the Western powers, such criticizm was less damaging than it had been before. For Roches, too, the expedition was important in several ways. By freeing the foreign representatives from their perpetual concern with maintaining a foothold in Japan, it allowed them to develop more positive and ambitious ideas about their role. Roches was extremely alert to this possibility, and the fact that he had been proved right over the action against Choshu gave him a strong hand in his subsequent dealings with his foreign minister. Moreover, the expedition also provoked the recall to London, and then the posting to Peking, of the able Alcock. Up to then, he had dominated the diplomatic scene. When the next British minister, Sir Harry Parkes, arrived in mid-1865, he was to find that Roches had laid claim to this position.[80]

3

LÉON ROCHES AND FRENCH SUPPORT OF THE BAKUFU 1864–68

THE BAKUFU – FRANCE SPECIAL RELATIONSHIP

THE SHIMONOSEKI Expedition marked the end of the first, turbulent, phase of Japan's relations with the Western powers following the signing of the 1858 treaties. Its success meant that demands for the expulsion of foreigners were henceforth confined to a minority of extremists and that the Bakufu was now willing to accommodate the French requests for the lifting of restrictions on the export of silk and silkworm eggs. The date on which Roches reported this – 15 October 1864 – may be regarded as an important turning-point in another way, for his dispatch also contained the following passage: 'I can even add that the *roju* have given me proofs of consideration and trust of which I believe it unnecessary to render account to the department but which give me hope of fruitfully fulfilling the mission which the government of the Emperor has entrusted to me.'[1] This intimation that Roches was being treated in a particularly favourable manner was the first definite sign of the emergence of a special relationship between Japan and France – a relationship which, as many historians have recognized, was to significantly influence the final years of the Tokugawa Bakufu and arguably play an important part in the latter's downfall.[2]

The new friendship between Roches and the Bakufu was soon in evidence at the diplomatic level. Following the Shimonoseki expedition, the Bakufu, anxious to avoid direct relations between the Western powers and Choshu, had accepted responsibility for Choshu's attacks on foreign ships and was given the choice of either paying a huge indemnity of three million Mexican dollars or opening another port to trade. Despite Britain's formal acquiescence in this decision, both Alcock and his stand-in, chargé d'affaires Winchester, had a strong preference for the latter; and with the support of the United States and Holland, Winchester was prepared to press for this option. The Bakufu, however, had good reasons for objecting to it. Even if the port were to be in Tokugawa-controlled territory, its opening would constitute an extension of the treaties which the Bakufu, by its earlier promise to the Court, remained in theory committed ultimately to terminate. Yet as it was in no position to pay the whole indemnity within two years, as required, the Bakufu could hardly have succeeded in resisting the Powers had they joined together in a common entente. Instead of backing his diplomatic colleagues, however, Roches persuaded Drouyn de Lhuys to opt for the indemnity, and without France's support the British government was reluctant to apply the strong pressure called for by Winchester.[3] As a result, the Bakufu was saved from another politically damaging surrender.

Roches' success did not long remain unchallenged, for in June 1865 the forceful Sir Harry Parkes arrived to take up his duties as British minister, and though Roches' junior in age by almost twenty years, he was less easily put off by his French colleague than Winchester had been. In November, backed by a powerful flotilla, he led his fellow diplomats to Hyogo. There they were not only close to Osaka, currently the location of the shogun and various of his leading advisers, but at an ominously short distance from Kyoto. With Parkes calling the tune, the diplomatic representatives presented the Bakufu with three demands – imperial sanction of the 1858 treaties, lower tariffs, and the opening of Hyogo and Osaka – in return for all of which they offered to waive payment of the remaining two-thirds of the indemnity. Were these to be rejected, there might, it was implied, be a direct approach to the Imperial Court or to the leading *han*. Notwithstanding the fact that France, in common with the rest of the Western powers, stood to make material gains if this new pressure met with success, Roches' pro-Bakufu sympathies led him to oppose the idea at first. Then, when he found Parkes adamant, and when it appeared that not only France but also the Bakufu might benefit if the demonstration of Western power and determination led to an imperial acknowledgement that the treaties with foreign countries were legitimate, he agreed to the *roju's* request that he accompany the British minister while contributing a restraining influence on him.[4] Claiming to be ill, he took no part in the negotiations on the British flag-ship; but when these seemed to have reached an impasse because the Bakufu was unable to concede the opening of Osaka and Hyogo, Roches helped to re-draft the final note with which the Bakufu partially satisfied Parkes.[5] His own dispatches make no mention of this.

Roches' concern for the Bakufu's position continued to influence his diplomacy in 1866. When a new Commercial Convention was negotiated, following the promise which the Bakufu had made to Parkes in November, Roches, in deference to his colleague's personal susceptibilities and Britain's predominant interest in Japan's import trade, allowed the British minister to act for him. Behind the scenes, however, his role seems to have been more positive, and in his report to the Quai d'Orsay he claimed a share of the credit for predisposing the Japanese towards more liberal ideas concerning international trade: 'The material question, if I may express myself thus, of tariff revision has been particularly dealt with by Sir H. Parkes; but I believe that I have greatly contributed to the success of the moral part of our convention. For a long time, as Your Excellency will have been convinced by reading my correspondence, . . . I have been preparing the high officials of the Japanese government for the adoption of liberal measures which have led to the abandonment of the last obstacles behind which struggled the spirit of isolationism – still yesterday the motive behind this Empire's politics'.[6] In the light of these comments, and in view of the influence which Roches had already acquired, it seems possible that he persuaded Bakufu officials that a reduction in duties would be the best way of securing an improvement in the British minister's attitude towards the Japanese government. The adoption of a uniform 5% import tariff may, therefore, have owed as much to him as to the blustering Parkes.

With regard to the other major diplomatic issue – the position which the Powers should take on the growing challenge to the Bakufu from the powerful south-western domains, and particularly the outrightly defiant Choshu – the difference between France's commitment to the established authority and Britain's more open position was less easy to disguise.[7] Here again Roches' pro-Bakufu sympathies were already marked, for he drew on his campaign experience in Algeria to offer military advice to Tokugawa officials and he persuaded his diplomatic colleagues to try to prevent the direct import of arms into Choshu by foreign traders.[8] His most striking demonstration of support for the Bakufu, however, came in mid-1866, when he agreed to a request by the *roju* that he follow Parkes to Nagasaki in order to counteract any impression which the latter might give of Western sympathy for the dissidents in the south-west.[9] Previously Roches had eschewed all contact with the powerful *han*, but now he welcomed the chance to encounter a Satsuma representative and, as he reported, leave 'no doubt in his mind with regard to the prudent and loyal policy which the foreign powers are determined to follow in regard to Japan'. He noted with some satisfaction that 'it was easy to read the disappointment on the face of the Satsuma officer'.[10]

Roches also succeeded in accompanying Parkes on his return from Nagasaki, although he failed to persuade him to join in an offer of mediation to Choshu when they passed through the Shimonoseki Straits. Parkes' reluctance was hardly surprising, since Roches' proposal was far from impartial: the note that he sent to Choshu spoke of the *han*'s illegal actions and offered to facilitate its 'submission' to the shogun.[11] How far the French would go in their support for the existing regime could not be known by the south-western domains, but concern that French aid might lead to a Tokugawa revival may well have helped to bring Satsuma and Choshu together in 1866 in an alliance which their erstwhile rivalries might otherwise have prevented.[12]

In reality, the fears of the south-western *han* were not without foundation, for by the beginning of 1868, when they launched their risky but successful challenge against the Bakufu, the latter was receiving not only diplomatic but also material assistance from France; and a few more years of French support might have transformed its position. The process had begun in early 1865 when the Bakufu officially requested French help in the construction of a naval dockyard and arsenal.[13] French assistance was by no means automatic, for suspicion still lingered that anti-foreign elements might yet regain influence in Japan, but Roches was a powerful advocate. His emphasis on Japanese admiration and preference for France could only be pleasing to his government; and when combined on the one hand with the warning that the Bakufu would turn elsewhere if rejected, and on the other with expectation that the materials would be purchased in France, it proved irresistible. The agreement of Paris was immediately forthcoming,[14] and the scheme, on which the Bakufu proposed to spend up to thirty – five million francs, was soon underway. A preliminary survey was entrusted to Lieutenant Verny, a French naval engineer; and after he had suggested Yokosuka as a suitable site, he was put in charge of constructing Japan's first major military installation. In March 1866 work was commenced with the aid of 45 French workmen, many of them from the French naval dockyards.[15] A small factory was established at Yokohama, and partly to provide interpreters, partly for more general cultural purposes, a French school under Roches' interpreter, Mermet de Cachon, was also set up there. Unfortunately for the Bakufu, its massive investment did not pay off, for the dockyard was completed only in 1876; but had the Tokugawa regime not been overthrown in 1868, the ambitious project would have given it a clear naval superiority over its internal rivals. Instead, the dockyard was to be inherited by the Meiji government and to become one of the main bases of the imperial Japanese navy.

Of more immediate value was another product of the Bakufu-French special relationship, the *Société Française d'Exportation et d'Importation.* The possibility of such an enterprise was first mooted by Roches on 17 October 1865, when he reported that he had been approached by the *roju* with a proposal that 'a powerful foreign company' should be formed in France for the purpose of 'entering into relations, outside of official channels, with an association of the same kind formed by Japanese subjects'. Although it was understood, Roches reported to Drouyn de Lhuys, that 'the Japanese government would renounce all action with regard to these companies other than that which European governments take with associations of this kind', he anticipated that as a result of 'the immense advantages which a company to which this government would simply accord its benevolence would be assured, Japan would be for us what China is for England, a French market'.[16] The idea was blessed by the Quai d'Orsay and the Ministry of Commerce, and a company was soon formed in France with the backing of the *Société Générale*, a bank which had recently been established with the intention of providing credit for new ventures.[17] Although a considerable amount of military equipment was purchased by the Bakufu through the trading company, however, the contacts made in Japan in the autumn of 1866 with Japanese merchants by its representative, Jacques Coullet, did not have time to come to full fruition, and the general pattern of Japanese imports and exports did not change very substantially.

The military power of the Bakufu might have been strengthened even more by yet another project which depended largely on French aid. During the final years of the Tokugawa period the inadequacy of the traditional military system was becoming generally recognized and several *han* experimented with foreign methods. The Bakufu, too, began to change its military structure in 1862, but it went much further when, early in 1866, a request was made to France, through Roches, to provide assistance in forming the nucleus of a new army.[18] While not prepared to supply as large a mission as the Bakufu and Roches wished, the French government did send to Japan a group of able young officers who, despite encountering various difficulties, applied themselves to their task diligently after they arrived in Japan in January 1867. Like the Yokosuka dockyard and arsenal, however, the military mission could not achieve a major transformation within the time available; and the reluctance of the last shogun to plunge Japan into civil war in early 1868 meant that the troops which had received French training were given little chance to prove how much they had learned.[19]

The Bakufu-French special relationship was even more far-reaching than the foregoing account might suggest, for Roches was also involved, especially in late 1866 and early 1867, in what has been considered by some to be the most significant of all the changes initiated by the Bakufu – the basic reform of Japan's political structure.[20] The reason why some historians emphasize this latter point is not so much the actual effects of the reform – even after the able and ambitious Tokugawa Yoshinobu became shogun in 1866, it was only implemented to a limited extent – as the evidence it provides for the view that the Tokugawa government was changing from a feudal organization into an absolutist bureaucracy.[21] Whether or not this view is justified is debatable. Roches' own observations about the reform of Japan in general tended to emphasize its progressive nature. In March 1867, for instance, he justified his actions to his government in the following words:

> Given the necessity of a rapid transformation, what is the best means of facilitating it and of introducing the Japanese people into the ranks of the civilized nations? Is it to stir up the embers of feudal attitudes and the rancours of the Daimyo? Or is it not rather to inspire and support the fertile reforms to which this country lends itself and to procure for it the instruments of civilization of which the European peoples are in full possession and of which they can teach others the conditions and usage.[22]

However much he expressed his concern for Japan as a whole, Roches certainly appreciated the need in practice for the strengthening of Tokugawa control. Basing his recommendations on his understanding of his own country's history, perhaps – in a later dispatch he claimed that feudalism was no match for a strong monarchy[23] – he urged the need to strengthen central authority and make it more efficient. An important item on his agenda – and an obvious one in the light of the challenge which Choshu and Satsuma were already posing to the Bakufu – was the limitation of the power of the more independent (*tozama*) daimyo. This was to be achieved by restoring the *sankin kotai* system, whereby daimyo spent alternate years in Edo; but the idea of eventually abolishing feudal domains seems to have been voiced by Roches as well.

Possibly to conceal the radical nature of his proposals, the French minister reported to Paris in approving terms a plan, which he attributed to Yoshinobu, for establishing some form of power-sharing in the immediate future: 'The Taikoun has, besides, indicated to me the intention of having the assistance, for making laws and adopting major policies, of a council of fifty persons chosen by election from among the daimyo in the Empire. The votes of these daimyo would be determined in proportion to their revenue. In that way the Tycoon would always be sure of a large majority.'[24] For their part, the direct retainers of the Tokugawa, the *fudai* daimyo and *hatamoto*, would be incorporated into a rationalized administrative structure. Bakufu institutions themselves were to undergo fundamental reorganization, the *roju* and *wakadoshiyori* (the senior and junior councils) being replaced by Western-style ministries headed by specialists and staffed by men of ability, with much less attention than before being paid to rank.

As Ishii Takashi comments, this was little different from the policy which was to be put into effect by the imperial government which replaced the Tokugawa regime in 1868, although it should be said that the post-1868 focusing of power on the Emperor contrasted very strongly, at least nominally, with Roches' scheme, in which the Emperor was to be returned to his former impotence and so educated and controlled that he would never again provide a rallying-point for anti-Tokugawa agitation.[25] To establish a better financial support for the new modernized structure, Roches emphasized the necessity for reforming the fiscal system also. New taxes on many items were proposed, with less dependence being placed on the major traditional levies on arable land, and a budget system based on the sale of all the Bakufu's rice revenues was also envisaged.

How far Yoshinobu intended to follow Roches' advice and to what extent Bakufu leaders had their own ideas of reform and looked to the French minister for support and encouragement rather than inspiration cannot be stated with certainty. That the last shogun did place great emphasis on friendship with France, however, was shown by his readiness to send his younger brother, Tokugawa Akitake, to Paris in 1867, not only to represent Japan but also, together with other young Japanese, for the purpose of receiving a French education. Yoshinobu's appreciation of Roches' efforts was expressed in several messages to the French minister, in one of which he declared: 'I am going to employ this time of suspension of activity [for official mourning] to follow part of the excellent counsel which you have not ceased to give to the Japanese government since your happy arrival in this country'. [26] If further proof of the exceptional position secured by Roches is needed, it can be found in a Quai d'Orsay assessment of Roches' position in February 1867 in which it was stated that 'M. Roches has been able to obtain so legitimate an influence in this country, which owes to him its transformation since 1864, that he corresponds directly with the Taikoun and on several occasions when the Japanese ministers have wished to have a plan adopted by their sovereign they have asked him to support it'.[27]

THE REPUDIATION OF ROCHES' POLICY

If the long-term plans for the re-establishment of Tokugawa power were to have a successful outcome, the immediate challenge of the south-western *han* would have to be met. As an important step to this end, agreement with the French trading company's representative, Coullet, was reached in 1866 for the supply of military equipment on a large scale.[28] Payment for this, however, presented the Bakufu with enormous difficulties. Not only were its revenues still limited, despite its adoption of various *ad hoc* devices, by its dependence on a traditional, mainly land-based, taxation system, but its expenditures had risen sharply since the opening of the country as a result of rapid inflation, defence expenditure, and the cost of suppressing *han* dissidence and popular uprisings, not to mention indemnities to foreign countries. The most tempting solution was a foreign loan, and this was decided upon in the autumn of 1866 when an agreement was reached with Coullet to raise thirty-five million francs in France and Britain.[29] Initially the project did not appear unrealistic. Within months, however, all hopes of a loan had disappeared, abandoned in the aftermath of the failure of the Franco-Japanese trading company to secure French public support.[30]

The collapse of the plan for a loan was a huge setback for the Bakufu. As Ishii Takashi puts it, 'bearing in mind the fact that the funds for completing the military preparations by means of which the Bakufu intended to suppress the powerful anti-Bakufu *han* were to come from this loan, one can say that it was on its success or failure that the Bakufu's existence really depended'.[31] Since the removal of such a key element of the Bakufu-French special relationship was so important, it warrants a fuller explanation; and to provide one it is necessary to take several factors into consideration, notably Roches' aims and methods, the extent to which his diplomacy was inspired or supported by the French government, and France's relations with Britain. These are all relevant because the abandonment of the loan followed shortly after, and was almost certainly partly caused by, the unexpected withdrawal of support for Roches by the Quai d'Orsay; and Paris's action was directly connected to its discovery that there was a danger of French policy in Japan incurring British disapproval. It is further arguable that when the Marquis de Moustier, who had become foreign minister in October 1866, instructed Roches on 18 May 1867 not to become involved in Japanese politics, he did not appreciate what France stood to lose – it is even possible that he was unaware that Roches had already established a special relationship with the Bakufu.[32] What is clear is that the effect of his action was to tie Roches' hands as far as further support for the Bakufu was concerned. Moreover, since it was accompanied by a failure to back the Tokugawa claim to be recognized as the sole legitimate governing authority in Japan at the Paris Exposition and since the *Société Française d'Exportation et d'Importation* was on the verge of a share flotation, the new French coolness towards the Bakufu could hardly have come at a less opportune time.

In support of the claim that the repudiation of Roches was prompted by the Quai d'Orsay's concern that French policy in Japan might embroil it with Britain, it can be argued that the policy which Roches had been following in Japan between 1865 and 1867 was largely his own personal creation, that it went much further than his government realized, and that it diverged significantly from that followed by Sir Harry Parkes. To do so, it is necessary to examine more closely the development of French and British policy towards Japan since 1864, since although, up until then, there were occasional minor disagreements between France and Britain, both countries subscribed to the proposition that the maintenance of foreign interests was closely linked with the preservation of shogunal power.

This shared assumption gradually came to be questioned, and it was the English minister, Alcock, who first diverged from the earlier view. Contacts with Satsuma, after the British bombard-ment of Kagoshima, persuaded him that the daimyo were by no means as anti-foreign as they had been portrayed; and he concluded from this, and from his awareness of Bakufu weakness, that the best solution both for Japan and for foreign trade was a constitutional compromise whereby the shogun would share his power with an assembly of daimyo.[33] What Alcock, and subsequently Parkes, inclined towards was not very different from the limited changes envisaged by Satsuma and other daimyo under the slogan of *Kobugattai* (union of Court and Bakufu) in the first half of the 1860s.[34] Contrary to the suggestions of a number of Japanese historians, however, not even Parkes went so far as to favour what the more radical samurai leaders in Satsuma and Choshu were working for after 1864: the overthrow of Tokugawa authority. Reform of the Bakufu, not its outright abolition, was what the British minister desired. To interpret Parkes' visits to the south-western *han* as meaning that he supported the latter is to ignore the fact that any attempt to achieve such a revolutionary aim would have been expected to lead to a civil war which would have injured British trade.

Not all British diplomats shared Parkes' views; the young interpreter, Ernest Satow, in particular, had much closer personal knowledge of the samurai activists, and his sympathy for their cause, revealed to historians by the publication of his 1860s' diary in 1921 under the title of *A Diplomat in Japan*, was long taken to represent the British position. The fact that Roches, with the obvious intention of encouraging greater reliance on France, did his best in his talks with Bakufu officials to portray Parkes in the same light, helps to explain why this opinion still remains common. Nevertheless, there is abundant evidence in Parkes' dispatches that he was significantly less committed to the anti-Tokugawa elements than were his subordinates. During his visit to the southern islands of Kyushu and Shikoku in July 1866, for instance, Parkes wrote that 'In regard to the political condition of Japan, the Tycoon's government appears, as far as I can judge, to be the only power in the State which is able to preserve general order, and secure the faithful observance of our Treaties'.[35] That he had no intention of seeking to encourage an anti-Tokugawa coalition is further indicated by a subsequent report in which he observed that 'It is by no means desirable that our communications with the Daimyos should be confined to that section who appear opposed to the existing government.'[36]

Further evidence that Parkes' sympathies did not wholly lie with the opponents of the shogun can be found in his acceptance of an interview with Yoshinobu early in 1867, even though he was conscious that such a meeting 'might be of material service to him at a time when a considerable section of the daimyos are not disposed to submit readily to his authority'.[37] In his private correspondence with the permanent secretary of the Foreign Office, Edmund Hammond, Parkes came out in support of the last shogun still more decisively in May 1867: 'At the same time I am quite disposed to give him all the support I can in whatever position he occupies; . . . he certainly appears to me to be the most superior Japanese I have yet met and it is possible that he will make for himself a name in History'.[38] Parkes' supposed alignment with the south-western daimyo also hardly squares with the fact that he made strenuous efforts to ensure that the shogun employed a British mission for the training of his naval officers, and that, not content with this, he also attempted to acquire a share in the training of the Bakufu army.[39] All in all, it is hard to avoid the conclusion that Parkes' sympathy for Satsuma and Choshu was limited, and that had he been fully aware of them, he would have been more likely to frown upon than to encourage the revolutionary aims of the younger samurai who were gaining influence in those domains after 1864.

In reality, then, the British attitude to the Japanese political situation changed much less than has often been assumed, and had Roches been content to continue in Bellecourt's footsteps, there need have been no significant friction between the two leading Western countries in Japan. If, though, French diplomacy remained more constant than the British in so far as there was not even a hint of deviation from support for the shogun, in reality it changed much more because that support became so active. The reasons for this development, however, have sometimes been misconstrued. It has been alleged, for instance, that the new policy was decided in Paris and that Roches was simply the agent who was entrusted with its implementation.[40] Such assertions are based on preconceived ideas rather than close analysis of the evidence; indeed, the latter indicates very clearly that Roches was expected to carry on the original policy of non-intervention from which Bellecourt had shown, to Drouyn de Lhuys' displeasure, signs of deviating. What seems to have misled the historians who have taken a contrary view is the assumption that France, as a great power, was naturally in competition with Britain, and that any attempt to promote French influence in Japan beyond its rival's must have been determined by the government in Paris. The apparent adoption of a policy of positive intervention by Drouyn de Lhuys at the time of the Ikeda mission's visit is taken as evidence that it was in early 1864 that the 'new line' was introduced.[41]

This view of French policy is superficially plausible, but misconceived. That the French foreign minister was engaging in bluff and had no thought of sending forces against Choshu – or any other enemies of the Bakufu – is all too apparent when one looks at Drouyn de Lhuys' reaction to Roches' agreement to French participation in the Shimonoseki Expedition. The severity of his strictures (until the expedition proved to be an indisputable triumph) make it abundantly clear that the Quai d'Orsay was still primarily concerned with avoiding what it perceived as unnecessary risks.[42] It is certainly possible – although there is no direct evidence for this – that the appointment of Roches reflected the concern of Napoleon III's government to extend France's commercial relations with Japan by sending there an enterprising diplomat who had special links with the French silk industry.[44] To treat his appointment as a 'new line' for this reason, though, is to ignore the fact that Bellecourt had already taken steps in this direction himself both by sending back to France some examples of Japanese silk-worms and by constantly urging the Bakufu to remove the restrictions on their export.[45]

The 'new line' theory also carries the implication that the initiative towards Bakufu–French friendship came entirely from the French side. This again rests on presupposition rather than evidence. While Roches' willingness to seize a favourable opportunity was to be a crucial factor in the development of a close relationship, his own dispatches suggest that the initial approaches came from the Bakufu. This evidence should not necessarily be accepted at face value: if Roches had departed from the official policy of caution by making his own overtures, he would hardly have admitted that he had done so. Nevertheless, even if he can be suspected of disingenuousness, there are other grounds for considering his views of the initial step towards a new level of cooperation to be substantially reliable. In particular, the record of the Bakufu's dealings with the Western powers since the opening of the treaty ports shows that the shogunal leaders were aware of the value of establishing a good rapport with one or more members of the diplomatic corps in Japan. Such a relationship could reduce the danger of isolation by providing a channel for information about the wider world as well as for the import of arms and other material requirements. Above all, gaining the sympathy of one or more Western representatives in Japan might temper the hostility of the Western powers at a time when the Bakufu's inability to execute the treaties made it highly vulnerable.

Until his departure from Japan in 1862, Townsend Harris to some extent played the role of friend and mentor, but the next American minister, Robert Pruyn, although willing to facilitate the purchase of arms, appears to have had too much of an eye on personal profit for the Japanese government's liking.[46] In any case, after 1861 the USA was too deeply involved in civil war to be of much use to Japan diplomatically. Neither Russia nor Britain could be envisaged in the role of protector, however, the one because of its supposed territorial ambitions, the other on account of its potentially threatening naval power and its unwelcome desire for the extension of trade,. For somewhat different reasons association with either Holland or Prussia offered little attraction. The former was now politically insignificant, and the latter had too little power and influence in East Asia. France, on the other hand, was a diplomatic heavy-weight and had a substantial military presence, without being strong enough to be a real danger. In 1863 Bellecourt had shown some disposition to give assistance to the Tokugawa regime – as, at least in appearance, did Drouyn de Lhuys in 1864 – and an approach to Roches would have been a logical move by the Bakufu.[47]

That the new relationship was so quick to emerge is partly explicable by the fact that Kurimoto Joun, a lesser Bakufu official who had served in Hakodate, was already on friendly terms with Roches' interpreter, Mermet de Cachon.[48] Ultimately what counted most, though, was Roches' own exceptional personality. Not only was he a man of great ambition and unusual vision, he was also exceptional in displaying goodwill towards Japan and respect towards Bakufu representatives.[49] The rapport which he was to establish with Japanese leaders arguably went well beyond that of any other diplomat in nineteenth-century Japan. It is important to note, however, that Roches did not evince an immediate sympathy for the Bakufu. During his first six months in Japan, indeed, he criticized the Japanese authorities in a manner not obviously distinguishable from that of his predecessor or his British counterparts. His early reports thus indicate that he did not arrive with any mission to create a special relationship with the shogun's government.

The crucial aspect of the Bakufu-French friendship, as far as the clash with British policy is concerned, was what it might lead to. Clearly Roches' policy held the promise of huge benefits for France, however much Roches might attempt to conceal them.[49] Not only would the modernization of Japan have a strong French flavour, but French strength and influence in the Far East stood to gain greatly from the acquisition of an ally (and perhaps a friendly naval base), from the immense increase in trade that would follow, and from a new outlet for French capital. These gains, had they ever been realized, would have presented a considerable challenge to British political and economic predominance in the Far East, and it would thus have been surprising if Britain had not attempted to sabotage the Bakufu-French friendship. Parkes, in particular, was bound to resent being unable to play the leading role in Japan after his very different experience in China; and hostility on his part to Roches' scheme may help to explain the failure of the trading company flotation and the collapse of the preparations for the crucial loan. Such a conclusion is suggested by a private letter from Parkes to Hammond, dated 14 November 1867, in which the former referred to Roches' position in a revealing passage:

> The Company which he and Coullet have endeavoured to form has proved an utter failure from their not being able to

get their shares taken. Their stock in trade would have been contracts with the Japanese Government and finance operations, in the way of loans on their account, but I have had something to do with checking these operations. Most of the contracts the Japanese Government thought of making have been abandoned as also the idea of raising a loan, and the proposed Company therefore find themselves without a field for their enterprise. I should, of course, not allow such a company to obtain any Exclusive privileges.[51]

Parkes did not, unfortunately, specify what steps he took to obstruct the French scheme.[52] It is clear that he advised Japanese officials against contracting any heavy obligations, but he could hardly have assumed that this would be effective.[53] It is possible that he also had a hand in what proved to be a significant action by the MP, Laurence Oliphant. Oliphant had served as a diplomat in Japan and had more recently developed close contacts with the young men from Satsuma who had come to study in Britain in 1866. In April 1867 he gave notice of a question in the House of Commons concerning French 'official trading'.[54] As a result, Lord Cowley, the British ambassador in Paris, was instructed by the Foreign Office on 19 April to bring to the French foreign minister's notice some reports in the *Japan Times* which had accused Roches of violating the treaties, and to request an explanation so that the parliamentary question might be answered.[55] Whether or not this communication was intended to warn the Quai d'Orsay that the British government was not happy about Roches' relations with the Bakufu in general is not certain. Whatever its intent, however, its effect must have exceeded expectations, for it was the need to make a response to it which led the Marquis de Moustier effectively to disassociate the Quai d'Orsay from the policy to which Roches had devoted so much effort. The latter was requested to provide the necessary information and warned that it was 'essential that your solicitude for our interests is exercised in such a fashion as not to furnish even the appearance of a pretext for our rivals to make an accusation'.[56]

Within France the fact that the government was distancing itself from Roches' commitment to the Bakufu was soon made evident when the Quai d'Orsay declined to issue a public statement that it accepted the shogun's claim to sovereignty over all Japan.[57] Such a lack of support was damaging because it followed an anti-Tokugawa propaganda campaign in the Paris press organized by the Comte de Montblanc (aided for a time, surprisingly, by Mermet de Cachon)[58] and because Montblanc had then outmanoeuvred a Tokugawa representative, Tanabe Taichi, at a meeting in April with the organizer of the Paris Exposition and secured a separate pavilion there for Satsuma on the pretext that its daimyo was also King of the Ryukyu islands. To make matters worse Montblanc then proceded to present medals decorated with the Satsuma crest to various French dignitaries, incluing Napoleon III. These blows to Roches' policy were further compounded by rumours of the impending overthrow of the Bakufu and, together with public awareness of the parliamentary question of which Oliphant had given notice, they spelled doom for the flotation of shares by the *Société Française d'Exportation et d'Importation*. Disastrously, only 1400 of the 40,000 shares initially offered were taken up.[59]

Whether Moustier intended his dispatch of 18 May as a reprimand as well as a warning is open to question. Lord Cowley's report on 23 May that the foreign minister had taken 'the opportunity of informing me that he had written very strongly to M. Roches in consequence of the communication which I had made to His Excellency' rather suggests the former.[60] But even if he was merely lacking in consideration of his representative's feelings, the fact remains that Roches was told in the plainest terms that what he had done already was quite enough and that he should not involve France too closely with a government which might soon be overthrown. It was made clear to him that he could expect no support for any independent action in the future and that British views on Japan were considered more reliable than his.[61]

How is it possible to explain this apparent willingness to abandon a successful policy at a mere hint of British displeasure? Two basic causes have generally been cited – firstly the worsening of France's position in Europe after the Austro-Prussian War and the Mexican Expedition, and secondly the replacement of Drouyn de Lhuys as foreign minister by Moustier who, it is held, was not committed to Roches and the Bakufu-France special link as his predecessor was, and who was more anxious not to offend Britain or become deeply involved in affairs outside Europe.[62] These arguments are not fully compelling. On the one hand, they imply that there was a greater sense of impending international crisis than actually existed, and on the other they fail to take account of the fact that Moustier's dispatch to Roches cannot be seen as especially personal since it closely followed a recommendation prepared by an anonymous Quai d'Orsay official[63]; and they further ignore the fact that, notwithstanding his display of firmness towards the Ikeda mission in 1864, Drouyn de Lhuys was no less concerned than Moustier to avoid involvement in distant parts. Had he still been in office in 1867, he, too, would have been likely to issue a warning, even though his tone would probably have been less cold and his attitude to the shogunal mission in 1867 more supportive. The point needs to be stressed, since attributing the reversal of policy wholly to international conditions and the change of minister has allowed historians to ignore a still more fundamental factor: that French policy was made in Japan and was to a large extent Roches' personal policy. It was this that made it so vulnerable to British pressure.

The clearest evidence that it was Roches rather than his foreign minister who masterminded the special relationship with the Bakufu is the fact that Roches spoke openly to both Winchester and Parkes of his *'politique personnelle'*, though, not surprisingly, these words never appeared in his dispatches to his own government.[64] Even without Roches' explicit acknowledgement of his personal involvement, the fact that it was he who provided the impulsion from the French side is evident from the Quai d'Orsay archives. These show that no significant initiative after 1864 was forthcoming from Paris; indeed the French government sometimes dragged its feet in responding to requests from Roches on the Bakufu's behalf, despite the efforts which Roches made to render refusal difficult by stressing both Japanese preference for France and the need to strengthen the power which guaranteed the treaties. For example, the Quai d'Orsay and the Ministry of War initially decided not to send as many military instructors as Roches had asked for, on the ground that 'it would be prudent not to give at first too great an importance to the mission which will be formed'.[65] Nor was Roches able in 1865 to persuade his foreign minister to ease the Bakufu's financial difficulties by renouncing France's share of the Shimonoseki Indemnity, an obvious action for the foreign minister to take had he been particularly concerned about the furtherance of the Bakufu-French link. The dispatch in which Drouyn de Lhuys first refused to make this concession is worth quoting, in fact, for in it he defined French policy in terms to which even a British minister would have found it hard to take exception:

> I believe that it is undoubtedly useful, in the present circumstances, for us to contribute to increasing the Taikoun's resources because I believe, like you, that we will thus aid him to triumph over the opposition of the daimyos who are enemies of the treaties. But the giving of arms and munitions, which we have already consented to, just like the assistance we are ready to accord for the creation of an artillery arsenal and for naval dockyards near Yokohama, sufficiently answer this end, and you will easily be able to appreciate the reasons which do not permit us to go further.[66]

If the fact that French policy was neither initiated nor positively developed by the French foreign minister was important, so, too, was the Quai d'Orsay's ignorance of the full extent of French involvement. Roches' dispatches were few by any standard, but their paucity is especially remarkable in the light of the numerous important developments taking place in Japan at this time.[67] He excused his infrequent reporting by pleas of ill health and by the claim that all his time was taken up by action; and the fact that his long silences were tolerated without question lends support to the view that there was, in Paris, only a limited interest in Japan. Such a situation made it easier for Roches to conceal those aspects of his policy for which he could not expect approval or which might reveal the depth of his involvement. His reports were not only uninformative, however, but also misleading. This may not always have been intentional: when Roches misrepresented the views of the south-western daimyo, it may have been at least partly because he himself had almost no direct contacts with them. The deception can scarcely have been anything but deliberate, however, when he reported Japanese requests for aid and advice as emanating solely from the Japanese side. This fact was particularly important with regard to Yoshinobu's governmental reform plans, for Moustier must have regarded them as something entirely Japanese in origin, for which France had negligible responsibility.

That Roches should have made so deep an impression on French policy in Japan can ultimately only be explained if one takes into account his exceptional character. A relative of Madame Roland, one of the Girondin leaders in the French Revolution, and a man whose flamboyant career in North Africa contained the ingredients of a romantic novel, he was not the kind of person to turn away from the opportunity – and challenge – of playing a key role when it beckoned, even if this necessitated unorthodox action.[68] He would have been all too well aware, however, from Drouyn de Lhuys' severe criticism of his involvement in the Shimonoseki Expedition, that caution and restraint remained the official watchwords. Only by playing down the political significance of his actions until his policy was firmly established and paying clear dividends could he hope to win for himself and his country a special position in a new Japan.

While, though, personal ambition and concern for French interests undoubtedly were Roches' primary motives, he also seems to have developed genuine pro-Tokugawa sympathies and to have really believed that the Tokugawa regime deserved admiration for trying to modernize itself. His pro-Japanese feelings, however, transcended politics, as can be seen from the remarkable speech which he made to Japanese students of French at Yokohama in November 1866, in which – commenting upon student essays on his chosen theme of climbing Mount Fuji – he imagined a future Japan (as seen from Japan's highest mountain) covered with roads, railways and factories, while its coastal waters teemed with steamships.[69] It is also significant that the Comte de Turenne, who later, as chargé d'affaires, was one of the few sympathetic French observers of Meiji modernization, gained his first experience of Japan as Roches' attaché. On his return to Paris in 1866 Turenne wrote a memorandum for the Quai d'Orsay which concluded a review of relations between the shogun and the Western powers with the words: 'We can count on [the shogun's] interested cooperation, and by this cooperation hope to civilize Japan'.[70] It would be reasonable to suppose that this attitude was inspired by Roches.

One further explanation of why Roches pursued a personal policy and why he kept so much from the Quai d'Orsay must also be mentioned: that he had a pecuniary interest in the Bakufu-French friendship. No direct evidence of such an interest appears to exist, nor indeed did an on-the-spot inquiry by the Yokohama Chamber of Commerce in 1866 find anything compromising.[71] Nevertheless, suspicions remain. The very fact that it was Roches' own banker, Flury Hérard, who was appointed Japanese consul-general in Paris and employed in all the Bakufu's financial transactions in Europe suggests that some sort of kickback would have been easy both to arrange and conceal. The same would apply, to a lesser extent, to Coullet's operations and to at least one silkworm egg transaction.[72] However, in the absence of more substantial evidence, the verdict must be 'not proven'. Even if a financial interest did exist, it need not have excluded other motives; and it would be difficult to account for all of Roches' activities in this way.

The fact that, for most of the time Roches was in Japan, French policy possessed a personal character has significant implications. It means, firstly, that the French government cannot justly be charged with actively pursuing an imperialistic aim of establishing an economic and political protectorate over Japan. Secondly, it goes a long way towards explaining the apparent volte-face on the part of the French foreign ministry. If the policy of close collaboration with the Tokugawa government had been initiated by Paris, it is hardly conceivable, even allowing for the change of foreign minister, that it could have been abandoned so lightly.[73] In fact, neither Drouyn de Lhuys nor Moustier was aware of the full extent of French involvement in Japanese politics.[74] Consequently, the Bakufu-French link was regarded as a peripheral enterprise which could be abandoned without much loss and without any sense of betrayal. It was this that made the interference of Britain so decisive.

ROCHES AND THE MEIJI RESTORATION

Though Moustier's 18 May dispatch was, in form, cautionary rather than censorious, it clearly meant the end of any personal policy in Edo; and in response Roches indignantly tendered his resignation. At the same time he insisted that all his actions had been approved by Paris and were entirely justified.[75] His words fell on stony ground, however. Indeed, from this time on any reference in Roches' dispatches to the shogun's need for help was assiduously underlined , and occasional marginal comments indicate that the French government now took such statements as confirmation that it should distance itself from a regime which was in trouble and quite possibly doomed. Despite the closer surveillance under which he henceforth had to operate, however, Roches remained in a position to give the shogun his moral support and help smooth any diplomatic difficulties that arose; and this could have been a major advantage for the Bakufu because in 1867 it was faced with a troublesome new problem involving Japanese Christians and French missionaries in Kyushu, not far from the south-western domains which were challenging Tokugawa authority.

The problem arose because in the area around the village of Urakami, near Nagasaki, several thousand Japanese Christians, whose families had preserved their faith (in diluted form) from the seventeenth century, had been rediscovered by French missionaries in 1865.[76] By 1867 their difficulties with local Buddhist priests and more open worship had created problems which local officials decided to settle by the imprisonment of some of their number. Lively protests by the Catholic priests were naturally forthcoming, and if these had resulted in French-led diplomatic pressure, the shogun would have been placed in an extremely awkward position. To alienate the foreign representatives by repressive measures at a time when he seemed at last to have secured their approval as a progressive ruler would have been to throw away a considerable asset and risk outside intervention. Yet to allow toleration to the Christians was impossible, for the enemies of Tokugawa power could have made great capital from the accusation that Yoshinobu was abandoning the traditional prohibition on what was still widely regarded as a pernicious religion.

Thanks to Roches, the dilemma never really had to be faced. The French minister did not entirely disregard the plight of the Christians or the pleas of the priests, but he readily accepted the shogun's promise that harsh measures would not be used and he stressed, in his communications with the missionaries, the limitations imposed by the 1858 treaty on their movements.[77] The fact that Roches' main concern was for the Bakufu's position, together with his evident preference for the Bakufu's version of what had been happening rather than that of the missionaries, led to bitter criticism from some of the latter.[78] Such attacks did not sway the French minister, however, and as a result the Urakami Christian question was not to play a part in the Tokugawa Bakufu's downfall. Instead it was to become one of the many problems inherited by the new Meiji government in 1868.

Even though Roches continued to provide some aid to the shogunate, the failure of the trading company flotation and, still more, the abandonment of hopes of a large loan were severe blows to the Bakufu. Setbacks of this magnitude could hardly fail to undermine Yoshinobu's trust not only in the French government's support but also in the French minister himself. Such a conclusion finds support in the fact that Roches was caught completely off-balance by Yoshinobu's resignation as shogun in November 1867. When rumours that this might happen first appeared in the Yokohama papers, the French minister greeted them with derision;[79] and his subsequent attempt to argue that Yoshinobu's action was a tactical manoeuvre which would not really weaken his position was, not surprisingly, less than convincing to the Quai d'Orsay.[80] Even when the south-western daimyo had gained the support of the Emperor by their coup d'état of 3 January 1868, Roches urged the ex-shogun to resist them, and assured him of France's moral support.[81]

Whether, as has been suggested, Roches made any offer of direct material support is, however, questionable.[82] His instructions so emphatically forbade any such involvement that he could have entertained no hope of official approval; and the most that he could have done would have been to allow the French military mission to advise the Bakufu military commanders on the best way to oppose the forces sent east from Kyoto.[83] As for French naval forces, the evident failure of Roches' policies meant that his influence over the new commander in the China Seas, Admiral Ohier, was negligible; and when Ohier had an audience with Yoshinobu in Edo in February, he did not, according to his own account, 'fail to affirm to his ministers, and then to Yoshinobu himself, with all possible firmness, combined with the consideration due to misfortune, that I would not intervene militarily in favour the Taicoun's interests'.[84] In such circumstances any promise of direct action by the French minister would have been of too little value to persuade the shogun to adopt a policy of active resistance.

Inability to offer military aid did not mean that Roches could not provide the Bakufu with any help in the period of uncertainty at the beginning of 1868. He had promised Yoshinobu France's moral support, and he endeavoured to persuade his colleagues not to make any diplomatic moves which would have favoured the anti-Bakufu forces.[85] In view of the fact that the south-western daimyo enjoyed the advantage of recognition by the Emperor, the foreign powers might not, but for his insistence, have issued a proclamation of neutrality. Roches was hampered, however, by the possibility that any decision calculated to benefit the Bakufu might, because of the exceptional fluidity of the situation, soon become a disadvantage. Later, when events had clearly turned against Yoshinobu, the French minister hoped to induce his diplomatic colleagues to intervene with an offer of mediation which would leave the Tokugawa in control of eastern Japan. After Parkes refused to cooperate, however, Roches made little effort to influence events.[86]

Despite the fact that Roches was constrained by his instructions and by Parkes' lack of sympathy, it is possible that he might have been able to take advantage of two anti-foreign acts of violence which occurred in the crucial months of early 1868. Perhaps surprisingly, he made little attempt to do so. In the first incident, in which nationals of several countries were fired on by samurai from the pro-Meiji Bizen domain in February, Roches was admittedly given little chance to act independently.[87] Parkes was quite as offended and disturbed as his French colleague; and when the foreign representatives took the drastic step of seizing Japanese ships, not only were apologies immediately forthcoming from the new government but punishment was administered with a speed which contrasted markedly with the impotence habitually displayed by the Tokugawa authorities. The second incident, however, was rather different in that France alone was directly affected and the incident more serious, no fewer than eleven sailors of the frigate *Dupleix* having been killed by anti-foreign samurai from Tosa near Sakai in March. Despite this considerable provocation, Roches did not use the incident to break off relations, and when the Meiji government offered apologies and compensation and promised to execute the offenders, he accepted without demur.[88]

The fact that Roches did not adopt an uncompromising line may not have been solely due to his awareness of Moustier's opposition to a policy of intervention and to the swiftness of the new government to make amends. By the time of the Sakai incident he was also aware of, Yoshinobu's unwillingness to fight, which meant that the Tokugawa regime was unlikely to survive and that the Meiji government was probably going to succeed. It was thus not in French long-term interests to risk alienating the latter. Such realism was facilitated by the fact that, thanks to the cooperation of the Comte de Montblanc, who was currently in Japan in Satsuma's employ, Roches was, for the first time, in possession of reliable information about the Meiji leaders.[89] It was against this background that, at the end of March, he joined with his diplomatic colleagues in accepting the Kyoto government's invitation to an audience with the Emperor, an act which, though it did not formally end the Western powers' neutrality, in a significant sense set the seal of foreign approval on the new regime.[90] He did not, before his departure in June 1868, entirely abandon hope that the Tokugawa might recover something of its former position, but to all intents and purposes he had reconciled himself to the existence of the Meiji government.

4

FRANCE AND THE CONSOLIDATION OF THE MEIJI GOVERNMENT 1868–80

FRANCO-JAPANESE relations would never again be of such critical importance as they were in the last years of the Tokugawa period. Nevertheless, the role of France in the consolidation of the Meiji government was not insignificant. This was so not only because of the legacy of Roches' support for the Bakufu but also because the new regime's position was for a considerable time precarious and its permanence unassured. There was no certainty that the victorious coalition, acting in the name of the Emperor and the Court in Kyoto (but effectively based on the military strength of Satsuma and Choshu) would hold together, nor that it would adopt policies that would ensure its stability in the long run. The able samurai from south-west Japan who had plotted the overthrow of the Tokugawa were faced by enormous problems, and these were made even more complicated by the fact that they were forced to work for more than three years through nobles and daimyo whose appointment to the highest offices in the new government was necessary in order to retain Court support and to dispel distrust of Sat-Cho ambitions.[1] Among these samurai leaders there developed from 1868 onwards the realization of the need for fundamental changes of attitude and for the construction of a strong central government to defend Japan against any threat to its independence, as well as to safeguard and strengthen their own political position. They were hindered, however, not only by the conservatism and prejudices of most of the Court nobles, but also by the *han* loyalties of many of their fellow-samurai, including some important leaders. Until they took the bold step of abolishing the domains in 1871, the control over policy of reformers with a national perspective (such as Okubo, Kido and Okuma) was far from secure, and they had generally to move cautiously in their pursuit of change.

In this situation the attitude of the Western powers remained of great importance, for the Meiji government, like the Bakufu before it, could not risk incurring their displeasure while there remained a danger of armed opposition or rebellion within Japan. Even after this danger was significantly reduced in1871, the new government was still dependent on the West for expert assistance and guidance in the achievement of its basic aim of *'fukoku kyohei'* (rich country, strong army). Although opportunities for playing an important role and wielding influence continued to exist, however, French policy during this period of transition was marked by lack of positive direction. Indeed, it would hardly be an exaggeration to say that for most of this period France merely had relations with Japan rather than a coherent policy. French diplomacy was, of course, concerned to maintain the rights and advantages which it had gained earlier.[2] Moreover, French diplomats were sensitive to the prestige which could accrue from Japan's use of French experts and French models, and usually lent support to Japanese efforts at modernization. However, in both these areas they were essentially reacting to Japanese approaches rather than positively pursuing a guiding role in the way that Léon Roches had done. There was certainly no sustained or coherent attempt by France to build up a favoured position in Japan by offering protection and friendship to the new government as it strove to develop Japan's resources and restore its full sovereign rights. Glimpses of both policies were seen, but in contrast to the United States not for long. Basically, French diplomacy lacked a sense of constructive purpose.

That France should have shown relatively little interest in pursuing a positive policy towards Japan is not entirely surprising. After the traumatic defeat at Prussia's hands in 1870-71 and the ending of the Second Empire, the first decade of the Third Republic was a period of cautious readjustment in international affairs, and it was understandable that France's diplomatic representatives should be strictly enjoined to avoid unnecessary entanglements.[3] This need not have prevented a more cooperative approach towards Japan, but the memory of Roches' failure remained to warn them of the possible danger of too active diplomacy. Had Japan been more strategically located, the situation might have been different. Geographically, however, it could hardly have been more remote, and the possibility that Japan might become powerful enough to act as a check on a rival Western power was as yet hard to imagine. Nor was there much economic stimulus for a positive policy. Rather the revival of the French silk industry after the massive import of silkworm eggs in the 1860s meant that what had been arguably the most vital French material interest in Japan diminished in importance.

In addition to these general factors, account needs to be taken of the fact that there was a lack of continuity in diplomatic personnel. Cabinet changes in Paris were so frequent that few French foreign ministers remained in office long enough to acquire more than a superficial understanding of Japanese developments. If governments had changed less often, though, it would still have been difficult for anyone in Paris to make a positive impression on French policy in Japan because detailed information about that country was limited. Even when significantly faster telegraphic communication became available, there was little inclination to use it – partly because of the cost – and much was left to the diplomat on the spot. However, during the twelve years which followed the Meiji Restoration, France was represented in Japan by no fewer than ten ministers or chargés d'affaires.[4] The one who stayed longest, Ange-Maxime Outrey, remained in position for no more than three years and four months, less than either Bellecourt or Roches.[5] By contrast Sir Harry Parkes remained as British minister, apart from furloughs, throughout the whole period Such lack of continuity inevitably affected France's ability to maintain a consistent and active policy. As a result French diplomacy played an even lesser role in the period of Japan's transition from a feudal to a modern state than might have been expected.[6]

RECOGNITION OF THE NEW REGIME

The negative character of French diplomacy was soon in evidence. The most important issue which faced Outrey after his arrival on 7 June 1868 was what attitude he should adopt towards the new Imperial government. The latter had already received a measure of recognition by Roches, when he agreed to an audience with the Emperor, and there could be no question of Outrey retreating from this position. Nevertheless, as long as the Powers' proclamation of neutrality of 18 February remained in effect there was room for manoeuvre. A strong show of sympathy for the Tokugawa would have given the new government cause for concern, and had it been combined with a determined French attempt at mediation, it might conceivably have forced the Meiji leaders to consider some modification of their demand for unconditional surrender. Outrey was tempted by this possibility, but only briefly. Basically, he had none of Roches' ambition and imagination, and his previous career as consul at Alexandria had accustomed him to cooperation with Britain.[7] As a result he shied away from recommending an independent line and made no serious attempt to obstruct the consolidation of power by the new imperial government.

Outrey's desire to avoid political complication was shown within a month of his arrival, when in early July he sent the Comte de Montebello to Osaka to convey to the Meiji government the most cordial assurances of his sympathetic feelings. That he had no expectation of a Tokugawa recovery is shown by the decided views he expressed a month later: 'The only thing which I can affirm without hesitation is that there is no chance of seeing the government of the Taicoun reestablished and that realistically he has disappeared from the scene, at least for a very long time'.[8] Admittedly, some private sympathy for the previous government was evident in September when, after the foreign diplomats were sent a manifesto by the northern daimyo who were refusing to accept the Kyoto government's authority, Outrey wrote that 'without departing from our neutral position, we must treat with some sensitivity a party which very probably had placed a great deal of hope on France's support'.[9] Despite the fact that the northern alliance's appeal opened a way to possible foreign mediation, however, Outrey never attempted to transform these faint pro-Tokugawa feelings into action. Even when the Meiji government itself appeared to be seeking his mediation in December 1868, he declined to be involved and on two other occasions he ignored similar opportunities.[10]

Outrey's unwillingness to respond to the rebels' appeal to mediate may have been partly due to his reluctance to offend the new government at a time when France had financial claims to make on it. One of the legacies of the Roches period was the claim for payment for the merchandise worth about three-and-a-half million francs which the Bakufu had ordered from Coullet, and this claim could only be satisfied by the new authorities.[11] The question was settled to the *Société Générale's* satisfaction in October, but the Meiji government's preference for paying off the whole sum with a loan from the Oriental Bank of Yokohama rather than by twenty monthly instalments, as Outrey suggested, caused the latter to reflect on France's uncomfortable position: '. . . it is easy to see the ardour which the British Representative puts into encouraging the Japanese to be distrustful about the intentions of France with regard to the Emperor's government'.[12]

Outrey's growing awareness of Japanese suspicion of France reinforced his natural tendency to caution. In January 1869, while remarking on Prussian and Italian jealousy of British influence, he outlined his policy as follows: 'In the present situation the only means of counterbalancing this influence is to have a policy directed in a parallel way to that of the English agents, to associate with them in everything which is equitable and in line with genuine European interests, and finally to convince the Japanese that we act without partiality and with entirely disinterested views'.[13]

In conformity with this prescription, France assumed a low diplomatic posture during the civil war in Japan. On only one occasion, when he warned it not to send warships to seize foreign vessels trading with the rebels, did Outrey adopt a strong tone towards the Meiji government, and in this he was safely following a British lead.[14] When, in January 1869, Iwakura Tomomi, the leading Court noble in the government, sought from the Powers the withdrawal of their proclamation of neutrality, Outrey did indeed make a tentative effort to act as mediator between Britain and Holland, who wished to accept the Japanese request, and Prussia and Italy, who opposed it. His compromise proposal of withdrawal after one month, however, met with favour from neither side; and although the Powers were ready to agree that the civil war had effectively ended, the legal position remained unchanged until 8 February, when Prussia and Italy finally gave way.[15] With this it was possible for diplomacy to resume a normal course, as was shown in May when the Powers presented to the Japanese government a request for the payment of the rest of the Shimonoseki indemnity.[16]

THE BRUNET AFFAIR

For all Outrey's caution, France could not avoid becoming drawn unintentionally into the Japanese civil war. The French legations's views carried little weight with Captain Brunet, one of the members of the military mission which had come to Japan in early 1867 to train the Bakufu army. This hot-headed young artillery specialist, like his colleagues, deplored the fact that he could no longer carry out his functions and was condemned to idleness, since in common with the British naval mission the French mission had been rendered inactive in April 1868 following the Powers' acceptance of neutrality (although its members continued to receive their pay from the Bakufu until July).[17] Despite the shogun's surrender of Edo in June, armed resistance to the new government both from Tokugawa forces and from some northern domains continued, and the French officers' sense of obligation and loyalty towards their previous associates made them increasingly frustrated.[18] When, in the autumn, it became certain that the mission would soon have to return to France, Brunet finally succumbed to the continual requests from Tokugawa officers to assist in the struggle against what they saw as a usurping clique. On 4 October he used the pretext of visiting Yokosuka to join the Tokugawa fleet, taking with him one NCO named Cazeneuve.[19] Two months later it was reported that Tokugawa forces had seized control of Yézo (Hokkaido) under his command.[20]

Outrey's reaction to these developments was predictable. After months of effort, his attempt to dissociate French policy from Roches' involvement with the previous regime was now being sabotaged by a young soldier acting with a reckless disregard for the diplomatic complications he was causing. The French minister's indignation was so plainly genuine that the incident never, in fact, assumed the proportions he feared, for it soon became plain both to the Meiji government and to Parkes that Outrey was not implicated and had no intention of siding with the rebels.[21] Not only did he refuse to have any dealings with them, he also did his best to have Brunet's resignation accepted, although in this he was disappointed for the Ministry of War instead chose to give its maverick officer leave, on condition that he abstained from using his military title.[22] Thanks to Outrey's consistent attitude the only adverse diplomatic effects of this episode were some momentary ill-feeling (which manifested itself in a number of attacks on French nationals)[23] and a few half-hearted attempts by the Meiji government to assert its right to an indemnity.[24]

The position taken by Outrey was a grave disappointment to Brunet and his sympathisers, among them the mission leader, Captain Chanoine. They felt that the seizure of Hokkaido under French guidance presented Outrey with an outstanding opportunity of emerging from the negative role to which he had so far been confined and of once more making France a power to be reckoned with. In one of two memoranda drawn up by Chanoine (now back in Paris) for the Ministry of War the erstwhile chief of mission reported that since the seizure of Hokkaido, Brunet 'had taken in hand ... the direction of political affairs; he is negotiating for a combined arbitration by France and England on the subject of Yézo [Hokkaido] which would become a fief held by Prince Mimbu Tayu under the overlordship of the Mikado'. His action, Chanoine suggested, 'can produce, from the point of view of French policy, the happiest result, if M. Outrey knows how to take advantage of it'.[25]

Exactly what Brunet really had in mind regarding the eventual position of Hokkaido is not clear, but unusual insights into his thinking and into the state of affairs in the northern island are provided by two extraordinary letters which he wrote to Chanoine in the early months of 1869. In January he was, by his own account, working for 'a political arrangement between my Tokugawas and the people at Yédo', but there is no suggestion that he was offering any concession other than the recognition of the Emperor's sovereignty, an act which might have meant very little in practice.[26] He evidently felt his position to be a strong one. In his force of 3,000, he claimed, there were 1,500 samurai who had received training from the French mission and among whom strict discipline was maintained. He doubted whether an army could be sent against them: 'for two months we have been waiting for an army <u>which does not come</u> and which, I am convinced, <u>absolutely cannot come</u>'.[27] [underlined in the original]. At least part of Brunet's confidence seems to have been due to the fact that he believed his influence in the Tokugawa camp to be dominant. He informed Chanoine that

'. . . the first thing on which I insisted is the necessity of strict order; I had translations made of the principal French regulations and of extracts from our code of military law, and I had copies of all these circulated among our various battalions . . . and one fine day I summoned all our officers and spoke to them in more or less this language: . . . "Promise to obey me blindly . . . your daily obedience will be my only guarantee of your absolute devotion on the day of common danger. I do not lead you alone, eight compatriots aid me, and I cannot let them share your peril with me unless you consent to hazard your best hopes on the adoption of French regulations. . . . in order to triumph, all your efforts must go into assimilating French ideas, even though at first you must do this without understanding; . . . choose between <u>my return to France</u> or your <u>consent</u> to what I <u>demand</u>"' [underlining in original]. His appeal succeeded. 'All the officers of the various ranks up to the commanding general gave me their signatures, and for the last six weeks the disciplinary results have been marvellous. Ah! If only that booby of a Taicoun had understood us better, dear Chanoine!'[28]

In hindsight it is all too apparent that Brunet allowed his hopes to get the better of him. Certainly he was too optimistic in his view that 'it only needs a helping hand to overthrow the new governmental edifice in this country' and that 'we are on the eve of a conflagration more terrible than the first', although his expectation that fear of Satsuma preponderance in the new regime might produce a new conflict was not uncommon at the time and arguably not far-fetched.[29] In the light of his lack of judgement about the political situation it is tempting to dismiss his boasts about his personal role and authority in Hokkaido as self-delusory posturing and to assume that the rebel leaders allowed it to appear that Brunet was in control in the hope of securing French government support. However, the evidence of an anonymous French officer who stayed at Hakodate for nearly two months on board a French ship offers corroborative evidence of Brunet's prominence. In a letter to Chanoine this unnamed officer declared that Brunet had taken complete charge of things – 'customs, municipality, fortifications, army; everything passed through his hands. The simple Japanese are puppets whom he manipulates with great skill'. More than this, 'he has carried out a veritable 1789 in this brave new Japan; the election of leaders and the determination of rank by merit and not birth – these are fabulous things for this country, and he has been able to do things very well, considering the seriousness of the position'.[30]

Brunet's letters make it apparent that his aims extended much further than his nominal objective of persuading the Meiji government to concede the right to colonise Hokkaido in return for acknowledging its authority. Inspired as he was by a bitter hostility to the south-western *han* who had overthrown the Bakufu with, he fervently asserted, Britain's aid, he plainly sought to make an unconquered Hokkaido a rallying point for those supporters of the Tokugawa who planned revenge and were waiting for dissension to appear in the victorious coalition. Paris itself believed that much more was involved than appeared on the surface. An anonymous note of April 1869 states that:

> M. Chanoine would like the initiative taken by Captain Brunet to be sanctioned by the Emperor's government and other French officers to be permitted to rejoin him; that is to say that we should take indirect possession of the island of Hokkaido, perhaps even of a larger part of Japanese territory. Instead of M. Roches' system, that is the exploitation of Japan by privileged French speculators, which he justifiably

blames, M. Chanoine would simply substitute conquest by force of arms. For he does not hide the fact that if there were several energetic men acting with him, and if it was conducted skillfully, the adventure begun by Captain Brunet would go so far as to throw a considerable, possibly decisive, weight into the balance of the civil war in Japan, and that our officers, transformed into daimyos themselves, would soon become the arbitrators and even the masters of the empire.[31]

To more sober men Chanoine's suggestions were bound to seem fanciful and imprudent; and they were rejected by Paris, just as they had been by Outrey. The anonymous note ended: 'If one let events take such a course, one could, of course, expect some strong reactions from the Powers, especially England. There is no need to add that it would mean a break with the Mikado's government which we have just recognized. It is not thought, therefore, that the Government of the Emperor can do anything which gives even the appearance of approbation to Captain Brunet's enterprise'.[32] Even if the decision had been different, it would have had no effect at that late stage. Contrary to what Brunet had predicted, the Meiji government quickly brought together a force sufficient to recapture the northern island, and Brunet was reduced to seeking refuge on a French ship, the Coetlogon, on 9 June 1868.[33]

THE URAKAMI QUESTION

The Brunet affair had arisen out of the ambiguous position in which the French military mission had been placed: condemned to await the outcome of the civil war from the sidelines even though its contract still had time to run. What was to be done with the mission was one of the numerous problems which Outrey complained privately had been left to him by Roches and which hindered the establishment of a satisfactory relationship with the Meiji government.[34] It was not, though, so difficult as the problem of the Meiji government's treatment of Japanese Christians – usually known as the Urakami question because, although arrests were also made in other places, such as the Gotō islands off southern Kyushu, most of those who suffered harsh treatment came from the Urakami valley near Nagasaki.

As has been seen, persecution of Japanese Christians had first occurred in 1867, but caution and restraint on the part of both Roches and the Bakufu, and then the outbreak of civil war, had pushed the matter into the background. It did not take long, however, to come to the fore again, since the new government adopted exactly the same policy towards the Christians as its predecessor, except for the fact that its execution soon became more heavy-handed. The resumption of persecution was a grave disappointment to the missionaries, who had to some extent moderated their activity in response to Roches' appeals and in anticipation of a more liberal attitude from the new authorities.[35] The action of the latter can hardly be considered surprising, however, in view of the strong xenophobic, and especially anti-Christian, strain within the anti-Bakufu movement and the new government's need to elevate Shinto as a means of providing ideological support for imperial rule; and although a number of the Meiji leaders now accepted that isolation was no longer possible and that to catch up with the advanced Western nations was an urgent necessity, they were not yet ready to tolerate the spread of a religion which had long been vilified and was traditionally associated with political dissent. Even those of them who, like Satsuma's Komatsu Tatewaki, claimed to have no personal hostility towards Christianity, were acutely aware of the danger to their cause which might result from concessions.[36]

Japanese objections were not regarded as baseless by the French either. Outrey acknowledged that there were good reasons for the government's annoyance at missionary zeal, since he held that 'Christianity necessarily brings with it ideas of equality and social independence which by their very nature would overturn the organization of the country by castes and professions'.[37] In addition, he felt that a struggle between Christians and Buddhists, leading to a social schism, would be inevitable. Similar observations were made by Captain Challié, who spent some time in Japanese waters during 1868 and had the advantage of discussion with the Comte de Montblanc, still a Satsuma adviser. Challié took the view that the Meiji government had been greatly disturbed by the appointment in 1868 of a bishop for Japan, who could serve as a rallying point for the spread of Christianity. This step might lead to even worse things. The government, he declared, 'is above all concerned lest foreigners should be able to scrutinize the interior of the country. The fear of seeing them, by means of Christians, spread their propaganda, penetrate perhaps into Japan and proclaim another master more powerful than the Mikado dominates all other considerations and gives to this question a very serious significance'.[38] It is possible that both Outrey and Challié exaggerated the extent to which theological considerations had a part in Japanese thinking, and a struggle between Christians and Buddhists was probably not a prospect which caused Japanese leaders much concern since Buddhism itself was currently out of favour. Whatever the validity of their arguments, however, it cannot be doubted that the possibility of the Japanese Christians providing a pretext for foreigners to go beyond the limits of the treaty ports, and for Western powers to interfere with Japan's sovereign rights as they had with China's, was one which in the new government's eyes called for speedy and drastic measures.

Although there was an urgent need, from the Meiji government's point of view, for measures to deal with the problem of the Urakami Christians, there was also a clear awareness that these measures might provoke the intervention which it was seeking to avoid. Indeed, until the religious issue was settled in 1873 by the acceptance, in practice, of toleration, the Japanese government faced the perilous task of steering a course between, on the one hand, an inaction which would allow the evil to spread and, on the other, an excessive rigour which would stir the Powers to action while the new regime was still insecure.[39] In the first phase, from 1868 to early 1870, the Meiji government tended, while occasionally lurching towards the second course, to favour a moderate approach. That is to say, while maintaining its right to deal with its own subjects as it saw fit, it did not, in practice, completely disregard Western sensitivities. In May 1868, for instance, when the foreign representatives protested at the (so far) limited persecution, it suspended its measures.[40] Nevertheless, there were clearly grounds for suspecting that the Meiji government would like to force the Urakami Christians to abandon their religious beliefs if only it could get away with a return to a more traditional approach, and this was to pose a particular problem for Outrey, when he took over from Roches.

The new French minister's ability to see something of the Japanese side of the question has already been noted. Even if more concerned personally than Roches about the fate of the Japanese Christians, he had no desire to make a major issue of what was still, in July 1868, a comparatively small affair, involving, as he understood, the arrest of only one hundred and twenty people. He had, in any case, a duty to avoid French involvement in Japan's internal affairs, and this duty was underlined with respect to religious affairs in September 1868, when foreign minister Moustier accepted that the stipulations of the treaties did not give France any means of intervening effectively in favour of the Japanese Christians.[41] Outrey was further inhibited by his fear that too direct an interference on the part of the Powers would compromise the missionaries and diminish their chances of eventual success. In view of France's special position as protector of Catholics in East Asia and the fact that all the Catholic missionaries were French, he could hardly remain completely inactive but his representations were, at least in 1868–69, not made with much force.[42] In July 1868, for instance, Outrey concurred in his diplomatic colleagues' decision not to make any written protest, and in September, after trying in vain to get an agreement to send a collective note, he again contented himself with expressing his views verbally to Komatsu. His reluctance to take a strong stance was, he explained to Paris, due to his concern 'to avoid an isolated intervention which in a short time would fatally give to our policy in Japan a special character of which it would be easy to take advantage to compromise our moral and material interests'.[43]

Despite the pleas of French missionaries and the failure to persuade the Meiji government to abandon its repressive measures, Outrey was still cautiously optimistic at the end of 1868. In November he found encouragement in the fact that there had been no complaints for two months, and although he believed that some new arrests had just taken place in Akashi, this was counterbalanced by the commentary in an official journal which, he claimed, 'seemed to want to prepare public opinion to accept the actions with expressions of moderation'.[44] In January 1869, however, he felt obliged to adopt a stronger pose when he was visited by the ex-daimyo of Uwajima, a vice-minister for foreign affairs, who was anxious to forestall any official intervention on account of harsh treatment of the Christians in the Goto islands. The French minister informed him that 'the European powers could not remain indifferent to odious actions which wound the religious feelings of their peoples and if the Japanese government did not take serious steps to stop the persecution, it must expect one day to see a general indignation take hold of public opinion and perhaps force the Powers to intervene, action which today they desire to avoid'.[45]

In his report to the Quai d'Orsay, Outrey was careful to note that this warning was couched in an essentially amicable form. Nevertheless, he claimed the credit for the fact that the Japanese government eventually sent the foreign Representatives an official note declaring that cruel penalties would be replaced by more humane ones. The note was unsatisfactory in some respects and was withdrawn in favour of a more acceptable one, but it was regarded as of great significance by Outrey. He saw it as marking a real change in the attitude of the government, adding that 'it recognizes in some measure our right to speak in the name of its Christian subjects, and once on this ground, European diplomacy cannot fail to make the principles of equality, justice and humanity which it invokes in favour of its co-religionists prevail'.[46]

In reality, it soon became clear that the government was not carrying out all its promises. The French minister's reaction to new reports of persecution was more in keeping with his habitual policy of caution, however, than with his veiled threats of January. He advised his foreign minister that 'the question of Christians in Japan is extremely dangerous and we must be highly circumspect in what we do'. Since, in any case, the Japanese government was probably powerless to give them complete satisfaction, he asked permission to 'act slowly and with great care'.[47] This cautious attitude was maintained throughout the year, but with the turn of 1870 the situation became more tense. There were increasingly signs of a reaction, especially in Satsuma, against the Meiji government's centralizing policy and support of reform, and a return to traditional policy towards Christianity came to seem advisable to the leadership. In January of that year Outrey reported that over

3,000 Christians had been forcibly taken from Urakami, dispersed among several *han* and set to work on public projects. Reports from missionaries alleged that families were being deliberately split up. All the Western diplomats joined in demanding a meeting with Meiji leaders and in insisting that 'orders to suspend the measures be sent to Nagasaki without delay, while we would reserve to ourselves what might be done for those unfortunates already deported'.[48]

Although the foreign representatives did secure a promise from such leaders as Saigo, Iwakura, Sawa and Terashima to stop the process pending further discussions, they were not deceived by their temporary success. Outrey pessimistically concluded that 'the Japanese government has decided not to tolerate this religion and and is returning to extreme measures to ensure that it remains in control of the country. It seems to me impossible', he added, 'to obtain anything henceforth by diplomatic means'. For the first time, however, perhaps encouraged by the unanimity of his colleagues' reaction to the intensification of the persecution, he was prepared to contemplate strong measures. 'I am very disposed to believe', he suggested to Paris, 'that the Japanese government would surrender in face of a threatening démarche if it was done in common, but it is necessary to be aware that it would have to be supported by an imposing demonstration'.[49] That he viewed the religious issue as important was shown by the dispatch he sent after a further conference, in which the Japanese representatives professed a liberal attitude but complained that the missionaries had infringed Japan's fundamental laws, had boasted of their success, and had tried to persuade Japanese Christians that they would be protected by the foreign powers. 'The Christian question', Outrey proclaimed, 'must fatally impose itself on European diplomacy because it is intimately linked to the progress of civilization in Japan. Now, the day this country is opened to foreigners, Christianity will penetrate it in their wake, or, indeed, Christianity itself will overcome the barriers which block the introduction of our commerce with the interior'.[50]

Outrey was not the only foreigner to favour intervention at this time. In a private unsigned letter of 20 February 1870 to the Comte de Montebello, a Quai d'Orsay official, a combined démarche was strongly advocated by someone who from internal evidence appears to have been a foreign representative in Tokyo, probably the Prussian minister Max von Brandt. The writer had been convinced by discussion with Terashima Munenori, a progressive official from Satsuma, that the Japanese government would abandon its repressive measures if it really believed that these were going to endanger its good relations with the Powers.[51] Despite this almost open invitation by a Japanese official to adopt a stronger line, however, there was little inclination in Paris to authorize a naval demonstration or make any sort of threat. Behind the French reluctance to act forcefully lay its awareness that Britain was not contemplating the adoption of a tougher line. In May a Quai d'Orsay review of the question concluded that the instructions sent to Parkes left very little doubt that he would not force the Japanese government to carry out its promises.[52] No further comment was necessary. That France could not act in isolation had by this time become one the basic assumptions of French policy.

Even if Paris had been more responsive and England more cooperative, it is doubtful whether any new step would have been taken, for within a short time Outrey again reverted to his former moderate stance.[53] What seems to have changed his mind was his perception of a more friendly attitude generally on the part of the Meiji government, and, more particularly, its intimation in June that it had decided to request further French assistance in establishing a new army.[54] This unexpected decision to renew the French military mission made Outrey both more cautious and more hopeful. On the one hand he now became more reluctant to press the religious question lest so welcome an opportunity of influence and prestige be lost. On the other hand, Japanese need of French help provided additional leverage. When Terashima presented the military request, the French minister immediately sought to take advantage of it by bluntly posing the question: 'Do you believe that France will be willing to help in the development of this force if it is to be used in persecutions which civilization and humanity abhor?' Terashima's reply was encouraging. According to Outrey, 'he let fall that they had surrendered to the public opinion of a large part of Japan which can not forget the events of the seventeenth century, but that in reality the government had no particular animosity against Christianity and would have no objection to departing from the rigour imposed by circumstances on the day when, feeling itself stronger and more solidly established, it could resist without danger the ingrained prejudices which existed in the country'.[55]

These arguments were persuasive; and Outrey also recognized that coercive measures would be dangerous, especially since he was inclined to believe that Parkes 'encouraged the Japanese in the thought that our missionaries' propaganda is a manoeuvre of French diplomacy. In this the British minister has met with tacit support on the part of my other colleagues who represent all the Protestant powers and it is on this account that I have avoided any isolated démarche with the greatest care'. He consoled himself with the conclusion that 'the best solution is that which will be obtained naturally and without effort by the diffusion of our civilizing principles through the mass of the population'.[56] Such a change of emphasis would undoubtedly have been welcome to the Meiji government, but evidently Outrey did not make himself clear, for a month later the French representative was visited by a higher-ranking official, Soejima Taneomi, who claimed that Terashima had reported that 'France would not agree to provide [military] instructors as long as Japan did not commit itself to proclaim the freedom of religion', adding that 'this demand being as dangerous as it is premature, had aroused the liveliest opposition within the government'. After some hedging, Outrey found Soejima still less than satisfied, so the French minister ventured as far as to concede that 'for us the development of intimate relations with Japan must lead infallibly to religious tolerance and, from this point of view it is possible that the Government of the Emperor will not insist on an immediate solution and will show itself disposed to be useful to you'. This admission achieved the desired objective. Outrey reported that 'the prospect of being able to let the Christian question rest until a new order came into being appeared to make more of an impression on Councillor Soejima than all the other arguments, and he departed declaring that having been sent by the great Council to learn my opinion, he was going to give an account of our interview'.[57]

Outrey's decision not to press Japan on the Urakami question was, in retrospect, a wise one; and it was not disputed by the Quai d'Orsay. In consequence, provided that it avoided any new outrage, the Japanese government was no longer in serious danger of intervention from the Power most concerned with the Urakami Christians. Further assurance was conferred by the outbreak of the Franco-Prussian War in August 1870. Even if Outrey had reverted to thoughts of religious intervention, France would thereafter have had insufficient means for enforcing her will. Not surprisingly, therefore, the religious question disappeared from the correspondence between Paris and Tokyo, reappearing again only in January 1872, when the new chargé d'affaires, the Comte de Turenne, reported that he had appealed to the Meiji government to release 70 Christians who had just been arrested near Nagasaki. A month later he was able to inform the Quai d'Orsay that his plea had succeeded.[58] On 1 April, he announced that the edict imposing severe penalties on native Christians had been revoked, and in May came news that Japanese were now permitted to practise Christianity so long as they did not seek to make converts.[59] Turenne's confidence in the Meiji government's liberal tendencies was strengthened by its release of more imprisoned Christians on his request.[60] In return he urged the missionaries, (whom he criticized in his dispatch for unthinking zeal) to maintain an extreme reserve.

Turenne's view evidently carried some weight with his foreign minister, but in December the imminent arrival in Paris, after a year's overseas investigation, of the top-level mission led by Iwakura Tomomi prompted the current foreign minister, the Comte de Rémusat, to adopt a sterner approach. The sufferings of Urakami, he informed the chargé d'affaires, had produced a 'a very deep emotion in the National Assembly'.[61] His concern about the strength of feeling was due to the fact that a demand for French intervention by a parliamentary deputy, the Comte de Richemont, on December 7 had been received with such applause that the foreign minister had felt obliged to assure the Assembly that he would take action.[62] He therefore instructed Turenne to remonstrate with the Japanese government, as he himself intended to do with Iwakura when the Japanese mission visited France.[63]

Iwakura was received by Rémusat on 24 January. A month later, the Japanese government decided to abandon the old policy of suppression. Despite the proximity of these events, however, and irrespective of the claim that the change of policy was the result of the experiences of the Iwakura mission, France's part cannot be considered decisive.[64] In his encounter with the Japanese leader, the French foreign minister adopted a statesmanlike attitude, simply advising Iwakura that 'the best means of drawing the sympathies of Europe and America to Japan would be for the Japanese government to abandon the errors followed by it up to today and show themselves well-disposed towards Christians';[65] and when the envoy replied that, though he could make no definite promise, the Japanese government intended to establish religious toleration as soon as it was opportune, Rémusat declared himself satisfied.[66] Notwithstanding his final reminder that the question was important to France, the tone of the interview was friendly and there was no hint of any recourse to force.

In Japan, Turenne was even more understanding of the Japanese position. Before receiving Rémusat's instructions he had pointed out that toleration would be delayed on account of the tension caused by samurai discontent;[67] and he strongly advised against any pressure being put on the Meiji government, which was continuing to act liberally.[68] He did, in February, inform the Japanese foreign ministry of Richemont's intervention and Rémusat's concern but accepted without demur a vice-minister's assurance that the accusations were distorted.[69] The whole question was settled a few days later, so far as Turenne was concerned, when he was informed that the Japanese government had decided to abrogate the anti-Christian edicts and return to their home village all the Christians who had been arrested and dispersed'.[70]

This was not quite, however, the end of the religious toleration problems. In March 1873 six deputies addressed to the Quai d'Orsay a letter demanding that France require from Japan not only complete religious toleration but also free access for missionaries to the interior; in it they referred ominously to the 'guarantees analogous to those which were given to us by the Chinese government in the treaty of Tientsin'.[71] Whether there was any direct connection between this letter and the subsequent change which manifested itself in the Quai d'Orsay attitude is not clear; but in August the Duc de Broglie, who had succeeded Rémusat, decided that the religious question should be raised in the forthcoming negotiations in which Japan's desire to revise its treaties with the Western powers were due to be considered, and the position which he directed the new French minister in Tokyo, Jules Berthemy, to adopt was essentially that which the deputies had advocated:

> We limit ourselves to considering as essential the adoption by the Japanese government of the principles of liberty of conscience consecrated by our conventions with other Courts less close to European ideas, that is to say, for the local inhabitants the right of embracing the faith and professing it freely, for missionaries the facility of teaching it without hindrance . . . you cannot insist too much, in the case of your encountering opposition which I do not wish to foresee, in order to ensure the victory of the principles which we hold it an honour to have constantly defended.[72]

Broglie's instructions, had they been carried out, would have created considerable suspicion of French motives in Japan, would have made the maintenance of good relations between the two countries extremely difficult, and might even have set back the cause of toleration for Christians in Japan. However, although Berthemy was far less sympathetic to Japan than Turenne had been, he perceived the danger. Even before he received Broglie's dispatch, he had expressed the view that the zeal of the missionaries, when exhibited prematurely, was prejudicial to the cause of religion in Japan; and he had even gone so far as to suggest that 'against the general opinion I think that the missionaries will delay the advance of civilization each time they wish to further it'.[73] When he heard that he was expected to seek new rights for missionaries, he warned that it would be imprudent to insist on any such provision. His reason, based on an analysis of events since 1868 which stressed the jealousy of Britain, was one which on past experience could be expected to carry weight with the Quai d'Orsay: no other representative would join him and the demand would be met with a blunt refusal by the Japanese government.[74]

Whether Berthemy's argument would have convinced Broglie is uncertain; by the time his dispatch reached Paris a Cabinet reshuffle had brought to the Quai d'Orsay a new occupant, the Duc de Decazes, whose opinions were less extreme.[75] Decazes acknowledged that his predecessor had been unrealistic in his demands and accepted Berthemy's view that the missionaries could make best use of their zeal by devoting themselves to teaching.[76] Thus what might have been disruptive and, as subsequent developments showed, unnecessary was averted. In practice, persecution was already at an end; and with the gradual surreptitious penetration of the country by missionaries, the issue of religious toleration vanished from diplomacy. Except in the late 1880s, when the challenge to the French religious protectorate in China had repercussions in Japan, the fortunes of the Christian religion were not henceforth to be a concern of French policy towards Japan.[77]

THE WITHDRAWAL OF FOREIGN TROOPS

The religious question was not the only problem in Franco-Japanese relations which stretched over several years. One which, though basically far simpler, took even longer to settle, was the problem of withdrawal of French and British troops from Japanese soil. First raised in 1869, it was only settled in 1875. The reason for this long delay was that, like revision of the unequal treaties, it was a question in which the status quo was unsatisfactory only to Japan. For the European powers concerned there was no compelling reason for change, especially since the Japanese government, though anxious to get rid of their humiliating presence, was not disposed to offer any inducement or compensation to hasten the troops' departure. Instead it placed its hopes on continual appeals to the two Powers' sense of justice. This policy might in certain circumstances have been successful but it ran up against the insensitivity and distrust that so often characterized European thinking about Japan. Indeed, had the cost of maintaining troops in Japan not operated in favour of the Japanese, the situation might well have remained unchanged for some years more.

The origin of the problem went back to the troubled years that followed the opening of treaty relations.[78] The violent hostility of the Japanese to foreigners made it natural for marines to be landed to protect the legations and residents in Yokohama; and in 1863 British and French forces became more permanently established when reports that the Bakufu had agreed to expel foreigners led the British and French admirals to fortify Yokohama.[79] This situation was tolerated by the Bakufu but subsequently the Meiji government was far less happy with the arrangement. The presence of foreign troops hardly represented a direct threat, but it did offend national sentiment and it did imply a want of confidence in the power and stability of Japan's new rulers.

Little could be done to alter the situation while the civil war continued in the north and while attacks on foreigners showed that old *joi* feelings persisted. By September 1869, however, there seemed ground for hope; indeed a tentative suggestion that the troops be withdrawn was made to Outrey by Parkes, who was then still enjoying his role as the Meiji government's mentor. It was met with a blunt rejection. The reason given by the French minister was security, but his report to Paris stressed a rather different factor. 'The equal footing here of France and England', explained Outrey, 'this superiority which the presence of their troops on the ground gives to the two powers without distinction, is at odds with his ideas of absolute predominance'.[80] Thus Japan was hindered, as later in its pursuit of treaty revision, not so much by the inadequacy of its case as by the mutual jealousies of the foreign powers.

In another form the French obsession with prestige was again shown when the Meiji government made a second attempt to secure withdrawal in December 1870. This time Outrey objected because Prussia had recently threatened to demand the expulsion of French forces from Japan. Withdrawal would therefore appear to be a surrender to France's enemy and would be wounding to French dignity.[81] As it happened , the financial burden of maintaining the current force of 260 French marines in Yokohama prompted reconsideration by the French navy before the Franco-Prussian war ended.[82] Outrey was informed of this in June 1871, but, ironically, when he consulted Parkes, he found that the British minister now claimed that Japan was undergoing a grave internal crisis and that such a move was premature.[83] Nevertheless, Outrey still concluded that the time for withdrawal would probably not be later than the following year.

This prediction proved too sanguine. Before 1871 was out, the Quai d'Orsay, too, began to have doubts about the wisdom of an early withdrawal. Since the Japanese government had declared its intention of revising the treaties in 1872, wrote Rémusat to the Navy Ministry in September, 'we might regret being deprived of a means of action which is not without value'.[84] In fact, no fresh approach was made by the Japanese government during 1872, probably because it placed its hopes on the Iwakura mission; and when the issue was raised again, it was Turenne who was responsible for doing so. Not only had he concluded that the Meiji government was now fully in control, he also believed that France might derive some credit from taking the initiative for withdrawal'.[85] The British chargé d'affaires, Watson, who was unaware that Turenne had already revealed his proposal to the acting foreign minister, Soejima, was then persuaded to urge this course of action upon the Foreign Office.[86] Turenne's manoeuvre proved unsuccessful, however, because for once the joint recommendation of the men on the spot was overruled. By the time it reached Europe the British foreign secretary, Lord Granville, had, as Rémusat explained to Turenne, already informed Iwakura that the troops could not yet be recalled because the security of the British representative required their presence.[87] There was no thought on the French side of acting alone and the only encouragement Iwakura received was the assurance that action would not long be deferred.[88]

A speedy settlement would certainly have been pleasing to the Navy Ministry, which in June 1873 raised the question for a second time. Its views were not wholly acceptable to the Quai d'Orsay but could not be disregarded. As the Duc de Broglie informed Berthemy, 'I believed that I could express the opinion that the measure awaited by it with a certain impatience would probably become possible in the not too distant future, without our acting in advance of Britain and without depriving ourselves of the faculty of making use of this concession in the course of our negotiations with the Japanese government'.[89] In line with this thinking Berthemy delayed taking any action, but when it became clear that this would not influence the treaty revision negotiations, he took the matter up in November. Again, however, the opposition of Parkes proved insuperable.[90] Nevertheless the pointlessness of the troops' presence was now so evident that in February 1874 one French company was allowed to leave.[91] The issue remained unsettled until January 1875 when the Foreign Office decided to withdraw the British contingent, and invited France to do likewise.[92] There was no further hesitation on the French side, and embarkation took place on 1 March. Seven years after assuming power the Meiji government had at last received the final Western recognition of its stability.[93]

FRENCH DIPLOMACY AND THE FRENCH CONTRIBUTION TO JAPANESE MODERNIZATION

No assessment of the influence of French policy on the consolidation of the Meiji government can afford to ignore the French diplomatic contribution to Japanese modernization. However well the Meiji government dealt with the problems of diplomacy, its hold on power in the long run depended on its success in carrying out fundamental political, social and economic reform. Only successful modernization would enable the central government to deal with the twin threats of samurai rebellion and peasant uprisings, both of which remained serious until the failure of the Satsuma rebellion in 1877 drove opposition into less violent channels. By no means all of the French contribution to Japanese modernization was connected with French diplomacy. Nevertheless, it was a French minister, Léon Roches, who first demonstrated the potential value for Japan of assistance from an advanced Western power,[94] and although no subsequent French representative matched him either in ambition or achievement, the cooperation of the French government after 1868 was to be significant in several of the more important aspects of Japanese modernization.[95]

Some of the ways in which French diplomacy was involved in Japanese modernization are obvious. To begin with perhaps the most important of all France's contributions to the establishment of a modern state – its role in the creation of an army – almost all the officers and non-commissioned officers in the two French missions (1866–68 and 1872–80) were seconded from the French army. Without going through the French legation and without gaining the approval of the minister of war, neither the Tokugawa Bakufu nor the Meiji government would have been able to secure these officers' services. Nor could the Japanese army have sent many of its own most promising officers for more specialized training in French military schools except with official French agreement. Similarly, the engineer who created the Yokosuka dockyard and arsenal, François-Léonce Verny, was a French naval lieutenant who could only be recruited through official channels. The same was largely true of his assistants and the numerous workers who served under his direction for over ten years from 1865. As Terashima Munenori, who was the foreign minister when the last of these Frenchmen left Yokosuka in 1878, wrote to the French representative at the time, the workers deserved credit for their zeal, 'but it was the benevolence of your government to our country which sent them'.[96] It was no less true that the engineer who in the late 1880s advised the Japanese Navy Ministry on the construction of state-of-the art warships, Louis-Émile Bertin, could be seconded only with the consent of the French navy minister.

Other Frenchmen involved in Japanese modernization were less obviously official in character. The eminent professor of law, Gustave-Emile Boissonade de Fontarabie, who played an enormously important role in the drafting of Japan's first modern legal codes, did not represent the French state in the same way that military and naval specialists did. Nevertheless, he did hold a position at the University of Paris, and it is unlikely that he would have been willing to leave this prestigious appointment had not the university, at the government's request, held open the option for him to return to it. That the French authorities were willing to do this is remarkable, since Boissonade not only remained in Japan for twenty-one years but worked strenuously to further Japan's aim of securing revision of the unequal treaties against the opposition of France.[97]

Boissonade was only one, albeit the most important, of a number of French lawyers employed by the Meiji government; and although this need for French expertise can easily be explained in terms of the general applicability of French law, it may also have owed something to the personal role of the French chargé d'affaires, Turenne. In March 1872 he claimed that for months he had 'neglected no opportunity of recommending to the Japanese government the adoption of our civil Code'; and the Meiji leaders' expectation that taking this advice would meet with encouragement and assistance from France may account in part for the fact that Turenne was also able to report that three government officials were just leaving to study the workings of French administration and to hire a professor of law.[98] The minister of justice, Eto Shimpei, whom Turenne deemed to be strongly pro-French was also scheduled to visit France in order to investigate its judicial system; and although this plan was aborted, Eto did request another French professor of law through official channels.[99] In addition Eto sought, through Turenne, the unpublished regulations relating to police organization in France; and although it was found that the multifarious documents embodying these regulations had never been brought together, the Ministry of the Interior offered to collect them specially for Japan's benefit.[100]

The French diplomatic contribution to Japanese modernization was mainly in the military and legal spheres, but in 1870 Outrey went beyond these when he played a part in the establishment of Japan's first machine-reeled silk filature at Tomioka. This factory, which was used as a model for demonstrating up-to-date technology, paved the way for standardized production of good quality and thus helped Japan to overtake China as an exporter of raw silk by the early twentieth century. Exactly what Outrey did is not clear – his report to Paris spoke vaguely of 'continuing to occupy myself with the erection of a model filature in the interior of the country'.[101] About his motivation, he was more explicit: it was meant to be a step towards opening the whole of Japan to foreigners. That he was encouraging the development of an industry which might in time compete with French silk products appears not to have crossed his mind.

The role of diplomacy as a channel for French assistance meant that the character of the diplomats themselves assumed a certain significance. When the Japanese government desired to employ Frenchmen in official or semi-official positions, the normal (though not invariable) procedure was for a Japanese official (or sometimes an unofficial intermediary) to make an informal preliminary approach to the French representative in Japan. If the latter's support was secured, the request would have a very good chance of being accepted by Paris. If, on the other hand, he discouraged the approach, the Meiji government could withdraw it without any loss of face. While such a mode of operation had obvious advantages, it also had one possible drawback: French representatives could either encourage or reject approaches as they saw fit, and since, if they were discouraging, there was little likelihood of a formal request being made, they need not fear Quai d'Orsay disapproval.[102]

The importance of this personal factor derives from the fact that the Quai d'Orsay did not give its representatives in Tokyo explicit instructions with regard to French participation in Japanese modernization, despite the fact that from the mid-1860s it normally approved the employment of French experts. Japanese requests for French help implied recognition of French excellence, and any show of preference for Frenchmen over Britons or Germans was particularly gratifying after the catastrophic defeat by Prussia in 1870–71. The involvement of French experts in Japan's development subsequently acquired a further significance, however, when in the mid-1880s Japan began to be perceived as a power to be reckoned with in East Asia. Rightly or wrongly, it was assumed that having Frenchmen as advisers there could enable France to influence Japanese policy.[103] To get Frenchmen appointed to such positions, though, had become much more difficult, because the Meiji government had now moved towards a more selective use of foreign expertise. To a considerable extent, therefore, the existence of such means of influence depended on earlier appointments and on the establishment of a pattern of looking to France as a model in particular spheres.

This being so, France was fortunate in that during much of the earlier period it was mostly represented by men who were sympathetic towards the progressive tendencies of Bakufu and Meiji leaders. Roches and Turenne were both enthusiastic advocates of Japanese modernization, and after two years in Japan Outrey also became convinced of its desirability. It is not surprising, therefore, that the years 1864–1873 saw a large number of requests for French assistance, as well as several study missions to France. When Turenne gave way to Berthemy, however, all such approaches ceased. That the new French representative was no supporter of reform in Japan emerges clearly from a dispatch which he wrote shortly after his arrival. In it he lamented that

... the foreign representatives who have aspired to the honour of creating a new society during their diplomatic service and of introducing it to the benefits of civilization, have forgotten, it seems to me, that it is difficult to construct an edifice when the base of that which is to be replaced has been destroyed. They have forgotten above all that, dangerous for the peoples of superior race, progress, as it is generally understood, is fatal to inferior races ... The history of the American continent since the end of the fifteenth century, the nationalities which have disappeared on contact with the white race, are the certain proof of this. If China, protected by the immensity of its territory, can defy this dissolving effect for a long time still, Japan is not in the same situation.[104]

The striking contrast between Berthemy's attitude and that of Turenne goes a long way towards explaining why the stream of requests for French help suddenly dried up. Moreover, bearing in mind that 1875 was to see the notoriously anti-Japanese Max von Brandt replaced by a more temperate German representative and that most succeeding French representatives came closer to Berthemy's than Roches' approach, it would not be unreasonable to suggest that the tendency that was apparent in Japan from the late 1870s to look towards Germany as a model may not have been due solely to Japanese perceptions of similarities in the two countries' political development or even to the fact that Germany proved more sympathetic than France to Japan's aim of treaty revision. It may also have reflected the different character and attitudes towards Japan of the diplomats with whom the Meiji government had to deal.[105]

FRENCH VIEWS OF THE DEVELOPMENT OF JAPAN

The differing attitudes of French ministers towards French involement in Japanese modernization can be better understood if their positions on the wider question of the changes and trends that were shaping the new Japan are also taken into account. The obvious starting point is the Meiji Restoration itself. The first serious thoughts about its nature and likely outcome were expressed by Outrey little more than a month after his arrival. In the circumstances, they were surprisingly acute. While admitting that the impact of foreigners had been partly responsible for the political upheaval in Japan, he added: 'But this is not, in my view, the primary cause of so complete an overturning of the secular institutions of Japan: the country is going through a most serious social crisis, and an intermediate class in the population seems to be substituting itself for the higher class which until today has alone occupied the political scene'.[106] The situation was too complex, however, for him to have any confidence about the outcome; and his inability to disentangle the thread of the future from the web of conflicting and overlapping political interests may have been partly responsible for the verdict he passed on Japan in a private letter: 'It is, in sum, a most mediocre country, from every point of view'.[107]

It took about two years for a more positive attitude to come to the fore. In the meantime Outrey was consistently sceptical, first of the declarations of the (mainly samurai) reformers within the Meiji government that a far-reaching transformation was being aimed at, and then, when he had become convinced that this was indeed their intention, of their ability to carry out their plans. In September 1868, for instance, he refused to believe that the main south-western *han* were aiming at a united Imperial government and were therefore willing to accept significant limitations on their own autonomy.[108] In April 1869 he found the actual handover to the Emperor of *han* registers by the Satsuma, Choshu, Tosa and Hizen daimyo inexplicable, adding that public opinion did not believe in their sincerity.[109] By May he had come to realize not only that 'the *karo* class' (the upper-level samurai) were governing in the name of the daimyo, but that it was 'dreaming of a complete reorganization which would dissolve all interests into one and permit the creation of a single, powerful government'. Nevertheless, he added, 'one asks oneself if the country is prepared for so radical a transformation and if these plans, without doubt laudable but too precipitate, are not such as to lead to inextricable complications'.[110] As for the experiment in public debate which the early Meiji government had inaugurated with the establishment of two deliberative assemblies, one of daimyo, the other composed of samurai representatives from each domain, Outrey, like his colleagues, was uninterested in any potential for representative government which these bodies might possess. On the contrary, the frequent expression of anti-foreign opinions in debates led the Western diplomats to raise with the Meiji government the question of the assemblies' status – with the intention of warning it that discussion of proposals contrary to the stipulations of the treaties was undesirable. Their intervention may have been a contributory factor in the Meiji leaders' decision to discontinue with the experiment with assemblies after 1870.[111]

Throughout 1869 and early 1870 Outrey persisted in believing that the Japanese leaders who proposed major change were over-ambitious and unrealistic. In March 1870, for instance, he described the Meiji government's plan to build Japan's first railway as 'an enterprise very problematic in its results'.[112] Then in June 1870 he struck a different note. 'Japan', he declared, 'is en route for transformation. Contrary to that which is happening in the other oriental countries and particularly in China, Japan is resolutely and with enthusiasm embracing European ideas'.[113] This conclusion significantly followed the first definite request by the Meiji government for a new military mission from France, a request which Outrey particularly welcomed (although he sought to conceal the extent of his gratification from the Japanese) because French advisers were being chosen in preference to Prussian. It was no doubt the case that the resulting conversations with Iwakura and other leaders had given Outrey a new insight into Japanese political realities. Nevertheless, the Meiji government still had some very important obstacles to overcome before it could be said to have firmly established both its own power and its programme of reform.[114] It would appear, then, that Outrey's assessment of the political situation in Japan was directly related to Japanese eagerness for French participation in the process of modernization.

Whether the same was true of the chargé d'affaires who took over from Outrey in October 1871 is much less certain. The Comte de Turenne certainly shared to the full Outrey's desire to increase French prestige by contributing to Japan's development, but the general tone of his dispatches suggests that he was in favour of Japanese modernization whoever was responsible for it. His approval was expressed without reserve, for example, in a report of November 1872 in which he wrote that 'each day brings a new proof of the progressive advance of the Government of the Tenno [Emperor]'.[115] What appears to have been a genuine sympathy for the Meiji government's efforts may have been one of the reasons why Turenne urged upon Rémusat a much more flexible attitude on important political questions such as the treatment of the Urakami Christians, the withdrawal of French troops, and revision of the treaties.[116] By 1873 the resulting cordiality between the two countries, during Turenne's service in Japan, was even approaching that of the years from 1864 to 1867, and, as in the Roches period, it was perceived to carry the promise of commercial advantage'.[117]

With the coming of Jules Berthemy in June 1873 this cordiality vanished. Whereas Turenne had welcomed every progressive move by the Meiji government and had willingly accepted that France should play a full part in promoting change, Berthemy showed nothing but distaste for the innovations that had been introduced: 'Undertaken without method, without effective study, pursued with feverish haste, this transformation', he almost immediately proclaimed, 'is such as to give rise to serious apprehensions about the future of the country'.[118] What probably lay behind this severe judgement emerged in his next dispatch, which discussed the problem of the Japanese attack on the privilege of extraterritoriality, the right enjoyed by foreigners as a result of the 1858 treaties to be tried in consular courts if accused of committing an offence in Japan. In the dispatch Berthemy lamented the

> . . . lack of entente which appears to exist among the foreign representatives with regard to the attitude which it is appropriate to observe towards the Japanese government when daily it raises new questions. Most of them appear to have no other object in view than to obtain for their own nationals well-paid positions. This results in a real rivalry, and in order to have their candidate succeed, they sometimes allow themselves to be party to compromising accommodations.[119]

The situation was the more objectionable to him in that he had been sent to Japan, after serving as minister in Peking and Washington, for the express purpose of securing treaty revision on Western terms, and without the full cooperation of his fellow diplomats his mission would have no hope of success. For him

France's role in Japanese modernization clearly had to be subordinated to a higher political interest.[120]

Berthemy's hostility to the Meiji government's treaty revision policy seems to have affected his attitude towards internal politics also. At any rate, after Soejima Taneomi and other ministers and councillors resigned following the rejection of their call for a strong Korean policy in October 1873, he showed more sympathy for them than for the victors in what was the first major split in the Meiji government. This, however, was not because several members of the new opposition group which some of the ousted men formed in January 1874 – in a move which is often regarded as marking the beginning of the movement for freedom and people's rights (*Jiyuminkenundo*) – called publicly for the establishment of a parliament. Indeed, Berthemy's comment on the proposal was typically scathing: 'The establishment of a Representative government', he wrote, 'will be, I fear, fatal for the country'.[121] In justification of this contention he provided a highly unflattering assessment of the Japanese character: 'The Japanese are quick to change and impressionable, easy to sway one way or another; they are at the same time superficial, as ready to imitate as incapable of creating . . . far from being in a position to govern themselves they consequently need, more than others, to be directed and held in check'.[122] His preference for the opponents of the government can only be explained by his belief that their manifesto was simply 'an arm of opposition' which would be forgotten when they came to power and that in the matter of treaty revision they would be more compliant than the existing leaders.[123]

Berthemy's views of Japan and the Japanese remained highly critical. In April 1874 he showed that he had no higher an opinion of the Japanese as workers than as potential democrats: 'The Japanese, and this is one of the causes of his inferiority towards the Chinese, does not think of the next day. If he receives higher pay for his work, he works fewer days per week or hours per day; consequently he produces no more. In short, he has no idea of economic saving and it will be the same as long as the family is not constituted here on better defined foundations'.[124] Perhaps more surprising even than these extravagant generalizations was his near-heresy in questioning whether the opening of Japan to the West had been to the former's advantage:

104

A glance back at the fifteen years which have passed since the opening of the port of Kanagawa makes it impossible to think that contact with the West has made the Japanese nation more prosperous or that the new field opened up to the enterprise of America and Europe has produced an abundant harvest. . . . The national civilization which, while not belonging to the same type as ours, had nevertheless attained a certain level of culture, has been replaced by a hybrid state of things as displeasing to the Japanese as to the foreigner himself.[125]

The diplomat who took over from Berthemy in April 1875, Ange-Guillaume de St. Quentin, was less decided in his opinions, but he, too, showed little liking for some of the changes taking place. He was quick, for instance, to point out that the experiment with more liberal laws had been followed by an increase in crime,[126] and he echoed his predecessor when he suggested that the advocacy of political assassination, atheism and full democracy by the recently established Japanese press was 'such as to raise doubts as to the good influence of European civilization on this country'.[127] His approval of the 1876 law which curbed the freedom of the vigorous new press revealed that he shared with most other French diplomats who served in Japan an almost instinctive distrust of any development which might threaten the authority of the Meiji government. Unlike Berthemy, however, he did not lack concern for the prestige that France derived from the military mission and the French personnel at Yokosuka, and much of his time was taken up in urging the Meiji government to retain them.

St Quentin's successor, Francis-Henri-Louis de Geofroy, who had earlier served as minister in China, also showed some disposition at first to condemn Japan for its haste in adopting new ideas. For example, in reporting the death of Saigo Takamori by *harakiri*, when the rebellious Satsuma ex-samurai whom he led were defeated by government forces in 1877 after a nine-month struggle, he praised him for wishing to 'return to the past, or, at least, curb the unconsidered movement of reforms into which Japan has thrown itself. The idea was right even if the means employed were not correct, and he would have rendered a great service to his country in trying to make it a reality in a more regular manner'.[128]

Closer acquaintance with Japan, however, led Geofroy to modify his views. In August 1878 he admitted in a dispatch that many reforms had proved useful and he actually criticized the Japanese for not going far enough.[129] With regard to the Japanese family system for instance, he claimed that 'as long as they have not legislated on this fundamental point, one cannot but maintain that their work is superficial and precarious'. His comment on Okubo Toshimichi, when this dominant figure was assassinated by admirers of Saigo, more than matched the compliment he earlier paid to Saigo. 'The story of his life is linked to that of the astonishing reforms which have transformed Japan', he wrote, proceeding to characterize him as 'the enlightened promoter of European civilization in his country'.[130] This change of attitude by Geofroy makes it less surprising that in his second year as minister, he questioned the French stand on treaty revision and showed a willingness to cooperate with Japan in Korean affairs, both of which ideas would have been almost inconceivable to Berthemy or St Quentin.

Such pro-Japanese tendencies were certainly unacceptable to Geofroy's successor, chargé d'affaires Marie-René-Davy de Chavigné de Balloy, who was swift to dissociate France from Japanese foreign policy.[131] Balloy's impressions of Japan were entirely unfavourable. In the harshness of his criticism he exceeded even Berthemy. His first dispatch declared that good relations would be difficult because 'The Japanese are vanity itself and see wrongs to their sovereign rights everywhere'.[132] His attacks were generally directed against the Meiji government, whose pursuit of treaty revision he attributed to the fact that it, 'like all governments which do not have deep roots in the country, periodically needs to make use of external issues to divert the attention of its subjects from its internal difficulties'.[133] He blamed the government's financial difficulties on its costly sponsorship of commercial projects and on its introduction in 1873 of a monetarized land tax, and he went so far as to describe the previous system as a golden age in which 'the peasant paid his daimyo a certain percentage of his harvest in kind. When the year was bad, not only was this remitted to him, wholly or in part, but he would even draw from his lord's reserves what he needed to live'.[134]

In one dispatch in 1880 the industrial programme of the Meiji leaders came under Balloy's severe censure: 'They did not know where they were leading the country, but they hoped that their venture would bring them honour and profit. In this they were not mistaken . . . it is thanks to their greed that Japan is covered today with all these associations which have as their purpose the monopolization of this or that branch of trade or industry and which weigh so heavily on the general prosperity'.[135] So seriously did he regard the financial crisis caused by the post-Satsuma rebellion inflationary expansion of the money supply that when he heard rumours that a loan of 100 million francs might be sought in Europe, he warned his foreign minister that if he should 'learn that the Japanese government is talking to any French bank, it would be prudent to caution it against the risk to its capital'.[136] He saw only one remedy – a stern retrenchment – which (failing to foresee the effective deflation carried out by finance minister Matsukata Masayoshi between 1881 and 1885) he believed to be beyond Japanese capability. His conclusion therefore was drastic: 'I believe I can predict that Japan is surely marching towards anarchy, perhaps even dismemberment – that will depend on the state of the main foreign powers, America included, at the critical moment'. [137]

The Meiji government's industrial programme was not the only aspect of Japanese government with which Balloy found fault. His criticisms of the workings of Japanese justice were scathing, and the fact that changes had been made to Boissonade's work gave him an excuse for judging the new penal and criminal prcedure codes harshly.[138] Yet for all his dislike of the existing administration, Balloy never wavered from the anti-liberal attitudes of previous French ministers. His comment in February 1880 on the agitation for a democratic government provides a good illustration of this: 'Japan does not appear to me to be sufficiently mature for parliamentary government, and from the point of view of the international relations of this country with foreign powers, I would not envisage without apprehension the inauguration of a system of government which would necessarily have the effect of diminishing, if not destroying, the principle of authority represented by the Emperor'.[139]

Balloy left Japan in December 1880. None of his successors quite matched the vehemence of his criticism and the depth of his pessimism, though Arthur Tricou, who was minister from mid-1882 to mid-1883, was almost equally anti-Japanese (at least until France's difficulties with China over Indochina prompted thoughts of Franco-Japanese cooperation). In 1882 Tricou went so far as to assert that 'the dignitaries who made the revolution of 1868 seek to borrow from us our methods of civilization only in the hope of being able one day to make use of them against that civilization and against us'.[140] This warning had not been voiced by any French minister since the time of Duchesne de Bellecourt, a fact which may indicate how little serious attention was paid to Japan by France in the decade and a half after the Meiji Restoration.

It would be difficult to avoid the conclusion that the on-the-spot views of Japanese progress by French representatives in Tokyo tended to be less favourable than those commonly held in Europe. This was remarked upon by Balloy in 1880. 'What I cannot explain', he lamented, 'is how Japan has been able throw enough dust into our eyes to make us believe in Europe that in adopting our customs and our civilization, it was going to be our champion, our vanguard in Asia'.[141] Whether or not Europe's reaction to Japan's transformation was excessively uncritical, the pertinent question here is how to account for the highly unsympathetic attitude of many French diplomats. One minor factor which might possibly have induced a jaundiced view was the physically trying environment in which diplomats worked at this time, at least in summer. Only in the 1880s does the practice of leaving Tokyo for the mountains to avoid the heat appear to have been adopted. A second possible cause may have been the speed of Japan's transformation, which meant that many reforms appeared incomplete or misconceived; and when the latter were guided by nationals of other Powers, they could hardly be expected to meet with French approval. More important than these considerations, almost certainly, was the French diplomats' awareness that one of their most basic tenets was being challenged. If Japan succeeded in raising itself to the level of the Western powers, abandonment of the cherished belief in Western uniqueness and inherent superiority which almost all foreigners held would become an unpleasant necessity.

These three factors alone, however, can scarcely account for the hostile or even contemptuous language to be found in

French diplomatic documents. One must also recall that during most of this period, and especially the later years, Japan was seeking to revise the treaties which had been imposed on the Bakufu. The Western powers would have liked to take the moral high ground and claim that Japanese backwardness and unwillingness to change made the abandonment of extraterritoriality impossible and unreasonable. The fact that Japan was openly seeking to emulate the West, however, made this argument much less satisfactory, and while it was still employed, the fact that it could not be used forever became increasingly obvious. Thus, Western diplomats were gradually compelled to have recourse to an essentially legalistic defence of their privileges. Nevertheless, they could not hide from themselves that the Japanese did see the question in moral terms. Their perhaps largely unconscious resentment at being unable to cloak their desire to maintain their countries' material interests with the justification that Japan refused to abandon its old ways may be inferred from the indignation which they sometimes showed at what were not unnatural demands on the part of the Japanese.

Tricou provides a good example of this mentality. In 1882 he wrote: 'I underestimated Japanese ambition but overestimated Japanese discretion. The Tokyo Court at last unveils its designs without making any attempt to conceal them. It throws aside the mask'.[142] His extravagant language was prompted by nothing more than the announcement by the Japanese government that it wanted new treaties which could eventually be terminated, rather than a mere revision of the old ones. Similarly Tricou described a Japanese plan to achieve tariff autonomy by separating the commercial from the jurisdictional aspects of the treaty as 'a puerile argument without doubt, but that much more Japanese in that it is puerile'.[143] Such feelings could not be totally concealed from Japanese leaders, and their existence may help to explain (though not wholly justify) the complaint to Roquette by foreign minister Inoue Kaoru in 1880 that the Western powers had given scant encouragement to Japan in its attempts to transform its civilization.[144]

5

FRANCE AND THE EMERGENCE OF JAPANESE FOREIGN POLICY 1870–85

THE MEIJI RESTORATION paved the way for the establishment of a centralized government and a wide-ranging programme of modernization, but it took a decade before the Meiji government had overcome all the reactionary or local-based threats to its authority and achieved real stability. Similarly the Restoration by no means secured for Japan instant immunity to external threat. The 1870s and early 1880s were years in which the widespread use by Japanese of the term 'the raging billows of Western advance' reflected a strong feeling that Japan was in danger of being overwhelmed by the Powers which had forced the opening of the country only a short time before; and it was not until the mid-1880s that Japan began to be taken seriously as an East Asian power.[1] In the intervening years French diplomats not only observed Meiji Japan's first tentative steps in foreign policy but occasionally had opportunities to influence the direction they took. Beyond the actions (or inaction) of individual French representatives in Tokyo, however, French policy in East Asia, especially when it entered a more forceful phase in the 1880s, was a factor which Japan could not ignore in the pursuit of its diplomatic objectives, and between 1883 and 1885 there was even a possibility that France might be largely responsible for a dramatic change in Japanese foreign policy.

THE FRANCO-PRUSSIAN WAR AND JAPANESE NEUTRALITY

It was not only French East Asian policy which Japan had to take into account. French policy in Europe could also be relevant. Indeed, it was France's war with Prussia in 1870–71 which first involved Japan in international diplomacy and provided the Meiji government with its earliest lessons in *realpolitik*. Initially the outbreak of war seemed an extremely propitious event for Japan. Not only did it make European intervention on behalf of the Urakami Christians less likely, it also presented the Meiji government with the opportunity of asserting Japan's rights as a sovereign state for the first time by proclaiming Japanese neutrality. Subsequent developments, however, proved that even apparently favourable circumstances might conceal unforeseen hazards; and while Japan undoubtedly benefited from France's inability to press for a change in Japan's religious policy, the war also served to confirm Japan's impotence and its inability to secure recognition of the rights it claimed under international law.

The question of neutrality was first raised with the Meiji government by the Prussian minister, von Brandt, on 18 August 1870, soon after news of the war reached Japan. Outrey also favoured the idea at this point, although the Meiji leadership would hardly have been happy with his reasoning, for in his report to Paris he emphasized 'the extreme importance of showing to the Chinese, as to the Japanese, that, even in a state of war the European powers will be always ready to unite in action to protect European interests in the two countries'.[2] The Japanese Foreign Ministry hastened to draw up and issue, on 24 August, a proclamation of neutrality which asserted Japan's rights and which Sir Harry Parkes described as 'the first State Paper of the kind that the Japanese Government have ever published'.[3] It stated that 'the contending parties are not permitted to engage in hostilities in Japanese harbours or Inland waters, or within a distance of three *ri* [seven-and-a-half miles] from land at any place', and that warships which were pursued into Japanese harbours would be allowed 24 hours start when they left port. An accompanying note emphasized that 'the inland waters of Japan are within our jurisdiction'.[4]

This proclamation did not meet with Outrey's full approval. In his report to the Quai d'Orsay he observed that he had 'had to indicate to the Japanese government that I could not accept the regulations which it proposed to establish'.[5] Nevertheless, he soon, on 24 September, accepted a new version which was not essentially different from the original.[6] That he did so was less surprising than that von Brandt also agreed to the second neutrality proclamation, for it failed to ensure a 24-hour start for any vessels when they left Japanese ports other than warships.[7] This meant that if France were to deploy a superior naval force – as it was in the process of doing during September – and if the French admiral chose to give European solidarity a lower priority than prosecution of the war – which Admiral Dupré, unlike Outrey, did – then no Prussian (or North German) merchant ships could safely depart from Japan.

It did not take long for von Brandt to realize his mistake, but in his attempt to correct it he made a serious miscalculation. Instead of consulting with his French colleague as before, he exerted pressure on the Japanese government and induced it to issue, on 12 October, additional regulations which gave 24 hours' start to merchantmen as well as to warships, while also prohibiting the use of any Japanese port as a base of operation by either belligerent.[8] Outrey's response to this *fait accompli* was to reject it outright and to insist that the previous proclamation was a tripartite international agreement which could only be altered with the consent of all the parties involved. His argument found favour with most of his colleagues, and on 16 October 1870 the Japanese government officially withdrew the additional articles.[9]

Though Outrey displayed considerable skill in his handling of this question, his diplomatic victory would have had little practical significance had it not been backed by French naval strength. Japan naturally favoured the Prussian version of neutrality, but with no navy of its own to speak of, it would have invited the humiliation of having its authority disregarded if it had attempted to implement the revised regulations in the face of Outrey's refusal to admit their validity. France was thus able to paralyse German shipping and gain some local prestige from the refusal of the German warships to meet the French challenge. Von Brandt himself refused to accept the Japanese retreat from the October agreement and strove continually to impose his view by making threats about an indemnity, although in the end no such demand was made.[10] While Japan escaped this penalty, however, it experienced a sharp reminder that if it was to carry any weight in international affairs, it would need to increase its military strength, and that in the meantime it would be well advised to display diplomatic caution. The domestic and foreign policies of the Meiji leaders in the next twenty years showed that they learned the lesson well.

FRANCE AND JAPAN'S RELATIONS WITH ITS ASIAN NEIGHBOURS

Although the difficulties arising out of the Franco-Prussian war were not without long-term significance, the circumstances which produced them were short-lived. By contrast, Japan's relations with its neighbours were a cause of frequent concern, involving as they did the continuing questions of Japanese control or influence over peripheral territory and the nature of Japan's relationships with China. The two questions were closely connected, since the central issue in deciding policy towards China was whether Japan should seek to cooperate with the Ch'ing empire in resisting further Western encroachment – the so-called Japan-China cooperation argument (*Nisshin teikei-ron*) or Japan-China alliance argument (*Nisshin Domei-ron*) – or whether Japan should try to take advantage of China's current weakness by denying the latter any share of authority over the Ryukyu Islands or by undermining its traditional claim to suzerainty over Korea. If the Meiji government were to choose the latter course, France might be expected to be at least an interested spectator, not just because of its active religious protectorate in China and its foothold in an area – Indochina – where China had a traditional claim to suzerainty but also as a result of French missionary activities in the Ryukyus and Korea. Moreover, in the case of the Ryukyus, an agreement with the local authorities had been signed in 1855 by a visiting French navy captain, and the islands clearly had potential strategic value.[11]

Despite these considerations, however, France showed relatively little concern with the Ryukyus and never questioned Japan's claim to them. At the time of the Paris Exposition of 1867, the daimyo of Satsuma had been recognised as king of the Ryukyus without any apparent discussion; and when the islands were forced by the Meiji government to accept a centrally appointed governor in 1872, the reaction of Turenne implied that this was a purely internal measure which the Japanese government had an indisputable right to take.[12] The Japanese action did not, at this stage, seem likely to be a cause of dispute with China, and no more thought was paid by French diplomats to the area until 1874, when it was decided to send what was essentially a Satsuma military expedition under Saigo Tsugu-michi to Taiwan to punish the aborigines on its eastern coast who had murdered some Ryukyuan sailors in 1871. By the time of the expedition Jules Berthemy had become France's representative in Tokyo, but despite his anxiety to avoid involvement in any Sino-Japanese conflict which might ensue, even he did not contest the legal basis of Japan's action. One probable reason (though it was never expllicitly stated) why France was inclined to favour Japanese control of the Ryukyus was that the islands were more likely to escape German attentions under the relatively firm hand of the Meiji government than under the distant control of China.[13]

Another reason for French inactivity in the Ryukyu issue is suggested by Berthemy's comments when Iwakura sought his opinion on the expedition in June 1874. Although the French Minister counselled the Japanese leader to withdraw the Japanese troops as soon as they had chastised the natives lest Japan find itself at war with China, his report to the Quai d'Orsay suggests that he would not have been sorry to see his advice disregarded:

> 'They write to me from Peking', he observed, 'that if Japan fails in its enterprise, the pride of the Chinese will know no limits and will become intolerable. Now it will be exactly the same in Yedo if success crowns the Formosan expedition. In

this situation I can see no other position to take other than to
allow events to take their course, while keeping close watch
on them and reserving diplomatic intervention until circumstances permit us to do so usefully. It is important, however,
not to lose sight of the fact that a war between China and
Japan, sufficiently prolonged to enfeeble the two adversaries
and halted before one or the other can justifiably claim
victory, may spare the maritime Powers the necessity in the
not too distant future of undertaking costly expeditions for
the purpose of preserving a situation in the Far East which
day by day becomes more difficult, in Peking as in Yedo, to
maintain intact'.[14]

Not all French diplomats were as Machiavellian as Berthemy,
and in general the French attitude was more sympathetic to
Japan, or perhaps one should say more hostile to China, than
would appear from this dispatch.[15] Nevertheless, if the wishful
thinking about intervention is set aside, Berthemy's views can be
considered representative in so far as they reflected, more or less
faithfully, the negative character of French thinking on Far
Eastern questions.

The Taiwan Expedition had been expected by the Meiji
government to provide an outlet for samurai frustration. It was,
however, very much a second best. The first hope both of many
restless samurai and of those government leaders who saw the
problem of national defence in primarily military terms, was the
conquest of Korea. In 1873, while Iwakura, Okubo, and many
of the young modernizers were still abroad, the advocates of a
Korean expedition had come to comprise a majority of the
government, and when the Iwakura mission returned, it was
only after a bitter struggle between Okubo, Iwakura and Kido
and their supporters on the one side, and Saigo Takamori,
Itagaki Taisuke, Soejima and Eto on the other, that Japan was
brought back to a policy of internal strengthening first.[16]

Since the foreign representatives knew of Japan's military
plans through Soejima, it might have been expected that the
possibility of war would have stimulated France to give the
question of Japanese policy towards Korea serious consideration.[17] Admittedly, France had shown negligible interest in
Korea since the failure of its 1866 naval expedition – the first
incursion in the peninsula by a Western power – and the

poverty of the 'hermit kingdom' was too well known for any great hopes of trade to be entertained. Nevertheless, missionary persecution there continued to be severe and France might well have seen in Japan's plans an opportunity of securing religious concessions.[18] Any expectations by missionaries that this would be so, however, were doomed to disappointment. Not only did the split in the Meiji government over Korea fail to prompt any reconsideration of French policy, but the whole question was regarded by Berthemy as no more than a side issue in comparison with his treaty revision negotiations. The sketchy information which he passed on was hardly of a nature to interest a Quai d'Orsay which was almost wholly preoccupied with European issues at this time.[19]

Though the Meiji government decided against invasion in 1873, it continued to seek the opening of Korea; and in 1876, after an attack on a Japanese surveying party, it secured by a show of force a treaty which made a first breach in Korea's traditional isolation policy. To St Quentin, the French chargé d'affaires in Tokyo, the opening of a few ports to Japanese trade seemed of little importance, however. He showed scarcely any interest in the commercial advantages the treaty might open up and none at all in its possible international repercussions. His main reaction was a negative one. The treaty would be welcome 'if only, unhappily, it was not to be feared that this success will increase still more the pride of Japan in such a way as to render relations with that country more difficult, if not precarious'.[20] The Quai d'Orsay, for its part, did not bother to respond to his observations.

About 1878–9 the era of cautious conservatism in French foreign policy began to wane, and this trend was evident in the Far East too, more particularly in Indo-China, but also to a certain extent in Korea. In April 1878, Geofroy, the French minister in Tokyo, began to show some concern about the plight of the missionaries in the peninsula. Having failed to secure the cooperation of the French navy, he was about to take the unprecedented step of asking the Japanese government to intervene when Terashima spontaneously offered his good offices and sent a letter urging the Korean government to release some missionaries who had been arrested.[21] The Japanese intervention had no apparent effect but it did go a little way towards producing a better relationship at a time when Japan

116

appeared to have decided that it was important to prevent Russian encroachment on Korea and that the way to ensure this was to open Korea to the world generally. Since this seemed to Geofroy to be in France's real interests also, he assured Iwakura of his support in December 1878, and at the same time urged his government to consider cooperating with Japan and other interested powers.[22]

Owing to the vagaries of French diplomatic appointments this harmony of views between France and Japan soon disappeared. Geofroy returned home on leave early in 1879, and his successor, Balloy, who had previously served as first secretary, at once enunciated an entirely opposite view of the Korean situation. He claimed that '. . . by associating ourselves morally with the Japanese eventual action in order to establish the right to claim a share of the advantages gained, we would have the air of receiving a tow from them. They are already', he continued, 'quite difficult enough to handle at present; after such a success, they would become impossible to deal with and would be only too disposed to make demands which would compromise international relations'. France should therefore, he concluded, appear to be uninterested in the question.[23] Despite his lesser rank and experience, the Quai d'Orsay preferred his analysis to Geofroy's and a further overture by Inoue, the new foreign minister, was treated with extreme reserve.[24]

How important this move away from cooperation may have been is hard to assess. Japan continued to favour the establishment of Western diplomatic representation in Korea, and even seems to have favoured an international treaty guaranteeing Korean independence along the lines of the 1839 treaty of Belgian neutrality; and the withdrawal of the French promise of cooperation, though a disappointment, did not mean that the Powers had decided not to seek treaties.[25] On the other hand, the French decision may have contributed to the delay in securing them and it was in this interval that China began to reassert its <u>suzerainty</u> over the states on its periphery. It is arguable, therefore, that the French failure to combine their efforts with those of Japan made it more likely that the West would play a negligible role in Korea and thus made a contest for dominance over the peninsula between the two Far Eastern powers more probable.

Before Geofroy's departure the other Sino-Japanese problem had unexpectedly emerged again. It had seemed to be solved when China's acknowledgment in 1875 of Japan's right to punish the Taiwanese aborigines had appeared to represent a tacit acceptance of Japanese sovereignty over the Ryukyus. However, the situation had become uncertain again in 1876, when the Ryukyuans, having resumed the tradition of sending a tributary mission to Peking in the previous year, sought Chinese support in a struggle against modernization by the Meiji government.[26] When China, which was currently preoccupied with its dispute with Russia over its Central Asian frontiers, proved unable to help, the Ryukyuans (at Chinese instigation) turned to the representatives of the three Western powers with which treaties had been signed. Their case was privately felt to be a good one by Geofroy. 'The good people of Lieou Kieou are interesting and their cause is just', he wrote to a Quai d'Orsay official.[27] But in his official report he recorded that he had 'not judged it useful to encourage the démarche of the Lieou-Kieou envoys', justifying his attitude by arguing that if the Ryukyus ceased to be Japanese, they would come under Chinese rule 'If we must favour the ascendancy of one or the other of the two powers', he suggested, 'it seems to me that it should rather be Japan, over which we have morally and materially more hold'.[28]

This was by no means the end of the dispute, for China was soon to reassert its traditional claims, and Japan even offered to hand over the southern islands, albeit only on terms which were unacceptable to China.[29] In 1883 there were constant rumours that China was preparing to use force to gain control of the Ryukyus, and this reflected the general toughening of its stance on its claims to suzerainty over bordering territories which already in 1881 had led Roquette to feel that Japan might be advised to give up the Ryukyus entirely rather than risk war. In February of that year he expressed the opinion that 'it would not be surprising if China emerged victorious from the struggle', and in October he gave Japan no chance: 'Japan can begin: China alone can finish'.[30] His views, however, clearly had no influence on Japanese policy. France's official attitude remained one of absolute reserve, which concealed, as Geofroy's comment showed, a partiality for Japan.

On this matter, as on Korea, the basic French attitude could not change, for France's own difficulties over its Annam protectorate meant that siding with China was out of the question. As Tricou, a later minister in Tokyo , wrote in 1882: 'The Peking Court's pretensions to suzerainty, pretensions which at present are visible in all directions, appear to me to require our vigilance, especially over Annam. I think, for my part, that, as a general proposition, we have an interest in discouraging them everywhere and on all occasions'.[31] Nevertheless, France's concern not to increase its difficulties in Indo-China by arousing Chinese hostility, together with its traditional caution and the personal inclination of its representatives in Tokyo, deterred it from supporting Japan openly. Thus the influence France exerted on Japanese foreign policy remained slight, even though in their East Asian positions the two countries had an important interst in common. It is arguable, therefore, that during the first decade-and-a-half of the Meiji era France neglected the opportunity to build up a position of goodwill and trust that might well have been useful later, most notably between 1883 and 1885.

FRENCH POLICY TOWARDS JAPAN DURING THE FRANCO-CHINESE DISPUTE OF 1883–5

The years 1883–5 deserve special attention because during this period there was a real possibility of a major change in Franco-Japanese relations. At issue was whether the two countries should establish a military and diplomatic entente which could well have turned into a formal alliance. In the end no such agreement emerged, and the whole episode was rapidly forgotten. Those historians who in more recent years have encountered evidence of it have been puzzled over what was actually involved. They have generally appreciated that it could be significant for an understanding of Meiji foreign policy, but have differed over what it really meant.

The lack of consensus derives partly from the uncertainty among Japanese historians as to how eager for an alliance France was: most have tended to assume that Japan was offered one, but the evidence available in Japanese sources does not provide irrefutable proof of this, and there are some contradictory indications which give room for doubt. Even on the rare occasions when French diplomatic records have been consulted, the picture has not become entirely clear, for the use of those records has been limited and selective. In addition, the ambivalence of French policy, not to mention its occasional inconsistency or lack of coordination, has not been properly appreciated by Japanese historians.[32] To understand the French position more fully, it is necessary to examine it in detail over the whole period of the Franco-Chinese dispute, taking into account also the surviving Japanese Foreign Ministry records (some of which remain unpublished and neglected) which relate to relations with France during these years.[33]

From an objective standpoint the development of the East Asian situation in the early 1880s made cooperation between France and Japan a logical means of pursuing their aims or protecting their interests. What stood out in this period was not so much the relentless advance of Western imperialism but China's more vigorous and successful efforts to resist further encroachment on its own territory – as it did against Russia in the Ili border crisis in the late 1870s and early 1880s – and to reassert its traditional (but never clearly defined) rights over the countries bordering its frontiers.[34] This claim to suzerainty by the 'Middle Kingdom' affected France and Japan more than any of the other powers with East Asian interests. It was, in fact, the issue that sparked off the Franco-Chinese dispute, which broke out in 1883 after the vigorous Jules Ferry formed his second cabinet.[35] Two decades earlier France had incorporated Cochin China (in southern Indochina) in its empire and in 1874 it had imposed on the ruler of Annam (which covered the main central region of Vietnam) a treaty which was not initially implemented but gave France what it regarded as a protectorate over Annam's external relations as well as the right to interfere on behalf of the Christians there. From the late 1870s French governments were concerned that the 1874 treaty might become a dead letter, and especially from 1881 there were tentative efforts to assert French authority over Annam, but Ferry was the first French premier who was prepared to act decisively by sending a significant force to the region.

Like most other Frenchmen, Ferry assumed that the Chinese would offer only token resistance to France's establishment of full control over both Annam and Tongking (the region of Vietnam which bordered China). He soon discovered that he had been indulging in wishful thinking. Instead of acquiescence, French forces met with stiff opposition from Chinese irregular troops. Though war was never formally declared, the conflict gradually escalated, and by the middle of 1884 the French were not only fighting on land in northern Vietnam but also attacking Chinese warships (some of which they sank in the naval port of Foochow in a surprise strike) and seizing Taiwanese ports.[36]

Japan kept a close watch on French actions, though not because it had any direct interest in Indochina at this time. Rather it was because French success might undermine China's claims to suzerainty over Korea and the Ryukyus. Although the latter were in Japanese possession, rumours that Li Hung-chang, the viceroy of the northern Chinese province of Chihli and China's most important foreign policy-maker, had plans to recover them by force were currently disturbing Inoue Kaoru, the Japanese foreign minister.[37] Korea, by contrast, was a country where Chinese influence had always been very strong but was now becoming irksome to an increasing number of Japanese.[38] Apart from the undesirability that an area of such strategic importance to Japan should be under another power's effective control, there were Japanese who regarded China as an obstacle to their own activities there. Notable among these were a number of progressive politicians and journalists who proclaimed the need to introduce Korea to the benefits of modernization under Japanese auspices, and who asserted that it should become truly independent. Some of the Meiji government leaders, particularly Iwakura Tomomi until his death in 1883, were content to leave Korea as it was, but even they could not completely disregard the possibility that the peninsula might again, as in 1873, become a cause of dispute.[39]

By itself Japan could not yet hope to make a successful intervention in Korean affairs, but association with a Western power would change the balance of power in its favour. For its part, France would significantly increase its chances of concluding its own dispute speedily and successfully if China were to be faced with Japanese forces as well as French. The French government, which, at a time of economic recession, was finding itself involved in a larger undertaking than it had anticipated, was not insensitive to the advantages which might result from an agreement, and there even existed some French-men – army officers who had helped train the Japanese army in its early stages and were now rising towards the higher ranks in France – who had some appreciation of Japan's possibilities, not only as a temporary friend, but also as a long-term ally.[40] While there were, as will be seen, reasons why not all Frenchmen and Japanese favoured such a development, it should not be assumed that an entente or an alliance was out of the question.

THE FIRST APPROACHES

The first definite suggestion by a French diplomat in Tokyo that Japan might be eager to join with France in a common cause was made in June 1883, when news reached the outside world of the defeat and death of the French commander, Rivière, at Hanoi the previous month. Although the forces responsible were the independent Black Flags, under the bandit leader, Liu Yung-fu, and not regular Chinese troops, the incident followed the Chinese government's rejection of the French claim that the 1874 treaty had ended Chinese suzerainty over Annam, and it indicated that if France were to overcome Chinese opposition, a stronger force might be required than France had at hand.[41] The excitement which the French setback aroused in Tokyo led the Comte de Viel-Castel, France's new chargé d'affaires, to report to Paris that the reinforcements France needed might well be found in Japan. Not only did he detect pro-French sympathies, but also a desire to join the French side: 'It would no longer be as spectators, but side by side, as brothers in arms, that the Japanese would consider following us in the struggle which they see us engaged in against the Celestial Empire'.[42] In support of this striking assertion Viel-Castel pointed to the fact that a vice-minister of foreign affairs had requested that Japanese officers be allowed to follow the operations of the French troops in Tongking, and that according to rumour three Japanese warships were prepared to cruise in Chinese waters, ready to protect Japanese nationals. He further claimed that public opinion appeared to favour war if it were possible to form an entente with France, termed by Viel-Castel 'the ally of their choice'.[43]

In retrospect it seems apparent that Viel-Castel, who had no previous diplomatic experience at this level, misread the indications of Japanese interest and indulged in wishful thinking. Japanese Foreign Office records, at any rate, give no indication whatsoever of any inclination towards war at this stage. By 3 July, the chargé d'affaires was backtracking, reporting that 'not only the dream of an effective alliance, but that of an entente based on common interests, seems for the moment to have been abandoned by this fickle people'.[44] It is rather more likely that in the intervening three weeks Viel-Castel had perceived that his initial reaction had been an exaggerated one.

However mistaken Viel-Castel may have been in his first impressions, his report undoubtedly encouraged the French government to suppose that Japan was eager for some kind of agreement. It was the more inclined to make that assumption in that the Quai d'Orsay had already been made aware that Japan was paying particular attention to events in Indo-China. Moreover, in March it had been approached by Frederick Marshall, an English adviser who had been counsellor to the Japanese legation in Paris for a decade , and who now led the French foreign minister, Challemel-Lacour, to understand that 'the objective of the Japanese government, preoccupied with the tendencies of China, is to join with the other interested governments in a concerted action to bring about a formal settlement of these various questions [ie. of Korea, the Ryukyus, Annam and Siam]'.[45]

Paris was at this point still hopeful that China would concede what France wanted, but before long its optimism faded, and in anticipation of Chinese prevarication or continued opposition, Challemel-Lacour concluded after another conversation with Marshall that 'we should neglect nothing which might be utilized if the need arises'.[46] More specifically, he recommended that 'we ourselves ought not to disdain the support which, at an appropriate moment, the attitude of Japan would be able to supply to our action'.[47] He therefore instructed Viel-Castel to consider 'what you can make of this without departing from the extreme reserve which the situation requires', adding that 'I count on your accurately communicating to me, together with the indications which reach you on China's intentions, whatever insights you can glean into the Japanese government's dispositions'.[48]

Further consideration of the possible support which Japan might provide and the means by which it might be secured was given by the Quai d'Orsay in early July, a month before Viel-Castel's sensational report of 13 June was received in Paris. 'The military and naval resources of the Mikado's Government', Viel-Castel was informed, 'are in effect considerable enough that, without wishing at present to lay down the bases of an effective alliance, we ought not to neglect to draw closer to it and to assure ourselves of a concurrence which circumstances may render of value. It is, then a matter of not losing sight of the various means of influence which we can employ to that effect and which create for us, at this moment, a somewhat favoured position'.[49]

Whether the sources of influence to which the dispatch referred were as valuable in the context of foreign policy as Challemel-Lacour seems to have supposed is questionable. The French military attaché and former member of the French military mission in the 1870s, Captain Bougouin, was acquainted with members of the imperial family and had access to top military officers but he was not in a position to offer them any inducements. It is doubtful, too, whether the French employed in the Japanese educational sector were of more than marginal relevance. The hope was expressed by the French foreign minister that 'living with the most intelligent and active sector of the population of Tokyo, these professors may be able to exert on opinion a real influence which it is a matter of concern to direct in line with our interests',[50] but precisely what was expected of them was not spelled out. When Viel-Castel received these suggestions from Paris in August, he observed that none of the French employees of the Japanese government had relations with the press;[51] and when the new minister, Joseph-Adam Sienkiewicz, arrived in Tokyo in October, he reported that Viel-Castel had hesitated for a week before attempting to carry out the instructions because he doubted that they would achieve their purpose. Such doubts, Sienkiewicz added, had been justified.[52]

The French Foreign Ministry did not, however, need to place its chief reliance on unorthodox means of influence. A more realistic way of preparing for possible cooperation was to adopt a less unsympathetic attitude towards Japan's demand for revision of the treaties which had been inherited from the Bakumatsu period. The Meiji government had sought to remove the most objectionable features of these treaties but had made little progress in the face of British unwillingness to give up the right of extraterritoriality and the low import duties which foreigners enjoyed. Hitherto, France's position had generally been as intransigent as Britain's, if not more so, but this now began to change.[53] On 6 June Challemel-Lacour invited the Japanese minister in Paris, Hachisuka, to discuss treaty revision with him; and he informed Hachisuka that he would 'study it, as soon as possible, with the intention of being favourable for Japan and for France'.[54] Over the following two months the French government did, indeed, move towards Japan's position, most notably by accepting that if a new trade treaty were concluded, it could include a clause which would allow Japan to renegotiate a more favourable agreement in due course. This change of position was the more significant in that it was made with the full awareness that it undermined Britain's treaty revision strategy.[55]

Important though the French change of tack on treaty revision was, it nevertheless failed to achieve its purpose. When foreign minister Inoue on 31 August 1884 communicated to Japanese ministers in Europe the news that 'France sympathizes with our views and will advance them with other countries', he did acknowledge that 'by utilising French goodwill the way will be open to reject the British counter-proposal and this of course will be favourable'. But he went on to note disadvantages:

> However, in the French chargé d'affaires' words was clearly evident the ulterior thought that since the French government would thus today be doing us a favour, France would demand alliance with us. . . . This runs counter to our country's strategy of always preserving the peace in the East and is undesirable. However, it will have a bad influence on the revision negotiations if we show an inclination to thwart the French government's wish, so I have judiciously steered a course between not rejecting and not accepting.[56]

There were good reasons for the Japanese government to be cautious at this time, and some of them were indicated in a report from Paris, dated 21 June, which reached Inoue on 4 August. In it Marshall noted that the strong reaction in France to Captain Rivière's death had lasted only for a few days and that soon 'people began to ask what was the use of Tonkin to France, and reports reached the government from the Prefects that public opinion was distinctly against war with China'. Despite this waning of belligerent feeling, just before the middle of June

'. . . the French Foreign Office reverted to warlike ideas, the [Foreign] Minister spoke personally to Mr Hachisuka about the common interests of Japan and France towards China, and the private information given day by day to Marshall showed much irritation against China'. However, the report continued, 'on 20 June the language of the French Foreign Office changed once more. Marshall heard that several European governments had urged France to be quiet in Tonkin and had manifested disapprobation of her acts there, that the affaire was beginning to be regarded with less confidence in Paris, that its risks were more clearly appreciated, and finally, he was told, confidentially, but distinctly, not only that there were two opinions in the Ministry as to the conduct which ought to be followed, not only that there is much doubt and hesitation, but also that the Minister for foreign affairs, (M. Challemel-Lacour) is personally in favour of strong measures and he will, very possibly, resign if a peace policy is adopted by the Cabinet. It was even said that the place of M. Challemel-Lacour may perhaps be taken by M. Jules Ferry, the President of the Council, who is at the head of the peace party'.[57]

Marshall's information was bound to prompt doubts about the strength of French resolution in the Tongking affair. Moreover, since French diplomats were still hopeful of the collapse of Chinese opposition and also suspected that the Meiji government might take advantage of a definite approach from France to improve its own bargaining position towards China, they were usually very circumspect.[58] Even Viel-Castel who, at least in June, appeared quite enthusiastic about the potential advantages of Japanese military assistance, acknowledged in the same dispatch that, 'on the other hand, the extreme reserve to which Your Excellency [Challemel-Lacour] refers has become the more obligatory in that there is no concealing that here, as perhaps elsewhere, the Japanese would proclaim very loudly the possibility of an entente which events would perhaps come to break before it had been sanctioned'.[59] Admittedly Viel-Castel did not always observe this precept religiously: Japanese records indicate that on one occasion he urged on Inoue that Japan and France aid each other like eternal friends if China attacked either Annam or the Ryukyus;[60] but it undoubtedly inhibited him and, even more, Sienkiewicz, from indicating clearly to the Japanese the advantages which might result from an entente.

The same hesitation was not shown by all French diplomats. When Tricou was hastily transferred from Tokyo to Peking in May 1883, he went with the conviction, as he wrote to Paris, that 'we have only to say a word, and we can be assured of the concurrence of the Japanese Government'. A force of twenty thousand Japanese would be enough, he maintained, to rout the entire Chinese army.[61] His distance from Japan did not prevent him from frequently exhorting Japanese diplomats in China to urge their government to join France.[62] Nor, in his attempt to influence the Meiji government, did he disdain to inform the Japanese consul-general in Shanghai that Li Hung-chang was aiming to make war over the Ryukyu question.[63] So long as Franco-Chinese negotiations continued, however, there was good reason for the Meiji government to suspect that Tricou was seeking to sow dissension between China and Japan and not to take his overtures seriously.

To explain fully why French overtures failed to evoke a positive response from Japan it is also necessary to examine Japanese foreign policy more closely. There is considerable evidence for the view that throughout his term as foreign minister (1879-87) Inoue Kaoru's main concern (together with treaty revision) was to maintain peace in East Asia and, if possible, remove potential causes of conflict.[64] Such a policy did not imply acceptance of the East Asian status quo in every respect, for Inoue did not believe that true harmony was compatible with China's refusal to recognize that Japan had a legitimate interest in Korea or with continued Chinese support for conservative factions at the Korean Court against the progressive (and supposedly pro-Japanese) elements who sought to assert their country's full independence.[65] To go to war with China in order to change its Korean policy, however, was in Inoue's view too dangerous to contemplate seriously, as was demonstrated by his cautious attitude after the attack on the Japanese legation guard in Seoul in 1882 by reactionary Korean elements. One, though not the only, reason for his caution was that China enjoyed, at least on paper, both military and, more particularly, naval supremacy over Japan. Fear of attack by China may, in the light of Japan's crushing victory over its neighbour in 1894-95, seem implausible, but there is evidence to suggest that it was real at this time;[66] and on more than one occasion it was implied by Japanese Foreign Ministry representatives that the seriousness of the Chinese threat made it impossible for Japan to entertain thoughts of a French alliance or even to officially accord France the favour of benevolent neutrality.[67]

In view of all the aforementioned factors – in addition to which should also be added the Japanese government's concern not to jeopardise the deflationary policy which the finance minister, Matsukata Masayoshi, had embarked upon in 1881 – it is scarcely surprising that Inoue was disinclined to resort to force. Even the approach to the Quai d'Orsay in early 1883 which had first made the French hopeful of Japanese action against China was only intended to lead to a joint protest against China's claims to suzerainty over the neighbouring states which had traditionally paid tribute to the Middle Kingdom. That the proposal appeared to imply something more was due to the fact that after Inoue had sent it to Paris, the situation in Annam deteriorated. The danger that his initiative might be misunderstood may have become apparent to Inoue by the end of April, when the Japanese minister in Peking, Enomoto, reported that the French minister in China, Bourée, appeared anxious for Japanese cooperation.[68] Soon afterwards a further alarm signal prompted Inoue to send Hachisuka a nervous telegram (in English) which read: 'Ito telegraphed France is completed [*sic*, ?compelled] by circumstances to take war measure against China; but we do not wish to go so far. What I . . . indicated in my private note to Marshall, was only to communicate mutually with France in regard to China and her minor neighbours and not at all intended to go as far as to take arms against China. So refuse as soundly as possible any warlike support of France against China'.[69] The Quai d'Orsay, however, was not informed that the Japanese foreign minister wished to correct the impression which he feared had been given.

Despite the persistence, at least in Paris, of the assumption that Japan would basically like to cooperate with France if only it dared to face the military consequences of challenging China, between the summer of 1883 and the final months of 1884 the question of a Franco-Japanese understanding was relegated to a much lower place on the diplomatic agenda.[70] It was hoped by the French government that the large credits for military reinforcements which were approved by the French Assembly in December 1883 would prove sufficient to bring Annam and Tongking under control. As for its perception of Japan's attitude, Ferry accepted that 'the lively repugnance which the Court of Tokyo appears to feel at compromising itself towards China bars us at present from seeking its concurrence with regard to a conflict which we, in any case, desire and hope to avoid'.[71] Meanwhile in Tokyo the new French minister, Sienkiewicz, made a point of emphasizing the undesirable consequences of the interest which had been shown in gaining Japan's support.[72] Like his predecessor, he acknowledged the potential value of an alliance with Japan; and he even anticipated that the time might come for him to 'make new overtures which ought then to be very clear and very positive with regard to their objective'.[73] Despite this willingness in principle to contemplate a future Franco-Japanese alliance, however, in practice Sienkiewicz proved signally reluctant to prepare the ground for it in any way.

Some French approaches were nevertheless made to Japan during this period. French diplomats in China were more concerned than their counterparts in Japan about Chinese 'arrogance' and made a number of attempts to raise the question of cooperation again, although they received no encouragement and met with no success.[74] At least one approach may also have been made by the French ambassador in Berlin through Aoki Shuzo, the Japanese minister there.[75] In addition to these conventional channels, however, there were also two attempts at unofficial diplomacy during 1884. When in that year the Japanese minister of war, General Oyama Iwao, visited Europe with a high-ranking military mission, one of the French officers assigned to accompany it was Colonel Descharmes, who had earlier been a member of two military missions to Japan. He had long favoured an alliance with Japan and he now urged his views on Oyama, who apparently 'encouraged him very strongly to raise it with the French government, while himself guaranteeing the absolute approval of his own country's'.[76] There must be considerable doubt as to whether Oyama really said – or meant – what Descharmes recorded; there is no such uncertainty about the reaction of the French minister of war. In Descharmes' words, 'When in 1884 I proposed to the minister (Campenon) that we make a firm alliance with Japan . . . and that we launch it against the flank of China, which was giving us in Tonkin the serious vexation which culminated in Langson in 1885, the minister responded to my proposals with derisive jokes about the value of the Japanese army'.[77]

This was not, however, General Campenon's last word on the matter. By September, the French failure to seize more than a foothold in Taiwan again aroused concern in Paris that China would be encouraged to hold out. As a result Oyama was invited to visit France again before leaving Europe and, although he did not himself return, the invitation was accepted by another member of the mission, the Chōshu general, Miura Goro. Miura was honoured by being received by the President as well as all the ministers but, unbeknownst to the French, the decision to send him instead of Oyama was apparently due to the latter's desire to avoid the anticipated French attempt to discuss an alliance. Nevertheless, Miura was not averse to making the most of his role. According to his memoirs, he led General Campenon on by telling him that a blow should be struck against China to make it open its eyes, thus leading the French minister to suggest: 'If that is so, how about using this opportunity, since France is now fighting China?' Campenon supposedly then offered French financial support, indicating that Japan would soon be able to repay such an advance from the proceeds of the indemnity which could be imposed on China; and when Miura rejoined that Japan would raise the money itself if it were necessary, the French minister stated: 'If so, that is still fine. I would definitely like to undertake joint operations (*dosaku*)'. Miura did make some attempt to dampen

Campenon's enthusiasm by arguing that alliances (*rengo*) between unequals worked to the disadvantage of the weaker partner, and that in fifty to sixty years Japan, not France, would be the butt of China's hatred; but at the same time he could not resist inciting Campenon further by expressing the opinion that China would surrender immediately if Japan joined France's side. By thus playing on French hopes of Japanese cooperation while avoiding any actual commitment, Miura secured, so he claimed, promises that French ministers would attend to Japanese grievances about treaty revision and lack of facilities for Japanese naval students in France.[78]

Unfortunately, Miura's account was published forty years after the event and is vague on dates. There is no reason, however, to doubt his clear denial that the Japanese government had any intention of entering into an agreement with France. Throughout 1884 Inoue continued to distance himself from the rumours of alliance that circulated in Tientsin and Shanghai, and through the Japanese minister in China, Enomoto, and the able young consul in Tientsin, Hara Takashi, he constantly assured Li Hung-chang of Japan's peaceful intentions. Indeed, not only did he do his best to maintain Japanese neutrality, but in late November 1884 he even offered to mediate between the two sides.[79]

On 4 December 1884, when the French government appeared to have abandoned hope of Japanese cooperation, an incident occurred which reawakened its interest. This was the attempted coup d'état in Seoul by Kim Ok-kiun and other radicals who, having previously entered into a conspiracy with the Japanese minister, Takezoe, assassinated several pro-Chinese ministers, secured control of the king, and then sought Japanese support and protection. The Japanese legation was then attacked by Chinese troops with some loss of Japanese life, and the Japanese diplomats were forced to flee. When news of the incident reached Paris on 15 December, Ferry immediately sent to Sienkiewicz a telegram which read as follows:

> A telegram from Patenôtre informs me of the clash which has just taken place in Korea between Chinese and Japanese. These events will perhaps decide Japan to depart from the reserve which it has maintained since the beginning of our

conflict with China and seize the occasion to take a resolute attitude towards the Court of Pekin. We are in a position to lend it useful support, by preventing, for example, the despatch of Chinese troops to Korea by sea. One can even envisage a final settlement where the question of Formosa comes into account. Japan can thus draw great profit from the situation and we, on our side, have powerful motives for enlisting it in action against China. Do discreetly what you judge possible with regard to this result, and keep me closely informed by telegraph.[80]

This telegram revealed that France was now ready to be positive in its pursuit of an agreement with Japan. It is noteworthy that Ferry, who had recently experienced difficulty in securing new credits for Tongking, referred merely to the need for discretion rather than extreme reserve. Clearly he felt that he had grounds for optimism about the outcome of a new approach. For the second time in three years Japan's representative in Seoul had been attacked and Japanese honour insulted. Surely now the Meiji government would realize that force was the only way to deal with China.

This view was understandable but mistaken. The Japanese government had not decided on war and still looked to achieve its aims by negotiation. Nevertheless, the need for caution was by now less imperative than it had been. With the escalation of the conflict with France, Chinese pressure on Japan to release its grip on the Ryukyus had faded and was no longer a cause for anxiety, while the destruction of China's southern fleet by Admiral Courbet in August 1884 greatly eased Japanese concern about Chinese naval strength. Moreover, the publication in Japanese newspapers on 1 December of the news that the French National Assembly had voted a new credit for the war provided powerful evidence of France's determination not to back down and clearly made it safer for Japan to push its own claims. It has even been alleged in connection with this demonstration of parliamentary support for the policy of the Ferry cabinet that 'the transmission of this news to Korea seems to have exerted a considerable influence on Minister Takezoe and to have caused his sudden action'.[81]

Even if the connection between events in France and Korea in December 1884 was not as close as this, Japanese policy towards

Korea may well have been affected by earlier French actions. Although in late 1882 Tricou had responded very cautiously to overtures by Korean reformers visiting Japan, Sienkiewicz was willing, when two more approaches were made in March and June, 1884, to suggest to Ferry that the idea of Korean military modernization under French auspices might be worth considering.[82] The French premier, however, rejected the idea, at least until diplomatic relations had been established. This might have been the end of the matter.[83] In September, however, Sienkiewicz was twice visited by Goto Shojiro and Itagaki Taisuke, two former government members who now led the principal opposition party, the *Jiyuto*.[84] Claiming to be motivated by hatred of China, dissatisfaction with their own government, and admiration for the French revolutionary tradition, they proposed that France should lend a million yen to facilitate the modernization of Korea by its young reformers.[85] Despite Sienkiewicz's earlier recommendation of assistance, his report to Paris on this occasion did not indicate any positive interest. That he gave Goto and Itagaki the quite different impression that French help might be forthcoming, possibly from private bankers, may have been a tactic designed to string the *Jiyuto* leaders along and maintain a useful channel of information.[86]

Before Goto and Itagaki had time to be disillusioned, the news of the supposed French interest was leaked by Goto, if the *Jiyuto's* official history is to be believed, to Ito Hirobumi.[87] This has led to supposition that concern about the links between the *Jiyuto*, the Korean reformers and France may have been a factor in the almost immediate sending back to Seoul of Takezoe, who had been on leave. As one prominent historian sees it, discovery of the Goto-Itagaki-Sienkiewicz interviews 'would build a sense of urgency in government circles that the intriguers, whom they had been ignoring, must now be weaned away from their French connections and kept under surveillance'.[88] Certainly the fact that Takezoe soon commenced the discussions with Kim Ok-kiun and his fellow conspirators which led to the attempted coup of 4 December provides circumstantial evidence that the Meiji government had decided to adopt a more positive policy.[89] Moreover, a further piece of evidence pointing in the same direction exists in a dispatch sent by Sienkiewicz on the very day of the coup. In it he reported that a French interpreter had been informed by Goto that the Meiji government, 'which hitherto was afraid of China, is today resolved to engage in struggle with this Power'.[90]

Goto's intriguing remark may appear to confirm that there was official Japanese involvement in the coup. Since, however, there is unambiguous documentary evidence that on 28 November Ito (acting as foreign minister) and vice-minister Yoshida, in response to a request from Takezoe for a decision as to whether he should assist the pro-Japanese party in an anti-Chinese uprising or maintain a policy of peaceful non-interference, instructed him not to encourage conspiracy against the Chinese by the pro-Japanese party, it seems more likely that Goto either misunderstood what the government's position really was or deliberately misrepresented it.[91] The fact that the coup took the Meiji leaders by surprise provides further evidence for such a conclusion. Even though Inoue and his colleagues were probably not directly involved, however, the dramatic events in Seoul created a new and volatile situation in which the idea of a Franco-Japanese alliance not only came to the fore again but had to be treated much more seriously.

Why then did an alliance not emerge?[92] Clearly, Inoue Kaoru's determination that Japan's differences with China should be settled by diplomacy remained a major obstacle to any resort to military action. Even so, as developments in later years were to reveal, modern Japanese foreign policy could be opportunistic; and there is some evidence to suggest not only that several of Inoue's colleagues were prepared to challenge China but that military action in Korea would have had public support. In the first three months of 1885, for instance, the reports of the British minister in Tokyo, Sir Francis Plunkett, frequently refer to a 'war party' (which he identified with Satsuma leaders); while the Japan correspondent of *The Times* wrote on 5 January 1885 of 'the large and powerful war party in the country'.[93] It is true that almost all the other Powers viewed the prospect of an enlarged conflict with disfavour, and that there was some danger that Russia might take advantage of a Sino-Japanese conflict to gain a firmer foothold in Korea.[94] Yet no foreign Power was likely to aid China,[95] and Japan's status would undoubtedly be significantly enhanced by alliance with a European power. Even without the additional inducement of French naval and financial help,[96] the opportunity presenting itself to the Meiji government ought to have been a tempting one.

There was, however, one less obvious factor which militated against alliance with France: the attitude of Sienkiewicz. Like several other French ministers who had served in China before coming to Japan, he had a poor opinion of the Japanese and distrusted them. Although he paid lip-service to the notion of an agreement with Japan, his real feelings were shown by a letter which he wrote to Rear-Admiral Mayer in January 1884. In it he argued that 'to tie ourselves, on the one hand, to Japan by a treaty would be to place ourselves between two peoples of yellow race, that is between two peoples who, despite the antagonism which exists between them, understand themselves much better than we shall ever be able to understand them'.[97] He further revealed his disinclination for an agreement by adding: 'The Japanese . . . are essentially changeable and, as they operate according to their own particular rules, which have nothing in common with European logic, one should always expect to be surprised by them'. His real desire was that Japan should undertake a completely independent war against China. As allies, he wrote later, the Japanese would have been worth little because of their vanity, fickleness, and unreliability.[98]

Given such views, Sienkiewicz was unlikely to welcome Ferry's order of 15 December 1884 to pursue the possibility of Japanese cooperation against China. Even allowing for his lack of enthusiasm, however, the way in which he chose to carry out his instructions was extraordinary. So exaggerated was his interpretation of his foreign minister's injunction to be discreet that vice-foreign minister Yoshida was able to inform Plunkett about a week later that Sienkiewicz had 'never touched the subject either before or since the Corean revolt'.[99] Firstly, while answering a query by Inoue about Franco-Chinese relations, he stated: 'We will then energetically pursue our campaign in Tongking; but above all we will give particular attention to the occupation of Formosa. This island will before long be entirely in our power. What we will do with Formosa is not yet decided, but it is definite that we will begin by taking possession of it. We will perhaps similarly make an excursion in the North'. Secondly he charged a 'reliable person' to say to a Japanese on close terms with members of the government: 'We are going to see what the Japanese can do and what they are worth. You have no idea, moreover, what you are in a fair way to gaining'.[100] This was to say nothing that was not already known, and was so imprecise as to be worthless.

How little in tune Sienkiewicz was with Ferry emerges clearly from the dispatch which the minister in Tokyo sent after receiving the 15 December telegram. In it Sienkiewicz revealed that rather than going to see the Japanese foreign minister himself, when the latter returned to Tokyo from the south on 16 December, he had waited for Inoue to visit him.[101] In reporting their encounter, he noted Inoue's comment that 'the Chinese will, if one lets them, fortify themselves in Korea and become a menace to Japan', and he observed that the foreign minister had seemed to expect Sienkiewicz to make a confidential overture. The French diplomat nevertheless concluded that what passed between them 'does not, however, allow one to discern a decision by Japan to have recourse to force to set right a completely lost situation', and that 'the Japanese desire to avoid a conflict with China is an incontestable fact'. While not overtly admitting that he had not behaved in keeping with the spirit of Ferry's instructions, he justified his conduct by insisting that 'it behoves me to act with the greatest circumspection', because 'the Japanese government would be very happy to see me make overtures at this moment. It would make use of them as a powerful argument to induce the Cabinet of Pekin to accept a friendly and satisfactory settlement of the Korean affair'. It was, he claimed, for the Japanese government to take the initiative since France's position was clear: 'The Japanese cannot doubt that we would be quick to offer them effective cooperation in a campaign against China'.[102]

Despite the fact that Sienkiewicz ended his report with the dubious claim that he 'would neglect nothing in order to profit from the slightest favourable opportunity which the events in Seoul may produce', he might have incurred a rebuke from his hard-pressed premier had not Ferry's hopes been dashed long before he received the dispatch on 31 January 1885, by the telegram which Sienkiewicz sent on 17 December. This read as follows: 'I follow closely the Korean affair. The excitement which was produced in 1882 has not manifested itself this time.

The gravity of the situation is being played down. The Minister of Foreign Affairs, moreover, returned to Yedo [Tokyo] after six weeks' absence only yesterday'.[103] In view of the fact that when he sent this telegram, Sienkiewicz had not yet spoken to Inoue, or indeed to any member of the government as far as either his own reports or Japanese records show, this was an extraordinary message.

Any doubt that Sienkiewicz was ultra-cautious, if not intentionally obstructive, in his interpretation of Ferry's injunction to be discreet becomes unsustainable when one compares his diplomacy with that of his counterpart in China, Jules Patenôtre. Patenôtre (who was Ferry's nephew) may have been no more optimistic than Sienkiewicz about securing an alliance with Japan, but he was far less reserved. On 17 December 1884 he reported that he had been visited and questioned at length by the Japanese consul in Shanghai, Ando Taro, and that 'without making positive overtures to him, I took care to make him understand that the Cabinet of Tokyo would act wisely in seeking to enter into an entente with France before China came to an arrangement with us which might be motivated by the sole desire to recover its freedom of action vis-à-vis Japan'.[104] Then, on 24 December, after reporting that he had had two further meetings with Ando, he informed Ferry that when the Japanese consul had shown him 'a telegram in which his Government requested him to ask me if I was positively authorized by you to make overtures to him with regard to an entente with France, I replied affirmatively'.[105] The contrast between Patenôtre and Sienkiewicz is further shown by the former's readiness to assure Ando that Japan would be able to raise a low-interest loan in France.[106]

Patenôtre's unequivocal language indicated to the Meiji government that France was now definitely interested in an alliance of some kind. Nevertheless, the reticence of Sienkiewicz, through whom any serious approach would be expected, was bound to introduce an element of uncertainty into the minds of the Japanese leaders.[107] It would have encouraged the impression that France sought, by inveigling Japan into making the first official offer, to secure an agreement on more advantageous terms than if France itself were to take the initiative. Even more disturbingly, it would have reinforced the suspicion that France was aiming to tempt the Japanese into an alliance proposal which could then be used to induce China to accept French terms.

It was, therefore, not altogether surprising that the Meiji government did not respond to the French hints and propositions in December 1884. Nevertheless, the possibility still remained, so long as China resisted concessions, that the two countries might yet come to some arrangement. There was, though, a noticeable change in their respective attitudes. On the French side interest in an alliance diminished as, on the one hand, their forces gained ground in Tongking and, on the other, the assumption that Japan was not prepared to fight China was again accepted. Sienkiewicz, of course, continued to emphasize that Japan was not ready for such a conflict; and he also put forward the interesting suggestion that 'the men who at present exercise a dominant influence in government councils would pass to the second rank if war came to break out'. His position was at the same time fatalistic and optimistic:

> If Japan decides to engage in struggle with China, it will be because it has been impossible to avoid a conflict. All the promises of cooperation which we might make it prematurely will have no influence at all on its decisions. It has never been in doubt about the haste with which we would support its action. On the other hand, if it accepts struggle with China, it will be absolutely necessary for it to turn to us. But then it will equally be for us to lay down the bases for an entente. So, to be in an advantageous position, we ought to be solicited by the Japanese and on no account make ourselves solicitors.[108]

There is no indication that Paris objected to this view in 1885.[109]

Ironically, as French interest faded, Japanese increased. Admittedly, the merits of an entente with France are not discussed within surviving Japanese Foreign Office records or in the correspondence of those Japanese leaders most closely involved in foreign policy. Nevertheless, there is compelling evidence, especially in the reports to London of the British minister in Tokyo, that the Japanese government was being forced to reconsider its position.[110] On 3 January 1885 Plunkett regretted 'that the war feeling here, and the prospect of a conflict with China, are undoubtedly increasing', while on 11 January he telegraphed: 'I am assured Cabinet desire peace but very extensive military preparations are already completed'.[111] A few days later he provided the further information that 'The Japanese Foreign Office continues to affirm that the leading members of the Cabinet desire Peace, and appreciate the grave objections there would be to an alliance with France, but they say at the same time that the war party is pressing hard for action against China, and that Government may have some difficulty in calming the public excitement here'.[112] These observations were supported by the comment of *L'Echo du Japon* on 2 January 1885 that Japanese public opinion was excessively excited and that all the newspapers were demanding that the government take vigorous measures.

The reason why public feeling ran high, in spite of Inoue Kaoru's return from Seoul in the middle of January with a Korean apology and agreement to pay compensation for the loss of Japanese lives, was that no settlement had yet been reached with China and there was no sign that China would either withdraw its troops from Korea or acknowledge that Japan had a legitimate interest there. Without such an acknowledgement, preferably in a formal convention, the Meiji government would not only remain open to nationalistic criticism but also face the continuing risk of renewed conflict in Korea; and it was to secure a formal agreement that Ito Hirobumi, accompanied by Saigo Tsugumichi, led a diplomatic mission to China in February 1885.[113] That he would be successful could not be anticipated with any certainty, however, so it was logical for Japan to put extra pressure on China by reviving the threat of of a Franco-Japanese common action. Such a move would also prepare the way, were Ito's mission to fail, for the Japanese government finally to commit itself to an alliance, if it could see no more satisfactory alternative.

An unmistakable hint that the Japanese government might shift its position was given to Plunkett by Inoue on his return from Seoul. When the British minister expressed the hope that the Japanese foreign minister 'was not allowing himself to be inveigled into an alliance with France against China', the latter's replies were 'vague and evasive'; it seemed to Plunkett as if Inoue 'personally disapproved of joining France, unless in conjunction perhaps hereafter with Great Britain in case we were also drawn into the conflict, but as if he feared the Cabinet might eventually decide on doing so very soon'.[114] Sienkiewicz, too, was soon receiving signals. In early February he reported that General Miura on his return from Europe had told him that, in his opinion, 'Japan ought to take advantage of circumstances to join with France', and shortly afterwards an interview with Inoue left him with the impression that 'without daring to raise the question of an entente between France and Japan, he would nevertheless like to prepare the ground for it in case events should make it necessary'.[115] Less than a fortnight later Hermann Roesler, the Meiji government's German legal adviser, made a transparent attempt to entice Sienkiewicz into making official alliance overtures.[116] About the same time Plunkett was reporting, after 'wonderfully frank' interviews with Ito and Inoue that, while so far French advances had not been accepted, 'if Count Ito came back empty-handed from Peking, war with China and an arrangement with France would ensue': 'Japan', he concluded, is 'on the fence', and it is still impossible to predict on which side she will finally decide to come down.[117] On 9 March he informed Sir Harry Parkes that Kuroda Kiyotaka, the supposedly belligerent Satsuma leader who had forced Korea's opening in 1876, had gone to Saigon, officially on a pleasure trip, but in public belief either to show his disapproval of Inoue's 'peace policy' or to be ready to combine future operations with the French commanders.[118] Finally, in April Captain Bougouin was informed by Miura that 'in six months, and perhaps even earlier, Japan will disembark an army in Korea under the protection of Admiral Courbet's fleet'.[119]

Miura's prediction proved to be premature, for Ito's mission was not unsuccessful. Japan benefited, as did France, from China's readiness to compromise rather than risk the formation of a dangerous coalition.[120] Treaties were signed in Tientsin with Japan on 18 April and France the next day. To the latter China abandoned all its traditional rights in Vietnam, although it avoided the imposition of the indemnity that had been demanded, and it also had the satisfaction of seeing the Ferry cabinet fall after a temporary French military reverse in March. To Japan, China implicitly acknowledged some share in its suzerainty over Korea. With the signing of these conventions the idea of a Franco-Japanese alliance vanished.

Did it, one must ask, ever really have a chance of becoming a reality? In addressing this question it must be recognized from the outset that neither the French nor the Japanese government actually wanted a formal alliance. What the former desired was always a simple military understanding whereby the deployment of Japanese troops in Korea would be coordinated with French operations; and it would have been reluctant to go further. Thus, for most of the 1883–85 period, what Japan stood to gain from France, was, at best, an undefined measure of military and diplomatic support against China, together with some help in treaty revision. Even if Japan's leaders had been more inclined towards military cooperation with France, the attraction of an arrangement which was both vague and limited would not have been overwhelming. To secure a military commitment from Japan, France would probably, at the very least, have had to commit itself not to make peace separately. Even this, however, would not have ensured that Japan would not subsequently be left to face China's displeasure alone. One of the prerequisites of Japanese cooperation might, therefore, have been that it should be embodied in a more permanent alliance. Until December 1884 this possibility seems not to have been considered on the French side and would probably have been regarded as undesirable and unnecessary.

Whether that would still have been the position after the attempted coup in Seoul is another matter. Had China refused to make concessions on Korea, Japan might have turned towards France, and in that case the disadvantages of a formal alliance might well have weighed less heavily in Jules Ferry's mind than the advantages of a quick settlement to a colonial war which, begun with little serious thought, had turned into a quagmire. The French prime minister was too much of a politician not to realize, long before his career was brought to an end on 30 March 1885, that the war in Indochina could put his administration at risk;[121] and there seems no reason why a man who had been willing to cooperate with Germany should have refused to pay the price which would have been demanded by Japan, however distasteful the latter's acceptance as a partner might have been to French diplomats in that country. Moreover, the offers of a low-interest loan by Patenôtre and the willingness of Ferry to contemplate naval support and the handover of Taiwan are strong evidence that the French government was prepared to go further than it had been ready to contemplate in 1883.

The fact remains that no alliance emerged. Quite apart from China's eventual willingness to make concessions, there were a number of reasons for this on both the French and Japanese sides. The French tended to overestimate Japan's eagerness for an agreement, while at the same time they did not, except in the cases of Descharmes and, perhaps, Tricou, foresee how considerable Japan's military potential might be. One should also not disregard, impossible though it is to measure, French reluctance to link their own country with one which was still not considered sufficiently civilized to exercise jurisdiction over foreigners.[122] The greatest impediment to alliance, however, was the Japanese government's policy of seeking security and stability through diplomacy and cooperation rather than war.[123] Japanese leaders still perceived Western expansion in East Asia as the main danger,[124] and Inoue Kaoru, in particular, did not wish to see China seriously weakened. In very exceptional conditions this reluctance might have been overcome, but at the moment when international circumstances seemed most promising there were always other factors – notably the diplomacy of Sienkiewicz – working in the opposite direction. Thus a Franco-Japanese alliance was to be nothing more than one of history's might-have-beens.

FRANCE AND THE REVISION OF THE 'UNEQUAL TREATIES'

FOR ALL THE INTEREST of the manoeuvres that took place during the Franco-Chinese war, the principal preoccupation of Japanese diplomacy in the late nineteenth century was revision of the treaties which in the 1850s had opened the country to trade on terms which had come to be seen as unjust. The importance of this issue can hardly be overstated. For the Japanese, revision of the treaties meant, above all, removal of the humiliating stigma of inequality; and the pursuit of this aim not only dominated diplomacy from the 1870s until the late 1890s, but was also one of the major factors in the acceptance of modernization. Legal reform, in particular, was prompted by the need to show the Powers that foreigners could abandon their special legal privileges without fear of the consequences, but many other changes also owed much to the same motivation.

The importance of treaty revision went beyond this, however. Under the 'unequal treaties' Japan's lack of tariff autonomy prevented the Meiji government using import duties to protect from severe foreign competition either its traditional industries or the new ones which it wished to see introduced. It was thus led to take the initiative itself by establishing factories and developing mines (many of which were sold off cheaply to chosen entrepreneurs in the 1880s) and by subsidizing favoured enterprises. The result was to encourage the growth of what became known as *zaibatsu*, great companies whose domination of the modern sectors of industry had far-reaching social and political consequences for Japan.

Treaty revision also became an important political issue, mainly because it provided the parties which emerged from the People's Rights movement in the early 1880s with a particularly dangerous weapon to employ against the government. The long drawn-out negotiations with the Powers in the 1880s and early 1890s were frustrating to politically conscious Japanese, and criticism of the handling of the negotiations proved a most effective way of uniting disparate opposition groups in assaults on the government. So strong were the feelings roused by this issue that in order to suppress political agitation the Meiji leadership resorted to the extreme measure of expelling hundreds of its most vociferous critics from the environs of the capital in 1887. More significant than this, however, may have been the tendency of the opposition parties to change the emphasis of their slogans from *minken* (people's rights) to *kokken* (national rights) as a result of the popular response to their criticism of the government's weak and ineffective handling of treaty revision.[1] In return for momentary advantage, it has been argued, they embraced a chauvinistic policy which in the long run was bound to strengthen the military, their main rival as heir to the power of the Meiji oligarchs. Finally, the seemingly unending treaty revision negotiations could only, in the view of many historians, undermine Western claims that they were guided by higher motives than the defence of vested interests and thus strengthen Japanese cynicism about the true nature of international relations.

In view of the immense importance of treaty revision to Meiji Japan and the length of the negotiations, the attitude of the Western Powers clearly demands close attention.[2] France's part in treaty revision, it should be made clear from the outset, was less important than that of either Britain, which had far more at stake commercially than any other country and too much power in East Asia for any solution to be possible without its agreement, or the United States, which was most forthcoming in accepting Japanese demands. Moreover, even though revision could not in theory be complete without France's agreement (since the most-favoured-nation clause in its treaty entitled it to claim unconditionally any new rights which Japan, in order to secure foreign concessions, might grant to other countries), once the Meiji government switched from multilateral to bilateral negotiations and seemed likely to win over (or wear down) even Britain, it was in practice impossible for France to contemplate resistance for very long. France's role thus merits attention mainly in the pre-1890 period, when a common front was basically still maintained by the Western powers. In these years France was able to exert influence because its cooperation and support was sought by Britain whenever the latter feared isolation, and because its own political and commercial interests, (or its representatives' conception of them) led it on occasion to further or, more usually, hinder Japan's cause.

France's attitude towards treaty revision was shaped by several factors. The most basic was its commercial position. Though not on the same scale as Britain's, French trade with Japan was substantial and France naturally had an interest in the maintenance of the low tariffs introduced in 1866. However, French exports to Japan were considerably less than Japanese exports to France, and since treaty revision would increase only Japan's import duties, France actually stood to lose much less than Britain, which had a very favourable balance of trade with Japan. It might therefore be considered surprising that for the most part France was no more accommodating towards Japan's hopes of tariff revision than Britain – and sometimes even less so. Part of the explanation for this can be found in commercial factors: France had a special interest in securing the abolition of export duties on silk and in selling Japan warships, and was reluctant to give up any potential bargaining counter. Perhaps even more important, however, were political and psychological factors.

Among the political factors the most obvious was the French involvement in Indo-China in 1883–85, which at one point led the Quai d'Orsay to initiate a reversal of its hitherto intransigent attitude. Because this tactic failed to secure the cooperation which France sought, it left a legacy of resentment which made France less ready to make concessions thereafter. Its eventual abandonment of its rigid opposition to Japanese demands in the 1890s appears to have been largely the result of another political factor – the growing awareness of Japan's increased military strength and of the difficulties that might be encountered when the Western powers had to deal with Japanese leaders who were under pressure from a parliament which was likely to be nationalistic, if not xenophobic.

France's change of attitude may also have owed something to its developing rapprochement with Russia, since it could not be uninfluenced by the latter's willingness to be accommodating to Japan over treaty revision. A more important consideration, however, at least in the 1880s, was French jealousy of Germany, the main effect of which was to produce hostility towards any concessions to Japan which Germany proposed and from which Germany could draw credit. Finally, there was one deeper influence which coloured the French attitude throughout the decades which followed the Franco-Prussian war: its sensitivity with regard to France's national standing. While on the one hand French diplomacy sought at all costs to avoid a humiliating climb-down, and thus did not press its opposition to Japan if there were a danger of being isolated, on the other hand it was so concerned with prestige that it tended, whenever possible, to resist even minor concessions, in the belief that firm resistance was the way to maintain respect for France.

France also had a cultural interest in Japan which might have been expected to make its attitude towards treaty revision less unfavourable. Much of the work on the new Japanese legal codes was carried out with the aid of Boissonade and other French experts and with the Napoleonic Codes as the chief model; and since France generally saw the propagation of its traditions and values as one of the main aims of diplomacy, the Japanese might have been pardoned for imagining that their legal reforms would be given an enthusiastic welcome and their aspirations to end extraterritoriality a sympathetic response. Any such hopes, however, were soon shown to be illusory. Whether through irritation at the number of changes that were made to Boissonade's drafts, or, alternatively, resentment that the French jurist had provided the Meiji government with effective arguments to deploy against the European powers, or whether, as was usually claimed, because French diplomats genuinely doubted whether Japan had judges capable of administering the new system fairly, France was as hostile as any Power towards every proposal to place foreigners under the jurisdiction of the Japanese courts.[3]

France would undoubtedly have found it preferable if the Meiji leadership had accepted the situation it had inherited and, like the Ch'ing government in China, allowed the treaty port system to be extended. From the Japanese point of view, however, the treaties contained major inequities which made their existence objectionable and their long-term existence intolerable. One inequity was that whereas the treaties all entitled the Western country concerned to enjoy any concession granted by Japan, this right was not reciprocal. Except that the most-favoured-nation clauses made it difficult to negotiate treaty revision with any country separately, however, this provision was of nominal rather than real importance, and was much less of a grievance than two other features of the treaties. Of these, the one which was voiced most in the earlier period of treaty revision was that Japan had been unfairly deprived of tariff autonomy, because its import and export duties had been fixed for the duration of the treaties. Not surprisingly in a period of enthusiastic Free Trade advocacy, these duties had been set at a fairly low level, but the situation had subsequently been made worse for Japan by the Bakufu's acceptance in 1866 of a new Tariff Convention which brought almost every item down to 5% (in practice closer to 3%).[4] Such nominal duties not only made it difficult to establish modern industries in Japan, but from the late 1870s, when protectionism returned to Europe in full force, were out of line with international trends. Nevertheless, although from the early 1880s the Powers were prepared to allow some increases, the price asked in return was so high that Japan was forced to put up with the 1866 tariffs until 1899.

The other great grievance related to the legal provisions of the treaties. These had established the bases of a system of extraterritorial jurisdiction similar in theory to that which had been granted to Europeans by the Ottoman Empire from a position of strength in the 16th century, but even closer to that which had recently been introduced after the Opium War in China. Under extraterritoriality, foreigners were not subject to Japanese jurisdiction, except in cases where they brought actions against Japanese; and in practice some of the offences committed by them against Japanese law went unpunished by consular courts. In the conditions of the 1860s and 1870s the system was more or less accepted as the only way of bridging the gulf between Japanese and Western legal standards, but with the drafting of the Western-style codes from the late 1870s onwards some recognition by the Western powers of Japanese progress was expected by the latter. When this was not forthcoming, or was given only grudgingly and with demands for extensive guarantees, it aroused deep resentment in a country where the growth of the press and the expansion and manipulation of education was spreading national consciousness far beyond the ex-samurai class.[5]

Some of the Japanese opposition to the treaties was also due to the way in which the ambiguity of some clauses was taken advantage of by the Powers. Until the time of Okuma, for instance, the Japanese government was obliged to defer to the Western view that the most-favoured-nation right was an unconditional one, which entitled any Power to claim for its nationals any privilege granted to another Power without having to make any corresponding concession. More important even than this, however, was the interpretation of the clause relating to the conditions of revision. Article 20 of the French treaty, which was not unrepresentative, stated: 'It is equally agreed that each of the two High contracting Parties will be able, after having given notice to each other a year in advance, from 15 August 1872, or after that time, to demand the revision of the present Treaty in order to make modifications or insert the amendments which experience will have shown to be necessary'. This provision was by no means as clear as that included in, say, the 1860 Commercial Treaty between Britain and France, but it gave the Meiji government grounds to claim that Japan had the ultimate right to denounce any clause which had come to appear unsatisfactory. This conclusion was one which France, in common with other Powers, chose not to accept. Except for a momentary initial hesitation about the legal position and a short-lived attempt in 1873–4 to insist that the revision clause gave the Powers rather than Japan the right to insist on new privileges, the standpoint which they consistently maintained was that no changes could be made without mutual consent. The unfortunate corollary of this for Japan was that the Powers were entitled to compensation for foregoing their rights, and were in a position to exact a high price.

THE FIRST PHASE OF TREATY REVISION, 1869–74

The first demand for treaty revision on the Japanese side was voiced almost immediately after the Restoration, when on 8 February 1868, at Iwakura Tomomi's instigation, an internal proclamation declared the new government's intention of revising the treaties.[6] This proclamation, however, was important mainly because of its implicit disavowal of the old xenophobic *joi* position, (which logically would have required the total repudiation of the treaties). It did not foreshadow any immediate challenge to the Powers, for, as yet, the inexperienced Japanese leaders had little idea of what to propose. Indeed, the Meiji government was not to formulate any clear plan of its own until 1876. Nevertheless, it did decide to intimate as early as possible to the Western powers its desire for treaty revision, and initially it received some encouragement from the United States.[7] Before long, however, it found that it had provoked the Powers to seek revision on their terms and had to struggle to prevent changes being made which would impair rather than improve Japan's position.

The earliest indication that Japan intended to invoke the revision provision was received on 23 February 1869. Like most of his colleagues Outrey informed the Japanese government that he could not discuss revision before fourteen years had elapsed since the signing of the treaties in 1858; and the fact that he asked it to specify the desired revisions 'in order that the government of the Emperor can examine the expediency of the proposals which will be made to his Representative' indicated that he did not accept that Japan alone could decide what those changes should be.[8] Not surprisingly, in the circumstances, the Japanese foreign minister did not provide the information requested, and the Japanese claim was not pressed again until 30 June 1871, when a communication from the Foreign Ministry spoke only of modifying 'a certain number of points which are presenting inconveniences'.[9]

The initial reaction of the French government showed that such caution was not misplaced. Though nothing specific had been said of unilateral denunciation, foreign minister Rémusat saw the Japanese note as reason for maintaining French troops in Yokohama.[10] The French attitude was not yet as rigid as it was to become later, however, for in May 1872, Rémusat requested Turenne to report on the working of consular jurisdiction;[11] and in his reply the chargé d'affaires admitted that it was 'an established fact that the existing system does not answer its purpose at all and that some modifications must be introduced' and expressed the conviction that 'an understanding with the Japanese Government in order to establish mixed courts should be sought'. Alternatively, he proposed a passport system which would allow suitable foreigners to visit the interior of Japan, in conjunction with the granting of the right of preventive arrest to the Japanese. Nevertheless even Turenne, who was unusually sympathetic towards Japanese aspirations, considered that any further measure of treaty revision would be premature; and his realistic assessment of Japanese hopes clearly indicated that complete revision would take a very long time.

> 'In reality', he concluded, 'although they are currently occupied in a serious way in codifying their laws, and in softening them to meet the claims of civilization, and although in principle we can admit with them that the right of jurisdiction which is conceded to us by the treaties is only temporary, and that it will be returned to them some day, it is very evident that we cannot for several years make a deal which abandons this jurisdiction, for our interests could not be safeguarded if they were entrusted to [the Japanese] before judges have been created who possess integrity and are capable of putting these new laws into practice'.[12]

This argument was to be constantly reiterated by French diplomats, usually in a much more rigorous and dogmatic form, in the next decade-and-a-half.

As far as France was concerned, the actual problem of devising some practical improvements in the working of the treaties which would go a little way to meeting Japanese grievances did not materialize at this stage, for the feelers that had been put forward by the Foreign Ministry in Tokyo in June 1871 were discontinued when the decision to send a high-ranking mission under Iwakura Tomomi's leadership to America and Europe was taken later in the year. The task of laying the ground for treaty revision was thus placed in Iwakura's hands. It was not envisaged, however, that he should actually commence negotiations, nor was he entrusted with formal powers to do so; and after the false start that was caused by the American offer to discuss a new treaty, the mission was not particularly eager to raise the question when it eventually arrived in Paris in January 1873. In reply to Rémusat's offer to examine any propositions that Japan might make, Iwakura stated that the chief purpose of the mission was to convey to the Powers Japan's feelings towards them, and that although it welcomed the opportunity of gathering the Powers' opinions on treaty revision no step would be taken until the mission returned to Japan.[13] When, in fact, the members of the mission did arrive back during the summer, they were too conscious of the extent of the modernization required to entertain hope of gaining much from renewed negotiations as things stood. Moreover, at the time of their return, they discovered that the idea of treaty revision had been hijacked by the representatives of the Western powers in Tokyo.

This attempt to revise the treaties to make them more favourable to foreign interests has received surprisingly little attention. Yet the pressure which the Meiji government experienced during 1873–4 goes some way to explain, firstly why it delayed until 1876 in taking up this prime diplomatic objective again, and, secondly, why the handling of the problem between 1876 and 1879 by Terashima Munenori, the foreign minister at that time, was so cautious. The attempt of the European powers to secure treaty revision on their own terms in the earlier period can only have served to warn the Japanese of the dangers of acting over-hastily. In teaching the Meiji government that treaty revision could hold risks as well as open the way to gains, the new French minister in Tokyo played a significant role.

Ironically, the European attempt to revise the treaties was, at least in the case of France, a response to the Japanese intimations, before and during the Iwakura mission, that they wished to commence negotiations. These intimations prompted the French government to make preparations for such an eventuality, and by the time the Japanese ambassadors had returned home, the Quai d'Orsay had taken two important steps to set the machinery of revision in motion. One was to consult the principal chambers of commerce in France, the most important of which predictably expressed the view that tariffs should be lowered if possible.[14] The other was the appointment of Jules Berthemy, previously minister at Peking and Washington, with the specific mission of accomplishing revision.[15] Berthemy's behaviour suggests that he may have believed the post in Tokyo to be incommensurate with his abilities and standing and that he felt that only a striking success could compensate him for this. Such an attitude would explain why he strenuously engaged in a campaign to remove the one great restriction on foreign penetration of Japan that the treaties had preserved – free access to the interior – even though informed French opinion had hitherto opposed rather than favoured the complete opening of Japan.[16] Unaware, or unconcerned, that any Japanese government which granted such a concession would jeopardize its very existence, for the next eighteen months Berthemy pursued this objective relentlessly.

For Berthemy and his British and German colleagues, Parkes and von Brandt, the question of opening the interior was that much easier to raise because a few months earlier Soejima, the acting foreign minister, had, in response to an Italian initiative early in 1873, offered free access to Italian traders under a passport system provided that Italy agreed to their being subject to Japanese laws and law courts outside the treaty ports. The plan failed when on the one hand the Italian government was pressed by other European governments to keep in line and, on the other, it was made clear to Soejima that the privilege of travel in the interior would be claimed as an unconditional right by the other Powers.[17] The very fact, however, that the Japanese government had shown that it was prepared to consider the opening of Japan, albeit conditionally, convinced the foreign representatives (and especially Berthemy when he arrived in June) that they were justified in claiming free access in return for conceding to Japan what they regarded as sufficient compensation – the right to deal with petty offences committed by foreigners outside the treaty ports.

Needless to say, the Meiji government would hardly give up its only important bargaining counter in exchange for so minor a concession, and even Soejima, whom the foreign Representatives considered sympathetic to some extension of foreign rights, became more reserved and declined to respond to the

Western diplomats' demand until the Iwakura mission returned. Although this was due within a few months, Berthemy was irritated by the delay. He held it to be wrong that a country which claimed to be entering the way of progress should restrict foreigners to a few ports, and he urged upon his colleagues the necessity of putting pressure on the Japanese government without delay.[18] In August he warned Soejima that the proposed deal with Italy was unwise, and 'sought to demonstrate to him that if one of the Powers should come, through ignorance of the situation, to accept the wishes of the Japanese Government, the latter would soon find itself obliged to renounce this gratification to its amour propre, under pain of exposing itself to the most serious embarrassment'.[19] He found the foreign minister's response encouraging and felt able to hope that the promised negotiations might result in European demands being met; but two conversations with Iwakura soon after his return on 13 September, together with the Japanese government's evident reluctance to engage in formal talks, soon reversed that favourable impression.[20] Before long Berthemy was beginning to doubt whether success could be achieved by what he deemed a reasonable approach. By November he was writing somewhat ominously to the French foreign minister:

> You will thus not learn without surprise, Duke, that the eager welcome, to say no more, of which the Japanese embassy has been the object in America and Europe has had a result diametrically opposite to that which the governments concerned expected, and that this result has just translated itself into a refusal pure and simple on the part of the new Minister of Foreign Relations to discuss the propositions submitted to his predecessor for examination. Treated as a spoilt child, Japan is abusing the position which one was pleased to give it.[21]

For a man of Berthemy's temperament, this situation was not one to be accepted without a struggle. Strong protests, and the hint that the remaining instalment of the Shimonoseki indemnity would have to be paid if the Japanese government were uncooperative, led Terashima, the new foreign minister, to suggest that a counter-draft incorporating the conditions under which Japan would allow free access might be forthcoming.[22]

This, however, had still not been produced by the end of the year despite pointed reminders by the foreign representatives that the final instalment of the Shimonoseki indemnity was now due. Indeed, Terashima's promise to meet Japan's obligation by July indicated that the Japanese leadership preferred to pay this financial price rather than accept any further penetration of the interior.[23] Thus a major diplomatic weapon had been blunted and Berthemy was forced by the end of the year to conclude that as long as Iwakura remained in power there was little chance of progress.[24]

This verdict was made to seem less pessimistic in January, when Terashima, reverting to the caution that normally characterised the Meiji government's conduct of diplomatic relations, gave Berthemy to understand that access to the interior would be allowed, though not for the purpose of trade.[25] While emphasizing the inadequacy of such a concession, the French minister again allowed himself to hope for a change of attitude on the more important question. Once more, however, disappointment followed. The Meiji government failed to implement its half-promise, and a number of incidents concerning foreign diplomatic rights occurred which were dealt with in what the foreign representatives regarded as an unsatisfactory manner. By late June it had become clear that the Japanese government had no intention of agreeing to any change in the jurisdictional situation until it was in a position to claim the total abolition of extraterritoriality. In an interview with Terashima and two other Japanese ministers, the foreign representatives were informed that the *Dajokan*, the highest government council, had rejected both the Western proposals and the Foreign Ministry's counter-proposals, plainly a move intended to end the negotiations.[26]

Notwithstanding the earlier indications of Japanese reluctance to open the country fully, the determined manner in which the Meiji government indicated that it was not going to yield to pressure seems to have come as a shock to the Western diplomats, particularly Berthemy and von Brandt. According to a letter, dated 20 July 1874, from the French officer, Captain Descharmes, to his former colleague, Colonel Chanoine, von Brandt was 'fuming' while Berthemy was 'completely furious'. Descharmes noted that 'Berthemy, who had on his arrival anticipated Japan's surrender, perceives today that some orientals are very different from others and that it is not sufficient to have been in China to play with [*jouer*] the Japanese'.[27]

The French minister was not yet prepared to give up, however. In reporting on the interview in which the Japanese decision had been communicated, Berthemy stated that 'on leaving Terashima I declared to him, as agreed with the ministers of Britain and Germany, that the Japanese government would oblige us to change attitude and claim as a right what up to now we had asked as a concession, if it persisted in confining themselves to a rejection of further discussion which is explained, but not justified, by its irritation at the refusal of the occidental Powers to renounce to its profit the principle of extraterritoriality'.[28] Following up their prior understanding, the foreign representatives had recourse to an argument which up till then they had no more than hinted at. Since the Japanese government employed several hundred foreigners to whom, in many cases, freedom of movement was necessarily allowed, the foreign representatives were able to claim that all their nationals were entitled to this privilege by right of their most-favoured-nation clauses, and at the end of their interview with Terashima they did so in forceful terms. By Berthemy, at least, this was intended to be more than an idle threat. The dispatch in which he reported his actions to the Quai d'Orsay ended with a recommendation that the Powers act firmly: 'The moment has nevertheless arrived for the main Powers to decide if they will accept the situation presented to their nationals by the unjustifiable obstinacy of the present counsellors of the Mikado, or indeed if they will give to their representatives the necessary instructions to overcome obstacles which will disappear, I am certain, in face of the clearly formulated expression of a common will'.[29]

This recommendation appeared to be an invitation to the French government to propose a joint démarche by all the major Powers in order to impose their will upon Japan. Whether other Powers would have responded to such a proposal cannot be stated with any certainty, since Berthemy's advice was very quickly made redundant by rapid Japanese action. There must, though, be considerable doubt as to Britain's readiness to collaborate, since Parkes was preoccupied with the possible consequences of the

Taiwan expedition and does not seem to have been so committed to the cause of free access as Berthemy, while the Foreign Office would probably have been cautious. Even the Quai d'Orsay, although initially sympathetic, in practice did little to implement the suggestion of its representative.[30]

Reactions might well have been less negative, however, had not the Meiji government heeded the foreign representatives' language. By a note of 13 July 1874 it conceded to foreigners recommended by their legation the right to request passports permitting them to travel within Japan for the purpose of health, study, or other important reasons, trade alone being specifically excepted. This compromise was welcomed by the British Foreign Office and, to a lesser extent, by Parkes,[31] although Berthemy was still dissatisfied enough to push his colleagues into drawing up another collective note reiterating their previous demands.[32] Negotiations were not resumed, however, and when positive instructions from Paris failed to materialise by December 1874, even Berthemy, whose energy had been a major driving force during this phase of treaty revision, gave up all idea of a renewed effort.[33]

Despite its inconclusive ending and its neglect by historians, this episode merits attention because it reveals the Meiji leaders facing renewed foreign pressure, and even the possibility of foreign action, for the first time since 1868. In hindsight the danger may not have been very great, and even at the time the threats that were made were veiled rather than open, but significantly the Japanese government did not adopt a wait-and-see policy. While not yielding on the key issue of opening the whole country to foreign traders, it moved quickly to minimise the risk of foreign action by making a strategic concession with regard to travel in the interior. In doing so it laid itself open to criticism, particularly by the still formidable xenophobic ex-samurai. That it was prepared to do so at a time when its position had been made more vulnerable by the deep divisions over policy towards Korea shows how high a priority it gave at this stage to avoiding a clash with the Western powers. Ironically it also demonstrates that however strongly Western diplomats might be tempted to push the Japanese around, their governments were very unlikely to abandon their traditional caution.

THE SECOND PHASE, 1877–89

When the issue of treaty revision was next taken up, the Meiji government , perhaps assuming that Berthemy's tough line would be followed by his successor, approached France only when extensive preliminary negotiations had been carried out with other powers. At the beginning of this second phase,[34] foreign minister Terashima, influenced by the Finance Ministry, confined Japan's demands to straightforward revision of tariffs,[35] and this strategy appeared to pay off when a new treaty which gave Japan tariff autonomy in return for opening new ports was signed with the USA, after two years of talks, on 25 July 1878. The treaty was to come into force, however, only when all other countries had similarly revised their treaties with Japan, so the problem of securing the assent of the major European powers still remained. Nevertheless, there were some hopeful signs for Japan at this stage. Both Russia and Italy were favourable to new treaties, the one for political, the other for commercial reasons. Unfortunately for Terashima, Britain and Germany were much less responsive and as long as these two countries took a common stand the chances of securing even tariff revision were slight given Japan's refusal to yield over the opening of the interior to trade. While this impasse lasted, France's attitude made little difference, but generally the French government was content to remain out of the front line and continue to enjoy the advantages conferred by the existing treaties.

Not all Frenchmen concurred in thinking that this negative line of policy was in France's best interests. Geofroy, who was minister in Tokyo when the first definite Japanese project of a revised tariff was presented in February 1878, saw some point in not incurring Japanese displeasure. A few months earlier he had concluded (after Terashima had assured him that the Meiji government would be reasonable when permitted to raise import duties and liberal in abolishing all export duties) that 'in principle . . . it seems to me that our role in Japan must be rather to incline towards American impartiality and condescension than to associate ourselves with Prussian haughtiness and English egoism and to accept a share in being hated'. While adding that there was no need 'to attach much importance to the grievances of the Japanese about their unrecognised sovereignty' and referring condescendingly to their 'slightly childish susceptibility', Geofroy admitted that they were suffering from the current trade imbalance, and he advised his government that 'we have no serious reasons for refusing to enter with the Japanese into the examination of arrangements which, while giving them satisfaction, will continue to safeguard our interests overall. It behoves us not to lose from sight that a refusal of the European Powers would probably result in precipitating the conclusion of a separate arrangement between Japan and the United States, an arrangement to which we would sooner or later be forced to rally'.[36] He was, in February, still inclined to make concessions to Japan without too much bargaining. Although he felt that the proposed new duties, which ranged from 5% to 30%, were not completely justified, he reasoned that so long as woollen muslins did not suffer, French interests were in no real danger and his advice to his government, therefore, was to offer 'a ready response to the overtures of the Japanese government and to not subordinate our acceptance to an agreement with England whose interests in Japan are essentially different from ours'. [37]

The view of the Quai d'Orsay on this question was somewhat different. Foreign minister Waddington replied that before deciding France's position on tariff revision he intended to find out how the British Foreign Office felt. 'I have not to reiterate here', he wrote, 'the general considerations which demand that we maintain in our contact with the nations of the Far East, particularly Japan, the harmony of views which have in all circumstances inspired the different European cabinets and which up to now have provided their strength and security'.[38] When the Quai d'Orsay was formally presented with Japan's demands by its minister in Paris, Samejima, it gave them an extremely cool reception.[39] The French government did not absolutely refuse to discuss the question, but it did inform Samejima, as a later memorandum by Geofroy put it, that 'to us, moreover, all negotiation seemed useless which did not embrace the measures appropriate for extending the commercial relations of the two countries by facilitating the access to Japan of French citizens and capital.[40] This was in line with the British position at the time. As Geofroy observed in 1878, to adopt such a standpoint was to reopen the question of extraterritoriality, which had proved insoluble in 1874, and would be even more so now that it was linked to the question of tariffs. This latter development made treaty revision inordinately complicated and was undoubtedly a major factor in preventing the achievement of even partial revision for a very long time.[41] Although Geofroy still felt that, general considerations apart, France would do well to align itself with the United States rather than Britain, he was forced by his instructions to inform Iwakura that France found the compensation that Japan was offering in return for higher tariffs insufficient.[42]

The advice forthcoming from Tokyo changed markedly when Geofroy was succeeded by Balloy in 1879. The latter completely lacked sympathy for Japan and saw the Meiji government's desire for treaty revision as an attempt to distract the Japanese people from its domestic grievances, rather than as a genuine national aspiration.[43] Although he was not, initially, totally opposed to tariff revision, he meant Japan to pay a very high price for it. His advice to the Quai d'Orsay in fact was:

> Let the Japanese Government make its proposals without responding to it. Once all of its demands are known, we will ask what they are offering us in exchange. Its proposals will probably be insufficient. We can then make counter-proposals in our turn, and as by the avowal of the the minister for foreign affairs, the Japanese government is obliged to create new resources, we can hold it by the money question and we will force it to submit to what we find just to exact from it in compensation for the higher charges with which they will hit our trade.[44]

This somewhat Machiavellian approach was superseded by an even harder line a few months later when the proposals of Inoue, the new foreign minister, were actually made known. 'Our reply', Balloy then stated, 'must be the rejection, pure and simple, of the present proposals as the base for negotiation'.[45] At the same time he informed Paris that he had been working with some success on his British, German, Russian, Austrian and Dutch colleagues to induce them to recommend the same response to their own governments.[46] Until this point, despite several other dispatches from Balloy bitterly criticizing the new draft codes and the workings of Japanese justice,[47] the Quai d'Orsay had kept its options open, and in June 1880 the French foreign minister had acknowledged that the 1866 tariffs were excessively moderate.[48] In the face of Balloy's strong advice and the apparent unanimity of the other important European powers, it was now decided to reject Inoue's proposals outright.[49]

Balloy did not remain long in Japan and was not an important figure in the history of treaty revision. His forthright language, however, reveals the essential character of French policy exceptionally clearly. Fundamentally France was content with the status quo, saw no reason to encourage Japan, and generally dragged its heels whenever concessions were mooted. Even those French diplomats who did not share Balloy's anti-Japanese feelings followed his line rather than that which Geofroy had tentatively suggested. Roquette, for instance, who replaced Balloy in December 1880, enjoyed relatively friendly relations with Japanese leaders and, as his painstaking and fair-minded analysis of the new penal and criminal procedure codes showed, was an unusually impartial observer of developments in Japan.[50] Nevertheless, he never felt able to give more than vague assurances of French sympathy in reply to Japanese appeals for advice and encouragement, and his assurances were always accompanied by advice to adopt a less demanding position, to appeal to the Powers for understanding of Japan's progress and needs, and to be content with minor improvements in Japan's position for at least the next twenty years. That he himself (after reporting that these points had left Ito Hirobumi still disheartened in August 1881) called them 'banal consolations' shows that he did not deceive himself about their lack of real substance.[51]

Roquette's one concrete proposal – made in conjunction with his British and German colleagues – was a European conference on treaty revision; but although this was welcomed by foreign minister Inoue, it was brought to naught by the opposition of the British and German governments.[52] The proposal did not, in any case, mark a real change in policy, but was rather intended to be a tactical ploy, as is evident from the way in which Roquette expressed his regret at the decision of the European cabinets:

If my colleagues and I believed that it would have been preferable to negotiate in Europe, it was in order to attempt to end up by giving away as little as possible and yet to satisfy the Japanese delegates, whereas here it is more than doubtful that we would arrive at an agreement. In reality, in future revision, it is a matter only of making concessions – we have nothing to expect since there is nothing to offer us – it is necessary therefore with a great deal of courtesy and eagerness to praise the progress of the last ten years and to allow, in recompense, some abandonment of our rights within a predecided limit. Self-regard [*amour-propre*] is here the great mover of all the statesmen, and finding themselves in Europe, enchanted by a compliment from the mouth of some illustrious personage, they would have insisted on much less and would have preferred the satisfaction of flattery to the reality of a concession.[53]

Roquette's attitude offered no great hopes for Japanese aspirations but at least it was not overtly hostile. The next minister, Tricou, who arrived in June, 1882, was adamant that the treaties must be regarded as permanent.[54] In common with his colleagues, he was prepared to accept minor tariff changes and the introduction of mixed tribunals in commercial matters, but these limited concessions were to be highly conditional. They would, in particular, only be granted if foreigners were permitted to travel in the interior for the purposes of trade.[55] To take this position was tantamount to rejection of the possibility of treaty revision, since the Japanese government would gain a mere fraction of its demands, while in return it would give up its main commercial bargaining counter and render itself open to the accusation that it was endangering national independence.[56]

During Tricou's stay in Japan, France was the most intransigent of the major Powers, but with his sudden transfer to China in May 1883 French policy was to swing briefly to the other extreme. This swing, however, was not due to the character of the new French representative, Ulric de Viel-Castel, but to the change in France's position in East Asia as a result of the outbreak of hostilities in Annam. With conflict between France and China looming, and the possibility that France might wish to seek Japanese cooperation, Paris now reversed the position adopted by Tricou by deciding not only to renounce the principle of the treaty's permanence but also to return to Japan gradually the right to impose administrative regulations binding on foreigners and to negotiate a separate commercial agreement.[57]

This change was the more significant in that it was taken without consultation with Britain and in the knowledge that it would undermine British treaty revision strategy.[58] Even though no concession was offered that could not be taken back if other Powers did not follow suit, it was France's first initiative in Japan's favour and may have influenced the governments of Belgium, Holland, Italy, Spain and Switzerland to express approval of a compromise proposal circulated by the German government in July 1883.[59] With other Powers more or less sympathetic also, Britain was forced to modify its position to the extent of accepting that, once introduced, the new commercial treaties could be terminated after ten or twelve years, provided that Japan had been opened to foreigners for a period of three years before notice of termination was given.[60]

This development proved less important than it promised to be because the French change of attitude was short-lived. When it seemed that the situation in Indo-China could be contained and that, in any case, Japan was unlikely to provide France with any military support against China, the traditional negative stand was, as far as possible, resumed. This was indicated by the Quai d'Orsay as early as July, when it informed London that it did not accept the argument that the new commercial treaties might be unilaterally denounced by Japan and showed distinct signs of reverting to the policy of entente with Britain.[61] The new French minister in Japan, Sienkiewicz, was even less inclined to favour any concessions. Displeased that, as he put it, 'we have granted Japan very important concessions in the matter of treaty revision and have obtained, in exchange, only evidence of the fear which the Chinese empire inspires in the Mikado's Ministers', he reacted by urging his government that France's interests would best be served by his leaving the initiative on treaty revision to Inoue and then making reservations, especially with regard to silk export duties.[62]

Sienkiewicz's determination to engage in obstruction was reinforced by the fact that Germany had now taken the lead in encouraging Japan. 'To accept the German proposals, that is to say to fix, from now, the time when the treaties will be able to be denounced in their entirety by Japan', he wrote in December 1883, 'would be not only to compromise the interests of our nationals but to serve German influence which, having taken the initiative in this exorbitant concession, would necessarily be alone in drawing advantage from the benefits it may have in mind'.[63] He saw no injustice to Japan in this, believing, like Balloy, that the Japanese leaders had raised the treaty revision question merely as a means of gaining popularity. In reply to the German claim that revolution might result from continued intransigence, Sienkiewicz maintained that the Meiji government would not dare to stir up agitation when they themselves might well be the victims.[64]

In line with Sienkiewicz's recommendation, French policy for the next few years sought on the one hand to limit any concessions contemplated by the Western powers and on the other hand to ensure that if concessions were made, France would receive appropriate compensation. Its particular objective – the abolition of the export duty on silk – was not in itself objectionable to the Japanese. Some loss of revenue would be involved but this would be offset by the higher duties which Japan could expect to levy on imports when the new tariffs came into force, and in any case there was advantage to be gained from improving the balance of trade by boosting silk exports and encouraging domestic production. The snag lay in the French requirement that Inoue should announce the abolition before or during the conference in Tokyo which was due soon to discuss treaty revision. If the Meiji government were to agree to this, it ran the risk of inviting similar demands from the other Powers – a prospect which, after the exhausting struggle to secure their agreement to the proposed new tariff, Inoue desperately wished to avoid.

Strenuous efforts were made by Inoue and by Hachisuka, Japan's representative in Paris, to persuade France to be content with a less formal promise that would bind Japan morally but would not be regarded as an acceptance of foreign interference with Japan's export tariffs. These efforts were to no avail, however. Although France moderated its demands slightly with regard both to form and timing, the essential feature remained: Japan must publicly state its intention to abolish the duties at a session of the conference.[65] In the end Inoue did make a declaration, though not until 1886, when a new series of revision conferences were being held,[66] and as it happened, there were no repercussions, possibly because the representatives of other Powers found the idea of reopening the one question that had finally been solved too daunting to contemplate. The fact remains, however, that even though removal of the silk export duty was of relatively marginal importance to the French silk industry, the French government persisted throughout these years in adding this potentially disruptive complication to the enormous problems faced by Inoue.

Part of France's insistence on a public undertaking with regard to the silk duty may have been due to the suspicion that once the Meiji government had secured its increased import tariff it might find some excuse for not implementing a merely moral obligation. Perhaps more important, however, was the French awareness that Japanese failure to comply with their demand provided a convenient pretext for avoiding further concession. French concern not to give anything more away was, it needs to be emphasised, determined by political as well as commercial considerations. In 1884, for example, Sienkiewicz justified his advocacy of resisting Japanese demands by arguing that since 'the exaggerated concessions which we might make would be attributed rather to the influence exercised upon us by the other Powers, we must, it seems to me, strictly maintain the principles which we must defend and the demands which we have formulated. It is , from another point of view, the one way of not losing standing in the eyes of the Japanese'. [67] From evidence such as this it is clear that treaty revision involved considerations of national prestige for France (and almost certainly for other Western powers) as well as Japan. In the light of this factor it is hardly surprising that treaty revision took so long to achieve.

However much France wished to assert its independent standing, it could not in practice stand completely alone. It generally felt the need to buttress itself by an entente with Britain, the Power least likely to abandon its rights in Japan;[68] and when Plunkett, the minister who had replaced Parkes in 1883, showed a disposition to moderate his demands in order to end the continual negotiations, France was reluctantly forced to modify its own position. This was recognized by Sienkiewicz when, after claiming to detect an Anglo-German entente in Far Eastern affairs in 1886, he advised: 'Hence, in regard to the question of revision, it behoves us not to show a lesser liberalism than the other Powers while yet reserving to ourselves the right to propose serious amendments to the projects submitted to the conference. A different attitude on our part would probably not hinder developments. The Powers, despite our opposition, would conclude with Japan treaties to which we would be obliged to subscribe sooner or later'.[69]

The limitations which fear of isolation placed on French action were shown clearly in the 1886–7 Tokyo conferences. After several changes of strategy in the proceeding years the Japanese government, against a background of rising feeling against both the treaties and the Meiji leaders themselves, attempted to achieve simultaneous revision of the commercial and jurisdictional provisions of the treaties. Its strategy did not suit the French minister. Though relatively little concerned about tariff changes, he was extremely reluctant to countenance any weakening of extraterritoriality, and had recently proposed that the two matters be treated separately.[70] He was more than dubious about the standard of justice that could be expected from the promised Japanese law courts and was specially anxious to preserve the strong foreign position in the existing treaty ports.[71] In May 1886 he alone opposed strongly the (German-supported) Japanese proposal to have the consular courts apply Japanese laws where the penalty was less than 5,000 francs fine or five years in prison.[72] When, however, agreement was reached between Germany and Britain, and France became isolated, Sienkiewicz backtracked by claiming to be sympathetic towards the principle of the plan if not to the plan itself.[73]

Sienkiewicz's tactical retreat was in accord with the strategy he had mapped out the previous month of avoiding blame for the breakdown of negotiations while seeking to modify or nullify any proposals which he considered dangerous. Such a strategy would only be workable, however, if France was able to find another Power or group of Powers to align with, and when, during later 1886 and early 1887, the details of the new project were being thrashed out, Sienkiewicz discovered that he was alone in maintaining his former position virtually intact. Not only was he forced to admit, as early as June 1886, that the abandonment of consular jurisdiction was a political necessity,[74] but, in the detailed discussion of the mixed courts which were to replace it, he was unable to secure from Japan what he considered a proper recognition of France's importance.

The French minister found particularly galling the fact that, supported by Plunkett, Inoue refused in November to accept French as an official language in Japan's new courts. When Sienkiewicz stated that he could only accept the unfavourable vote of the conference under an *ad referendum* formula whereby all decisions would have to be subsequently approved by the French government, he was advocating a procedure which other Powers would have been tempted to take advantage of and which could have made much of the conference's work meaningless. It was not only the Japanese government which found his attitude unacceptable, however, for he was also challenged by Plunkett. As the discomfited French representative reported to Paris, the Japanese delegates, encouraged by the British minister, 'pushed things to the extreme and declared that they would suspend the sessions of the Conference until I was able to give a formal response to the Conference on the question of languages. While drawing attention to the abnormal character of the procedure to which they had recourse, I gave the votes which I was not free to refuse. . . . To say to a foreign delegate that the sessions of a Conference will be suspended because of him', he complained, 'is to say, is it not, that the consequences of this measure will likewise fall upon him and to exercise particular moral pressure on this delegate'.[75] Sienkiewicz clearly resented the position in which he found himself, but he was, it may be felt, experiencing a taste of what Japanese leaders had had to suffer, sometimes from him.

Thereafter, Sienkiewicz adopted the policy of voting for every conference decision, even those to which he publicly objected, hoping thus to make the other delegates aware that his assent was nominal and that he still basically adhered to the *ad referendum* formula.[76] His later claim that this had made Inoue reconsider his earlier attitude was to some extent justified by the Japanese readiness to promise France a generous share in the allocation of foreign judges to serve in the proposed new Japanese courts which would have jurisdiction over foreigners.[77]

Nevertheless, the fact that Sienkiewicz, despite his government's expressed displeasure at the pressure to which he had been subjected, dared not risk a disruption of the conference indicated that France would have found difficulty in subsequently rejecting its decisions if the conference had ended with a general agreement.

As it turned out, an unexpected development delivered the French government from the necessity of choosing between unpopular isolation and ignominious retreat. Inoue had been prepared to pay for the recovery of tariff and jurisdictional rights by not only establishing tribunals with a proportion of foreign judges but also by agreeing to submit Japan's new legal codes to foreign approval (as well as by accepting the complete opening of Japan), but when these plans were leaked, first to other members of the Meiji government, and then to the public, they provoked a political crisis.[78] Organised opposition, which had faded when the People's Rights movement was hit by governmental counter-measures and internal dissension in the early 1880s, began to revive; and the fear that treaty revision on the terms which had been accepted would impede the achievement of full national independence was used by Inoue's critics to undermine his position.[79] The foreign minister endeavoured, by attempting to withdraw the provision for a foreign veto on the Japanese codes, to meet the objection that he was yielding Japan's sovereign rights to foreigners, but this provoked opposition on the part of the foreign representatives. He was thus unable to counter the attacks of either nationalists, who advised that treaty revision be postponed until Japan had proved the extent of her progress and could negotiate from a stronger position, or radicals, who claimed to believe that the 1858 treaties could be denounced unilaterally.[80] As a result Inoue adjourned the conference *sine die* on 19 July 1887, and a month later admitted defeat by resigning.[81]

As Japanese foreign minister from 1879 to 1887 Inoue Kaoru had devoted an enormous amount of time to securing treaty revision. Although in the end his efforts came to naught. It is possible that he might have achieved a limited agreement if the European powers had been more accommodating. As has been seen, the fact that France, while not the major stumbling-block, was particularly obstructive owed not a little to the views of most of its representatives in Tokyo, especially Sienkiewicz. If further evidence of the latter's personal role is needed, it can be found in a dispatch of August 1885 in which he outlined his attitude and strategy:

> I must, moreover, recall here once more that all my colleagues are disposed to make greater concessions than we are to the Japanese. I know, indeed, that I am reproached for holding up the solution of the revision question by the difficulties which I raise concerning jurisdiction. The course which I have followed up to this time seems to me, however, to be very easily explained: being convinced that from the political point of view we have no interest in staying completely outside this movement which leads the Powers to make concessions to the Japanese, I concentrate on moderating these concessions, as much as possible, where they may go too far, while maintaining a very firm opposition to measures which would be directly harmful to us.[82]

Except for the brief change of tack in 1883, this was the line of policy which French diplomats tried to follow throughout the 1880s.

THE THIRD PHASE, 1889–96

Inoue's successor, Okuma Shigenobu, may have been chosen in the hope that public opinion would be conciliated by the inclusion in the government of an ex-minister who had become a political party leader. From the standpoint of the Western powers, however, Okuma could be expected to improve his own position by pressing harder for revision and by seeking better terms for Japan. While following Inoue by retaining the safeguard of having foreign as well as Japanese judges in cases involving foreigners, he aimed to reduce their numbers and to have them adopt Japanese nationality. He deviated far more basically from Inoue's approach, however, by abandoning the pursuit of agreement at a conference of all the Powers concerned in favour of separate bargaining. The logic of this change of strategy was that if he persuaded the more sympathetic Powers to accept his terms, he could hope to create an atmosphere in which revision was seen as inevitable, even by the Powers who were less disposed to make major concessions.

At first this new approach seemed to receive an encouraging response from every Power except France.[83] It was unfortunate for Japan that the request to consider Okuma's new proposals came at a time when Sienkiewicz felt that the Meiji government had behaved badly over the ending of the contracts of the last French military advisers. The French minister's apparent uncooperativeness, according to Japanese records, certainly caused Okuma concern. Not only did he show reluctance to send Okuma's proposals to Paris, but he presented the Japanese foreign minister with a long list of detailed questions which the latter regarded as obstructionist and even insulting. Moreover, when Okuma offered to answer them orally, Sienkiewicz did not respond; and the Japanese Foreign Office was placed in the position of having to provide a point-by-point legalistic response.[84]

Clearly the personal characters of the two men jarred, for Sienkiewicz later complained of Okuma's absolute lack of tact,[85] while Okuma informed the Japanese minister to Paris, Tanaka Fujimaro, in February that 'the French minister in Japan, judging from the situation up to now, has no sympathy for the [Japanese] imperial government'. So unhappy was the Japanese foreign minister with Sienkiewicz that he went so far as to add: 'Japanese-French treaty revision negotiations are due to open in Tokyo as previously mentioned, but M. Sienkiewicz is not, at any rate with regard to this matter, trying to help or bring things to a conclusion, and it is difficult to estimate whether he will engage in profitless obstruction in the negotiations and in the end damage relations between Japan and France, so I propose that we now bypass him and move the negotiations to Paris'.[86] While no formal complain was lodged with the French government about its representative's conduct, Tanaka did seek to discuss treaty revision in Paris; but the Quai d'Orsay sidestepped this move by informing him that Sienkiewicz had been told to engage in talks in Tokyo and would soon be sent detailed instructions.[87]

Sienkiewicz's own reports present the situation in a quite different light, but it is not difficult to see how Okuma found his attitude cold and unhelpful. When the French representative first received official notification of the resumption of Japan's pursuit of treaty revision, he inveighed against the Powers

which had encouraged Japan by making ill-considered concessions, especially with regard to jurisdiction, in order to gain
Japanese favour, and in his advice to his government he
combined resignation with a recommendation not to be
generous: 'To draw from this situation, regrettable as it is, the
least bad possible, and especially not to remain isolated, seems
to me our principal concern'.[88] Similarly, in the following
month, he expressed to Paris the opinion that 'if we must not
adopt towards Japan an attitude different from that of the other
great Powers, we do not have to put too much haste into
accepting a treaty which is, so to say, imposed on us by the
circumstances'.[89]

Although Sienkiewicz obviously intended to drag his feet,
however, he was not as big an obstacle to treaty revision as
Okuma assumed; and had he known of it, Okuma would have
been gratified by Sienkiewicz's advice to the Quai d'Orsay in
March that France should reject Britain's request for cooperation in opposing various aspects of the Japanese government's
proposals on jurisdiction.[90] His experiences in the mid-1880s
had led him to believe, he argued, that France could easily be left
isolated again if the British government were to decide on a
policy of concession. More fundamentally, though, he had now
become convinced that consular jurisdiction was doomed to
imminent abolition and that it was more realistic for France to
resign itself to the loss of jurisdictional rights and concentrate
on securing substantial compensation on the commercial side. In
May the Quai d'Orsay expressed its complete agreement with
these recommendations.[91]

It is impossible to single out any one factor as decisive in this
reversal of the previous, long-standing, French attitude.
Undoubtedly the old fear of isolation was present still, and
the disposition to concession which it encouraged was
reinforced, momentarily at least, by the advice of the Russian
minister, who, in accordance with his government's policy of
removing Japanese distrust, urged Sienkiewicz in 1889 to
execute a master-stroke of diplomacy by accepting the Japanese
project without reserve.[92] On a different level the French
minister seems to have finally recognised that Japanese
modernization was a factor which could not be ignored: by
May 1889 he was prepared to urge: 'Let us then neglect nothing

to avoid being the last to sign the emancipation of the only people in the whole of the Orient which is seriously committed, using its own strengths and its own ways as best it can, to the assimilation of Occidental civilization'.[93]

It is often assumed that the development which did most to change the Western image of Meiji Japan was the establishment of constitutional government, and that this was also decisive in the achievement of treaty revision. Sienkiewicz's last-quoted dispatch, written as it was not long after the promulgation by the Meiji Emperor of a constitution, would appear to lend support to that assumption. This view cannot, however, be accepted without two significant qualifications. The first is that the introduction of a representative assembly was important not so much because it was seen as a mark of progress – it was criticized as over-ambitious by Sienkiewicz – but because it opened up a channel for popular nationalism and (since the Meiji government would now be able to claim that if the Diet was not satisfied, power might fall into the hands of the less amenable opposition parties) provided the Japanese foreign minister with a powerful new argument for demanding treaty revision on terms that were more favourable to Japan. The second qualification is that the constitution was only one of many modernizing reforms. It was because these together had endowed Japan with a new strength – although military modernization arguably stood out in this respect – that the Western powers were now aware that if they refused to negotiate revised treaties, Japan might dare to abrogate their rights completely. In such a case the threat of force might no longer be sufficient to compel Japan to back down, and the actual use of force, even if practicable, would be prohibitively costly.

In such a situation it was virtually inevitable that France would sooner or later choose to compromise, but its change of approach was surprisingly rapid. Not only was the emphasis quietly switched to commercial matters[94] but unusual care was taken to inform the Japanese government of France's willingness to negotiate.[95] What really mattered to Japan, though, was the fact that the French government did not attempt to bolster its position either by seeking cooperation with Britain or by responding to the latter's overtures. This weakened the latter's

171

stand, because it meant that Britain had to shoulder the main burden of resistance, and thus risk a rupture with Japan, at a time when the British position in the Far East seemed threatened by the Russian decision to go ahead with the Trans-Siberian railway. London therefore persisted in making approaches to Paris, even after its March 1889 initiative was rebuffed.

The Quai d'Orsay was evidently less averse than Sienkiewicz to cooperation, for in July of the same year it urged him to discuss joint action with his British colleague over the treaty which Japan had just persuaded Mexico to accept.[96] This treaty opened the interior to Mexicans in return for recognition of Japan's right of jurisdiction, and Sienkiewicz objected verbally to Okuma's insistence that the most-favoured-nation clauses in the Western powers' treaties did not entitle them to the same privileges that were being granted to the Mexicans.[97] Nevertheless, he declined to present a written protest in combination with the British chargé d'affaires, Fraser. Although informed by the Quai d'Orsay that Fraser was empowered to act in common, Sienkiewicz claimed that Britain appeared to wish to act alone in the matter.[98] Whether this was justified is questionable: that his true motive for avoiding joint action may have been different is suggested by the fact that he also put forward the argument that strong action would place France in an awkward position. His justification, however, was accepted by the Quai d'Orsay without question.

In January 1890 the possibility of an Anglo-French entente was raised again, on this occasion by Fraser, but his initiative withered in the face of Sienkiewicz's bitter memories of the mid-eighties.[99] The same fate met a further attempt in June, when Lord Salisbury requested French support for his counter-project.[100] Even though Japan's terms were by then much higher than in January, Sienkiewicz still discouraged the idea, this time on the ground that the British project was not a practical basis for negotiation.[101] Yet again the Quai d'Orsay accepted his reasoning and this third failure brought Britain's efforts to an end.

In the meantime, France had come close to reaching agreement with Japan. Although the negotiations between Sienkiewicz and Okuma during the summer of 1889 left some problems unresolved, foreign minister Spuller felt able to inform Sienkiewicz that as far as commercial issues were concerned, it seemed as if a definite understanding with Japan could be reached without great difficulty, and as early as July Sienkiewicz himself had anticipated in a report to Paris that France would sign a treaty with Japan towards October.[102] The expectation that agreement would soon be forthcoming was shattered on 18 October 1889, when Okuma lost a leg in an assassination attempt by a young Japanese who was indignant at the concessions still being made to foreigners (and who committed suicide immediately after throwing a bomb). Prime minister Kuroda Kiyotaka at once offered his resignation, and the new foreign minister, Aoki Shuzo, soon put forward for the approval of the new cabinet of Yamagata Aritomo a proposal to negotiate on a significantly different basis, including jettisoning the provision for foreign judges.

Aoki, and his successors (Enomoto Takeaki and Mutsu Munemitsu) in the following cabinets of Matsukata and Ito, also chose to concentrate on reaching a settlement with Britain, assuming that if the most important Power in East Asia accepted a new treaty, the other difficult Powers would fall into line. Most of Japan's subsequent treaty revision negotiations with France therefore took place after the signature of the new British treaty in July 1894.[103] By this time Sienkiewicz had been succeeded by Harmand, who, despite being relatively pro-Japanese, was in no hurry to open discussions. Though aware that the state of feeling in Japan made it impossible for treaty revision to be postponed indefinitely, he anticipated that an apparent willingness to withhold agreement might prove useful in securing special advantages.[104] In this view he was not mistaken, judging from Mutsu's complaint, in March 1895, that 'Japan's tariff proposals are already more favourable to France than to any other power'.[105] Nevertheless, more than a year was still to elapse before agreement was reached, because France continued to press for further concessions, in particular for reductions on the proposed import duties for woollen muslins, wines and perfumes. Its demands were strongly contested by Mutsu, who feared that the other Powers would follow suit, but eventually Japan did give way on a considerable number of points.

Despite this bargaining success, French opposition might well have taken longer to overcome had Japan not made one more concession: it agreed, secretly, to buy warships from France. Warship orders had been linked with treaty revision in the French view since 1894, when they received considerable emphasis in the instructions given to Harmand;[106] and on several occasions in 1895 and 1896 hints had been dropped to the Japanese government that, if treated favourably on this score, France might be disposed to generosity on other matters.[107] In April 1896 there was a suggestion of possible success when, after long interviews on the subject with prime minister Ito and navy minister Saigo, Harmand telegraphed the Quai d'Orsay to urge it to postpone its signature of the new treaty until it heard from him again.[108] Then, in June, the French minister reported that orders had been given to the *Société des Forges et Chantiers de la Méditerranée*.[109] There was no open admission by Japan that any bargain had been reached and no documentary evidence appears in the voluminous Japanese printed sources, but in view of the delicacy of the issue in terms both of Japan's relations with other countries and Japanese domestic politics, this is hardly surprising.

The treaty between Japan and France was ratified without difficulty by both the Chamber of Deputies and the Senate, on 29 October 1897 and 23 December1897 respectively, and came into effect on 4 August1899.[110] It was substantially the same as the treaties which most of the other Powers had already signed, and its commercial provisions did not impose significantly heavier tariffs on the main French exports to Japan. Since, however, Japan was free to denounce them after twelve years, and since they neither retained an unconditional most-favoured-nation clause nor any element of extraterritoriality, they were clearly no longer founded on an unequal relationship. By dint of colossal efforts, Meiji diplomacy had finally achieved its first objective.

Despite the complexity of the treaty revision process – both in terms of the number of countries with which Japan had to deal and the mind-numbing minutiae of the negotiations about tariff duties – France's position was basically simple. Enjoying, as it it did, considerable advantages under the unequal treaties, it was only prepared to abandon them when no other course seemed safe. Moral justification for this position, on those occasions when it was needed, could always be found in the argument that if Japan had really Westernised itself sufficiently for foreigners to be subjected to Japanese jurisdiction, then it would act in a liberal Western manner and allow foreigners to travel, trade, and set up their own establishments anywhere in Japan.[111]

If the basic French attitude was simple, though, the length of the negotiations meant that there was room for changes of emphasis and even, in a few cases, for a complete reversal of the French position. This was true of silk export duties: whereas in the 1880s, Sienkiewicz had, with Paris's backing, frequently demanded that the Japanese government promise to abolish them, by 1894 foreign minister Hanotaux was informing Harmand that their removal was now regarded as a potential threat to the French silk industry rather than an advantage.[112] It was also partly true with regard to an even more fundamental issue. In 1874 one of Berthemy's main arguments in favour of the complete opening of Japan was that the existing situation compelled foreign merchants 'to submit to the ruinous mediation of native corporations which monopolise, with the assistance of the authorities, all branches of trade. . .'[113] By 1895 circumstances had so changed that the French vice-consul at Nagasaki, Steenackers, stressed the negative side of the approaching opening of the country. 'As for the merchants', he wrote, 'the right to buy silk and other products in the interior themselves will only take away the guarantee which the buyer previously had when working with Japanese intermediaries'.[114]

In recent years historians have been less inclined to stress the unfairness to Japan of the 'unequal treaties'. The treaties clearly did not prevent Japan's economic modernization and in some respects may even have stimulated it. Nevertheless, a judgement on them needs to take account of all their features, and how they actually worked. In this regard it should be noted that for many years French representatives interpreted the treaties to their advantage and did not hesitate to pounce on any Japanese infringement of its provisions, however slight. Yet in 1893, after thirty-five years of treaty relations, Sienkiewicz could write to the Quai d'Orsay:

In my reports of 24 July and 10 August, 1885 . . . I had the honour of calling the attention of the Department to the strange and dangerous privilege which the French enjoy in Japan, of not having to observe the laws of the police and public safety. Only being answerable to the consular tribunal, they can obviously not be published by penalties provided for by the Japanese laws, and, on the other hand, they do not have to fear the laws of the French police, the jurisdiction of which does not extend beyond the national territory.[115]

Clearly it was not only in their provisions but also in their execution that the 'unequal treaties' were unequal; and in the light of Sienkiewicz's report it is hard not to conclude that there was a distinct element of hypocrisy in the repeated insistence by France in common with other Powers that Japan must live up to its treaty obligations.

7

THE DECLINE OF
FRENCH INFLUENCE
1885–95

EVEN THOUGH the Franco-Chinese conflict over Indochina did
not lead to a Franco-Japanese alliance, it did focus the attention
of the French government on Japan in a new way. For the first
time there was a recognition in Paris that Japanese support in
East Asia might be of real value. Whether France would again
have need of it could not be predicted with any certainty, but
although a willingness to compromise had eventually led to the
settlement of both the French and Japanese disputes with China,
lasting stability seemed unlikely. This was clearly the view of
Sienkiewicz when, less than three months after the conclusion of
the Tientsin conventions, he referred in a dispatch to 'this Far
Eastern question which has opened up so abruptly and which
threatens to superimpose itself, so to say, on the old Eastern
question'.[1] Only weeks earlier, a similar awareness had led the
British foreign secretary, Lord Granville, to raise the possibility
of a further British alliance with Japan.[2] France, too, it might
therefore be argued, ought to have been awakened to the
potential advantages of good relations with Japan and to have
fundamentally reconsidered its policy.

Whatever the merits of this argument, in practice French
policy was to change only very slowly. Any serious attempt to
cultivate Japanese goodwill would have involved making
concessions over the revision of the unequal treaties, and a
move of this kind would have been perceived to be not only

economically disadvantageous but also – and probably more importantly – undesirable from the point of view of French prestige. Other factors were also involved, however, not the least of which was that there remained in the French legation in Tokyo, certainly until the end of the 1880s, a tendency to regard Japan as a third-rate power whose aspirations to modernize should not be taken too seriously.

This low estimate of Japan was usually implicit in French diplomatic dispatches but from time to time received explicit expression. In November 1885, for instance, in reflecting on mooted cabinet changes, Sienkiewicz wrote: 'The Japanese choose to rank themselves among European nations; in reality they are really Asiatics' His comment on the quality of the Japanese army the previous month was equally dismissive: 'Our officers, who were present at the manoeuvres two days ago, were profoundly surprised by the clear evidence of incapacity and ignorance which the Japanese generals gave'.[3] The officers to whom Sienkiewicz referred, incidentally, included Captain de Villaret, who in 1889, after the end of his service in Japan, in a book entitled, somewhat inappropriately, *Dai Nippon* (Great Japan), was still prepared to express the view that Japan could not expect to rise to a level higher than that of a Scandinavian country and would never be able to challenge China.

Criticism of Japanese deficiencies went beyond the political and military fields. In March 1886 Sienkiewicz also asserted that the Meiji government's education policy had been inept: it had, as he saw it, 'paid no attention at all to finding out which programmes would best meet the country's needs; it sought to learn what ones were followed in Europe and America and straightaway adopted them'.[4] From this he went on to claim that the Japanese masses had been almost completely untouched by the process of reform in the previous decade and a half, and that the quality of Japanese conscripts was doubtful. He buttressed these otherwise unsupported judgements by declaring that 'the present cabinet ministers, who all know the old régime and who have an idea of what the European countries are like, are perfectly well aware of the progress which Japan still has to make', condescendingly adding that 'one can admire the progress which Japan has made; one must certainly encourage its development. But from the point of view of education, commerce, agriculture and industry, this country will have to make very great efforts before playing in the Far East the role which is marked out for it today by those who know it only superficially'.[5] In the same dispatch he made it clear that he saw Japan not as a potential ally but as a country whose security was still in jeopardy. 'The great powers', he observed, 'have, in recent times, become very expansionist. Their operations bring them close to Japan. . . . Japan is making enormous sacrifices to provide itself with an army and a navy, but before its forces are organized, incidents can happen. Japan is so rich in islands'.

Because Japan was seen as weak and vulnerable, French diplomats found it natural that the Meiji government should adopt a low-posture foreign policy which primarily reflected concern at the possible actions of other countries, notably China and Russia. In reflecting on the Japanese agreement with China at Tientsin, for example, Sienkiewicz expressed the opinion that 'the Japanese government desired no more, with regard to Korea, than to arrange for itself an honourable retreat', supporting this by adding that 'Count Inoue in effect clearly declared to me that it would be very desirable that China should place Korea under an effective protectorate'.[6] In October of the same year he anticipated that Japan would continue to follow a peaceful, friendly policy toward all countries as long as its army and navy remained weak;[7] and in the following January he judged that 'the foreign policy of Japan seems to consist at present in avoiding with the greatest care all difficulty with Russia and with China'.[8] Nor was this view of things peculiar to Sienkiewicz. When, in 1888, chargé d'affaires Bourgarel suggested that Japan might have entered into a secret agreement with Germany to allow the latter the use of Japanese naval facilities in the event of war with another European power, he based his suspicions on 'the fear which Japan has at all times shown on the Russian side'.[9]

Occasionally French diplomats noted the continuing Japanese interest in a special relationship with China referred to by Japanese historians as the *Nisshin Teikei-ron* or the *Nishin Domei-ron*, and this too they tended to attribute to Japanese concern about their own weakness and the vulnerability which they shared with other East Asian countries. When, for example, Sienkiewicz sought in 1890 to explain what he saw as Japan's complaisant attitude towards China's reassertion of influence in Korea, he suggested that 'In reality it would be a question of creating between the two empires a union designed to preserve them both from the attempts which might be made against them by the Western powers, notably Russia'.[10] The existence of popular support for Sino-Japanese understanding did not escape his attention. In July 1891, for example, he noted the formation of an anti-Western society, with the Chinese minister to Tokyo as a member;[11] and in October, after he had discussed recent anti-foreign incidents in China with foreign minister Enomoto, he was led to conclude that 'if foreigners are the object, in the Chinese empire, of the open hostility of at least part of the population, their situation in the empire of the Rising Sun has been, for about four years, far from as favourable as it was formerly'. Posing the question of whether 'this double anti-European action should be connected with some general, but not easily grasped, cause whose influence is at work throughout the Far East', he came up with the answer that in the case of Japan the reaction was caused partly by resentment at failure to secure treaty revision and by the disturbing effects of indiscriminate Europeanisation, but also by 'the fear inspired by the expansionist tendencies of European powers'.[12]

Despite the customary allusion to Japanese fear of the Western powers, the focus in the above dispatch was more on the problems of anti-foreignism. In the course of the 1890s concern about this and about ideas of Asian solidarity became more common in French diplomatic assessments of Japan's foreign policy. In 1893, for example, Sienkiewicz noted that the Japanese deputy foreign Minister, Hayashi Tadasu, had appeared uneasy when informed of the French decision to blockade the Siamese coast;[13] and Sienkiewicz subsequently explained this reaction by observing that 'Siam is part of that Far East over which Japan has given itself the mission, platonic so far, of keeping watch with a jealous concern'.[14] Instead, however, of dismissing this as empty pretension, as he probably would have done in the past, the French minister evidently took it seriously, for he proceeded to warn that the Governor-General of Indochina should keep a close eye on the military mission which Japan had requested to send to the French colony. 'Under the pretext of studying the organization of our colonial troops in Cochin-China and Tongking', he cautioned the Quai d'Orsay, 'the mission would try to penetrate into Siam'.[15]

This was to be only the first indication of French concern about Japanese intentions in South East Asia. In November 1894 Sienkiewicz's successor, Jules Harmand, was writing in an alarmist vein that

> ... in effect, the Japanese government regards as an obligatory consequence of its accession to the ranks of the civilized nations, and as a preparation for the role which it intends to play in the future, the organization of an espionage agency embracing all the Far Eastern countries, and if I indicate this fact to Your Excellency, it is to beg him above all to put on their guard our colonial authorities in Indochina against being led by courtesy to accord too great facilities to Japanese travellers bearing recommendations who may ask to visit our military or naval establishments.[16]

The level of concern on the French side was yet more marked in May 1895, when Harmand was sufficiently disturbed by rumours of a Japanese-Chinese alliance plan to inform Hayashi that 'at this moment such a combination would attract thunder on to the Japanese empire and would ruin, before much time had elapsed, all the ambitions which it nourishes; I told him that nothing would do more to efface very promptly all the wrangling and rivalries of the European nations and in bringing their forces together against the two Oriental empires, with the prospect of a war, the outcome of which could not be doubtful'.[17]

This greater sensitivity towards Japan's possible ambitions was undoubtedly in part the product of Japan's demonstration of its military prowess in the Sino-Japanese War. Even before the war, however, there had been a growing awareness that Japan could not be taken so lightly as it had been. In particular, as early as 1890 Sienkiewicz's observation of the grand manoeuvres had led to a significant reappraisal of the Japanese army. Although he prefaced his remarks by stressing that 'without doubt the Japanese army is still far from matching up to a serious European army', he felt obliged to concede that when the officers who had received training in Europe reached the higher ranks, it would be a redoubtable force, and that already 'one can almost affirm that Japan is safe from invasion'.[18] This judgement was effectively repeated in 1893, when he observed that 'Japan seems to be applying a certain haste to becoming a very serious naval and military power'.[19]

Sienkiewicz sounded an even clearer warning note in January 1894, when he cautioned that Europe was too inclined to consider Japan 'merely as a country which produces an abundance of trinkets and curious or strange objects. Now, this country of forty million souls, strongly organized and powerfully armed, will soon be able to stand up to the immense China'. The situation, however, was complicated, in his view, by Japanese internal politics. Whereas up to that time, 'the opposition politicians were in favour of an attitude of resistance, of aggression even, and did not draw back in face of the prospect of a war, the Cabinet members were supporters of an entente with their powerful neighbour'. But the growth in importance of popular opinion left the future in doubt, and he concluded: 'this country seems bound to experience violent agitation in the future. What will be its effect on Japan's external action? Nobody can say'.[20]

Sienkiewicz's uncertainty about the impact on Japanese foreign policy of internal politics marks another significant change in French assessments of Japan between the mid-1880s and the mid-1890s. In 1885 it was possible to feel confident that the policy of caution which the Meiji government was seen to favour would remain essentially immune to the pressure of popular feeling because Japan was an oligarchy. Not only that, it was also an Oriental oligarchy. As Sienkiewicz put it, 'what characterises it is the mystery with which it surrounds itself; but perhaps it is also because it is almost impenetrable to all investigation that its prestige among the population at large is considerable'.[21]

While this was in one sense a disparaging judgement, it should not be assumed that French diplomats – or indeed most resident foreigners – were so critical of the Meiji system that they wished to see Japan emulate the most advanced countries of Europe by moving towards representative government. On the contrary, there were regular warnings – certainly in diplomatic dispatches and doubtless also in their discussions with Japanese leaders – of the dangers attendant upon any dalliance with democracy. One week before the promulgation of the Meiji constitution in 1889, for instance, Sienkiewicz condemned what he termed 'the enlightened classes' for demanding a constitution, attributing such rashness to either their illusions or vanity; and he insisted that, whatever its faults, the system which was about to be replaced had merit. 'While there was ample scope for personal ambitions, the Emperor, unchangeable, dominated the situation and maintained intact the principle of authority', he asserted, and he went on to ask, rhetorically, 'Will it be equally so in the future? One may doubt it'.[22] Moreover, in condemning the *Japan Herald's* criticism of the Emperor's behaviour after the attempted assassination of the Russian crown prince at Otsu in 1891, Sienkiewicz argued that 'foreigners as well as Japanese have a major interest in not impairing in any way the Mikado's prestige, in as much as it would not be impossible, were that power destroyed, that Japan might find itself a prey to anarchy'.[23]

However much French diplomats might have wished that Japan would not engage in political experiments, it proved difficult to dismiss these as merely superficial. Sienkiewicz himself, in the same dispatch in which he expressed his unhappiness about the introduction of a constitution, acknowledged that 'it would be puerile to wish to deny that Japan, if one takes into account the shortness of the period which separates it from its medieval era, has made, especially in the field of administration – and I use this term in its broad sense – astonishing progress'. He was evidently surprised by the fact that Japanese statesmen 'expatiate today on constitutional rule, necessary liberties, the best of constitutions, the rights of man and the citizen, all as if, in their youth, they had followed the courses of a school of political science. To such a point has this come that one would be tempted to believe that they are going to resolve the great political problems which have agitated Europe for so long'.[24]

In September 1890, as the opening of the first Diet session approached, Sienkiewicz continued to find the political situation remarkable, observing that 'Japan has for several months offered the curious spectacle of a Far Eastern country which, with an ever-increasing intensity, is agitated by political passions of which only the West can offer the equivalent',[25] and after the conclusion of the first Diet session he was still astonished by the speed with which the most extreme European ideas had spread. In other respects, however, he had modified his views. He now claimed not that the constitution had been brought in too soon but that it would have worked better if it had been introduced before 1887, at a period when the government's standing had still been high. Because it had led to intense conflict, with the Diet succeeding in reducing the budget by over six million yen, he felt that before long the government would either have to abolish the Lower House or form a political party of its own. Nevertheless, he was now prepared to envisage the possibility of a cabinet formed by the existing party leaders without undue alarm, since he argued that they would, if in power, have to modify their extreme attitudes.[26]

Such a readiness to contemplate a political party cabinet with equanimity was something of an aberration from Sienkiewicz's normal stance. In his belief that a shift in power was taking place, however, he hardly wavered; and he came to the same conclusion as recent historians when, in March 1893, he wrote perceptively that, 'if one looks more closely, one cannot fail to observe that, when everything has been taken into account, it is the Diet which, in this as in preceding sessions, has triumphed'.[27] Such an assessment may well have been passed down to the next French representative, chargé d'affaires Dubail, who just before the outbreak of the Sino-Japanese war, was to venture the suggestion that 'the cabinet of Count Ito has launched itself a little quickly into this adventure, desiring to seize the occasion to divert opinion from the internal difficulties which have led to the dissolution of the Lower House'.[28]

Slow though it was, there was clearly some increase in French awareness of Japanese progress and potential strength, and this at times prompted thoughts about the desirability of establishing and cultivating French influence in Japan. In May 1886, for instance, foreign minister Freycinet, responding to a dispatch from Tokyo in which Sienkiewicz had referred to 'the struggle for influence among the foreign representatives which intensifies each day', affirmed that 'you are right to draw attention to the fact that we ought to neglect none of these means of action to ensure the maintenance of French influence in Japan.[29] It is significant, however, that his emphasis was on defending the position which France had already won rather than on trying to extend it, and also that such expressions of concern from Paris about France's general influence in Japan are rare. The Tokyo legation, too, rarely displayed a broad interest in developing French influence. No really clear example of this can be found until late 1894 when, following Japan's initial victories against China, Harmand suggested that the conquest of Taiwan by Japan was not something to which France should object, and that 'it can show us in a still clearer manner all the value which our diplomacy ought in future – and without wasting time in achieving it – to attach to earning, more completely than our rivals, the trust of the Japanese government, and all the usefulness which a more or less definite entente with it can have for us'.[30]

For the most part French preoccupation with influence was either defensive, especially where any threat to French prestige was perceived, or limited, in that it was rather narrowly focused on particular individuals and institutions. A fundamental reorientation of French strategy was never considered, and in many respects French policy represented merely a continuation of previous attitudes. In no case was this more notable than in French sensitivity to the danger that German influence might oust that of France in the Japanese army. The general principle was succinctly reiterated by Commandant Berthaut when, in a report to the French minister of war, he referred to established policy as being that 'our influence must check that of the German officers in Japan, where we must conserve the place which rightly belongs to France and its representatives'.[31]

Such an aspiration relied on the strength of the legacy of French military assistance, and in particular on the pro-French sympathies of officers who had received a French training. Among such officers Prince Kanin stood out. He had been allowed, after some misgivings, to study at the École Supérieure de Guerre, the French staff college which had been founded, on the German model, in 1880, and after he returned to Japan, he presided over dinners held at the French legation for Japanese officers who had similarly been sent to France for advanced instruction.[32] Other members of branches of the Imperial family were also regarded as pro-French, including Prince Komatsu and his son, Prince Yorihito, who had also been admitted to a French military school.[33] The importance attached to these, mostly up-and-coming, officers was such that as late as 1895 the French military attaché, Lieutenant de Labry, felt able to assert that 'French influence is still considerable in the Japanese army; the number of officers having been in France, either in our schools or on study missions, amounts to more than a hundred colonels or commandants, occupying in general the most influential posts (Colonel Murata, aide de camp of the Chief of the General staff; Commandants Oshima and Watanabe, aides de camp of the Minister, etc.), several hundred officers speaking French, about half belonging to the artillery, the duties and establishment of which they direct'.[34]

French hopes of retaining influence within the Japanese army rested not only on the officers who had received French training but also on some who were regarded as sympathetic because they opposed the German-oriented Choshu clique which seemed to be emerging as the dominant group within Japan's military leadership. In 1886 military attaché Bougouin raised hopes by reporting the appearance of a new group, based mainly on officers from less favoured areas than Choshu and Satsuma, and headed by Prince Komatsu, a high-ranking officer, and Generals Horie, Miura and Soga. The latter three had all resigned recently rather than accept transfers out of Tokyo to lesser posts, but they had formed an unofficial opposition which Bougouin expected to have some impact, especially if General Tani supported it on his return from Europe.[35]

Bougouin's hopes proved to be over-optimistic, for the opposition faction was to fade away with the disbandment in 1889 of the society, the *Getsuyokai*, which had been formed to give their opposition the veneer of legitimacy.[36] Nevertheless, rivalries based on *han* origins within the Meiji political leadership continued to engage the attention of French diplomats because of their supposed implications for French influence. In 1887, for instance, chargé d'affaires Bourgarel anticipated that the return of Kuroda Kiyotaka and Saigo Tsugumichi from foreign trips would revive Satsuma opposition to Choshu; and he welcomed this not only because Kuroda had expressed admiration for France and maintained relations with the French legation but also because he regarded Satsuma as

186

hostile to Germany.[37] Bourgarel was also gratified that Tani (from Tosa) was criticizing the Choshu leadership from within the cabinet and had told him that Japan should be Japan and not the Germany of the Far East.[38] Not surprisingly, when Ito Hirobumi under pressure resigned as prime minister and was replaced by Kuroda in 1888, Bourgarel commented that 'from our special point of view . . . we can only applaud the change of front which has just come about'.[39]

Similar views were still being expressed in the mid-1890s, although when Harmand criticized a subsequent Choshu-led administration in 1895, it was not because of any supposed pro-German orientation but because he saw it as pro-British. 'I am led to think', he wrote, 'that as things stand now any new cabinet . . . would be more in our interest, as well as in the interests which we have with Russia, than the Ito cabinet, the head and several members of which are personally too engaged, and for too long a time, with the English to be able hereafter to extricate themselves from their influence'.[40] It was thus consistent with French long-term attitudes that when this third Ito cabinet gave way to one led by Matsukata in 1896, Harmand expressed his satisfaction: 'It cannot, however, be regarded as unfavourable to our views, for preponderance in it belongs incontestably to this great clan of Satsuma, which has always been seen as rather sympathetic to French ideas and influence, or whose members at least do not blush to recognize or recall the disinterested services which our country has rendered to theirs'.[41]

There were other indications of French interest in influencing Japan, but these were more sporadic in nature. When, as happened occasionally, the services of Frenchmen other than army officers were sought by the Meiji government, this was invariably seen as likely to be of value to France. In welcoming the request for the naval officer, Bertin, to be seconded to the Japanese navy, for instance, the Quai d'Orsay congratulated itself that 'our influence and our interests can only benefit from the appeal thus addressed by the Japanese government for the cooperation of one of our engineers, so Admiral Galiber, in accord with me, has authorized M. Bertin to accept the duties which have been proposed'.[42] And when the expertise of the legal expert, Gustave Boissonade, was required for an extended period, Sienkiewicz supported the request by pointing out that 'the ideas and the principles which he propagates in Japan can only be French ideas and principles, and hence we must see with a lively satisfaction that the Japanese government attaches so high a price to assuring itself of his services'.[43]

Concern for French influence can be seen in attempts to censor writing about Japan which might cause an adverse Japanese reaction. One such case involved the expulsion from Japan by Mgr. Osouf (on chargé d'affaires Collin de Plancy's advice) of a young Catholic priest whose letters home criticizing Japan had, indiscreetly in the diplomat's view, been published by his parents in France.[44] A similar fear of incurring Japanese displeasure was displayed by Harmand four years later when he complained to the Quai d'Orsay of 'the deplorable effect produced by the Letters from Japan which *Le Temps* publishes periodically'.[45] And on at least one occasion Harmand took preemptive action by means of informal censorship to avoid upsetting Japan, as he explained when he reported: 'I have believed it to be my duty to invite M. Villetard de Laguerie, correspondent of *Le Temps*, to throw a discreet veil over the excesses, which in any case were understandable, committed at Port Arthur, and to avoid singing the same tune as his colleagues in the British and American press, since I am of the opinion that this difference of attitude cannot be harmful to us'.[46]

FRENCH EFFORTS TO MAINTAIN THEIR MILITARY POSITION AND INFLUENCE

It will have been evident from the preceding survey that French diplomacy showed only limited interest in building up its influence in Japan, especially before the Sino-Japanese war, and that there was only occasional awareness of the need for a far-reaching and sustained effort to achieve an improved position. It is therefore not surprising that the pursuit of influence was uncoordinated and confined essentially to three areas. The first of these, both in the sense that it aroused the deepest concern and in that it was a carry-over from earlier years, was the military. Its significance was indicated by the fact that France was the first country to station a military attaché in Japan with the appointment in 1880 of Captain Bougouin, a member of the second French military mission.[47] The role of a military attaché, however, was inevitably limited; and the real key to the maintenance of French military influence was clearly seen to be the continuation of French involvement in the development of the Japanese army. If this proved not to be feasible, the next best outcome to be sought was that Germany should not step into France's shoes.

The fear that Germany might supplant France and deprive the latter of both its influence and the prestige which attached to it as the chosen model for the Japanese army had already been felt for some years before 1885. In 1882 chargé d'affaires Conte, reporting that a staff college might be set up in Tokyo, added: 'I must not hide from Your Excellency that there exist here, in the army as much as in the government, strong German tendencies, and that, if one were to let a favourable occasion escape, there would be the danger that the Tokyo cabinet, forgetful of services rendered, might call upon the German General Staff to organize its staff college'.[48] The fact that Conte could ask whether the French legation should offer Japan French good offices or wait for them to be asked for, however, suggests that at this stage French concern about German rivalry was tinged with complacency, and the expectation that Japan would turn again to the French army seemed to be justified in February 1883 when the new French minister, Tricou, informed the Quai d'Orsay that the Japanese minister of war, Oyama Iwao, had expressed his wish for France to send to Japan a captain, a lieutenant and two non-commissioned officers. This request, Tricou added, he could 'in the interest of our influence only support', the more so since Oyama, without being encouraged in any way, had insisted that he wanted to 'degermanise' the Japanese army and might seek further instructors.[49]

That there really was, nonetheless, cause for alarm was shown less than two months later when foreign minister Inoue informed Tricou that unexpected difficulties had led Oyama to shelve his plans.[50] The French received a temporary reassurance when in July 1883, on instructions from Paris, chargé d'affaires Viel-Castel approached Oyama directly and was told that Japan would ask France for new military instructors even though the signing of contracts would be deferred until mid-1884 and would be settled in Paris. Viel-Castel noted, however, that

Oyama's pro-French tendencies were meeting opposition from Choshu leaders, such as Ito and Inoue;[51] and it was soon apparent that while the minister of war still seemed intent on appointing French officers, the Japanese wanted individual instructors who would be fully under their control and not a new military mission. Sienkiewicz, as soon as he arrived, recognized this but was able to persuade himself that 'with time a veritable French military mission will find itself in being, in fact if not in name', and he took the view that any such concession would be justified if it enabled the German threat to be resisted: 'In sum, Germany, whose influence has made noticeable progress in Japan during recent years, covets a domain which up to now has morally belonged to us; it is for us to neglect nothing to keep it'.[52]

The question of foreign military instructors was not quickly resolved. The rivalry which it engendered was again explicitly referred to by Sienkiewicz in January when he expressed his belief that 'the major powers attach a very particular price to gaining the trust of the Mikado's government and especially to contributing to the organization of its army' and he warned that 'in France there is, perhaps, too great a disposition to nurture illusions about Japanese sympathies towards us'.[53] He urged, therefore, that contracts should be settled before the mission which Oyama was shortly to lead to Europe left France to visit other European countries; and the doubts which he evidently felt about either Oyama's true intentions or his ability to overcome opposition from less Francophile leaders were shown to have some justification in April 1884 when Captain Bougouin informed him that Oyama had been secretly charged with engaging in Germany an officer who would be at the same time a General Staff adviser and a professor at the Staff College.[54]

The seriousness of the Japanese decision was immediately perceived. Bougouin was sent to warn the leading Japanese generals 'in the most energetic manner' of the consequences which might result; and Sienkiewicz himself remonstrated with foreign minister Inoue. The French minister, in trying to explain to Paris what had happened, attributed the Japanese change of position to three factors, one being the triumph of Yamagata and Ito after Oyama's departure, another the fear of depending on a single Power, while the third was 'the excessive vanity which characterises the Japanese'.[55] That there might be good military reasons for turning towards Germany for military help was ignored. To prevent the decision from being implemented the French pleaded that the proposed employment of a German in the Staff College and Frenchmen in lower-level military schools was both unwise and incompatible with the dignity of French officers and that it was 'inadmissible that officers of different nationalities should be employed in the same service'. The crucial question, however, was whether France would sever all connection with the Japanese army if the Meiji government persisted in its intention; and a thinly veiled warning that this might happen was dropped by Bougouin when he told General Yamada that the Japanese mission's reception in Paris might be affected, that new French instructors might not be forthcoming, and that in future Japanese military students might not be admitted into French schools, regiments and military establishments.[56]

Whether such reprisals would have caused a revision of Japanese army policy is highly dubious. War minister Campenon may well have understood this, for he did not hesitate to sign contracts with Oyama in July for the engagement of two officers, Captain Berthaut and Lieutenant de Villaret, and two non-commissioned officers.[57] Four years later, chargé d'affaires Bourgarel was to imply that Campenon had done so in the hope that French influence might revive, but that this had been a mistake; and when Sienkiewicz returned to Japan in September 1888, he too argued that reprisals should have been taken in 1884 because of the Japanese government's breach of faith.[58] This criticism may have owed something to the benefits of hindsight, however, for it is not evident that at the time either Bougouin or Sienkiewicz pressed for such strong action. What does seem clear is that a difference of approach existed between Paris and the French legation in Tokyo, with the former placing the chief emphasis on the maintenance of French influence and the latter being primarily concerned with French prestige. It is conceivable therefore, that if Oyama had not led a mission to Europe and the issue had been settled in Tokyo, the French legation might have found some way of blocking a new arrangement which left their country in an inferior position.

Although concern for French influence prevailed in 1884 over sensitivity about French prestige, Campenon's decision by no

191

means removed the scope for conflict between the two objectives, and it was a continuing source of irritation for the French legation that Major Meckel, the German officer, was superior to Berthaut both in rank and in terms of his functional responsibilities. Despite this inequality, however, the French position suffered less than had been feared, for although Berthaut never acquired the influence which Meckel enjoyed, he did set himself up as a serious rival by including strategy as well as tactics in his lectures at the Military Academy and by encouraging higher-ranking Japanese officers to attend. As Sienkiewicz later put it: 'Instead of conducting a course for the students of the Military Academy, as he was required by the letter of his contract, he transformed into students the same academy's instructors. In a word, to the courses taught by Major Meckel he opposed courses which were as advanced and which have here had no less a following'.[59]

When, therefore, the Japanese sought to extend Berthaut's and Villaret's contracts in 1886, Sienkiewicz raised no objections but rather drew the flattering conclusion that the French officers 'must have given proof of exceptional merit for the Japanese government to wish to retain them'.[60] This assessment seemed to be justified by the Japanese request for another French officer to replace Villaret at the end of the latter's contract in 1887. However, when in the summer of 1888 Bourgarel approached Oyama with the intention of securing a further renewal of Berthaut's contract, he received the unwelcome news that military education was now the province of Yamagata as inspector-general (a post instituted at Meckel's advice); and he was subsequently taken aback by a letter from Yamagata stating that Berthaut's services would no longer be required after the completion of his current course of instruction.[61]

Although Yamagata's letter indicated that no other foreign officer would be appointed to the Military Academy, the ending of Berthaut's service was a major blow for France. Not only would his departure leave in Japan two French instructors who would be distinctly inferior to the two current German instructors, a situation which would be 'contrary to the dignity of France and of the French army', but the opportunity for exercising influence would be considerably diminished.[62] In these circumstances Paris was easily led to accept the French legation's recommendation for a strong response, and the only question was the exact nature of that response. In his initial reaction Bourgarel suggested that Berthaut should be allowed to remain beyond the term of his current contract to finish his course, as Yamagata was requesting and Berthaut himself wished. If, however, French hopes of Yamagata's removal had not been fulfilled by that time, then all the French instructors should be recalled and at the same time all Japanese military students in French schools, military establishments and regiments should be sent back to Japan. 'Such a resolution', he added, 'would moreover, we are all convinced here, have an immense and salutary reverberation in the Japanese army; it would equally have the probable consequence of preparing for our instructors an honourable return, the day when the "French party" is in its turn triumphant . . .'[63]

Bourgarel's proposal commended itself to the French government and in September the Quai d'Orsay informed Sienkiewicz (who had resumed his duties on 1 September) that its implementation had been authorized by the war minister.[64] Sienkiewicz, however, was both less sanguine about the possibility of French officers ever again playing a more important role in Japan than German officers and less disposed to alienate the Japanese government by carrying out reprisals. The latter, he objected, would be both undignified and, since the preference often shown to France in naval matters might be jeopardized, unwise. His advice, therefore, was to recall the French officers on the grounds of the Japanese government's breach of its commitments, and to inform Japan that no more Japanese military students would be allowed to complete their studies.[65] The French government again broadly accepted the advice from Tokyo and this time action was taken: on 20 November 1888 Sienkiewicz notified foreign minister Okuma of the decision and reported the latter's surprise.[66]

Various Japanese attempts were made to have the French officers serve out the remainder of their contracts, but the French stood firm. There was even some thought of toughening the French position on existing Japanese military students. In November foreign minister Goblet had left their treatment in suspense, and in December he inquired of Sienkiewicz whether Japan's attitude necessitated the students' return – while authorizing the French minister to reassure the Japanese that Prince Kanin and Prince Komatsu would be allowed to remain.[67] Already by this time, however, Bougouin had told General Tani that the Japanese students would be sent back, while Sienkiewicz, without going quite so far, stated when initially reporting his announcement of the French decision to Okuma, that he expected the Japanese government to recall them itself in order to preserve Japanese self esteem.[68] The Quai d'Orsay, however, took a more judicious attitude. Sienkiewicz was informed that 'we must limit ourselves to the recall of our military instructors: to go further would be to go beyond the proper measure, and we have no interest in pushing things to an extreme'. The French government's intention, it was added, was 'to permit these officers to pursue their studies without even requiring from them a formal request. . .'[69] Despite this apparent imposition of Paris's will, however, it was the legation's wishes which prevailed. Statistics produced by the military attaché in 1895 recorded that whereas there had been eighteen Japanese military students in France in 1888, there were only two by the end of 1889, and thereafter no more than one in any year.[70]

1888 marked a watershed, but the potential for French influence was not totally eliminated. In 1890 Sienkiewicz reported that the Emperor had personally thanked him for France's benevolent treatment of Prince Komatsu and Prince Kanin and the French representative commented that 'this démarche, which departs from normal custom here, seems to me to be motivated by the Emperor's keen desire to see Prince Kanin admitted to our École Supérieure de Guerre'.[71] The Quai d'Orsay's initial response was to regret that such a request would have to be rejected because of the confidential nature of the instruction; but in June foreign minister Ribot communicated the news that Prince Kanin had been admitted as an exceptional favour.[72] It was not long, though, before that decision was being questioned. In January 1891 Sienkiewicz discovered that, contrary to an assurance given to him in December 1888 by Oyama, it had now been decided to engage a new German officer for the Staff College; and not content with a mere protest, the French minister wished to know if his government was disposed to eject Prince Kanin.[73] Again a difference of approach between Paris and Tokyo was apparent.

In a marginal comment on the dispatch in which Sienkiewicz reiterated his suggestion someone at the Quai d'Orsay wrote 'But no!',[74] and in March Ribot confirmed and explained the rejection of Sienkiewicz's recommendation. To add insult to injury, the foreign minister stated that the admission of Japanese into French military schools was now to be encouraged as 'a means of propagating our influence in Japan'.[75] In Paris, at least, the resentment produced by the Japanese treatment of Berthaut appeared to have been forgotten.

In the light of the foregoing survey it would be hard to rate French efforts to maintain influence in the Japanese army highly. Admittedly, the odds were against the French in that pro-German tendencies were particularly noticeable in the Choshu leaders who were emerging as dominant figures after Okubo Toshimichi's assassination in 1878 and Iwakura Tomomi's death in 1883. Within the army, especially, the strong position of Yamagata Aritomo and the rising influence of Katsura Taro were factors which worked in Germany's favour.

Even allowing for this, however, it can be argued that the French achieved less than they might have. It is clear that French officers mostly tended to underrate their Japanese students and were unwilling, until Meckel showed the way, to satisfy Japanese interest in learning about strategy;[76] It also seems likely that the Japanese were more reluctant to engage French officers after 1880 because the French initially showed themselves anxious to send another military mission – with its own chain of command and at least some autonomy in deciding what it should do – rather than provide individual instructors. Nor was it likely, after the display of spleen in withdrawing all French instructors after Berthaut's contract was not renewed in 1888, that the Japanese army would be disposed to consider any further employment of French officers.

In retrospect, therefore, it would seem that the French sensitivity about the loss of dignity and prestige militated against a rational policy. On top of these failures to adjust to Japanese ambitions or to take a longer-term view, it also needs to be recalled that French diplomacy showed no awareness that Japanese decisions on military matters might be affected by policies in other areas; and it was probably no coincidence that when the German star was rising, Germany was taking an accommodating line on treaty revision. By contrast France was resisting concession at least partly because such a policy was supposed to be important to the maintenance of French prestige.

CHRISTIANITY AND THE RELIGIOUS PROTECTORATE

In 1885, when France had just suffered a significant setback to its military position in Japan, the prospect of extending its influence in another, broader, sphere suddenly opened up. The event which sparked new hope was the granting of an audience by the Emperor to Mgr. Osouf, the French vicar of northern Japan, on 12 September 1885. Osouf was the bearer of a letter from Pope Leo XIII which expressed the latter's admiration for the progress made by Japan and his appreciation of the religious liberty which missionaries had been allowed to enjoy since 1873.[77] In his report on the audience, which he had been instrumental in setting up, Sienkiewicz stated that he had told foreign minister Inoue Kaoru, when the matter was initially broached in August, that the Pope's action 'would contribute to making Japan rank among the Western powers', and he noted that 'Count Inoue, who has a sharp and quick mind, immediately perceived the consequences which the Pope's démarche might have for Japan and did not even attempt to disguise how pleased he was.' The potential significance of the event for France, however, was only indicated fully when Sienkiewicz quoted the words which Inoue had used on 10 September:

> Japan has borrowed everything from the West, its adminis-
> trative system, its laws, its military organization, and
> especially its teaching and education methods. In the near
> future it will be endowed, like the countries of Europe and
> America, with a constitution. One step more remains to be
> taken – to borrow in the same way from the West the
> Christian religion. It is prepared to accept this great change.[78]

This remarkable pronouncement – which was shortly afterwards reinforced by a similar expression of opinion by Ito
Hirobumi – provoked some lengthy reflections by Sienkiewicz.
He began by emphasising the need not to jump to mistaken
conclusions:

Would the Japanese government ministers have suddenly been struck by the superiority of Christian teaching or Christian morality? Not at all. In matters of religion they are absolutely indifferent. What has led them to show themselves favourable to Christianity is the fact that Europe and America profess this religion which is, as it were, the undiscussed attestation of the most advanced existing state of civilization. Furthermore, in Christian countries one does not encounter parcels of territory where foreigners enjoy extraterritorial privileges. That is, for the Japanese statesmen, the most appreciable consequence of Christianity.

On this basis, he concluded, it was possible to expect that the Pope's letter would prompt a declaration of complete religious freedom in the near future.[79]

A follow-up dispatch indicated that Sienkiewicz believed that whereas in other Eastern countries missionaries were mostly faced with unconvertible Moslems and had to contend for those groups which were originally Christian, in Japan they could set their sights on the whole population – 'a unique situation, if I am not mistaken, in modern times'. Moreover, the Meiji government's attitude was uniquely favourable also, so that 'were it not for a fear of stirring up the mass of Buddhists against them, the Japanese ministers would proclaim Christianity this very day'. All that was in doubt was the exact period when the Japanese would have become Christians – 'an event still distant, but foreseen and inevitable' – and which branch of Christianity the government would choose to adopt. Perhaps not surprisingly, he recorded that his Russian diplomatic counterpart, Davidov, thought that the Orthodox Church would be the most acceptable, whereas the British minister, Plunkett, though himself a Catholic, insisted, against Sienkiewicz's own arguments, that Roman Catholicism had no chance of acceptance.[80]

Some Japanese historians have lent indirect support to Sienkiewicz's views by stating that by the 1880s 'the Japanese realized that Modern Catholicism did not oppose monolithic government', that 'a catholic's attitude towards his Pope was similar to the attitude the Japanese Government wanted to inculcate with respect to the Emperor', and that in the secular realm their own power would be strengthened if the number of

Catholics increased.[81] In retrospect, however, the assumption by Western diplomats that the Meiji government would make Christianity an official religion appears excessively optimistic, if not naive. Even if they were unable to perceive in the mid-1880s (when the Japanese élite was mimicking Western fashions and high society more than at any other time) that Japanese modernization was a much more complex process than simple imitation of all things Western, they ought to have been aware that a strong core of traditional suspicion of Christianity survived, albeit in a less intense form.

The Japanese government also had good political reasons for not favouring too great a dissemination of Christianity. One was that it 'could easily provide an ideological basis for opposition to authoritarian government, as was indicated by the disproportionately large number of Christians among the activists in the People's Rights movement. Less obvious, but no less important, was the fact that in the 1880s the Meiji oligarchs were beginning to construct the so-called 'emperor system' (*tenno-sei*).[82] This meant that amongst other things the government consciously strove to inculcate unquestioning loyalty to the Japanese state and emperor by such means as the Imperial Rescript to Soldiers of 1882 and the Imperial Rescript on Education of 1890, and that in doing so they drew heavily on traditional values associated with Confucianism, Shinto and *bushido*. In such an environment there might be room for individual conversions but certainly not for the wholesale adoption of Christianity.

Whether or not Japan became a Christian country, Sienkiewicz attached considerable importance to the spread of Catholicism. This was not because of any religious enthusiasm on his part but rather because he saw it as a valuable channel for French influence. If Catholic missionaries became more numerous and more involved in primary education, they could, he felt, play a crucial role in disseminating a knowledge of French (which was currently being challenged by German as the second foreign language in Japan) and thus help to overcome the disadvantages which resulted from the relatively small number of Frenchmen in Japan. As Sienkiewicz put it, 'it is precisely because our modest colony is not sufficient to spread the French language that it would be so desirable that our missionaries should do here, as far as they can, what the religious orders do in the East'.[83]

There was, however, another dimension to the relationship between the expansion of Catholicism and French influence in Japan. For a considerable number of years – and more particularly since its 1860 treaty with China – France had asserted its right to protect Catholic missionaries, whatever their nationality, in East Asia. This religious protectorate had no juridical basis, but it had hitherto been accepted by the Vatican. In Japan it had not come into play because all the Catholic missionaries in that country were French and all were members of the Paris-based *Société des Missions Etrangères*. In China, however the situation was quite different. Catholic missionaries there represented various religious organizations and in many cases were not French. Not all of them were happy about the French protectorate, and the Franco-Chinese war of 1883–85 created apprehension that missionaries might suffer rather than gain in China from the French connection. Moreover, the governments of Germany, Belgium, Spain, Italy and Britain had each expressed dissatisfaction with the French protectorate. In addition, by 1885 Pope Leo XIII may also have felt that the arrangement had outlived its usefulness, for when the letter which he sent to the Chinese Emperor on 1 February of that year, thanking him for the scrupulous respect shown to Catholic missionaries during the current war, led to a proposal by the Chinese leader, Li Hung-chang, for the establishment of permanent diplomatic relations between China and the Vatican (thus removing France's key role as diplomatic intermediary), the Pope responded positively.[84]

That such a serious challenge to its religious protectorate was in the wind was not fully apparent to the Quai d'Orsay, and scarcely suspected by Sienkiewicz, when the Pope's letter to the Japanese Emperor was delivered by Mgr. Osouf in September 1885. Quite a strong hint of Leo XIII's intentions might have been discerned, however, in Osouf's formal address before the letter was ceremonially delivered: 'The Sovereign Pontiff . . . has desired to place himself in relations with Your Majesty, just as with the sovereigns of the other great world powers'.[85] Even if Sienkiewicz had been better informed, he might not have been excessively alarmed, for his attitude towards the religious protectorate appears to have been ambivalent. This may explain why his comments on the significance for it of both Osouf's audience and the possible religious developments failed to display his usual clarity of argument. While acknowledging that the influence which might be derived from the protectorate was not to be disdained, he expatiated on the fact that it existed in Japan only notionally, but then implied vaguely that it might now assume a certain importance:

> The Buddhists will defend themselves and struggle for their existence, and complications which today it is impossible to foresee may arise. It will then not be a matter of indifference that the protection which we owe to our French missionaries is still consecrated by the Holy See. . . . As for the direct advantages of our protectorate, they will result from the fact that among the future Christians the Catholics will clearly be the most numerous and that they will be directed by our missionaries who are themselves simultaneously administered and protected by us.[86]

Sienkiewicz's comments on the possible future relevance of the religious protectorate in Japan could not have been very convincing, but it was not the weakness of his reasoning which caused the Quai d'Orsay to give a critical reception to his report. Nor was it his view that 'from the political point of view, and it is from this point of view alone that we must consider the question, the protectorate's importance is directly proportional to the difficulties and challenges which it provokes'.[87] Rather it was the relative indifference towards the protectorate displayed by the French legation in Tokyo that concerned Paris. Although the French government was distinctly anti-clerical at home, it had no doubt whatsoever that the defence of the religious protectorate was essential. As the Quai d'Orsay informed the French legation in Pekin in 1880, 'if we were to renounce the protection of the Catholic missions, our role in the Celestial Empire would in practice be singularly diminished; any change in the policy which we have followed for twenty-four years would without doubt be interpreted as a sign of great weakness, for the abandonment without compensation of the right which we acquired at the cost of a war could in no way be understood'. Even worse might follow: 'there would be reason to fear besides that if France renounced its protectorate over the missions, it would be taken up without delay by some other power . . .'.[88]

Given such an attitude, it was evident that the French government would resist any move which might threaten its protectorate in Japan, however nominal this might be, lest its position should be weakened in Japan's more important neighbour. Hence, when Sienkiewicz remarked that 'it was with reason that M. Berthemy, about ten years ago, discontinued the practice of receiving the honours of the church', a rare marginal comment observed tartly: 'I disapprove of M. Berthemy. It was our right and we ought to maintain it'.[89] And when Sienkiewicz proceeded to argue that 'these honours, being the distinctive and manifest sign of the protectorate, are useful, necessary even, there where the religious protectorate is exercised in a constant and effective manner, but are difficult to justify any longer when the protectorate remains, so to speak, theoretical, and especially when the circumstances are such that it cannot even be challenged', another marginal comment again expressed disagreement: 'I do not understand this naturalistic conception of law at all. It is with its theory that Germany has made itself and become the arbiter of Europe'.[90] Foreign minister Freycinet immediately informed Sienkiewicz that France had no intention whatsoever of relaxing its protectorate over all Roman Catholic priests in the Far East.[91]

By February 1886 the French government had become fully aware of the seriousness of the challenge which the scheming of the Vatican and China posed to its established rights, and the next six months saw a determined counter-attack which culminated in August in a threat to withdraw its ambassador from the Vatican unless Leo XIII renounced his proposed decision to send to China an apostolic delegate with diplomatic functions. The appointment of such a delegate, Freycinet informed the ambassador, would not only be 'in the opinion of other nations a diminution of prestige and, consequently, influence for France' but also 'a demonstration of lack of goodwill, I was going to say an act of hostility, towards our country'.[92] The stiff French warning achieved its purpose; on 12 September 1886 the Pope suspended *sine die* the departure of the apostolic delegate, and although he never renounced the appointment formally, no papal representative with a diplomatic character was sent to China until many years later.

Such was the importance of the religious protectorate that it almost totally eclipsed any interest in increasing French influence through the spread of Catholicism in Japan. Apart from an expression of satisfaction at the Emperor's liberal views on religion, the Quai d'Orsay devoted almost all its attention to checking the threat to France's position on its Japanese flank. In February 1886 it informed the legation in Tokyo of the French government's surprise and indignation at the Vatican's negotiations with China, describing them as 'an enterprise which manifestly tends to put at issue one of the elements of our influence in the Far East'.[93] Even before Sienkiewicz received this, he showed that he was now more alert to the danger, since he had secured the Japanese government's agreement that the formal letter of response which the Emperor intended to send to the Pope would be presented to Leo XIII by the Japanese diplomatic representative to Paris.[94] Scarcely a week later, however, Sienkiewicz felt obliged to send a telegram warning that 'the Japanese government seems to wish, although it denies this, to enter into direct and lasting relations with the Holy See. Austria probably serves as intermediary'.[95] As his next dispatch related, he was trying to nip the idea in the bud by persuading the Japanese government that, on the one hand, a papal nuncio might show more zeal than French diplomats and revive the religious question in a controversial way and, on the other, that countries without France's experience and skill would try to establish their own protectorates.[96]

By September, however, Sienkiewicz's growing awareness that the religious protectorate had become difficult to defend led him to express doubts which hitherto had been latent or disguised: 'Is it not permitted to ask oneself if it suits our interests to maintain a doubtful situation which will soon be worth only enemies and difficulties of all sorts?' Perhaps fortunately for Sienkiewicz, this almost heretical questioning of the status of such a sacred cow only reached Paris after the Vatican had given way on the principal issue. A pencilled comment on his dispatch reads: 'Write to M. Sienkiewicz to make known to him how the affair has turned out. It is profitless to discuss his report – for all that it is very discussable'.[97]

The frustrating of the Vatican's bid to emancipate itself from French tutelage in China did not actually resolve the question of the Meiji Emperor's reply to the Pope's letter, for the Japanese government clearly did not wish to encourage French belief in the validity of a protectorate which had never been exercised meaningfully in Japan, and it was thus reluctant to transmit the Imperial message through its minister in France. Moreover, it also sought to use the content of the communication to further its purpose. Bourgarel learned in December 1887 that, in addition to the previously announced inclusion of a formal assurance that the old anti-Christian edicts were now officially abrogated, the still undelivered letter would now include the following sentence: 'We will be pleased to see the Head of Your Church in Our country address himself directly to Our Foreign Minister whenever he has to make a communication to Us on your part, or an arrangement to make with Us'.[98]

Seeing this not as the result of foreign scheming but as an expression of Japan's desire for complete independence and equality, Bourgarel made no protest. But when, subsequently, the letter was delivered by none other than the Japanese minister to Germany, Sienkiewicz could not refrain from recrimination – first by letter from Paris to foreign minister Inoue; then, when he returned to Tokyo, to Inoue's successor, Okuma, who absolved himself of responsibility by blaming his predecessor.[99] The French minister wisely did not pursue the matter, which in any case was effectively put to rest in February 1889, when the Quai d'Orsay made known that despite German and Italian attempts at interference, France had received assurances from both China and the Vatican that they accepted the existing situation.[100]

It was only after the question of the religious protectorate had been settled that the more fundamental issue of the growth of Christianity in Japan again attracted serious attention. In September 1889 the Quai d'Orsay sent Sienkiewicz a request for information which was based, rather curiously, on the understanding that 'it seems to be feared in the Vatican that Russian Orthodoxy may succeed in having itself adopted by the Mikado's Government: thus the Pontifical Court is extremely desirous that we exert ourselves to outdistancing rival confessions and bringing about the triumph of Catholicism'. The minister in Tokyo was told that 'the views of the Holy See are in this matter perfectly in accord with the interests of France in the Far East: it is in effect evident that our influence can only be affected favourably by the development of the Catholic religion in the Empire of Japan', and he was reminded of the hopes of success which had been expressed earlier.[101]

Sienkiewicz's response demonstrated how greatly his expectations had changed in four years. As he saw the situation, the authority of the Meiji government had been so eroded, mainly as a result of quarrels among the oligarchs themselves, that even if they still favoured Christianity, any official action would have much less effect than it would have had in 1885. The recent reaction against foreign influence, however, made any such action unlikely. As for the speculation in Europe about Russian Orthodoxy, he dismissed it with the remark that it had never worried French missionaries. 'What deserves, with infinitely more reason, close attention', he added, 'is that emancipation of mind which is beginning to reveal itself in Japan and which the opening of the Diet will doubtless help to develop in a manner which could become disturbing'. He held that missionaries should concentrate on individual conversion, but he noted that although there were now 40,000 Catholics in Japan, the number of Protestant converts had recently been increasing more rapidly, partly because the American missionary societies had far larger resources. His pessimistic conclusion was that Protestantism had the best prospects of eventual success, especially if a Japanese Protestant should found a new, purely Japanese, sect.[102]

FRENCH EDUCATION AND THE FRENCH LANGUAGE

If religion was seen as the major potential source of influence, apart from the army, in the late 1880s, it was education on which French hopes mainly rested in the 1890s. Here again French interest dated back to an earlier period, at least to 1864 when the Quai d'Orsay transmitted to Roches a request from the Ministry of Education for information as to the extent of French teaching in Japan.[103] Such interest was relatively casual, however, and especially after the overthrow of the Bakufu, the whole question of encouraging French teaching and the French language in Japan was ignored. At the end of the 1870s, admittedly, Geofroy began to complain of the prevalence of the English language; and in 1882 Conte noticed and lamented that despite being necessary for attendance at the military school and the study of law at Tokyo University, French was steadily losing favour.[104] Until the arrival of Sienkiewicz, however, French ministers did not perceive the progress of the French language to be of sufficient significance to justify diplomatic action.

Sienkiewicz himself had been in Japan for two years before he first evinced any concern. Then in his report on Mgr. Osouf's audience, he expressed regret that the French missionaries had inadequate funds for educational purposes and stated that, as a partial solution, he had arranged with Osouf to introduce into Japan one of the orders which devoted themselves to teaching.[105] He had good hope of success in such a venture since, despite the progress of German, French was still the language most studied after English. However, it took Osouf over a year to find an order – the *Congrégation des Marianites* – willing to take a chance on what was inevitably a somewhat hazardous commercial venture;[106] and in the meantime German was perceived to have made more headway than French.[107]

At the end of the 1880s this relatively casual approach was abandoned, at least by the Tokyo legation. The first substantial report by Sienkiewicz was dispatched to Paris in December 1889,[108] and thereafter Sienkiewicz, his successors, and various French teachers regularly grappled with the issue of how best to promote the French language in Japan. The fundamental problem was the very limited extent of the existing provision of French education. This consisted of three main elements: the small elementary schools established by missionaries, which numbered 66 at the end of 1889, had 3,400 pupils (compared with 10,000 pupils for American missionaries), taught the basic Japanese primary school curriculum (but with the catechism after hours) and received a 600-franc subvention from the legation; the Marianites, whose *École de l'Etoile du Matin* (Morning Star School) catered for the sons of the wealthy and influential, both Japanese and foreign, and had only 11 teachers and 60 pupils in 1888, but who had major expansion plans; and two schools – the *École du droit français* (School of French

Law) and the *École de langue française* (French Language School) – which had been founded by the *Sociéte de langue française* and for which the latter had been allotted by the Japanese government a subvention of 5,000 yen to encourage the study of law and to pay its two teachers of French.[109]

The basic issue for the French was what segment of Japanese society and what stage of Japanese education France should attempt to influence. Arrivet, a teacher at the First [Tokyo] Higher School, ignored the Marianites' school when in 1891 he put forward the suggestion that the *École de langue française* should be the focus of attention because it provided the best route to higher specialized education.[110] Sienkiewicz too, although he had more sympathy for the Marianites and wanted to encourage French education at all levels, emphasized the need for more students with French language qualifications to enter the First Higher School and then go on to the Imperial University in Tokyo, where the study of French language, history, literature and philosophy had recently been expanded, thanks partly, he claimed, to his own efforts. To rely on a combination of private initiatives and on the Japanese government's actions, however, no longer seemed sufficient, and Sienkiewicz consequently urged his own government to reverse the suppression of the legation's previous small subventions by the commission of the Chamber of Deputies and provide financial support at the fairly modest level of 1,800 francs for missionary schools and 6,000 francs for the *École de langue Française*, with a strict surveillance being placed on the employment of these funds.[111]

Scarcely a fortnight later this suggestion had to be reconsidered when Sienkiewicz was informed, prematurely as it happened, that the *École de langue française* might be closed down. As an alternative he suggested the provision of scholarships to encourage students to enter the French section of the First Higher School.[112] This idea was supported by Collin de Plancy, the chargé d'affaires in 1892, but he added the new suggestion of a regular publication in the French language for Japanese readers.[113] Thanks largely to the support of the *Société de langue française*, such a periodical, the *Revue Française du Japon*, appeared the same year; and the energetic involvement of Boissonade meant that it did not lack for contributions initially.

These various recommendations were not unconnected with the belief, which Collin de Plancy reported, that French had not only been outstripped in popularity by German but was even being rivalled by Italian. In August 1892 foreign minister Ribot showed that the French government shared his concern by promising 4,000 francs (for one year) for the *École de langue française*, together with 500 francs each for missionary schools and the Marianites.[114] That seemed, for the time being, as much as could be hoped for, but in 1894 Sienkiewicz sought an increased subvention of 8,000 francs for the *Société de langue française* and 1,500 for missionary schools, only to be told that his request had come too late to be included in the next Budget.[115] Three months later, however, a new report, produced by Michel Revon, a young professor of law at the Imperial University, provided a detailed and convincing warning that although the position of French in the University had improved as a result of its being made, with German, one of the two principal languages in the Law Faculty, there remained cause for anxiety: 'unfortunately, it must be acknowledged that we are not ready, and that great efforts will be needed to raise the French language, in the Higher Schools and others, to the high level of the new role which it is called to play in the University'.[116] After receiving this foreign minister Hanotaux requested Harmand to suggest practical measures for remedying the situation.[117]

Not surprisingly, Harmand sought advice from Revon and Arrivet. The former, concerned that the private French schools had succeeded in getting very few of their pupils into the five Japanese higher schools, felt that France's efforts should be concentrated on the state school system, since this provided the main route to the University. To introduce French courses at all levels was 'simply a matter of undertaking to persuade the Japanese authorities', who would 'always be disposed to develop French studies if one proves their usefulness to the country'.[118] Arrivet agreed with much of this. He, too, advocated the virtual abandonment of help to private schools, including those run by the missionaries, which he refused to take seriously; but in contrast to Revon he advocated firstly the establishment of a club for French-speaking Japanese; secondly, the improvement (aided by French subsidy) of the *Revue*

Française du Japon, which had declined since Boissonade's departure in 1894; and thirdly, the establishment of bursaries in France or Indo-China for Japanese students.[119]

Neither of these reports had any immediate effects, for Hanotaux, while commenting that he regarded the matter as very important, decided to request Harmand's opinion before taking action,[120] and the minister in Tokyo was too preoccupied with the Sino-Japanese war and its aftermath to formulate considered conclusions until January 1896. When he did, he showed himself in agreement with Arrivet in favouring the establishment of a new Franco-Japanese club, which he hoped would have several members from the Imperial Family, and the improvement of the *Revue Française du Japon* – or at least its reorientation as a more effective organ of French propaganda. As he saw it, the best hope for the French language lay in the existence of a pro-French élite. 'Our ambition', he wrote, 'must consist of influencing Japan *through ideas*, and we will arrive at that only through the medium of a certain number of superior men, drawn from the heart of the nation, rather than by the direct action of teachers'. Nevertheless, he also considered it essential to extend to as many Japanese children as possible the teaching of French at an elementary level and to send to France on scholarships those who showed the greatest promise. Japanese who spent several years in France, he asserted, could be considered 'our natural clients, the willing partisans or unconscious propagators of our intellectual and moral influence'.[121] His plea, however, fell on stony ground; and in 1897 the hopes of propagating French culture suffered another blow with the demise of the *Revue Française du Japon.* In effect the French government was not prepared before 1898 to offer the sort of support which could have compensated for the relatively low number of Frenchmen in Japan and for the rising political, military and scientific importance of Germany.[122]

What exactly was hoped for from the propagation of the French language and culture? One aim was commercial advantage. In April 1894, for instance, Sienkiewicz, in reporting that some the students of French at the First Higher School were seeking the establishment of a chair for a French professor of civil engineering at the University, noted that it 'could have, at some time, a serious importance for our industry'.[123] Revon, too, maintained that there would be concrete benefits:

> There is no need to insist on the very important practical consequences which a larger development of French studies at the University could have. In the Faculty of Law these studies would in due course give us valuable support in the Government, the magistracy, the bureaucracy, the great bodies which direct the public life of the Empire; in the Faculty of Medicine they could produce, apart from a desirable extension of our scientific reputation, practical results for the trade in pharmaceutical products and medical instruments; in the Faculty of Civil Engineering they will provide awareness of our machines, our boats, our constructions of all kinds, and, to cite only one example, one might see returning to France the large orders for warships which are now going to England.[124]

Such references were less frequent, however, than more general expressions of French concern for influence, coupled often with an open desire for admiration and a keen ambition to be emulated. Revon himself, for instance, in speaking of French studies in the Faculty of Literature at the University, claimed that 'they could have a profound moral influence on the mind of the young, and by instilling a love of our literature, they will instil a love of our national spirit and genius, brother of the national spirit and genius of Japan in so many noble facets'.[125] Harmand's language in 1896 was less lyrical, but he too, clearly revealed his belief that cultural links would have a wider value when he urged that 'it is undeniable by any Frenchman that our own country has the greatest interest in attracting to it, in view of its future political and even economic action in Japan, the greatest number possible of outstanding young men and in thus removing them from the literary, scientific and artistic attraction exerted by Germany'.[126] François, a teacher at the Military Academy, expressed similar aims, even though they were stimulated by the fear that Japan, having proved itself by its victory over China, might be tempted into an anti-French alliance by the promise of Indo-China. 'These formidable uncertainties are to be anticipated', he warned, 'and from today we must take, in order to exorcise them, all the necessary measures, both in our Indochinese possessions and in Japan, by creating for ourselves sympathies, and if possible, friends, who by the study of our language will have learned to know us, to judge us themselves, to see us with their own eyes'.[127]

French concern for the expansion of the study of the French language and for a wider and deeper knowledge of French culture clearly increased in and after 1894. This was a logical result of the Sino-Japanese war, as François indicated when he wrote that 'this question of influence has suddenly assumed a considerable importance since the brilliant military successes won by Japan over China'.[128] Nevertheless, in practice the Quai d'Orsay was not very responsive to its representatives' suggestions of ways in which the situation might be improved or remedied.

Why this should have been so is not easy to determine. Budgetary considerations cannot be completely disregarded but these alone should not have prevented the expenditure of a few thousand francs more a year if the objective had been regarded as important. More plausibly, perhaps, it might be argued that the desire to extend French influence in Japan was over-shadowed in the early and mid-1890s by a much higher priority in French foreign policy – the achievement and maintenance of alliance with Russia. While the Quai d'Orsay was not prepared to abandon hope of maintaining French influence in Japan, it clearly made little sense to invest heavily in schemes which could easily be rendered ineffective if French support for Russian policy towards Japan damaged France's image and prestige there. That such a choice was a real one was demonstrated by the Triple Intervention of 1895.

THE FRANCO-RUSSIAN ALLIANCE AND THE TRIPLE INTERVENTION

From well before1895 there were indications in the relations between the French and Russian legations in Tokyo that the two countries were drawing together. Indeed, as early as 1887 it was the Russian minister to Japan who informed the French of the contents of the Emperor's letter to the Pope.[129] Moreover, when this new relationship was developing into alliance in the early 1890s, the awareness that Russia currently favoured a generous policy towards Japan may have encouraged France to make its reluctant concessions over treaty revision.[130] However, Japanese distrust of the Tsarist empire remained acute, and Sienkiewicz was complaining as early as 1891 that French friendship with Russia, although not yet confirmed by a formal alliance, was compromising France's position.[131] His misgivings, however, carried scant weight with the French government, for local considerations mattered little beside Russia's ability to rescue France from its long isolation. That this was so was to be abundantly proved by the Sino-Japanese war.

When Japan went to war with China over control of Korea in late July 1894, the French were not greatly concerned. Their attitude had already been indicated by Sienkiewicz six months earlier: 'far from taking the lead in conflicts with China and the powers which support China in Korea, we have the greatest interest in avoiding complications in the whole Far East and in departing from a strict reserve only where this may be required by concern for our dignity'.[132] Inaction was also seen to be in France's interests by Harmand. Hardly had he arrived when he was expressing his personal opinion that 'we have substantial interest in seeing China occupied for a long time in the North on account of Indochina and that we can let events follow their course, while contenting ourselves with benevolent neutrality towards Japan'.[133]

Harmand soon discerned other potential advantages in the war. One was the possibility that Russia would have the opportunity to strengthen its position in northern China by securing a port which could be used in war. Such a development, he commented, 'could only be profitable to us; it is England alone which will complain, and the recriminations of our eternal and hateful adversary will never be painful to us'. Another was the prospect of increased exports of war materials, not to mention the chance for Indochina to supplant China as a supplier of rice to Japan. 'For those reasons and for others', he concluded, ' . . . I judge that we have more to gain than to lose in the struggle which has begun, that our interest must lead us to desire its prolongation and even its aggravation and that, if we can, without openly violating the rules of neutrality, favour one of the two adversaries, it is for Japan that we ought to keep all our encouragement'.[134]

Harmand's attitude goes a long way towards explaining why France was perceived as being pro-Japanese by the British chargé d'affaires in Tokyo, Le Poer Trench, who on 14 September commented on the friendly and cordial relations between Japan, Russia and France adding that 'It is now generally believed that there must be some secret understanding between Russia and Japan and that France has lately been invited to become a party to it'.[135] However, the French minister's sympathy for Japan reflected his particular experience as a colonial administrator in Indochina and was not fully shared by the Quai d'Orsay, where his reference to 'benevolent neutrality' was queried. That there was some difference in approach between Paris and Tokyo was indicated by the fact that the French government joined in the initial, but ineffective, diplomatic move by the major powers to persuade China and Japan to resolve their dispute peacefully, and also by its at least token support in August for a Chinese proposal that Japanese forces should evacuate Seoul and withdraw to southern Korea as a condition of opening bilateral negotiations.[136] In both cases, significantly, France followed the line taken by Russia, just as it did when declining to join in British démarches on 10 July and, more importantly, 6 October.[137]

With the unexpected military success of Japan, however, the Tsar's government moved away from its initial waiting position towards a policy of intervention intended to prevent Japan from making continental gains which might hinder Russian future advances. The first intimation of this change came at the end of January 1895 when Russia proposed that Britain and France join it in making separate, but identical, communications to the Japanese government expressing the hope that the peace talks which the Chinese government had now agreed to engage in would be brought to a rapid conclusion.[138] Harmand made no open objection to this démarche, which was carried out in a non-threatening manner, but a few weeks later he pointedly reported that rumours of an alliance between Russia, France and Britain to limit Japanese conquests had dealt a blow to the popularity which he had earlier been congratulating France on acquiring.[139]

The conclusion of a peace treaty at Shimonoseki in April 1895 made it impossible for French policy any longer to embrace both the regional considerations stressed by Harmand and the broad international perspective of which the Quai d'Orsay was far more conscious. On 8 April Russian foreign minister Lobanov, aware that the German government was now not only ready but eager to check Japan's gains (as well as align itself with Russia in the hope of weakening the newly forged Franco-Russian alliance) invited France to participate in a joint intervention, the main objective of which was to deprive Japan of the foothold which it had just secured in Manchuria by pressurising it to return the Liaotung peninsula to China. The French government quickly agreed, its sense of priority being clearly shown by foreign minister Hanotaux in a telegram of 9 April to the French chargé d'affaires in St. Petersburg: 'Although, in the question of the cession of southern Manchuria and Port Arthur, France has no immediate interest, its alliance considerations rank first among its concerns'. How far it was prepared to go was less evident. Hanotaux expressed the hope and expectation that an exhausted Japan would give way in the face of a combined, albeit amicable, démarche; if it was necessary to have recourse to force, that would, he recognized, be a much more serious and complex matter, but he did not envisage such an eventuality.[140]

At this stage, Hanotaux was not yet aware that Germany had made clear to Russia its intention of joining in the proposed intervention, and when he discovered this on the next day, he was both surprised and uneasy.[141] He was even more unhappy when the British government, whose involvement he had described as decisive on 9 April, unexpectedly declined the Russian invitation; and after failing to secure a British change of mind, Hanotaux momentarily wavered to the extent of suggesting that it might be sufficient to have Japan neutralise the strategic points which it was insisting upon retaining.[142] Moreover, before acting he sent Harmand, on 19 April, a telegram which read: 'We may be led to participate in a démarche by the powers with the object of advising Japan to renounce certain of its demands, and notably Port Arthur. Make known to me by telegraph the probable impression in Tokyo and your personal opinion'.[143] Harmand's response, not surprisingly in view of his previous attitude, emphasized the desirability of caution: 'Judge that prescribed démarche is very delicate and has little change of achieving its end even made with energy for publicity given by Japanese government to conditions, the latter very badly received by a national party, renders withdrawal dangerous or impossible for it. Would be better if possible to advise China not to ratify than to act by ourselves'.[144]

The chance that Harmand's view might influence his government's thinking, however, was even less than it might have been, because Hanotaux's 19 April telegram had strangely taken two days to arrive in Tokyo and Harmand's response was thus only sent on 21 April. By the time the latter reached Paris on the following morning, the crucial decision had been taken. Indeed on 20 April Hanotaux had already sent a second telegram which informed the legation in Tokyo that the Russian government had taken the initiative in concerting a démarche and that the French government had agreed to participate. For Harmand's guidance, the exact words of the telegram from St. Petersburg to the Russian minister were included: 'We find that possession of the Liaotung peninsula would be a permanent threat to capital of China and would render illusory independence of Korea; in consequence would become a perpetual obstacle to any lasting peace in Far East'. The French minister was instructed to reach an understanding with his colleagues as to how to give the démarche a most friendly character.[145] Clearly the need to maintain the alliance with Russia had prevailed.

Although the decision had been taken, it was not readily accepted by the French legation. In acknowledging his receipt of a third telegram which Hanotaux had sent on 22 April reiterating his instruction of two days earlier, Harmand stated rather equivocally: 'I am in constant relations with two colleagues and confirm to you their hesitation and mine'.[146] His uncertainty was short-lived, however. Later the same day he dispatched another telegram reporting that 'the German minister having received this evening the order to proceed prescribed démarche as soon as I received my instructions, we had no more hesitation possible', and he confirmed that the three diplomats had gone to see the deputy foreign minister together. He congratulated himself on having, in contrast to the German minister's brusque manner and insensitive language, conveyed his communication in a sufficiently friendly manner 'to retain Japanese trust and not offend Japanese self-esteem'.[147]

Harmand's approach may have been more amicable than Hanotaux wished, for his language did nothing to discourage the hard-line elements within the Japanese government from hoping that if Japan held out against concession, the unity and resolve of the three interventionist Powers might collapse. While Japanese leaders debated inconclusively, Western governments became more anxious. On 28 April Hanotaux showed his concern in another telegram: 'I have no news of the concerted démarches. Can you not give me some idea of what their result will be?'[148] To this plea Harmand only replied that the Japanese government had asked for more time for reflection when the three foreign representatives had made another démarche on 29 April, but he expressed his hope of a satisfactory solution when foreign minister Mutsu Munemitsu returned to Tokyo in a few days.[149] It is clear, however, that Harmand's attitude continued to give the Meiji leaders some encouragement, especially when, on 1 May, Japan offered to give up most of the Liaotung peninsula provided it was allowed to retain the part which included Port Arthur. In passing on a Japanese request for Hanotaux' good offices in persuading the Russian and German governments that any new concession was politically impossible for the Japanese government, Harmand did not conceal his own feelings: 'In consideration of the advantages which this honourable commission can give us, I join my entreaties to [the Japanese government's] and I judge that solution offered is acceptable'.[150]

Hanotaux would not himself have been entirely unsympathetic to Harmand's advocacy, for he had already on the same day made a vaguely favourable response to a similar approach by the Japanese minister in Paris, Sone Aresuke.[151] His apparent willingness to compromise would have been strengthened by a telegram from the French admiral in East Asia, Admiral Beaumont, warning that a naval demonstration could easily, given the high feeling on both the Russian and Japanese sides, escalate into war.[152] Once again, however, France bowed to the wishes of its partners in the intervention. A draft telegram from Hanotaux to Harmand (which was apparently not sent) stated that 'everything leads to expect that the Powers will maintain their original demands' and included the interesting assertion that 'there are certainly in Europe men in politics who seek an opportunity to destroy the nascent strength of Japan'. Hanotaux took care to add that 'our sentiments are different, Japan has understood this'. The most significant sentence, however, was the one which followed: 'But we will follow the line of conduct dictated by our general policy'.[153] That French policy towards Japan had hardened is shown by another telegram which was evidently drafted by Hanotaux personally on the same day and was presumably intended for St. Petersburg, although again it was not sent. For the first time, it went into detail about naval action, including the blockade of Japanese ports.[154] On the following day Harmand was informed that he must insist on Japan's cession of the whole Liaotung peninsula and on 5 May the Meiji government gave way.[155]

The aftermath of the Triple Intervention confirmed not only that France no longer felt able to pursue its own interests in East Asia when they ran counter to Russian policy but also that Russia was little inclined to offer reciprocal support. Having dutifully gone along with Russia's and Germany's insistence on the return to China of the Liaotung peninsula, France now hoped to gain for itself commitments from Japan with regard to Taiwan and the Pescadores, the islands off the southern China coast which had been ceded to Japan at Shimonoseki and which were regarded as lying within the security perimeter of French Indochina. Some thought had been given by France to the inclusion of its own desiderata in the three Powers' demands in April and early May, but the idea had been set aside because it would have complicated the intervention.[156] As soon as Japan had accepted the three Powers' 'friendly advice', Hanotaux sent Harmand a list of points to be pursued in the forthcoming negotiations on the questions which remained outstanding. The most important were a guarantee that the Formosa channel, the strait between Taiwan and China, be kept free for navigation and that Japan should further commit itself not to fortify the Pescadores.[157]

Although Hanotaux was unaware of the fact, discussions between Russian and German diplomats in Europe had already shown that neither of France's partners shared its concern about the Formosa channel or the Pescadores and that both were anxious to avoid new demands which might present Japan with a pretext for backing away from its commitment to evacuate the

Liaotung peninsula.[158] As it turned out, their lukewarm attitude did not affect the Formosa channel proposal since the Japanese government was preoccupied with the question of increasing the indemnity which it was to receive from China and readily gave an assurance that it recognized the channel as an international waterway not subject to its own exclusive control.[159] To the demand for the non-fortification of the Pescadores, however, the Japanese leadership was less amenable, and Harmand understandably blamed his fellow-diplomats for his failure to overcome Japanese resistance on this point : 'The two ministers, but especially the Russian minister, appear to believe – and let it be too easily seen – that France alone is interested in this matter'.[160] Eventually France had to be satisfied with a Japanese promise never to cede either Taiwan or the Pescadores to another power – very clearly a second best.[161]

The Triple Intervention was an important landmark in Japan's relations with the Western powers. The Meiji government was given a dramatic lesson in *realpolitik*, and learned – or was provided with new proof – that Western protestations of friendship were not to be relied upon, especially if great power interests were involved. France did not escape Japanese resentment; and although Harmand continued to try to cultivate friendly relations and occasionally managed to persuade himself that Japan was less disenchanted with France than with other European countries, he was compelled to register a marked deterioration in the French image. In January 1895 he had been able to report that the *Yomiuri* newspaper was proclaiming that 'on every occasion the great voice of France, in advance of that of any other nation, has made itself heard on our side', and that the *Kokumin* was urging that 'it is absolutely necessary that Japan in its turn finds a way of showing clearly both its friendly feelings towards France and its gratitude'.[162] By contrast, in May he was deploring that most Japanese, in expressing their hatred and disappointment after the Triple Intervention, did not distinguish between Russia, Germany and France.[163] Even worse was the *Nippon's* criticism – made more difficult to bear by the fact that it was essentially true – that France's 'participation in the work of intervention in the Far East must be regarded as the result of its subservience to Russia and Germany'.[164] Attacks such as this were by July 1896 to lead

Harmand to conclude that, far from diminishing, Japan's bitterness towards France, as towards Russia, had actually grown deeper. 'Even the upper-class Japanese more and more keep their distance from us, and despite all the efforts which I make to attract them I am obliged to state that their visits are becoming rarer and their manner less open, even among the military officers'. France's situation, he felt, had suffered more than Germany's since 'we are at present regarded as the definite allies of the Russians and as determined to espouse all their disputes to the limit'.[165]

In time the difficult atmosphere of 1895–6 was to disappear, and after 1907 the realignment of great power relationships with the Anglo-Japanese alliance, the entente between Britain, France and Russia, and the rapprochement between Russia and Japan, together with the attraction of the Paris money market, brought about a new cordiality between France and Japan. Nevertheless, there was a crucial difference between the decade preceding the First World War and the years which followed the Franco-Chinese War of 1883–5. From the signing of the 1858 Treaty up until the final stages of treaty revision, France, for all its weaknesses and embarrassments, had retained an independent role in Japan. Once the alliance with Russia was signed that was no longer possible. The verdict of the *Nippon* that 'France's reputation belongs only to the past; its glory is no longer of this era',[166] may have been over-harsh, but as far as France's position in Japan was concerned, it was uncomfortably close to the mark.

8

FRENCH TRADE AND ITS INFLUENCE ON FRENCH POLICY

THE VOLUME AND PATTERN OF FRENCH TRADE

WHEN FRANCE joined with the other leading Western powers in opening Japan in 1858, trade was the chief obstensible purpose. Yet few tangible signs of interest in securing a treaty had been shown by French traders themselves and there was little expectation that Japan would become a significant trading partner.[1] Consequently, it is not surprising that there was no great rush by Frenchmen to engage in commercial activity in Japan in the years immediately following the opening of the ports. Statistics for those early years are, of course, both unsystematic and unreliable, especially on the French side. The French government refused to appoint a full-time consul at Yokohama until 1870, despite the appeals of its diplomatic representatives and the French merchants there, and thus it was left to a member of the Legation Chancellery to attempt to unravel the affairs of a port which accounted for about three quarters of the entire trade with Japan. This was a far from easy task. The Japanese customs officials were inexperienced and unhelpful, and the traders themselves notoriously made false declarations about the values of their goods.[2] Since in addition, a good deal of smuggling was carried on and much French trade was conveyed in foreign ships, it took a considerable time to formulate even rough estimates of the volume and value of French imports from, and exports to, Japan.

Nevertheless the overall pattern and growth of Franco-Japanese trade are not hard to discern. Its development was initially sluggish. Although Bellecourt had arranged for French interests to be looked after by nominating British traders as consular agents in Yokohama, Nagasaki and Hakodate, there were still, by March 1860, only four Frenchmen at Yokohama (out of a total of 120 Europeans) and Bellecourt was doubtful about their ability to compete with the large English and American houses.[3] To ensure the development of French trade he therefore persuaded the Bakufu to extend the foreign settlement to twice its former size and allocate one-fifth of the new area to Frenchmen.[4] Despite this official encouragement the French community did not establish a definite position for itself for several years and at the end of 1862 the number of Frenchmen in Yokohama was still only eight.

For this unsatisfactory state of affairs Bellecourt blamed French caution. As he saw it, 'it is probable that before setting up distant establishments, the French houses will have wanted to begin by making an exact tally of the advantages which they could obtain by using Japanese silks, and that they will initially have preferred to leave to others the hazards of the first risks while themselves limiting their efforts'.[5] 1863, however, marked a turning-point in French trade with Japan. Between January and October the number of Frenchmen at Yokohama rose sharply to 32 and before the end of the year it had reached 41;[6] in the same year the French shipping line, the *Messageries Impériales* decided to extend their service to Yokohama, thus releasing French traders to a large extent from their dependence on English shipping and shipping routes.[7]

The cause of these developments was the sudden rise of the silk trade. Before 1859 it had not been realized in Europe that Japan might prove to be an important silk exporter,[8] and the instructions given to Bellecourt by the Quai d'Orsay had ignored the entire subject, concentrating only on possible French imports, which, in the event, found it difficult to make much impact.[9] Only champagne among French wines met with much favour and *articles de Paris*, another category in which hopes were placed, proved very disappointing.[10] By contrast, Japanese silk soon showed that it had the potential to become a major export. In 1861, for instance, the first year for which any overall estimate of French trade was attempted, silk exports to France direct from Yokohama alone amounted to about 2,600,000 francs, compared with only 500,000 francs for all imports from France.[11] The following year saw a decline in exports but they still easily outweighed the 871,023 francs worth of imports.[12] Then in 1863 came a steep rise in silk exports to France: one estimate put the figure at 8 million francs.[13] This total does not appear to have increased by much in the following three years,[14] but in 1867 and 1868 Japanese exports to France again took a colossal leap. In the former year, they more than doubled to 20,221,000 francs,[15] and in the latter, despite the civil war being waged in northern Japan, they almost trebled to 56,800,501 francs.[16]

The reasons for this rapid growth lie partly in the more liberal attitude of the Bakufu but also in the development of a new item of trade – silkworm eggs – which for a few years was to rival raw silk in value.[17] Silkworm eggs accounted for 6,941,000 francs in 1865, 3,771,150 francs in 1866, for 7,163,557 francs in 1867, and for 25,232,962 francs in 1868.[18] This increase, it should be noted, was not matched by an equal increase in volume, since higher demand meant that prices rose steeply during this period.

The second half of the 1860s also saw French imports to Japan flourish. The 1865 figure of 546,000 francs quadrupled to 2,025,000 francs the following year, and in 1867 soared to 7,480,000 francs.[19] About half of this resulted from the orders given to Coullet,[20] but other sides of commerce evidently profited from Roches' good relations with the Bakufu too, for the level was not sustained after 1867.[21] In fact, it was not approached again until the mid-1870s and was only exceeded in the 1880s.

Trade statistics for the Meiji era remain unsatisfactory and need to be treated with caution. There are major discrepancies between standard Japanese secondary sources and some contemporary French sources which may be explained by the fact that one refers to 'general commerce' (which includes good passing through France) and the other 'special commerce' but which may also be due to other factors such as the use of the financial year rather than the calendar year in the period measured. Despite these difficulties it is fairly clear that Japanese exports to France fell considerably after the Restoration (though this drop, like the earlier rise, partly reflected a change in the price-level).[22] It is also apparent that there was in the early 1870s a temporary drop in French imports of Japanese raw silk as well as a permanent decline in the silkworm egg trade.[23] Thereafter the pattern of trade saw few sudden changes. Raw silk and silk products remained by far the most important Japanese exports to France. In 1885 they accounted for 23,837,740 francs out of a total of 29,254 771 francs, and as late as 1901 raw silk alone was worth 40,446,000 francs out of a figure of 77,060,000 francs.[24]

As regards French imports into Japan, a staple finally emerged in the mid-1870s in the form of woollen muslins, which by 1876 exceeded in value all other items put together and continued to take an ever larger share in Franco-Japanese trade.[25] With the expansion of the Japanese navy in the mid-1880s another item of considerable importance also appeared. Munitions and warships were sought in large quantities from Europe, and France made a considerable, and not unsuccessful, effort to share in these orders. However, military items remained far inferior in value to woollen goods in the list of French exports to Japan; and they did little to alter significantly the overall balance of trade, which had always favoured Japan and from the 1880s did so overwhelmingly. Indeed, from 1875, which was a disastrous year for Japanese silkworm dealers, right up until 1951, there was no peacetime year in which Japanese imports from France surpassed Japanese exports to France.

Although the use of trade statistics is fraught with difficulties and liable to be misleading, they can give a very rough idea not only of changes in the balance of exports and imports but also of the periods when Franco-Japanese trade grew, stagnated or, occasionally, declined. The picture is complicated, however, in that each country experienced inflation and deflation in quite different ways and the value of the yen in terms of the franc dropped by almost half between the early 1870s and the late 1890s (when Japan went on to the gold standard). If one looks at Japanese exports to France in terms of yen values, the annual average between 1873 and 1879 was 4,800,000.[27] Between 1880 and 1889 this rose sharply to 9,440,000 yen and between 1890 and 1899 it accelerated to 19,759,000 yen. In the first decade of the twentieth century it went up to 32,962,000 yen, and in the four years before World War I the average reached 48,150,000 yen. Estimates of the value of Japanese exports to France in francs, based on the rates of exchange current at the time, indicate a less impressive rate of growth. Between 1873 and 1879 the average annual value was, very approximately, 25 million francs, between 1880 and 1889 40 million francs, between 1890 and 1899 65 million francs, between 1900 and 1909 99 million francs and between 1910 and 1913 144 million francs.

Compared with the relentless growth of Japanese exports to France, the record of French exports to Japan is unimpressive and uneven. In yen terms their average annual value from 1873 to 1879 was 3,030,000, and thereafter the imbalance in Franco-Japanese trade increased still further. From 1880 to 1889 they averaged no more that 2,432,000 yen,[28] and although they picked up between 1890 and 1899 to 4,874,000 yen, between 1900 and 1909 to 5,299 000 yen, and from 1910 to 1913 to 5,618,000 yen, this final figure was little more than one tenth of the figure for Japanese exports to France. Estimates of the value of French exports to Japan in francs present an even less impressive picture. After achieving between 1873 and 1879 an approximate average annual value of 16 million francs they sank between 1880 and 1889 to 11 million francs, recovering to 16 million francs between 1890 and 1899, but remaining stagnant between 1900 and 1909, and only just exceeding their 1870s' level between 1910 and 1913, when they reached an average of 17 million francs.

This imbalance in trade between the two countries was almost inevitable, given the French demand for Japanese silk, and it cannot be said that the French government showed any great concern about it. It was, after all, small in terms of overall French trade and a good deal less substantial than that caused by trade with China.[29] Nevertheless, French traders, and the French commercial mentality, did occasionally come under criticism from French diplomats in Japan for their lack of enterprise and their inefficiency. Some of these criticisms may, perhaps, be dismissed as prejudiced or ill-informed, but others seem fairly well founded. Roches' unfavourable comparison of French silkworm buyers in Japan with those from Italy,[30] for instance, is supported by the fact that the Italian silkworm-rearing industry recovered more strongly from the pébrine disease which had ravaged European silkworms than did the French.[31]

In the early 1870s criticisms of this kind are no longer encountered, but they make a definite return in the mid-1880s with the campaign to secure naval orders for France. The French government's concern about selling warships to Japan was shown by the memorandum from the Navy Ministry which the Quai d'Orsay passed on to Sienkiewicz in October 1885:

> At a time when, as a result of the crisis which weighs so heavily on the naval armaments industry, it is no longer possible to count on the support of the merchant navy to maintain the French shipyards, the *Compagnie des Forges et Chantiers,* whose bad reputation is now well in the past, has not hesitated to enter the lists with the aim of obtaining a share of the orders which the Japanese Government intends to entrust to foreign industry with the a view to augmenting its military power. The interest which we attach to the success of the *Compagnie des Forges et Chantiers'* negotiations does not need to be spelled out.[32]

In view of Paris's concern the failure to secure as many orders as Britain required some explanation by French diplomats, and they found it, fairly consistently, in the deficiencies of French companies. In 1886, when the race to supply the Japanese navy had already begun, Sienkiewicz complained that only one French establishment was directly represented in Japan,[33] and in 1892 the fact that his predecessor's complaint had not been heeded was seized upon by Collin de Plancy to explain why French prestige had declined even though three large orders had actually been gained.[34] Some improvement both in expert knowledge of the market and in construction certainly seems to have been called for. Even the French chargé d'affaires admitted that one ship had taken longer to build than the contract stipulated and was further reported to be unseaworthy; that another had had two accidents on the way to Japan and had still not arrived after 60 days; and that a third had failed by three knots to reach the required speed.[35]

Since, in addition to these failings, French ships tended to be more expensive than those of France's rivals,[36] at least some of the successes which French industry achieved probably owed something to special factors. The French adviser, Bertin, for instance, helped to persuade the Japanese navy to equip itself with cruisers, which the French could build fairly well, rather than large battleships, in the construction of which French shipyards could not compete.[37] It was also hoped that the Japanese navy minister from 1890 to 1892, Admiral Kabayama, might be tempted to favour French companies with the lure of the Grand Cross of the Legion of Honour,[38] but whether this method ever contributed to French success is doubtful. The one probable case of Japanese purchasing policy being affected by considerations which were neither commercial nor military occurred in 1896, when Japan's concern to cut short the protracted treaty revision negotiations presented France with a bargaining opportunity of which it did not fail to take advantage.[39]

COMMERCIAL INFLUENCES ON FRENCH POLICY

The French government's concern with the sale of warships raises the question of the extent to which French diplomacy was dictated by commercial considerations. In theory, of course, the safeguarding of trading rights was the basic mission for the diplomats who were first sent to Japan, but after 1868, and arguably as early as 1865, the existence of the treaties, and therefore the continuation of commercial relations, was no longer in question. Even before this, trade may have been used by France as a cloak for other motives, and after the Meiji Restoration commercial considerations in general seem to have weighed less heavily in French policy than in British. This does not mean, however, that particular commercial needs or pressure groups did not operate at particular times, and the possibility that such forces influenced French policy needs to be examined.

The questions which, above all others, suggest themselves in this context are to what extent the motivation behind Léon Roches' pro-Bakufu policy was commercial and what exactly were his commercial aims. Most historians have been inclined to accept the argument first developed by Otsuka Takematsu that Roches had a mission to develop French trade and that it was this which led him into blind support of the shogun.[40] It cannot be denied that Roches was greatly interested in making commercial gains and that the Bakufu's lifting of restrictions on the silk trade and cooperation in the provision of silkworm eggs did much to convince Roches of its good faith and friendly feelings towards France. Account needs to be taken, however, of the fact that he was not the first French diplomat to show a concern with trade, that such a concern need not have excluded other motives and that the initiative for the Bakufu-French special relationship did not come only from the French side. More importantly, the superficially plausible assumption that the extension of French trade was only possible if monopolistic rights were acquired needs to be subjected to closer scrutiny.[41] While conceding that Roches relished the prospect of France enjoying a preeminent position with regard to the exportation of Japanese silk and that he anticipated Bakufu favour with regard to the importation of arms and munitions, one may question whether the evidence is sufficient to justify the allegation that he sought to go further than this.

To take the silk question first, there were undoubtedly rumours in Yokohama that Roches had monopolistic intentions with regard to silkworm eggs, and possibly raw silk itself, and these were to some extent accepted by both the British chargé d'affaires, Winchester, and von Polsbroek, the Dutch Minister.[42] Furthermore, their suspicions were not unreasonable in the circumstances. In the early 1860s the vast bulk of the silk exported from Japan went to London, whence it was largely re-exported to France. This state of affairs was a constant source of irritation to the Lyons market and the *Messageries Impériales* were encouraged to extend their services to Yokohama largely in order to remedy it.

It was against the background of the *Messageries'* decision that Roches arrived in Japan. His ill-disguised ambition and secretive nature were hardly calculated to allay British fears of new, and possibly unfair, competition. One of his first actions, after the political impasse had been removed by the Shimono-seki Expedition, was to request the Bakufu to supply him with 15,000 eggs for the purposes of regenerating the French silkworm rearing industry.[43] The Bakufu's response was astonishing in view of its previous lack of cooperation. About 40,000 eggs were brought to Roches, and a French expert, named Barlandier, was allowed to select the best specimens.[44] This move was followed, early in 1865, by a Bakufu request, which Roches supported, that the French government supply the Shogun with sixteen of the new French rifled cannons.[45] Their arrival in June did not go unnoticed.[46] Finally, in the autumn of 1865, Roches accepted a further gift of silkworm eggs from the Bakufu.[47]

These three actions were seen as connected in British eyes and given an sinister interpretation by some.[48] But if solid evidence rather than mere suspicion is taken into account, it is plain that they presaged no attempt to establish a French monopoly. To begin with, it should be noted that Roches' original purchase came under fire from French merchants as well as British. An editorial in the *Moniteur des Soies* of 28 January 1865, for instance, referred to 'the recriminations made from all sides on the subject of this sale which the Government took care of'.[49] The editor, however, sought to dispel suspicion by adding that

> . . . we can affirm, on the basis of our particular information, that the circumstances which motivated these purchases were well intentioned. If the eggs had suffered damage, the losses would have been borne by the Government's agents; if they turn out well, what is left over from the outlays of money will be deposited with the agricultural societies which have the greatest need. In the final account, this operation will certainly not have harmed the importers of eggs, since the unlimited confidence in their value has pushed prices to a very high maximum.

Roches' second acquisition was also received with mixed feelings in commercial circles in France. The complaint was made that he was competing on unfair terms with genuine traders, and that once the restriction on the export of silkworm eggs had been lifted at the start of 1865 any further official action was unnecessary.[50] Still more significant, although Roches was warmly congratulated by Drouyn de Lhuys on the success of his first initiative, he was informed in 1865 that silkworm eggs should henceforth be left to the industry itself.[51] With both his foreign minister and his own traders demanding an end to official intervention, it is hard to see how Roches could ever have thought of creating a monopoly, even if he had wanted to.[52]

Nor is the case of the import of arms by the *Société Franco-Japonaise* much more incriminating. It is true that Roches spoke of Japan becoming a French market, but it is important to observe that he saw this prospect in terms of the British position in China, which, in so far as it was largely a British market, was so mainly because of British investment and established connections with Chinese merchants. The *Société Franco-Japonaise* was a short-cut to the same end, but Roches expressly stated that it did not imply an actual monopoly when he wrote:

> It has been well understood, moreover, that the Japanese government would renounce any action towards these Companies other than that exercised by European governments on associations of this kind and that it would carefully avoid giving any motive for complaint, either to commerce in general or to any of the other Powers in particular, by barring itself from granting to the Companies in question privileges incompatible with the complete liberty reserved for the commercial operations of foreigners.[53]

The Company appeared likely to secure a large share of the Japanese government's orders of foreign manufactures but Winchester himself had earlier conceded that 'a Government going beyond its own territory to trade is a private individual and can suit itself as to the market'.[54] There remained, however the worry that direct imports by the Bakufu itself might be paid for 'by consigning all the available silkworm eggs to France and as much silk as may be wanted to cover the contracts'.[55] On this point, however, Winchester, at least, had his mind set at rest by Roches, who declared, after raising the topic himself, 'that no such schemes were in contemplation and that if he pursued such vicious commercial relations he would deserve to be shown the door [*à la porte*] by his government'.[56] In view of the Quai d'Orsay's evident caution and the criticism by French merchants of Roches' two, very limited, operations, not to mention the fact that silk exports to France far exceeded French exports to Japan in value, the allegations against Roches appear implausible and ill founded.

There is further evidence that Roches was not aiming at a monopolistic position for France. It should be remembered that Roches' connections with Lyons would have inclined him towards free trade and on various occasions he made declarations and proposals that show him, in diametrical opposition to the usual view, as a firm believer in that creed.[57] To judge by some of Roches' language in fact, free trade was almost as much a conviction with him as it was with Cobden or Bright. It is not hard to discern an ideological element in a communication which he sent to Choshu in July 1864. In it he stated that 'as men are all brothers, the Most High has decided, in His supreme mercy, that they will have between them amicable intercourse and trading relations which will enable them all to profit from the advantages which He has given to different nations and to different regions'.[58]

Further evidence of Roches' convictions is to be found in his claim in connection with the approaching tariff revision negotiations in 1865 that 'my colleagues will adopt, without difficulty, a base of 10% to 12 % but I hope to bring the Japanese government to consent to levy in future only 5 % on all types of merchandise, without distinction'.[59] That this was eventually achieved arguably owed much to Roches and suggests that Sir Harry Parkes may not have been justified in suspecting his colleague of duplicity when the latter (unsuccessfully) proposed to Drouyn de Lhuys that the French government should support a plan to make Nagasaki and Hakodate free ports.[60]

All this is not to argue that Roches' protestations need always be taken at face value; and it has also to be acknowledged that in one respect he was definitely opposed to complete freedom of trade. The desire of many silk merchants for complete access to the Japanese silkworm areas found no sympathy with him. The reason for this, however, was no nefarious scheme to make a monopoly possible but rather Roches' acceptance of the belief held by Edmond Duseigneur and many other experts that the disease which had struck the silkworm-rearing industries of Europe, and even much of Asia, was caused by *'grainage industriel'*, the excessive commercial breeding of the silkworm.[61] Their anxiety lest the Japanese silkworm should have its quality impaired before the French varieties recovered may also have contributed to Roches' reluctance to see any new ports opened.[62] Other than this, however, he did not attempt to restrict the export of eggs, and in general it may be said that the view that Roches' policy was decided by the pursuit of monopoly rights is based on supposition rather than hard evidence.

Other possible cases of French diplomacy being influenced by specific commercial or economic pressures are conspicuous by their rarity. In fact, it is just as easy to find examples of commercial interests failing to make themselves felt. For instance, although the need for Japanese silkworms was already apparent in 1864, the French government made no special effort to coerce the Bakufu into relaxing its prohibition on their export, even though this prohibition was contrary to the Treaty. It is possible, as a contemporary claimed, that Drouyn de Lhuys did instruct Bellecourt and Roches to facilitate the purchase of silkworm eggs.[63] There is nothing in the archives to support this, however, and it is worth noting that the French foreign minister himself specifically referred to Roches' 'initiative' with regard to the first consignment of 15,000 eggs.[64] Moreover, on the very same day in 1863 that the *Moniteur des Soies* was proclaiming that 'the next consignments from Japan are going to have a great influence on our markets',[65] Drouyn de Lhuys was reining back Bellecourt and informing him that France did 'not have at the moment great interests to protect in the Japanese seas'.[66] This was entirely consistent with his rejection, a few months earlier, of Bellecourt's request for the establishment of a consulate at Yokohama. The expense, he stated, 'would in no way be justified by the degree of importance of our commercial and maritime interests in Japan'.[67]

French economic interests were, of course, taken into consideration when the 'unequal treaties' were being revised, especially during the final stages of the negotiations, but there is only limited evidence of consultation with the French community at Yokohama or with the French chambers of commerce. The views of the latter were, admittedly, sought by the Quai d'Orsay in 1873, but this was exceptional.[68] Finally it needs to be noted that the image of advanced Western countries seeking opportunities to invest surplus capital in undeveloped areas which could easily be exploited is not supported by the evidence of France's relations with Meiji Japan. Rather the reverse was the case. Not only was there little direct investment but from 1868 until the mid-1890s the idea of a loan to the Japanese government was only mentioned once by a French diplomat in

Japan, and that with the object of warning French banks about Japan's financial instability.[69]

Against this, the examples that do exist of specific economic issues acquiring diplomatic significance are all, with the single exception of shipbuilding, connected with the silk trade, and for the most part they were of no real political importance. In 1870 the Quai d'Orsay informed Outrey that the chambers of commerce of Lyons and St. Etienne had advised the Ministry of Agriculture and Commerce that the Japanese government proposed to restrict (to 1,000,000) the number of cartons of silkworm eggs which could be exported in the coming year. 'If this eventuality materialised', it stated, 'it could have, for France, very regrettable consequences'.[70] The minister in Tokyo was instructed to check on the reports and 'in the case that the Japanese Government really should have the intention which is attributed to it to do what rests on you to prevent so regrettable a measure'. What might have turned into a diplomatic incident, however, disappeared when Outrey reported the rumours were without foundation.[71] Eleven years later a report that the Japanese government had established a company with a monopoly on the sale of silk led to telegrams and a protest from the Quai d'Orsay, but Roquette allowed himself to be satisfied with a government promise that the company did not possess official protection.[72] Three years later a more important instance occurred. In this case France demanded the removal of the Japanese export duty on silk in return for French agreement to a revised tariff, an act which complicated foreign minister Inoue's already difficult task of achieving revision of the unequal treaties and contributed to his failure.[73] Finally in 1897–8 a law passed to encourage the direct export of silk by Japanese merchants was abandoned when the British and French ministers responded to the anguished protests of their merchants, and when France threatened to impose a duty on Japanese-imported silk equal to the bounty which the Meiji government was proposing to offer.[74] None of these incidents had any significant effect, however, on other aspects of France's relations with Japan.

THE ECONOMIC IMPORTANCE OF FRANCO-JAPANESE COMMERCIAL RELATIONS

In considering the economic importance of Franco-Japanese trade, it is immediately apparent that this was not equal for the two countries. For France it was naturally less than for Japan, since it formed a much smaller fraction of the country's total overseas trade. For instance, whereas in 1876 France accounted for approximately 27% of Japan's exports, and 15% of Japan's imports (and, in 1892, 20% and 5% respectively), the comparable figures for Japanese exports and imports as a proportion of French trade were, in 1876, 1% and 0.25% and, in 1892, 1.5% and 0.37%. Nevertheless, the value to France of trade with Japan was greater than such figures alone would suggest. Silk was one of France's most important industries, and Roches was hardly exaggerating its parlous state when, in 1864, he claimed that: 'one of the principal sources of our national wealth will be in danger of drying up if a new and healthy element does not come to regenerate that which is defective today.'[75] As early as 1860 the hope that Japanese silkworms could play the chief part in regenerating the French industry after it had been devastated by *pébrine* induced F. Bourret, the representative of Rémi Schmidt (the first French company to engage in major purchases of Japanese silk), to make tests of Japanese silkworms, and on the basis of this evidence he reported to Bellecourt in 1862 that 'European commerce has found with the opening of Japan a source of provision which, without harming the trade of China but in conjunction with it, can largely fill the deficiency in the production of silk in Europe'.[76]

French expectations emerge even more clearly in the pages of the *Moniteur des Soies*. In 1865 this Lyons-based periodical published a letter from Duseigneur in which he asserted that 'today the Japanese seeds have gained such a favour and reputation that it is necessary to consider them henceforth as secured for European agriculture. Many people envisage them as our only future resource, and I am of that number'.[77] The following year it recorded a statement to the Senate which showed that the French government accepted the views of experts like Bourret and Duseigneur: 'the silk industry, having already experienced many bad harvests, has vainly counted on that of 1865, which, even less favourable that the previous ones, has shown that it is only the Japanese eggs which, at least for the present, can produce good results'.[78] The *Moniteur des Soies* also, in its issue of 27 April 1867, pointed to the fact that Japanese silkworms were providing useful material for the study of *pébrine* by Louis Pasteur. It included a letter from the celebrated scientist in which he stated that 'there was a great interest in being able to compare Japan and France' and that the samples which he had received from the Ministry of Agriculture and which had come through Roches ('whose services to sericulture are praised by everyone') had given him 'the certain confirmation of the ideas which I have expressed'.

By the 1870s reports of the promise of Japanese silkworms had mainly given way in the *Moniteur des Soies* to complaints about the deterioration of their quality. This did not, however, mean that the promise had not been fulfilled. An article of 8 July 1871 declared that 'the Japanese eggs have been a powerful help to France, Italy and other countries, in preserving an industry which, otherwise, would have been ruined'.[79] It has to be added that French silkworm-rearing never recovered to its former level, and that, faced with competition from Chinese, and to a lesser extent, Japanese silk producers, it soon entered into a slow decline. Nevertheless in the 1860s and 1870s imported Japanese silkworm eggs provided many of the 180,000 French families who produced cocoons with a means of continuing an important by-employment. Since these silkworm rearers were concentrated in one region – the Midi – the social implications were significant.

Not only did Japanese silkworms rescue the French silk-worm-rearing industry from almost complete extinction as a result of over-intensive exploitation, but large-scale imports of Japanese raw silk (together with imports from China) helped to fill the gap in the supply of material for processing. Had the French silk-weaving industry, which, like the Japanese silk industry, was largely organized on a domestic basis, not been sustained by these imports, Lyons and the surrounding area would have suffered severe hardship. On top of this, finished silk was one of France's key exports.[80] Without a supply of (relatively cheap) raw silk and silkworm eggs from Japan which could be given added value by further processing, the balance of trade, which in the 1870s was becoming unfavourable to France, would have deteriorated further. Japanese silk and silkworms, therefore, provided a cushion against the shock of *pébrine*. This was for France the most valuable result of the Japan trade – more important than the additional outlet for woollen muslins and warships, which affected the French economy only marginally.

It was in the 1860s and 1870s too that trade with France was most important for Japan. Its impact was more double-edged, however. Whereas Japanese silk was wholly beneficial to the French industry, French demand had some adverse effects on the Japanese industry. The desire for quick gains led to the export of many better-quality eggs, and to a tendency to over-produce which led to a rapid drop in the quality of Japanese silk. Even the willingness to export silkworm eggs on a huge scale represented a failure to foresee that the recovery of French production would limit the export market for Japanese raw silk in the longer term.[81]

On the other hand, Japanese direct and indirect exports of silk to France were crucial in providing Japan with a favourable balance of trade in the 1860s and in reducing the drain of specie from the country in the 1870s. Japan needed to counterbalance the sharply rising demand for Western manufactures, as well as pay for foreign experts, model factories, and subsidies for new industries, and the only special advantage which it enjoyed was the capacity for producing silk. The existence of an exceptional demand from France and Italy meant that peasants in the silkworm-rearing areas of central Japan had a strong incentive for expanding their output, while the French and Italian need for higher quality and better consistency helped to promote the Meiji government's decision to promote a modern silk-reeling industry by establishing the mechanized filature at Tomioka with French help in 1872.[82] It can, therefore, be reasonably claimed that the trade brought appreciable advantages to both France and Japan and was a significant factor in the establishment of the foundations of Japanese economic modernization.[83]

9

THE BROADER PICTURE: MODERNIZATION AND CULTURE

TRADE MAY HAVE BEEN the nominal justification for France's establishment of relations with Japan, and the maintenance of France's standing and position as a major Power may have been, in reality, the chief objective of French diplomacy in Japan, but to limit an examination of Franco-Japanese relations to trade and diplomacy would be to ignore a much wider set of influences and contacts between the two countries which were arguably of greater and more lasting importance. Some of these were known to French diplomats and were seen as being beneficial to French interests; others appear to have entirely escaped their attention. In most cases they involved Japanese learning from Frenchmen, but the process was not entirely one-sided. The late nineteenth century also witnessed a discovery of Japan by French artists and critics which was in some respects comparable with the fascination which China held for French thinkers in the previous century. A full exploration of these non-diplomatic aspects of the Franco-Japanese relationship would require a separate study, but their extent and significance will, it is hoped, be indicated by what follows.

FRANCE AND THE BEGINNINGS OF THE MODERN JAPANESE ARMY

Some of the influences between the two countries operated at the individual level, but the most important involved governments and diplomats. This was very much the case with the French role in Japan's military modernization: it originated with the strong encouragement of Léon Roches and could not have been maintained without the active support of the Quai d'Orsay and the French War Ministry. Ironically, it had an unpropitious beginning and an unhappy ending, and its contribution to Japan's meteoric rise as a military power has been overshadowed by the later role of the German officer, Major Meckel, who helped to establish an effective General Staff and introduced his own ideas about military strategy. Even allowing for Meckel's outstanding qualities, however, it remains the case that a far greater number of French officers were employed by the Japanese army, that many of them were enthusiastic and talented, and that Meckel would not have had a base to build on had it not been for their preparatory work, which was carried out in less favourable conditions than those which the German officer encountered.[1]

The fact that French military guidance was not very successful in its initial phase, and indeed left what in some respects was an unfortunate legacy, was due primarily to the outbreak of civil war within a year of the first French mission's arrival on 13 January 1867. The result was the suspension of its training activity and then, after several months of enforced idleness, its repatriation (minus the defecting Lieutenant Brunet, who had, much to the discomfiture of the French minister, joined the remnants of the Tokugawa forces in their last-ditch stand against the new imperial government).[2] Even if the mission had had a longer period in which to work, however, it is not certain that it would have been very effective. Although support for military reform certainly existed among Bakufu leaders, the willingness to change traditional methods was not shared by all the elements on which the Tokugawa regime depended; and without the degree of commitment shown by the renovationist Meiji government later, the work of the first group or French officers might have proved less productive than its sponsors hoped. Such an outcome was the more likely in that the French government had chosen to send a considerably smaller mission than the Bakufu had requested and Roches had urged.[3] Only five officers and ten non-commissioned officers were selected – less than half the number originally envisaged – and the officers, although talented, were not men of great experience.[4] Even the mission leader, Captain Chanoine, was only 31 years old.

Notwithstanding the obstacles it faced, the first mission did make some headway. A foundry for manufacturing rifles and guns was established, and at Chanoine's behest a military academy was set up to instruct youths between fourteen and nineteen years old.[5] Well over a thousand existing troops were given some basic training, and although they in no way covered themselves with glory during the crucial period of fighting in January 1868, neither did they disgrace themselves.[6] More might conceivably have been achieved if Tokugawa Yoshinobu, the last shogun, had opted to fight to hold the eastern part of Japan, as he seems to have been advised by the mission members. Had he chosen to resist, the superior theoretical knowledge of the French officers might have enabled the Bakufu to test severely the imperial army, which itself lacked both experience and homogeneity. Given the French government's concern to avoid any potentially costly commitment, however, or any action which would cause friction with Britain, it is unlikely that even surreptitious French military involvement in the civil war would have been permitted for long.

Even though the first mission's record was not a glorious one, and even though its reputation was tarnished by Brunet's hot-headed behaviour, its legacy proved far more important than seemed likely at the time of its departure. Some of the soldiers it had instructed switched their allegiance to the new government after 1868 and were themselves employed in the latter's military training programme, the most notable example being Tajima Oshin, who joined the staff of the military academy (*heiga-kuryo*) which was set up by the effective head of the Military Affairs Ministry, Omura Masujiro, in Osaka.[7] Another result was that a significant number of feudal domains adopted the French drill system in imitation of the Bakufu and became familiar with French methods. British methods may have been even more widely practised, and no less important a domain than Satsuma (despite hiring some ex-soldiers from France through the Comte de Montblanc in 1867) wished to continue with them. However, when the Meiji government decided that it, like the Bakufu, needed foreign help to develop a new Western-style army, its dominant elements, and especially the Choshu military specialists, were not tempted to seek British assistance instead of French, because the British army recruited through voluntary enlistment. This meant that the choice in practice was between turning to Germany, which had impressed Yamagata Aritomo when he investigated European military systems on the spot in early 1870,[8] or reverting to French guidance, which Omura advocated until his assassination in late 1869 and which Yamada Akiyoshi and others associated with Omura continued to press for. In the eventual decision to take France as Japan's model (which was formally announced by the Meiji government's ruling council, the *Dajokan*, on 26 October 1870, although it had been anticipated by an approach to Outrey nearly six months earlier) what seems to have carried particular weight was the very practical factor that, as a result of the first mission's work, there were far more Japanese who were capable of acting as interpreters for French instructors than for German.[9]

One other legacy of the first French mission may also have played a part in the decision to invite a new one – the presence of Captain Dubousquet, the only member of the original team of French officers (except for Brunet) who chose not to return to France in 1868 but to become an interpreter for the French legation. Despite being wounded in May 1869 by a xenophobic samurai, Dubousquet seems to have had a genuine liking for the Japanese: he married one (Tanaka Hanako) in 1869 and continued to reside in Japan until his death, at the age of 45, in 1882. While still working for the French legation, he acted as an adviser to the Military Affairs Ministry (*Hyobusho*) from early 1870 until early 1871 before becoming a full-time Japanese government employee. In those positions he was able to obliterate, by his dedication, any surviving impression that the French could not be trusted because they had earlier worked for the Tokugawa cause.

Apart from providing the Meiji government with invaluable help in initiating the process of revision of the 1858 treaties,

Dubousquet, in response to the Japanese authorities' request for information on how to bring Japan to the level of the advanced countries of Europe, compiled a lengthy series of reports in Japanese on various aspects of military organization and methods in France and other Western countries.[11] His commitment is evident not only in the sheer volume of his reports, which provided a very substantial supplement to the Meiji leaders' existing knowledge of Western military systems, but also in the language he used. In one proposal which he presented in the spring of 1872, for instance, he emphasised that 'in order to put the government's orders and instructions into effect' it was necessary to establish 'military forces which in the cause of the government are not deterred by water or fire'.[12]

Dubousquet was well placed to encourage and participate in an approach to the French minister for a new mission, and also, through his reports, to predispose the Meiji government towards a more wholesale acceptance of the French model. It may well be that he slanted his presentation in a way that favoured his own country (and ignored the widespread feeling in France itself that the French system and methods were inferior to Germany's), for in the view of one Japanese historian, the Army Ministry (when it was separated from the Navy Ministry in 1873) was reorganized in such a way as to resemble Dubousquet's description of the French War Ministry.[13] The same historian further suggests that Dubousquet had a hand in the formulation of the conscription system which the Meiji government brought into effect in 1873, although he also gives credit for this hugely important reform to Lieutenant-Colonel Marquerie, the head of the second French mission.[14] Whether either of them played a key role, however, is doubtful. Marquerie may have recommended the French system to Yamagata, and Dubousquet did provide a detailed description of it in one of his reports, but others were closely involved, including Nishi Amane, the scholar-cum-bureaucrat who is supposed to have drafted the conscription law.[15] In any case, even though the new law seems to have followed French practice – at least before France itself in 1872–3 moved away from the idea of a basically professional army based on a long period of active service – in allowing a considerable number of exemption categories, its adoption of the principle that all adult males were liable for military service probably reflected Prussian influence.

Dubousquet also seems to have been involved in late1870, together with Tajima, in recruiting three of the first mission's non-commissioned officers (who were currently in Saigon) to give instruction at the military academy in Osaka. Prior to that there had been two French teachers, both of whom were ex-lieutenants (unconnected with the first mission) who had been transferred from an official French language school at Yokohama, but one of them, Buland, returned to France towards the end of 1870 (accompanied by ten Japanese military students). Dubousquet was similarly involved in the recruitment to the Military Affairs Ministry in 1871 of another Frenchmen who had previously been hired by Tosa to change that *han*'s military system for the British to the French style in 1870.[16] He was often engaged in non-military matters, however, and after its arrival on 17 May 1872 the second French military mission became the main channel for French military influence. Its direct contribution to Japan's development was almost inevitably greater than its predecessor's. For one thing, although its size (sixteen) was almost the same, its six officers were less inexperienced, including, apart from Lieutenant-Colonel Marquerie, three captains (two of whom, Descharmes and Jourdan, had served in the previous mission) and only two lieutenants. More importantly, it lasted much longer. While some of its members did not serve for the full period of their contracts – notably Marquerie, who suffered a riding accident and was replaced by Lieutenant-Colonel Munier in 1874 – and others did not have their contracts renewed at the end of their three years' term, several newcomers were brought in to fill gaps, and a nucleus of military advisers, including the mission leader, remained until the middle of 1880.

That the second mission would make a significant mark was not a foregone conclusion. The Japanese army was an unhomogeneous force, with a very large Imperial guard drawn from the three old domains of Satsuma, Choshu and Tosa, and, in the main body of the new centralized army a mixture of fresh conscripts and samurai drawn from the other ex-domain troops. In terms of how it would respond to external guidance it was something of an unknown quantity. On top of this a substantial number of Japanese officers and military officials did not welcome the French presence or were anxious to impress the foreign officers that they were advisers with no prerogative of command.[17] This situation was described by Marquerie in a letter to Major Chanoine of 23 September 1872:

> We arrived preceded by a reputation as invaders, determined to change everything and turn everything upside down. At that time a coalition determined on a last-ditch defence was formed in the War Ministry. To attack this head-on at the outset would, I think, have been bad tactics. Without compromising principles, I believed it preferable not to engage in confrontation. The results which have now been obtained show that this approach was not unwise. Today, instead of declining our help, as almost everyone did when we arrived, the majority of officers seek out our instruction, and I have hope of a new success which would make me really happy.[18]

The optimistic note which Marquerie struck cannot, in the light of the mission's subsequent achievement, be dismissed as wishful thinking. Apart from devising plans for coastal defence, the mission played a crucial part in establishing some important facilities: a training school for non-commissioned officers (and initially for officers also); the Toyama school for teaching infantrymen to shoot; a major arsenal comprising workshops, an arms factory and a pyrotechnical school employing 2,500 workers (4,000 during the Taiwan expedition); an artillery range; a gunpowder factory; numerous barracks; and, probably most important, a Military Academy (*shikan gakko*) for training Japan's future officers.[19] This Military Academy, it has been claimed, was modelled entirely on the French officers' school at St Cyr, and Captain Jourdan, the acting head of mission in early 1874, is said to have been deeply involved in its planning. The length of the course was two years in the case of infantry and cavalry officers, and three in the case of the artillery and engineers; and, under the supervision of Lieutenant Colonel Munier and Captain Vieillard, no fewer than thirteen Frenchmen (two of them civilians) were involved in instruction.

An unusual feature of the Military Academy was the inclusion of 35 hours of debating under the chairmanship of an instructor. This has been attributed to French influence and has been used, together with the fact that soldiers were free to leave their barracks after their training hours and on Saturday afternoons and Sundays, to support the claim that French ways were helping to make the Meiji army relatively democratic until it became more fashionable to follow the German model.[20] While this claim appears difficult to justify fully, it is generally accepted that the knowledge of French practice encouraged the idea of civilian control over the military, with power over both command and routine administration residing in the army minister. French influence in this area did not last long, however, for the establishment in 1878 through the efforts of the Germanophile officer from Choshu, Katsura Taro, of an independent General Staff, answerable only to the Emperor as supreme commander, sunsequently changed the basis of civilian-military relations in Japan.[21] Ironically Katsura had once studied French at the Yokohama language school.

By 1879 it was apparent that the Meiji government wished, for reasons which were partly financial, to dispense with the services of as many of its foreign employees as possible. The French military officers, who had already been in Japan for a relatively long period, were not exempt from this policy, even though they themselves felt that Japan's military leaders overestimated their own capabilities and underestimated what still needed to be learned. Their views were echoed by Dubousquet when he wrote:

> I find it truly distressing that the inept war leaders do not wish to take account of the mistake which they are committing by not keeping at least our officers who teach specialised skills. It means the ruin of a very well organized military School, and the ruin of their cadres, because there is no Japanese officer capable of replacing our artillery and engineering officers as a teacher. All that is the consequence of a deep-lying fault, namely, the stubbornness and self-conceit of the Japanese army's generals who have preferred to live in ignorance of their profession rather than sacrifice their self-conceit by turning for help to our mission.[22]

Nevertheless, French military influence did not come to a final end with the departure of Colonel Munier in 1880. For one thing France appointed Captain Bougouin, one of the officers who served in Japan in the latter half of the 1870s, as military attaché, an unprecedented move which implied that Japan now possessed military significance, while the Meiji government sent Major Tajima to Paris as the first regular Japanese military attaché in any country. More importantly, Japan's military leaders before long tacitly acknowledged the validity of the French claim that Japanese officers were not yet ready to dispense with foreign help by requesting two more French instructors, Commandant Berthaut and Captain Villaret, for the military academy and Toyama school in 1884, and one non-commissioned officer, for training in gymnastics and fencing.[23] The gratification which the French gained from this was reduced, however, firstly by the fact that their officers would serve as individuals rather than as a formal mission, and, much more, by their discovery that Berthaut and Villaret would not be the only foreign officers hired. Even worse, the appointment of Major Meckel, as a General Staff adviser and as chief instructor at the newly established Staff College (which operated at a higher level than the Military Academy) would give Germany an edge over France in the competition for influence. Although French officers remained in Japanese service for another four years, this third phase of French involvement in Japanese military development was marked by tension and ended in rancour when the Japanese Army Ministry declined in 1888 to renew the contracts of the French officers.[24]

It is clear from their careers that the officers sent by the French War Ministry were men of ability. Berthaut was the son of a general (who had served as War Minister) and he himself subsequently rose to that level. Villaret was similarly promoted to that rank, as were Chanoine, Descharmes and Brunet. Their letters bear testimony to their dedication, and many of them were decorated with the Order of the Rising Sun.[25] On the basis of this evidence, it seems reasonable to accept as more or less genuine (even while acknowledging an element of flattery) the various indications of Japanese appreciation of French efforts which were reported by French diplomats and soldiers. The Meiji emperor may, of course, have been prompted to compliment the French officers, after he had attended manoeuvres at Kamakura, on 'the perseverance and intelligence which they deploy in the exercise of their functions', and it was certainly the case that Turenne had to manoeuvre to secure for them in January 1873 the formal imperial reception which the French war minister had asked for.[26] Five years later, however, Geofroy was able to report that 'first minister Sanjo, and princes of the blood Arisugawa and Fushimi, who particularly concern themselves with military matters have on several occasions . . . made flattering declarations, the sincerity of which is attested by the step [of again extending the duration of the military mission] taken today'. He attributed the praise to the French officers' 'dignity in their deportment, their diligence, their tact and their reserve in their relations both with the Japanese and with foreign residents . . .'[27]

The good impression made by the French may have been helped by the interest which other officers, in addition to Dubousquet, showed in Japanese culture. Descharmes had already, by 1868, become an admirer of Japanese art, while a Japanese newspaper reported in August 1873 that one French officer was composing Japanese poems.[28] Even the Germanophile Yamagata was prepared after the Sino-Japanese War, according to an ex-member of the second mission, to 'attribute to the instruction received from the French army the greatest part of the successes of his army'.[29] Allowance has to be made for the fact that this statement was made to an old associate while Yamagata was visiting France in 1896. While it undoubtedly was a deliberate overstatement, however, the tribute was still not worthless. Perhaps of more value, though, was the favourable assessment of the American Major-General Upton in 1877. Despite finding the deportment and appearance of the Japanese soldiers deplorably sloppy, he was effusive in his praise of the French officers' zeal, intelligence, spirit of initiative, and success.[30]

One further aspect of French military influence needs to be noted although it seems never to have been studied, and its importance is particularly difficult to assess – the sending of Japanese military students to France. When French amour-propre was wounded in 1888–9 by the termination of French military instruction in Japan, the French minister, Sienkiewicz, sought to punish the Japanese for giving France what he chose to regard as a humiliating brush-off, and he recommended the termination of the admission of Japanese to French military schools. His recommendation was not completely accepted, for it was considered impolitic to deny access to Prince Kanin, a member of the Japanese imperial family, but in general a ban was imposed. It was by no means insignificant, for in each year from 1878 to 1889 from five to eighteen Japanese students had attended French military schools.[31] Some of them, at least, may have taken back to Japan with them a certain admiration for things French.[3]

FRANCE AND JAPANESE NAVAL DEVELOPMENT

When, in October 1870, the Meiji government announced that it intended to adopt the French system for the Japanese army, it also proclaimed that it would model the Japanese navy on that of Britain. This was logical and predictable, given that Britain was the premier naval power and that, matching the French military mission, a British naval mission had already begun to train the Tokugawa naval forces.[33] Nevertheless, it would be wrong to suppose that France played no role in Japanese naval development, for Léon Roches' close links with the Bakufu meant that Frenchmen were already helping to lay one of the foundations of future Japanese naval power in 1868. In contrast to French military cooperation, however, French naval assistance did not involve the training of naval officers but rather guidance and instruction in designing, building, and repairing modern ships. In further contrast, it continued after the Meiji Restoration without a break.

The origin of the French naval connection was a Japanese request for assistance from Admiral Jaurès in the repair of one of the Western-built ships which the Bakufu had purchased. Jaurès' response was favourable and the work was carried out with impressive speed and efficiency. From this emerged the idea of a major naval installation: a dockyard and arsenal. With the encouragement of Roches, the Bakufu requested French assistance in January 1865, and the French government agreed to this with unusual rapidity, influenced perhaps by Roches' warning that if France did not help, another country would.[34] The choice of the Frenchman who was to run the project was made, however, by Jaurès and Roches, both of whom were aware of a person who in many ways was ideally qualified:

Lieutenant François Léonce Verny, a naval engineer who had shown his ability since 1861 by building naval facilities and ships for the Chinese at Ningpo and who happened to be a distant relative of Roches. Verny was easily lured to Japan in September 1865 by the prospect of having a good salary ($10,000 a year) and masterminding a scheme on which the Bakufu had contracted itself to spend $2,400,000 over four years. After agreeing with Roches and Jaurès that Yokosuka (which resembled Toulon) was a better site than the one chosen by the Bakufu previously, Verny departed for France with the authority to determine what equipment should be purchased for the dockyard (and its associated foundry at Yokohama) and what other personnel should be recruited.[35] He returned to Japan in June 1866, having selected another engineer, a doctor, and 42 workers drawn from Brest, Toulon, Cherbourg and other French shipyards[36].

The Yokosuka dockyard turned out its first vessel (the tiny, 30 horse-power, Yokosuka-maru) as early as November 1866, but the planned two repair yards, three ship-building yards,and the iron-works and repair yard at Yokohama were not fully completed by the time the Bakufu fell. French fears that Verny and his French workers would be replaced by British personnel as a result of the change of regime proved groundless, and Frenchmen continued to be employed exclusively at Yokosuka until 1878, when 25 remained.[37] Verny himself departed at the beginning of 1876, having built, by his own account, five ships (only one of them a warship), and repaired 263 (101 foreign and 162 Japanese).[38] Rather higher figures – six ships constructed, 305 repaired – are given by Edouard Clavery;[39] while Tanaka Sadao offers yet another set of figures; four ships built, four under construction, and one, a larger (1,200 tons) vessel, on which work was about to commence, but only 86 ships repaired.[40] Tanaka also lists some other undertakings – three lighthouses (one built when Verny was on leave for ten months in 1869 by his deputy, Thibaudier), and four 110-horsepower machines for use in the Ikuno copper and silver mines.

The completion and effective use of what was to remain for many years Japan's principal naval dockyard clearly represented a very considerable achievement, and reflected well on France's reputation. By the time Verny left, however, the French engineer's own reputation had become slightly tarnished. Great though his devotion to duty was, it was matched by his impatience at anything which seemed to stand in his way, especially laziness on the part of the Japanese workers. Various written complaints about his displays of rudeness and anger survive in the Japanese records.[41] Similarly, his ability as an engineer and an organizer was counteracted by a marked tendency to behave in an autocratic manner. The large measure of authority which had been entrusted to him at the beginning of the project evidently encouraged him to resist Japanese interference: in 1868, for instance, he insisted on keeping the dockyard in operation during the civil war, claiming that it was a French government undertaking, not just a Japanese responsibility and that its purpose of repairing foreign ships could not be set aside.[42] When he was away on leave for most of 1869, the French minister, Outrey, commented on how much better a relationship his deputy, Thibaudier, had established with the Japanese.[43] In November 1875, when the Meiji government decided to give Verny, Thibaudier, and the French doctor, Savatier, three months' notice, as it was entitled to do, the current French diplomatic representative in Japan, St Quentin, expressed the view that this regrettable step might not have been taken had Verny 'known how to maintain easier relations with the minister and officers of the Japanese navy'.[44] His criticism of Verny did not prevent St Quentin from appealing against the Japanese decision, however; and his argument that Dupont, the engineer who was scheduled to continue, would be unable to cope with both the training school and construction and repair work secured a renewable ten-month extension for the deputy director, Thibaudier.[45]

Six months later Verny was again criticized, this time for his 'strange forgetfulness'. He had, it seemed, been negligent of French interests in his failure to ensure that, in their new contracts with the Japanese, those Frenchmen who had, until his departure, had contracts with him directly, were not made subject to the authority of the new chief French engineer at Yokosuka. St Quentin felt that the consequences were 'most regrettable', because without such clear subordination, it would be impossible to maintain French unity. Already two French civilian employees at the dockyard were 'in league to refuse all obedience to the [French] naval engineer', a 'division of the personnel into two enemy camps' which 'satisfied the secret desires of the Japanese authorities'.

What worried St Quentin was not just the assumption of total control by the Japanese but 'the rapid and complete breakdown of organization, as a result of which it was easy to foresee the arrival of a personnel of a different nationality'. This disturbing prospect had fortunately been kept at bay by Japanese acceptance of an arrangement which, while no longer allowing the French chief engineer to make purchases or contracts, or determine the pay and promotion of the Japanese personnel, or decide what work should be done, and when, nevertheless gave him the right to exercise authority over all French personnel. This was only secured, however, after 15 March, when Verny was no longer present to cause difficulties.[46] Significantly Thibaudier's new contract prescribed that 'in the exercise of the functions entrusted to him M. Thibaudier will never lose from sight that the present objective which the government purposes to attain is to develop the initiative of the Japanese chiefs, by giving them practical familiarity with directing works and administering a large staff of workers'.[47]

Needless to say, the French sought to maintain their position at Yokosuka, but after Thibaudier's departure at the end of 1876 the odds were stacked against them, the more so because Dupont did not wish to remain at Yokosuka much longer. Hearing this, foreign minister Decazes was again alarmed at the possibility of other countries' gaining a foothold there, and St Quentin was instructed to secure a new arrangement to prevent this from happening. If he failed, Decazes warned, 'the consequence would, according to all appearance, very shortly be the abortion, or at least the diminution, of a considerable enterprise whose success, due to our persistent efforts, constitutes a real and precious element of influence in these countries'.[48]

If Decazes expected the situation to be restored, he was soon disabused by the newly-arrived Geofroy, who realised that the Meiji government wanted to dispense with foreigners and acquire total control over all enterprises in which they were involved. He too, however, could not resist joining his predecessors in laying some of the blame at Verny's door: 'At

Yokosuka, one must recognise, the excessively personal administration of M. Verny, the seeds of division which he left after him among the French personnel, and the difficulties which followed, have served [the Japanese] aims only too well'.[49] When Geofroy sought the appointment of a new French 'chef hiérarchique', the Japanese foreign minister declined to countenance such a suggestion and even gave the impression of being pleased that Dupont was about to leave.[50] Terashima was presumably jaundiced at being subjected to yet more pressure. When the last of the contracts signed in 1876 expired in late 1878 he showed that he appreciated the value of what Verny and the other Frenchmen had done at Yokosuka by writing to Geofroy that 'they founded the art of naval construction, and it is to them that we ought likewise to acknowledge today the achievement of all the services relating to naval construction'.[51]

Except for the continuing service of a few Frenchmen as individuals at Yokosuka, it may well have seemed as if France's involvement in the creation of the modern Japanese navy had come to an end in 1878. Such was not the case. Although its prestige may not have matched that of the French army, the French navy pioneered most major naval developments in the last quarter of the the century.[52] It was, therefore, not so surprising that in 1885 the Meiji government asked the French government to lend the Japanese navy a French naval architect. In doing so, navy minister Kawamura acknowledged, in language clearly calculated to attract French sympathy, that 'the Japanese constructors at the Yokosuka arsenal ... who were formed in the school of M. Verny, at first worked very well; but left to themselves, being no longer in the current of scientific progress, they need at present to be guided'. Kawamura asked specifically for Louis-Émile Bertin, a 45 year-old graduate of the École Polytechnique, who had specialized in naval technology, studied in Britain, worked at the Cherbourg school of naval engineering, and, as Kawamura stated, had 'had the kindness to direct the young Japanese engineers who are sent to France to perfect their art'.[53]

The choice of Bertin was also, however, due to his reputation as an innovative designer. In the Japanese navy's original request to the Japanese first minister for permission to employ him, Kawamura described Bertin as one of the top two naval architects in Europe, whose services were badly needed because of recent improvements in European ship-building technology. From this description it seems clear that Bertin's innovations in ventilation, stabilisation, and protective armament – innovations which were so quickly copied that by 1896 as many as 220 ships had adopted them – were known to Japanese naval officers. He was initially contracted for three years, from February 1886 to February 1889, and charged, as counsellor of the minister, with the direction of studies relating to naval construction and with general surveillance of Japan's arsenals. The high value placed on him was shown by his being awarded the highest official status (*chokunin*) and by his exceptional salary of 22,800 yen a year (substantially more than Verny, even allowing for inflation, and about fifteen times higher than the average for foreign employees).[54]

Bertin's appointment was favoured by Sienkiewicz in Tokyo and quickly approved by Paris. There can be little doubt that he made a good impression, for, unlike Verny, he was never the object of complaints, and his contract was extended for one year. During the time that he was in Japan, the Japanese naval attitude towards France seems to have been cordial. In July 1889 navy minister Kabayama was effusive in his praise of both Bertin and the French navy, telling Sienkiewicz that after his long stay in France in 1888, 'he had applied himself to reorganizing the Japanese navy in line with the principles and regulations of the French navy so well that he hoped that soon the navy of Japan 'would follow in the wake [*serait comme une suite*] of the navy of France'.[55] The previous year Kabayama's predecessor as minister, Saigo Tsugumichi, had also visited France and received a favourable impression.[56]

Bertin helped to bring the two navies closer together partly because his advice that Chinese naval superiority should be countered by building smaller, but heavily armed, cruisers and other fast ships opened the way to Japanese orders from French yards. Possibly, as Shinohara has suggested, the Japanese navy was also influenced by concern that Britain might not be a reliable supplier of warships because of its large Chinese interests and possible support of China in war. He further notes that in at least one case, a French shipyard responded to a Japanese tender for a cruiser with a lower bid than its British competitor.[57] Whatever the cause, the result was that the 4,217 ton cruisers *Itsukushima* and *Matsushima*, which were to be two of Japan's future front-line warships, were built to Bertin's design in France (with the similarly designed *Hashidate* being constructed at Yokosuka), while the parts for sixteen 54-ton torpedo-boats (which were to be assembled in Japan) were ordered from Le Creusot at Chalon-sur-Saone in 1888.[58]

This partial turn towards French yards was the more surprising in the light of the disappearance in December 1886 after leaving Singapore of another French-built cruiser, the *Unebi*, and it might be supposed that Bertin had succumbed to the temptation to indulge in favouritism. If there was such a tendency, however, it was probably due in part to the fact that he knew his own country's shipbuilding capabilities best. He did not always order from France, but also had one cruiser, *Chishima*, built in Britain and another at Yokosuka. According to his son, he put Japanese interests first: 'I served Japan like my own country, I considered and treated the Japanese in my entourage as I would have Frenchmen of old civilization, high culture and elevated rank'. His additional comment that he never encountered difficulties is not without significance.[59]

While Bertin's commitment to the Japanese navy seems beyond dispute, the value of his contribution is more difficult to measure. It has been argued that his policy of making cruisers the major Japanese warship was flawed, because they were unable to sink the Chinese battleships in the 1894–95 war. Their quick-firing guns, although effective, proved to be no substitute for heavy guns, while their single 12.6 inch large gun played only a small part in the 1894 battle of the Yalu because it could only fire one shot in five minutes. His designs also suffered, it has been alleged, from other defects: 'M. Bertin was a very competent designer, but even so too much had to be sacrificed to get the heavy guns to sea on the small displacement. Protection was on a very light scale except for the barbette and shield for the large gun, the rest of the ship being vulnerable to shot above 4.7 inch calibre. Sea-keeping qualities were poor and the designed speed was never reached'.[60] Against this verdict, however, there is evidence that the ships which Bertin designed did perform well in both the Sino-Japanese and the Russo-Japanese wars. The day after the decisive naval battle of the Yalu in December 1894, the Japanese commanding admiral, Ito

Yukio, wrote to Bertin that his ships had lived up to expectations: 'They constitute . . . the formidable elements of our fleet; thanks to their powerful character and the informed ideas which presided over their construction we have been able to win a brilliant victory against the Chinese ironclads'.[61] However one balances these opinions, it should be noted that designing warships was not Bertin's only claim to Japanese gratitude. He also extended Japan's naval capacity by pressing for the creation of two new arsenals at Sasebo and Kure to supplement Yokosuka; and he played a major role in introducing the most up-to-date steelmaking techniques, to ensure that Japan got the best out of his state-of-the-art designs.[62]

FRANCE AND THE DEVELOPMENT OF JAPANESE INDUSTRY

Bertin's pressure for the introduction of up-to-date steelmaking technology was significant not only for naval construction but for the general modernization of industrial technology. In this he was following in the footsteps of Verny, for the Yokosuka dockyard and foundry represented Japan's first major venture in the field of heavy industry. The operations at Yokosuka, together with those at the associated foundry at Yokohama, introduced the Japanese to practical engineering on a large scale; and with over one thousand Japanese workers regularly employed at Yokosuka, and well over one hundred at Yokohama, new skills were widely disseminated. According to one historian, the French trained several thousand workers who 'took their skills to newer and smaller factories and emerged as leaders of working-class society'.[63] In addition to on-the-job training, there was also some attempt to provide technical education in schools for some of the workers, although Verny himself, at the end of his ten years in Japan, felt that this was the one area in which more could have been done.[64]

The number of French workers employed at Yokosuka did not exceed 45 at any one time, although over the whole period a considerably larger number of Frenchmen worked there. By the painstaking reckoning of Saigusa Hiroto, Nozaki Shigeru and Sasaki Takashi it was as high as 98.[65] This helps to explain why as many as 177 Frenchmen are listed (out of a total of 1392 foreigners) as contributing to Japan's industrial and technological modernization between 1860 and 1914, a figure which ranks France equal second (with the United States) to Britain (which could boast 649) and ahead of Germany (135).[66] In qualitative terms, however, it is doubtful whether France really played such an important role as these overall figures suggest, and it is significant that among the 290 Westerners whose contributions are individually outlined by Saigusa, Nozaki and Sasaki, no more than eighteen Frenchmen are featured (6.2%, as compared with 12.75% of the overall number).

Some Frenchmen, nevertheless, did make a noteworthy impact. The best known was Paul Brunat, who was involved in the modernization of the silk industry. Like many foreigners he was young (29) when he went to Japan in 1869 to work as a quality inspector for a silk-trading company in the Yokohama after acquiring experience of various aspects of the silk industry in his native prefecture, Drôme, in Lyons and in Spain.[67] He quickly acquired a reputation for his ability to detect poor-quality silk and his tough attitude toward merchants who tried to sell it. In 1870 he signed a contract with the Meiji government to organize the establishment of a modern filature.[68] After selecting Tomioka, in what was to become Gumma prefecture, as the site, Brunat apparently spent a month watching spinners using existing methods because, he is supposed to have said, 'his aim was not to utilise European machines in disregard of traditional ways, but to operate a simple transition between the two techniques, in order to make the most of the qualities of the Japanese workers'.[69]

Brunat went back to France to buy machinery in early 1871, returning a year later with a team of nine French men and women. The plant was completed in June 1872 and although the size of the reeling machines and the black smoke emitted from the filature apparently made recruitment of local girls difficult, official pressure ensured that before long over 400 women operators, a majority of them from samurai families, were employed there.[70] Brunat's regulations established conditions of work (eight hours in a nine and a half-hour day, no night work, and Sundays free) which were less harsh than those imposed by private filature owners later;[71] and this may partly explain why, as more recent historians have been inclined to stress, Tomioka was not commercially profitable. Such a criticism is beside the point, however. What mattered was rather the demonstration that modern filatures producing silk of consistent quality could be operated in Japan. Together with this went the dissemination of operating skills. Many of the women who had been trained became instructors in privately established filatures, and by the time Brunat returned to France, his work finished, in 1875, the process of modernization of Japanese silk-reeling, gradual though it was to be, had clearly got under way.

The only other Frenchman who might be compared with Brunat was François Coignet. A graduate of the School of Mining in his native St. Étienne, Coignet had worked in Madagascar, California and Mexico before coming into contact at the age of 32 with the Satsuma representatives at the 1867 Exposition in Paris and accepting a rather vague offer of employment by their domain. Having arrived in Japan, however, he transferred in the late summer of 1868 to the service of the Meiji government which, having only limited sources of revenue, was anxious to extract as much specie as possible from the mines which it had taken over from the previous regime. Coignet inspected and surveyed several mines and analysed ores, but his main effort was concentrated on redeveloping the Ikuno mine near Hyogo, which had appeared to be exhausted by the mid-1860s after producing gold and silver for almost a thousand years. On his advice the policy of extracting copper first was adopted. Western machinery (or, more commonly, Western-style machinery manufactured at Yokosuka) was acquired to deal with the problems of tunnel drainage and ventilation, and French miners were hired, as well as a geologist.

By the spring of 1871 Coignet had proved that inactive mines could be revived by the use of modern technology, even on a small scale, but he then put forward a proposal that more could be achieved by larger-scale improvements (notably a lengthy rail track for easier transport) and was allowed to go to France to buy equipment and hire more personnel in the late summer of 1871.[72] On 4 October 1873 the *Moniteur des Soies* recorded the fact that 'a little colony' of fifteen Frenchmen existed in the village of Ikuno, and on 25 March 1876 it noted that the mine's silver output was worth 200,000 francs (c.40,000 yen) a month.

Altogether 24 French miners and mining specialists were employed at the mine down to 1881. By that time Coignet had himself been for four years back in France, where he suffered from poor health but wrote a highly rated treatise on mining before his death in 1902.[73]

Of French contributions to other areas of industrial technology, the only one which has a clear claim to attention is the pioneering work by Henri Pelegrin, another young man (he was born in 1841), in developing the production of gas and introducing gas lighting.[74] There had been an initial effort in this direction under the impulsion of the governor of Yokohama, but not until Pelegrin's arrival in 1870 (after involvement in the setting up of gas lighting in the French concession of Shanghai) did things start moving. He effectively took over the running of the gas company headed by Takashima Kayuemon, secured a commission to go to Britain to buy equipment, and on his return supervised the introduction of gas lighting in the streets of Yokohama. The work was completed in October 1872, and between January and December 1874 Pelegrin also oversaw the installation of street lighting in central Tokyo. He remained in Japan until the end of 1878 and, together with Japanese associates (with whom he seems to have established a relationship of trust), he developed the manufacture of clay firebricks. Unfortunately for his reputation, however, the attractiveness of gas was severely limited firstly by the easy availability, through imports, of kerosene oil, and secondly by the development of electric lighting in the 1890s.

Most of the French involvement in Japanese industrial modernization was channelled through French experts in Japan. In some cases, however, Japanese learned about advanced techniques by studying them in France. This happened as early as 1872, when the Kyoto city government sent two Nishijin silk-weavers to Lyons, together with a skilled tool-maker, to master the use of Jacquard looms, six of which were to be purchased. After they returned to Kyoto, the weavers taught the techniques which they had learned to local craftsmen. Five years later, in 1877, eight more young men from Kyoto were sent to Lyons to study weaving, thread spinning, flax spinning, dyeing, and pottery.[75]

FRANCE AND THE MODERNISATION OF
GOVERNMENTAL INSTITUTIONS

The French contribution to Japan's technological modernization was not insignificant, but in general France was not the country to which the Japanese turned first in their efforts to develop their economy. There were, however, areas in which France was either the principal or the initial model. French institutions, in particular, were attractive to a Japanese government which was aiming at the elimination of the deeply rooted, and potentially dangerous, traditions of localism which the division of the country into more or less autonomous domains for several centuries had reinforced. Although both Germany and Italy had recently achieved national unification, neither could yet offer examples of successful integration based on strong central control. France could. No other major country came near to rivalling it in the extent of its centralization, and its institutions had survived various changes of regime. It was natural, therefore, that Japanese leaders, in seeking to build a modern state, should look to France and Frenchmen for model and guidance.

One of the institutions which the Meiji government sought to emulate was the French police system. This was stated explicitly in a letter of 31 July 1876 from Ito Hirobumi to Okubo Toshimichi: 'the *Keishi-cho* (Metropolitan Police Board) entirely follows the French police rules, and it is desirable these should be imitated in both spirit and form'.[76] The nature of the Japanese debt to France in police organization is spelled out by the one Western scholar, Eleanor Westney, who has studied the process of Meiji institutional adaptation in depth: 'By the end of the Meiji period Japan's police system exhibited an evident kinship to the European police, especially to its French model. The dual structure of the judicial and administrative policing; the gendarmerie, or military police, whose primary role was as an auxiliary civil police force; the wide range of functions; the mode of financing; and a powerful and centrally administered police organization for the national capital – all these features were derived from France. The speed with which the Japanese government was able to construct the national police system owes much to the fact that it had a 'blueprint' at hand, in the form of the French system itself and of the French-modelled Tokyo police'.[77] Westney takes care to point out that imitation inevitably required adaptation, and that the *Keishi-cho* also innovated, most notably in establishing training schools for police recruits in 1880, three years before the first police school was set up in the West (in Paris). Even this innovation was partly imitative, however, for it was modelled on the military academy which the French army officers had helped to introduce, with St. Cyr in mind, in 1874.[78]

While Westney stresses that the French police system was selected as a model chiefly because of its general attractiveness and suitability, she also notes that the choice was influenced by other factors, among them the existence of 'networks of personal contact that made it easier to find the right advisers to help build organizations in other fields'.[79] Both personal contacts and personal experiences were certainly relevant. To begin with, the Japanese were first made aware of the efficiency of the Parisian police through the published account in 1868 by Kurimoto Joun of his experiences in the French capital in 1867. The reputation of the French system was further enhanced by the 1869 report which the Meiji government requested from another, albeit earlier, visitor to France, Fukuzawa Yukichi.[80] Positive support for the adoption of the French system was forthcoming from another traveller, Saigo Tsugumichi. He urged it on his elder brother, Saigo Takamori, and this prominent figure in 1872 suggested to one of his followers, Kawaji Toshiyoshi, that he should go to Europe to study its police systems. Of the ten months that Kawaji stayed there, four were spent in France. He was to return to France on a further study mission in 1879–80.[81]

Other personal connections were also involved. The interpreter for Kawaji's mission was Numa Morikazu, who had been attached to Chanoine's military mission. More importantly, Georges Bousquet, a French legal adviser, included information about the different functions of the judicial and administrative police in a series of lectures on the French legal codes and courts which he gave to Justice Ministry officials in 1872 Since the Justice Ministry was at this time wholly responsible for the existing rudimentary, and partly traditional, police system, Bousquet was well placed to influence the process of creating a new structure.[82] Even more relevant in this context was the fact that the justice minister, Eto Shimpei, was an admirer of France who had already received encouragement from French chargé d'affaires Turenne in his effort to acquire French legal expertise and a better understanding of the French legal system. During Kawaji's absence in Europe, Eto was himself actively pursuing knowledge of the French police by asking the French government, through its Tokyo legation, for details of police organization. The French government went to some lengths to provide these.[83]

In contrast to the normal pattern of Meiji modernization, the Japanese made very little use of foreign advisers, the only one whose name is reasonably well known being Wilhelm Hoehn, a German who had some influence in the 1880s. The man who above all created the modern police system, Kawaji Toshiyoshi, did, however, personally seek the services of one foreigner, and he was a Frenchman, Prosper Gambet-Gross. An experienced lawyer who came to Yokohama in 1873 at the relatively advanced age of 53, he impressed Kawaji in 1875 by his successful presentation of the Japanese government's case against one of its British employees in the British consular court. After becoming a *Keishi-cho* adviser in 1876, Gambet-Gross assisted in many court cases involving foreigners. His help was sought because it was feared that Japanese inexperience in such a sensitive area might lead to the loss of police jurisdictional rights under the ill-defined extraterritoriality system. Gambet-Gross went further than this, however, by lecturing to police officers on French criminal and criminal procedure law, showing how these were important to Japan and also urging the need to respect basic human rights and abolish torture as a method of extracting confessions. The lectures were published and attracted public as well as police interest. His dedication to the safeguarding and extension of Japanese police rights was matched by his devotion to Kawaji. When he died in 1881, he was, at his special request, buried in Aoyama cemetery next to his former chief, who had died a year before.[84]

One of the main reasons why the French police system was so attractive to the Meiji government was that the Paris Prefect of Police was directly responsible to the Minister of the Interior and could thus be reliably used for political purposes. Such a role was even more important in Japan, where the danger of revolt and assassination was all too real in the early Meiji period, and it was logical that the *Keishi-cho* should be set up in 1874, soon after the establishment of a Home Ministry (*Naimusho*) by the Meiji government after the 1873 split over Korean policy led to major dissent. This new ministry, which was headed by the strong leader, Okubo Toshimichi, not only took over the function of maintaining law and order but also became closely involved in economic development and the introduction of a new tax system. It resembled its French counterpart in many of its features, partly, no doubt, because Dubousquet had provided an outline of the French Interior Ministry's organization.

The prefectural system through which the Home Ministry mostly controlled the country undoubtedly was influenced by French local government (even though the Meiji government could also call upon Japan's own Chinese-based earlier tradition). Not only was a mission sent to France in March 1872 to examine the workings of French administration in general, but in June of the same year the governor of the recently created Tokyo metropolitan district deemed it of sufficient importance to learn about the municipal system of Paris to visit it personally.[85] In a letter to *L'Echo du Japon* of 25 November 1881, an anonymous Japanese went so far as to claim that 'Japanese institutions are, in general, an imitation of French institutions' and he asserted that 'after the great revolution of 1868 the han (principalities) were replaced by *ken*, which are absolutely as your departments are in France', adding that subsequently 'there have been created arrondissements (*gun* and *ku*), district councils, municipal councils in the towns and villages, departmental commissions, and in order to organize all these one has literally imitated France'. Even *L'Echo du Japon* felt that the writer might be exaggerating slightly, but the tribute could not have been paid if there had been no ground for it at all.

Another important sphere in which the French tradition of centralization provided an attractive model was education. It is generally accepted that the Fundamental Education Law of 1872, the first attempt by the Meiji government to introduce a modern system of compulsory primary education, was based on French practice, particularly in establishing close central control over the new elementary schools and the content of their teaching. Few, if any, historians, however, would claim that the new system worked well in Japan. In the words of Nagai Michio, 'the government had succeeded in devising an educational system after the French model but the Japanese economy was still too weak and backward to make the implementation of such a grand plan feasible'.[86] Although a new Education Ordinance was issued in 1879, however, and although there were further adjustments in the 1880s, one of the features of the 1872 law which was distinctively French – the high degree of state control over basic education, and hence its marked uniformity – largely survived; and the aim of universal education for all children, which French ideals encouraged, was to be achieved by the end of the Meiji period. What survived less well was 'the French and American notion that the purpose of education was the advancement of the individual, materially as well as intellectually'.[87] As a result of this imbalance the long-term effects of French influence on the Japanese education system may not have been wholly beneficial.[88]

FRANCE AND THE MODERNIZATION OF JAPANESE LAW

If institutions were the building-blocks of the modern structure which Meiji Japan was so intent on erecting, one of the chief elements which supported them was a modern system of law. It was in providing both a legal model and expert advisers that France made one of its most durable contributions to Japan's modernization. Much of what was involved is well known. Certainly, the story of justice minister Eto Shimpei's 1869 suggestion that the Napoleonic codes might be translated and then applied, just as they were, has often been used to illustrate Japan's early awareness of the advantages to a newly unified state of a comprehensive body of law which had been tried and tested and which would make possible the elimination of outdated custom and local particularism.[89] It hardly needs to be added that a further imperative reason for adopting Western-style legal codes and systems existed in the universally accepted desire to revise the 'unequal treaties'. Over and over Meiji leaders were told by foreigners, when they sought to regain the right of full jurisdiction over them, that this would be only possible when they had introduced a new legal structure.

With such strong motives operating it is not surprising that the Meiji government was quick to hire foreign legal specialists. It was initially prompted to do so in 1870, when the Justice Ministry official, Mitsukuri Rinsho, who had been ordered to translate the French civil code into Japanese, requested that he be allowed to study in France because of his difficulty in understanding some of the terminology. Since this would mean the suspension of the translation, his request was denied. Instead, Eto decided that it would make more sense to hire a French expert who could not only clarify the meaning of the text but also teach Japanese law students. It took some time for the Japanese minister in Paris, the youthful Samejima Hisanobu, to find a candidate, but in early 1872 Georges Bousquet, a lawyer who himself was only 27 years old but whom Samejima commended for his good character and academic strength, arrived in Japan.[90] He stayed for only four years, and is best known for the readable and wide-ranging two-volume work, *Le Japon de nos Jours,* which he published in 1877. From one of Captain Lebon's letters, it seems that he was not the most hard-working of men;[91] but he did provide useful information and his lectures at the law school (the *Meihoryo*) within the Justice Ministry were apparently well-prepared and clear.[92]

In both these respects he differed from the legal expert who joined the Justice Ministry in late 1873, Gustave-Émile Boissonade de Fontarabie (1825–1910). Boissonade was a mature scholar who had held a chair at the University of Grenoble before returning in 1867 to the University of Paris and had published extensively.[93] Like his younger colleague (who seems not have welcomed his arrival), Boissonade was known to Samejima, who had sent Japanese students to his lectures, but the Dean of the Faculty of Law at Paris also seems to have played a part in his selection.[94] He was clearly expected to be away for only a limited period, and not the 21 years which he did spend in Japan and which brought him to the age of retirement. The faculty-based journal which he had jointly edited, the *Revue de Législation Ancienne et Moderne Française et Étrangère,* reported that a fellow had been attached to the Paris Law Faculty 'in order not to permit any adverse effects during the temporary absence of M. Boissonade, who is going to carry to Japan our ideas and our traditions, and aid it in providing itself with legislation which is in line with European civilization'.[95]

Whoever was responsible for selecting Boissonade chose well. Not only did he train many students within the Justice Ministry, he also taught at the *Meiji Horitsu Gakko* (the forerunner of Meiji University) and in another private law school, the *Wa-Futsu Horitsu Gakko* (subsequently Hosei University), which he himself helped to set up. His lectures may have been discursive and hard to follow at times, but he probably did more than any other foreign legal specialist to encourage Japanese to think about the foundations of law and he certainly propagated universal values through his championing of the idea of natural law. His was also one of the most strenuous voices calling for the abolition of torture (achieved in 1879) as a means of securing confessions. Through his published commentaries, which were extensively used in the examinations taken by would-be bureaucrats, as well as by legal specialists, his approach to law reached a significant proportion of Japan's future élite.[96]

Important though his teaching was, Boissonade's fame rests more on his role in compiling Meiji Japan's new legal codes. He was largely responsible for the Criminal Code and the Code of Criminal Procedure, both of which were published in 1880 and promulgated in 1882; and it has been suggested that a draft by him, although discarded, prepared the ground for the 1890 Code of Civil Procedure, which is normally seen (like the Commercial Code) as wholly German in inspiration.[97] Boissonade's major undertaking, however, – the Civil Code – is better known for the controversy it provoked after its promulgation in 1890 than for his monumental achievement in authoring most of its 1762 articles. Such was the weight of opposition that a committee had to be set up to produce a new version, and when the Civil Code was eventually put into effect in 1899, it had a much more German appearance (although much of its substance remained unchanged).[98]

This setback undoubtedly tarnished Boissonade's reputation, but it needs to be noted that much of the opposition was prompted by the imminent opening of the Diet, which meant that party politicians (and newspapers) were looking for ways to embarrass the government and force it to make concessions.[99] They would certainly have found it much more difficult to make an issue out of the Civil Code had there not been also a chorus of criticism from legal specialists, but much of this arose from the way in which the teaching of law in Japan had come to be divided between rival French, German and British schools. Academic lawyers, in particular, had a vested interest in having the tradition in which they had been trained predominate, and some them were prepared to make what Boissonade, at any rate, regarded as exaggerated accusations against his draft.

Boissonade presented his defence in the *Revue Française du Japon*, a periodical to which he was a prominent contributor. Some of the allegations – such as the claim that the code could not admit the existence of inequality between sovereign and subject, parent and child, or master and servant – he dismissed as scarcely worthy of comment. Others – for example, the argument that the section of the code dealing with Persons had been subordinated to that dealing with Property – he rejected by pointing to the fact that some provisions in the latter had been changed to make them consistent with the former. On the central issue of whether too little account had been taken of the special nature of the Japanese family system, he altered the ground of his defence. While claiming that the new civil code did indeed 'respect the longstanding organization of the family, except for slight modifications, and the right of succession, with its privileges, by the eldest son', he was not prepared to accept that 'the authority of ancestors should influence the distribution and administration of wealth [fortunes]', since he maintained that 'if the nations of the Orient have remained behind modern civilization, the principal cause is that the present generations have their eyes turned towards the past, instead of having them turned towards the future'. Similarly, at the same time as he objected to those who denounced the code for paving the way for 'a revolution in the family and hence in Society', he justified the provision which allowed a widow to become the legal guardian of her child's interests by arguing that her affection was likely to be stronger than anyone else's and also because 'the woman's role in the family ought to be raised, and the civil code raises the mother and the wife, as is appropriate in a civilized country'.

One other criticism which Boissonade contested was even more general – that he had 'admitted, like the French code, a natural law which preceded positive law'. On this point he had no truck with his critics. They might, he pronounced, have discussed whether the Civil Code gave better expression to natural law than the Commercial Code, 'but one cannot seek another foundation for civil law and for commercial law since, without it, there would remain only the arbitrary'. Plainly Boissonade was not willing to abandon his most basic principle. Nevertheless, he was not inflexible in practice, and he was certainly not a slavish follower of French precedent. Indeed, he was at pains to stress that in order to give Japan the most advanced legal system in the world he had borrowed freely from countries which had improved upon the Napoleonic codes.[100]

To what extent Boissonade's progressive ideals were forced to accommodate Japanese traditional practices and inclinations emerges clearly from a review in 1881 of the changes made to the French legal expert's much earlier draft Criminal and Criminal Procedure Codes. The author of the review was Roquette, the minister in Tokyo, but its level of detail, and the insight it revealed, strongly suggest that he was expressing Boissonade's own opinions. To begin with, Roquette showed that he had inside knowledge of how Boissonade's original drafts had come to be modified. As he presented it, the process of amendment reflected a background of bureaucratic in-fighting: the Justice Ministry had resisted the efforts of the *Dajokan* (Council of State) and the *Genro-in* (Senate) to participate in the drafting of the two codes and had had to pay the price for this when the drafts had to be submitted to those two bodies for approval. Perhaps surprisingly, he found some consolation in this explanation of the tampering with Boissonade's work: 'I have the satisfaction of thinking that there is, in the circumstances, no reaction against the spirit of French legislation, which, moreover, remains manifestly dominant in the new Japanese codes; there is only a simple rivalry between organizations, only a wholly internal struggle'.[101]

Although he played down the significance (for France) of the revisions, Roquette had to acknowledge that although many were purely formal or trivial, others were, or might be, important. One was that the death penalty was allowed for political crimes, whereas the original draft had limited it to attempts on the life of the Emperor. This was regretted by the French minister, but he found it understandable in the light of the Takehashi mutiny by part of the Imperial Guard – 'the terrible insurrection of 1878, which was grave just when this part of the draft was being discussed'. He recognised that the change reflected the fact that 'the Japanese government cannot yet have on certain points of public law the same views and the same principles of conduct as the majority of the governments of Europe and America'. Another alteration, which Roquette hoped would in time be revised, was the strengthening of the provision relating to defamation of officials; whereas the original scheme had allowed a newspaper to justify its alleged defamation by furnishing proof, no such provision remained in the approved code. Above all, however, Roquette deplored the abandonment of the proposal for juries in criminal trials. Seventy articles had been devoted to this innovation, and he was convinced that ultimately, when treaty revision had been achieved, it would have been in the interests of French nationals. He noted the Meiji government's claimed concern that there were too few enlightened Japanese outside the official class to sustain the burden of jury service, but he voiced the suspicion that there was a further reason: that the government, 'which believes it premature to admit the Japanese people to participate in public affairs, has seen dangers in its involvement in criminal justice'.[102]

From Roquette's account it is plain that the decisions on the jury system and capital punishment for political crimes were felt deeply by Boissonade. This fact is not evident in the latter's preface to his *Projet de Code de Procédure Criminelle pour l'Empire du Japon,* which he published in Tokyo in 1882. In that volume he briefly mentioned that his project had been revised; but while stressing that he had consulted the Belgian and Austro-Hungarian codes, and while expressing the hope that the new Japanese codes would so effectively embody generally applicable legal provisions that they might offer a sort of international common law, he also noted (like Roquette) that the alterations had not been intended as a reaction against French ideas. Roquette's dispatch, however, reveals that when Boissonade's wishes on the jury and capital punishment did not prevail, he opted out of the review process. In that way, Roquette observed, 'he disengaged himself from all the other modifications. Doubtless, a great number of faults of detail would have been avoided; but it is difficult to blame him'.[103]

Notwithstanding his regrets about the opportunities missed, Roquette ultimately gave the new codes high marks. He listed many examples of liberalisation, including the removal of the death penalty for many offences and the opening of trials to the public; and in acknowledging that 'the Japanese legislator has evidently kept in touch with modern science and has assimilated in large part our French ideas of justice and humanity', he paid the leading Japanese jurists an unusual compliment. His overall verdict was similarly generous: 'these codes constitute, not only a considerable advance on the existing Japanese legislation, already much softened since the Imperial Restoration; but they even realise several reforms which Frenchmen have urged for a long time'.[104]

Boissonade's role in Meiji legal modernization was his most notable achievement, but his services to Japan went well beyond this. Some of these related to Japanese foreign policy and are fairly well known. The first came in June 1874 when, scarcely six months after his arrival in Japan, he provided Okubo Toshimichi with arguments to justify Japan's sending of a military expedition to Taiwan and helped to reassure the Emperor by answering the latter's questions.[105] That his advice was regarded as valuable was shown by Okubo's taking him to China so that he could consult him during his negotiations there. Much less well known is the fact that Boissonade's views were sought in 1875 after an incident involving a Korean attack on a Japanese ship. Most of the points he made were incorporated in the instructions given to the Japanese envoy who was sent to secure a diplomatic settlement and who, adopting the same strong line that Boissonade had advocated, returned with a treaty which opened three Korean ports to trade.[106]

In the light of Boissonade's support for Japan's assertion of its interests against China and Korea, it may appear surprising that subsequently he advocated a much closer relationship with the former country. He did so, however, very emphatically in 1882, when an attack on Japanese diplomats and soldiers in Seoul prompted thoughts of war with China (which possessed a dominant influence in Korea). In a discussion with the influential Inoue Kowashi, Boissonade criticized the latter's opportunistic approach to foreign policy, arguing that Russia was a much bigger danger than China and that to cope with this danger, Japan should aim at cooperation with China and establish a Japanese-Chinese-Korean alliance (*domei*). Japan and China, he claimed, were 'natural allies' which shared a common race, writing system, customs, and religion and were also both looked down upon by the Europeans.[107]

Although its factual basis was not entirely accurate, this view was similar to that expressed shortly afterwards by the high-ranking Iwakura Tomomi, to whom Inoue was an adviser, and it may also have influenced foreign minister Inoue Kaoru in his policy towards China. The historian, Watanabe Ikujiro, suggests not only this, but also that Boissonade was the person who first prompted the Meiji government to think about a Japanese-Chinese alliance.[108] The possibility of such an alliance, it should be added, had provoked alarm among Western diplomats in East Asia in the early 1870s, when most of them had attributed to the signing of the first treaty between China and Japan more significance than was justified. That Boissonade, a Westerner himself, should put it forward shows that his nationality did not interfere with his loyalty to his 'second country', as he described Japan.[109]

If any doubts remain about Boissonade's devotion to Japan, his position during the treaty revision negotiations in the 1880s should remove them. The testimony of the French minister in Tokyo in 1889 is in this case incontestable. Boissonade, he pronounced,

> . . . has deserved well of Japan. He has combatted, by all the means at his disposal, the policy of the foreign Powers, and notably that of France, in the matter of treaty revision. He readily claims the credit for having made the Japanese more demanding in the questions of jurisdiction. I even have reason to think that he will devote the last part of the leave which he has just commenced to campaigning in France on behalf of the Japanese government's views in this same matter of revision.[110]

It was not only the Western powers which Boissonade combatted. His belief that Inoue Kaoru was giving too much away to foreign demands in 1887 by accepting foreign judges in Japanese courts led the Frenchman to present the reasoned objections which ignited the opposition to the foreign minister's proposals and eventually caused their abandonment.[111] Boissonade was no doubt partly influenced by a not unnatural sense of grievance, in that the legal code which he had put so much effort into preparing was to be subjected to the Powers' approval. Even so, his action was courageous.

Boissonade's expertise was not confined to law. He had also written about political economy and taught it in the University of Paris for three years; and this may have become known to Okubo during their time together in China. As home minister, Okubo concerned himself with Japan's economic development, and it was he, together with industry minister Ito Hirobumi, who organized a series of lectures by Boissonade in 1876.[112] They were initially delivered in the *Sei-in*, the policy-making division of the *Dajokan*, and subsequently in the *Genro-in* (Senate), and the audiences included members of both bodies and other officials, in addition to Okubo and Ito. Boissonade undoubtedly saw the lectures as more than academic exercises, and he used them to put over his pro-free trade ideas. In view of Japan's current lack of tariff autonomy, his advocacy of the eventual abolition of import and export duties may not have seemed of particular relevance, but his call for the suppression of all regulations which might hinder internal commerce would presumably have been generally approved, while more progressive Japanese would have welcomed his assertion that 'political economy will demand of Japan that individual ownership of land replaces, more and more, collective ownership, whether of the State or of pubic administrative bodies'.[113] How much impact the lectures had can hardly be estimated, but the fact that Boissonade gave another series in 1877 suggests that they were appreciated.

Boissonade's total contribution to Japan certainly was appreciated. When he finally departed, after nearly 21 years, in 1894, he was sent off with a glowing tribute by the Germanophile Inoue Kowashi, who, on the basis of personal knowledge, praised his unremitting application to work. The tribute seems to have been fully justified: on 21 November 1884 *L'Echo du Japon*, reporting that Boissonade had gone to take the waters at Atami (not very many miles from Tokyo), added that the Japanese newspapers who announced this 'observe that it is the first time that he has taken leave during the twelve years that he has been in the Japanese government's service'. Other foreign employees served Japan with real commitment, but few matched Boissonade in this respect, and the award of a pension of 2,000 yen indicates that the Meiji government recognized his dedication. What made him so dedicated for so long a time can only be guessed at. However, judging from his statement (in his funeral oration for Gambet-Gross) that he himself wished to be buried next to Okubo, it may not have derived only from a desire for achievement or a deep sense of duty but also from a much more personal admiration for, or empathy with, at least some of the Japanese with whom he worked.[114]

THE FRENCH LANGUAGE IN JAPAN

Boissonade's role in the transformation of Japanese law would not have been possible had there not been Japanese available to interpret for him and translate his writings. Indeed, since not only Boissonade but most foreigners were unable to communicate in Japanese, Japan's modernizing enterprise in general depended heavily on the willingness and ability of a substantial number of Japanese to learn foreign languages. Moreover, if foreign ideas and foreigners' proposals were to be examined intelligently, not only linguistic skills but also more specialized knowledge of Western institutions and traditions were required. By the mid-nineteenth century Japan, despite its political isolation, had already made large strides towards acquiring knowledge about the West, but the medium through which this learning had come was principally the Dutch language. In 1807 no Japanese was able to translate a letter written in French by a Russian emissary;[115] and when Mermet de Cachon, who had spent some years in the Ryukyus as a missionary, acted as interpreter for Baron Gros in 1858, there was still no one who could perform a similar role for the Bakufu.

This situation was soon to change dramatically, especially after the establishment of a French school at Yokohama with

Bakufu support in 1865. Although it was the arrival of Frenchmen which was mainly responsible for the rapid development in the 1860s, however, some pioneering efforts by Japanese also deserve recognition. The earliest of these was the production by Motoki Shozaemon and two other Dutch-language interpreters in Nagasaki in 1814 of a French manual (*Furansu-jihan*), which contained some vocabulary and basic grammar.[116] Because the Bakufu soon lost the interest in promoting the study of French which the 1807 incident had stimulated, this manual proved of little immediate relevance, but it may have been of some help, over thirty years later, to the first serious student of French, Murakami Eishun. Murakami, a friend of the celebrated Dutch scholar, Sakuma Shozan, seems to have acquired, mainly through an old Dutch-French dictionary, a basic grasp of the language by 1850; and his 1854 manual in French, English and Dutch (*Sango Benran*) was the first work by a Japanese to use French. He followed this with a series of further writings and translations, including, in 1864, the first alphabetical French-Japanese dictionary (*Futsugo Meiyo*) to appear in Japan.[117]

From 1860 Murakami taught French at the Bakufu's institute for foreign study, the *Bansho Shirabesho* (renamed *Kaiseijo* in 1863), where some teaching was also done from 1861 by Irie Bunro, who had learned the elements of the language from Murakami's writings.[118] Irie had also received lessons from a French legation official, Weuve, just as another early student of French, the ex-doctor and Bakufu official, Kurimoto Joun, had the benefit of contact with Mermet de Cachon in Hokkaido. The real upsurge in the study of French, however, came after Léon Roches, with Mermet de Cachon and Kurimoto playing key roles as intermediaries, established a special relationship with the Bakufu from the second half of 1864. With this as a stimulus the number of students of French at the *Kaiseijo* in 1868 rose as high as 200, according to one estimate.[119]

This was not the only way in which the Bakufu-French relationship had an impact on the study of French, for by early 1865 Roches had prompted Japanese leaders to provide a site for a school which would enable Japanese to communicate with and learn from the large number of Frenchmen who would be employed at the naval dockyard and arsenal which was soon to be built at Yokosuka. The school itself was established at Yokohama.[120] Mermet de Cachon, who had already acquired some pupils in Hakodate, readily agreed to take charge of it, and Roches himself helped to plan the curriculum. When it commenced operations in early 1865, it had 47 Japanese students, most of them aged from fourteen to twenty. Examinations were held every three months, and the turnover of students appears to have been rapid, for it was later claimed that several hundred were taught there. Some of them were of fairly high status, for the Bakufu saw the school also as a nursery for practitioners of diplomacy.[121] Despite the change of regime in 1868, its graduates' skills were appreciated by the Meiji government: fourteen of them found positions in the Army Ministry, nine in the Navy Ministry, seven in the Foreign Ministry, five in the Education Ministry, three in the Home Ministry, three in the Public Works Ministry, and others were scattered through the bureaucracy.[122] In 1866 the educational provision was expanded when Verny, the engineer in charge of the Yokosuka project, initiated some separate instruction in naval design and in technical skills, but this, like the teaching at Yokohama, was suspended with the fall of the Bakufu.[123]

One other school taught French to a considerable number of students in the Bakumatsu period – the *Saibikan*, which was established in Nagasaki in 1865 by the French priest, Petitjean, with the encouragement of the French consul there, Léon Dury.[124] Although the school changed its name (to *Kounkan*) in 1868, teaching there seems to have been only briefly interrupted by the Restoration. Over the 1868–71 period it had 48 students of French (in addition to 111 of English and 22 of Russian), among them Saionji Kimmochi, a Court noble and future prime minister, and Inoue Kowashi, a later minister of education.[125] French also continued to be taught at what had been the *Kaiseijo* but in 1868 became the *Kaisei Gakko* before being incorporated in the new *Daigaku* from 1869 to 1871. In 1869 the French school at Yokohama was reopened, with an ex-Bakufu official as director. It was then transferred to military control, and in 1870, when it had 35 students, eleven of them from Choshu (including Katsura Taro, a later army minister and prime minister, and Sone Arasuke, a later minister to Paris), it was incorporated in the *Heigakuryo* in Osaka.[126]

Other government ministries also felt a need to train their personnel in an appropriate language in order to prepare them for specialized study, and in the case of the Justice Ministry this meant a four-year course in French, with Frenchmen as teachers.[127] The Education Ministry too was naturally a major hirer of foreign teachers: of its 71 foreign employees in August 1873, eleven were French. Some of these taught at the Foreign Languages School (*Gaikokugo Gakko*) established in Tokyo in 1873 and converted in 1877 into a four-year preparatory division of the newly constituted Imperial University in Tokyo.[128] The Education Ministry was also responsible for a French-language school in Kyoto (notable partly because Dury had transferred there and partly because the 72 pupils who were learning French there in 1872 included nine girls) until 1874, when government cuts forced its closure.[129]

The boom in French study after 1869 also produced a number of private schools. In 1871–2 there were five in Tokyo which taught French (four exclusively). One of them was Murakami's *Tatsurido* which between 1868 and its closure in 1877 had 429 students.[130] Another private teacher immediately after the change of government (although he also acquired an official position as a French teacher at the *Daigaku* in 1870) was Nakae Chomin.[131] A samurai from Tosa, Nakae had studied French at Nagasaki from 1865 and in Edo and Yokohama in 1867 before serving as interpreter for Léon Roches in the troubled early months of 1868. He then became interested in French law and in 1871 managed to be sent to France by the Justice Ministry, although once there he devoted his attention to philosophy, history and literature. After returning to Japan in 1874 he, not surprisingly, did not re-enter the Justice Ministry, but instead became head of the recently established Tokyo Foreign Language School. His insistence on making classical Chinese a compulsory subject (comparable to the classical languages in European schools) resulted in his removal after after only three months, and he only lasted for eighteen months in his next job as a translator at the *Genro-in*. This allowed (or forced) him to concentrate on his writing and, more immediately, upon his revived career as a private teacher. According to one study of his life, his academy (the *Futsugakujuku* or *Furansu Gakusha*) 'was important in Meiji Japan not only because of the large number of students it trained – nearly two thousand in twelve years – but also because of the attitudes it fostered. Chomin did not simply teach a series of disconnected courses; he taught the world view he had learned in France'.[132]

It would be difficult to estimate how many of Nakae Chomin's students were more interested in French ideas than in the French language, but the latter alone was undoubtedly valued as a passport to a rewarding career. Hara Takashi, whose fame was to surpass that of Nakae, was one who perceived the benefit of learning French in his teens. His commitment, it should be added, was greater than that of his fellow-students at a French-run school in Tokyo for in order to improve his understanding he alone was prepared to undertake the duties (which the others considered too demeaning) of attendant to a French priest on a journey to Niigata.[133] Within little more than a decade Hara was serving as chargé d'affaires in Paris, one of the stepping-stones which ultimately led to his appointment as Japan's first non-noble prime minister in 1918.

By the end of the 1870s Frenchmen and Japanese Francophiles could not ignore the fact that the French language had lost the unequal struggle with English. In January 1879, France's diplomatic representative, Geofroy, noted that there were only three French professors at the Imperial University (out of eighteen foreigners) and that only one school in Tokyo taught French exclusively (and only one jointly), compared with the 87 English-language schools. The minister pessimistically concluded that 'The study of Our Language is daily less in favour. In language, science and method, Japan today asks America for almost everything'.[134]

What was even more concerning was that there now seemed to be a real danger of being overtaken by German. It seems to have been this fear, at least in part, which prompted the creation in October 1880 of the *Société Japonaise pour la propagation de la langue française au Japon (Futsugakkai)*. Boissonade made a speech praising Japan's progress at the society's inaugural meeting, and by January 1882 it had 210 members.[135] Its influence may have played a part in the decision of education minister Fukuoka in 1882 to maintain the requirement for applicants to (the élite) secondary and higher state schools to have a knowledge of either English or French, rather than limit this to English. It was also largely responsible for the establishment in 1886, with a Japanese government subsidy of 5,000 or 6,000 yen, of a new French school.[136] Initially the school had 140 students, and the teaching staff included two Frenchmen, but in 1889 the higher section of the school was separated to form the successful *Wa-Futsu Horitsu Gakko.* The junior section, however, did not flourish on its own, and by the mid-1890s had scarcely any pupils, thus mirroring the decline of the *Futsugakkai* , which had launched it. At that time French was still taught at the Military Academy, and also had gained a foothold in the First Higher School's medical faculty and in the Naval Academy. Only one Frenchman remained on the staff of the University, however, and in the much expanded middle-school sector French had fallen further behind, being taught at only fourteen schools, whereas English was studied at 437 and German at 26.[137]

JAPANESE STUDY IN FRANCE, AND FRENCH CULTURAL INFLUENCE

Far fewer Japanese studied in France than received instruction from Frenchmen or learned French in Japan. According to the figures compiled by Ishizuki Minoru, the number who went to France for study amounted to 33 in the Bakumatsu period and to 60 from 1868 to 1874.[138] It may be significant that none were sent to France in 1873 or 1874, when Berthemy was taking a strong diplomatic line towards Japan. In 1872, when France was at the peak of its popularity, 58 students aged from 16 to 28 (except for one nine-year old) were currently there, of whom thirteen were being trained in military science, ten in law, six in mechanical engineering, five in mining, four in architecture, four in agriculture and chemistry, four in political economy, four in book-keeping, four in physics, four in mathematics, and one in medicine. Some were applying themselves to more than one field, and ten had no speciality.[139] After the early 1870s there was a general diminution in overseas study, as the Meiji government became more selective, but the flow by no means dried up. Between 1875 and 1897 France alone received 30 students sent just by the Education Ministry (just behind Britain's 34, though well below Germany's 104).[140]

Japanese who studied, usually at an impressionable age, in another country were naturally likely to be more strongly influenced by it and to gain more from the experience than from study at home. In some cases the results were tangible. One of Dury's ex-pupils, Tomii Masaaki, for instance, became a Doctor of Law at the University of Lyons in 1883, and soon after his return became a law professor at Tokyo University. In the 1890s he was one of the three legal specialists involved in the revision of the Civil Code.[141] Another Japanese who studied law in France, although in this case in Paris in the late 1870s, was Kinoshita Hiroji, who became headmaster of the Tokyo First Higher School from 1889 to 1894.[142] The career of Maeda Masana, who served in three government departments and became a vice-minister, was probably advanced by his seven years' study in France and by the reputation he gained for organizing Japan's much admired presentation at the 1878 Paris Exposition.[143] At a rather different level, it would be hard to imagine that Nakae Chomin's three years in France did not contribute significantly to the development of his thinking. He was undoubtedly impressed by the teaching of Professor Émile Acollas, whom he listed as one of the leading European political philosophers, and without this stimulus he might not have become so important an intellectual leader of the People's Rights and Freedom Movement in Japan in the 1880s. It can hardly be doubted, also, that without a common background of study in France, Nakae would not have collaborated with Saionji Kimmochi in 1881 in publishing one of the more radical organs of the early 1880s, the *Toyo Jiyu Shimbun* (Oriental Freedom Newspaper).[144]

In some ways the French influence on Saionji was clearly similar to that on Nakae. In particular, both men were notable for their political sophistication. While both men scorned narrow nationalism, however, Saionji arguably went further than almost any Japanese in espousing internationalism. When he became education minister in 1894, he broke, albeit temporarily, the trend towards the inculcation of narrow patriotism in school textbooks, and his support for cooperation rather than conflict between nations was evident in his later career as senior counsellor to the Emperor in the 1920s and 1930s. Again it would be hard to doubt that this owed something to his studies in France (also with Acollas) and even more to his immersion in French social and cultural life. His ten years in France from 1871 to 1881 gave him ample opportunity to savour the many pleasures of Parisian life, including close acquaintance with literary leaders. His involvement even went so far as collaboration with Judith Gautier in the 1885 publication, *Poèmes de la Libellule*.[145]

French culture was too rich and complex for its influence on Japan to be simple. French missionaries to Japan, for instance, were not noted for their liberal views. However, while the French government favoured the efforts of the *Société des Missions Étrangères* to spread Catholicism in Japan, the French tradition of religious scepticism provided ammunition to use against the missionaries. As early as 1873 the French minister in Tokyo noted that a Buddhist priest had returned from Europe bringing with him, among other books acquired in Paris for anti-Christian purposes, Renan's *La Vie de Jésus* and several works by Voltaire.[146] French writers certainly made their mark on Japan, although much more in the Meiji than in the Tokugawa period. The Bakufu accumulated quite a number of French books, but they tended to be those which expressed conventional ideas rather than innovative thinking and were probably not much read.[147] For many Japanese before 1868 knowledge of France may well have been limited to awareness of Napoleon I, whose exploits had been recounted in a number of Dutch books imported into Japan.[148]

Even in the Meiji period far fewer French works than English were translated into Japanese, and as late as 1895 Michel Revon, a professor of law at the Imperial University, bemoaned the small number of French works among the 180,000 in the library of Japan's highest academic institution.[149] Nevertheless, one French novelist – Jules Verne – was sufficiently popular to have ten of his works translated between 1878 and 1888 (only two fewer than Shakespeare). According to one of the leading scholars of Japanese relations with the West, 'the Japanese with modern inclinations thus preferred the genre of contemporary European adventure novels, well exemplified by Jules Verne, in which the heroes employed all the strategies at their command, and especially money, to overcome the obstacles which hindered the achievement of their plan'.[150] This was not the only style which appealed to Japanese readers, though. Another novel translated was Fénélon's *Aventures de Télémaque* which, though written two centuries earlier and not describing the wonders of modern technology, demonstrated moral values still felt to be worthy of emulation. Alexandre Dumas' novels also appeared in Japanese, his historical romanticism being particularly attractive in the 1880s when the People's Rights Movement's fascination with the French Revolution gave French history a special interest.

Some of the French literary works which reached the Japanese public may have helped to create an impression of France in the 1880s as a source of dangerous ideas – a far cry from the image of a strong centralized state which had attracted Meiji government leaders in the previous decade. The bogey of a French-style revolution was certainly used by conservative oligarchs to stir up concern about the current pressure for popular participation in government. Much more important in creating that image, however, were the writings of French political philosophers. In the words of Ito Hirobumi, who was in the early 1880s emerging as the leading figure in the government, 'the opinions in the country were extremely heterogeneous, and often diametrically opposed to each other . . . the educated politicians, having not yet tested the bitter significance of administrative responsibility, were liable to be more influenced by the dazzling words and lucid theories of Montesquieu and Rousseau and other similar French writers'.[151]

To lump Montesquieu and Rousseau together like this suggests that Ito may not have read their works, but in so far as he identified Rousseau as an inspirer of radicalism in Japan he was not wide of the mark. Moreover, according to one historian, it was Nakae's serialized translation of, and commentary, on *Du Contrat Social* which made Rousseau influential in the early 1880s. With it, he claimed, 'Nakae Chomin contributed most of the ideas for the development of the theory of popular sovereignty'.[152] Nakae's denial that the Emperor was the repository of sovereignty and his assertion that the government held its mandate in trust and should obey the people's will certainly reflected, albeit imperfectly, Rousseau's thinking; and the association of such ideas with famous Western names may well have given them an extra appeal in Japan.

FRENCH INTEREST IN JAPAN

Although Japanese, such as Saionji, who lived for some years in France in the late nineteenth century would have acquired insights into French life and culture, those whose knowledge was derived only from literary sources would have had little idea of what made France different from other European countries. Some accounts by travellers such as Fukuzawa Yukichi and Kurimoto Joun provided useful information, as did the record of the Iwakura mission, but this was limited. Essentially Japanese at this time were interested in the West in general rather than any particular country, and although there were a few with specialized interest in French law or painting, or more rarely, the French army or French naval shipbuilding, there were at this date no general students of France.

With regard to French interest in Japan the position was quite different. To begin with, Frenchmen went to Japan to trade, to preach or to teach, not to study, and very few of those who lived in Japan would have been less than 25 years old. Those who visited the country more briefly were likely to be sight-seeing tourists rather than fact-finding officials. Japan was also of less importance and interest to Frenchmen than France was to the Japanese, and there were almost certainly fewer Frenchmen who knew anything of Japan than there were Japanese who had at least some awareness of what sort of a country France was. On the other hand, the Frenchmen and Frenchwomen who were drawn towards Japan were more likely to emphasise its distinctiveness from other Oriental countries than Japanese were to stress the differences between France and its neighbours.

This point should not be overstated. There were certainly many books by Frenchmen, usually accounts of their travels, which lumped Japan together with the other countries which the authors had visited, although even then they might highlight Japan's more unusual characteristics. It must also be acknowledged that when Japanese were portrayed in French novels, plays, operas and ballets, as they began to be (albeit only occasionally) in the 1870s in Paris, a very imperfect understanding of Japanese customs, behaviour and names was usually revealed, including, inevitably, some confusion with China.[153]

Nevertheless, articles devoted to Japan alone did appear in the widely read *Revue des Deux Mondes,* as well as in newspapers; and a number of books, most notably Georges Bousquet's two-volume *Le Japan de Nos Jours* (1877), sought to explain Japan at a reasonably intelligent level.

Admittedly, by comparison with Britain serious scholarship was slow to develop.[154] Whereas there were a number of Britons of intellectual stature, such as Satow, Aston, Gubbins, Longford, and Chamberlain, who acquired a serious interest in Japanese history, literature or religion and the linguistic skills to pursue this, there was only one Frenchman in the late nineteenth century – Léon de Rosny – who could even claim to be on the same level. Born in 1837, he first studied Chinese in Paris but soon became curious about Japan, and by using Abel-Rémusat's *Élémens de la Grammaire Japonaise*(which was basically a French version, dating from 1825, of an original 1604 Portuguese work by Rodriguez) he picked up enough Japanese to be able to communicate in that language with Fukuzawa Yukichi and other members of the 1862 Japanese mission to Europe. In 1865 he entered into an agreement with the Shibata mission to supply the Bakufu with regular news from Europe, although it does not seem that any attention was paid to his information. More significantly, he began to teach Japanese in Paris in 1863 at the *École des Langues Orientales,* where he was made a full professor in 1868 and remained until 1907.[155]

It would appear that some of Rosny's later students became interpreters for the French legation in Tokyo, but except for Maurice Courant, the later biographer of Okubo Toshimichi, details about them are lacking. Rosny himself only visited Japan briefly, in 1872, but he was a prolific translator and among other Japanese classics he tackled the difficult *Nihon Shoki* (1887). As a scholar he has been criticized for excessive imagination and lack of rigour, but it is to his credit that his *Anthologie Japonaise* (1871) made available to a French audience some of the most celebrated poems in the Japanese canon. He was the leading figure in the *Société des Études Japonaises, Chinoises, Tartares, Indo-chinoises* (from 1887 the *Société Sinico-Japonaise*), and his translations and researches figured prominently in the eight volumes of papers produced between 1873 and 1891 by that first group of Frenchmen with a more scholarly, albeit still somewhat amateur, interest in Japan. In 1883 he published his lectures on Japanese geography, ethnography, and history in a 400 – page volume, *La Civilisation japonaise,* having earlier helped to disseminate knowledge about a wide range of aspects of Japan, both ancient and modern, by ensuring that the first Congress of Orientalists, which met in Paris in 1873 and included ten Japanese among the 88 foreigners in attendance, focused especially on Japan.[156]

JAPONISME AND ARTISTIC INTERACTION

There was one cultural area in which French interest in Japan exceeded Japanese interest in France – the visual arts. By 1900 a large proportion of the French people had in their homes art objects which had been made in Japan or copied from Japanese models or influenced by Japanese design and many had seen examples of Japanese art at exhibitions, such as the Paris Exposition of 1900, which attracted 50 million visitors. Moreover, for a significant number of artists Japanese art was no mere source of casual enjoyment but a major inspiration. In France, more than anywhere else, Japanese works of art and craftsmanship proved so fascinating and stimulating in the last third of the century that, to describe the phenomenon, the term *Japonisme* was coined – by a French critic and connoisseur, Philippe Burty, in 1872. Without this external influence French art – and Western art in general – would have developed differently, and probably changed less radically, than it did.[157]

Just as the reviving effect of Japanese silkworms on the French silk industry was not foreseen before the opening of the Japanese ports in the 1850s, so there was no awareness at that time of the role which Japanese art might play in breaking the stultifying grip which the *École des Beaux Arts* and its acolytes maintained, through its annual Salon exhibitions, over French painting. This was not because Japanese art was entirely unknown, for through the Dutch a selection of high-quality works in various branches, notably porcelain and lacquer ware, had been made available, and members of the French Court, such as Madame de Pompadour and Marie-Antoinette, had been among the most avid collectors. Indeed, in the eighteenth century French porcelain factories paid their Japanese counterparts the compliment of imitating them.[158] In addition to the normal route – the Dutch East India Company – objects acquired in Nagasaki by one notable Dutch visitor, Titsingh, were sold in Paris in the early part of the nineteenth century; and in 1837 Philip von Siebold established a museum in Leiden to house and display the very extensive Japanese collection which he had put together during his lengthy stay in the country. Some of this collection was reproduced in his multi-volume account of Japan, a French version of which appeared in five volumes in 1838–40.[159]

Despite this background, however, awareness of Japanese art was still, in the 1850s, limited to a few collectors who would probably not have differentiated between Japanese objects and those (much more numerous) from China. Not only were the former still unusual but they included few examples of what was to be the most significant form of Japanese art – the woodblock print. Exactly when Japanese prints first became known in France remains in doubt. The claim that the etcher, Felix Bracquemond, came across an album of Hokusai's *Manga* in 1856 at his printer's, and was so fascinated that he subsequently acquired it and showed it to his friends, has been questioned in terms of its chronological accuracy;[160] and the fact that there was little apparent awakening of interest in Japanese prints until the 1860s makes 1856 an unimportant date even if the (much later) account of Bracquemond's discovery is correct. Similarly, the inclusion of depictions of birds by Hokusai in a series of designs which A. de Beaumont and E. Collinot recommended artists to use as models was probably of limited relevance, since this was a specialized publication (and also because nobody followed their advice until Bracquemond himself designed a dinner service using Hokusai's illustrations in 1867).[161] Of more significance in terms of capturing public attention were the still small but growing number of general books about Japan which were addressed to a wider audience and included comments on Japanese art, as well sometimes providing copies of prints that had achieved popularity in Japan. That they had some effect is indicated by the praise which Japanese art and taste received from such perceptive literary figures as Baudelaire and the Goncourt brothers.

Some dealers in antiques or art curios in Paris responded to this burgeoning interest. In particular, a shop was opened,

281

probably in 1862, by a husband and wife who had come back from Japan with many objects which were soon snapped up by budding connoisseurs, such as the Goncourts. The low price of prints – from one to five francs each initially – must have added to their attraction and meant that even impecunious artists could afford them.[162] Even so, the real breakthrough to wider popularity only came with the 1867 Exposition (which nearly seven million visitors attended). Although the presentation of Japanese exhibits left something to be desired – which was hardly surprising in the light both of Japanese inexperience and the political manoeuvring over separate representation for Satsuma – they still made a strong impression.[163] What was actually exhibited is not exactly clear, but one commentator described the Bakufu section as 'literally a revelation' and stated that Japan had 'conquered the world of artists and collectors', a claim which may have been hyperbolic but received some justification from the fact that Japan won four of the 64 top prizes.[164]

After 1867 the taste for things Japanese became firmly established, partly because many of the Exposition exhibits were bought by collectors. The appreciation of Japanese art was further promoted by a number of influential afficionados who formed the *Société du Jing-lar* immediately after the Exposition.[165] Some of them played a prominent part in organizing an exhibition of Oriental art in 1869. The growing popularity of Japanese art was reflected in the appearance of articles by critics like Ernest Chesneau which generally praised its qualities and sometimes came close to being ecstatic. One by Zacharie Astruc in *L'Étendard* in 1867 with the arresting title, 'L'Empire du Soleil Levant', extolled the Japanese for their ability to combine naturalness with artistry; and called on French painters to display a creative spirit like theirs. 'Let us make ourselves Japanese!', Astruc urged.[166] Occasionally, there were more dismissive voices. Duchesne de Bellecourt, in a review of the 1867 Exposition for the *Revue des Deux Mondes,* was one such, and Edouard Duranty, who unfashionably preferred Chinese art, was another. Moreover, even among those who were impressed, appreciation was occasionally accompanied by concern that the French might be turning into facile imitators. Émile Zola, for instance, writing in 1880, warned that 'if the influence of Japanese style has been excellent in extricating us from traditional bitumen and showing us the blond gaieties of nature, a sought-after imitation of an art which is neither of our race nor of our surroundings, would finish by being no more than an unbearable fashion. Japanese style is good, but it must not be used everywhere or art will become a bauble'.[167] His note of caution, to which Renoir, among others, would have subscribed,[168] is ironically reminiscent of the worries expressed by Japanese conservatives about what they, much more generally, considered uncritical acceptance of Western culture.

Such views, however, ran counter to the rising tide of admiration which was produced by increased imports of a wider range of Japanese art. Notable in this context were the large-scale purchases by an admittedly small number of collectors and dealers who went to Japan themselves. Henri Cernuschi and Théodore Duret did so in 1871, the former acquiring the works which later formed the basis of the Cernuschi museum (established in 1898), the latter bringing back 1350 print albums. Three years later Philippe Sichel brought back 450 chests containing over 5000 works of art which he had picked up cheaply and were to earn him very large profits; and in 1875 a dealer of German origin, S. Bing, sent his brother to Japan, before himself making, in 1880, the fruitful visit which helped him to emerge as probably the major figure in the popularization of Japanese art in Paris in the next two decades.[169]

Another significant visit to Japan was made by the Lyons businessman, Émile Guimet, who also returned with numerous works of art, after spending several months there pursuing the interest in Oriental religion which had absorbed much of his attention since he had visited Egypt a decade earlier. Guimet was a member of the *Société des Études Japonaises,* and his contact with an influential figure in the Japanese Ministry of Education gave him privileged access to religious institutions. His collection, which was even richer in Chinese art, was to be made available to the public, however, not by being put on sale but by being displayed at the *Musée Guimet* which was first established in Lyons in 1879, but transferred to Paris in 1889, becoming also an important centre for religious research. Possibly more important in terms of drawing public attention to Japan, though, were the books which described his experiences, *Promenades Japonaises* (1878) and *Promenades Japonaises – Tokyo – Nikko* (1880), both of which were illustrated by the artist who had accompanied him – Felix Régamey.[170]

The publication of Guimet's first book on Japan came in the same year as the third Paris Universal Exposition (1878), perhaps the single most important landmark in the French discovery of Japanese art. Not only was this huge exhibition attended by thirteen million people, considerably more than that of 1867, but the contents of the Japanese pavilion were both more substantial and chosen with more care than had been possible previously. As well as Maeda Masana, the art experts Wakai Kenzaburo and Hayashi Tadamasa, as well as the Mitsui company, were involved in organizing the Japanese contribution, and their efforts won great acclaim. One contemporary commentator observed that 'Japan has just won a complete and decisive victory at the Universal Exposition in the exhibition of its arts and industries of the past and present'.[171]

Japan's success stimulated more serious interest, and the fact that Hayashi remained in Paris as a dealer meant that at least some of the expertise that had previously been wanting was now at hand. It was against this background that Louis Gonse, with help from Bing, Burty and Edmond de Goncourt, produced the first comprehensive study of Japanese art in French in two volumes in 1883. In the same year he also organized, with the help of other collectors, the first exhibition devoted solely to Japanese art. It included not only paintings, ink drawings and print albums, but also bronzes and lacquers, some dating back to the ninth century, and was prominently and enthusiastically reviewed in the press.[172]

Not all Japanese art met with a favourable reception. An exhibition later on in 1883 of mainly contemporary paintings, which particularly featured artists who belonged to the *Ryuchikai*, a society dedicated to maintaining traditional Japanese styles of painting, was compared unfavourably with the work of the old masters and most of the 73 works sent from Japan had to be sent back unsold.[173] In addition, Japan's reputation suffered from the diminishing supply of high quality art and from the tendency of Japanese exporters to exploit foreign demand.[174] At least as early as 1874 a Japanese company, the *Kiritsu Kosho Kaisha,* had specialized in exporting artistic products, both old and new;[175] and from the early 1880s there were complaints about the lower level of Japanese workmanship, a problem which was accentuated by the growth of competition from cheap French imitations.[176] The fact that Japanese wares, even before the 1880s, had begun to appear in department stores meant that ownership of Japanese curios no longer carried quite the same mark of distinction as formerly. Nor did the Japanese contribution in 1889 to the fourth International Exposition held in Paris enlarge the appreciation of Japanese art as those of 1867 and 1878 had done.[177]

The 1880s did not, however, see the end of *Japonisme.* In the final years of the decade, in fact, a new phase of fascination with Japanese art began with the publication by Bing, from 1888 to 1891, of a magazine with serious articles and impressive illustrations, *Le Japon Artistique* (with English and German versions as well). It helped to extend French awareness of the merits of Japanese painting beyond the colour print, which had enjoyed a disproportionate prominence even after the 1860s. At the same time, appreciation of the range and quality of woodblocks was increased by the major exhibition (of 725 prints) at the *École des Beaux Arts* which Bing mounted in 1890 and by the studies of Utamaro and Hokusai which Edmond de Goncourt produced with Japanese help and published in 1891 and 1895 respectively. Official recognition of Japanese art was conferred when the Louvre established a Japanese section in 1893;[178] and the opening by Bing two years later of a shop devoted to the sale of Japanese decorative art and work influenced by Japan reflected not only the popularity which the former had long enjoyed but also its role in stimulating *Art Nouveau.* By this time Japanese art no longer seemed so exotic, but the fact that it could still surprise and impress was demonstrated in 1900, when the Meiji government drew upon the private collections of the Imperial family and Court nobles to send to the fifth Paris Universal Exposition an exhibition which in its diversity and quality surpassed even those of 1878 and 1889.[179] Since eighteen million more people attended the Exposition than the 32 million in 1889, Japanese art almost certainly reached a wider public than ever before.

The 1900 exposition was not only a landmark for Japanese art in Europe but also for Japanese painting in Western style. Commenting upon this part of the Japanese exhibition, a contemporary Austrian art historian, Richard Muther, noted that 'the main room shows how European art developed in Japan has become the standard in Japan. . . . There are very skilled, very fine paintings'; and he went on to mention Kuroda Seiki, Nakagawa Hachiro, Okada Saburosuke, Wada Eisaku, Watanabe Shinya and Yoshida Hiroshi specifically.[180] This plaudit constituted recognition that Western-style painting had had a real impact on Japan and that some artists, at least, had achieved respectability through the creation of distinctive works. In so far as this success was the result of formal guidance by foreign teachers in Japan, France had played little part in the flowering of the new style, for the Meiji government had turned mainly to Italy for instruction. Some of the outstanding artists, however, had studied abroad, and Paris, with its artistic milieux revived, proved particularly attractive. Kuroda Seiki, perhaps the best-known of the painters in the Western style, spent several years there, and more artists of note were drawn to the French capital, probably, than to Rome or Venice or Munich.[181]

Japanese artists who had spent time abroad not surprisingly played a part in 1889 in organizing the Meiji Art Society to promote Western-style art, in response to the traditionalist reaction led by Ernest Fenollosa and Okakura Kakuzo. Interestingly, the society was headed by the man who had just returned from serving as Japan's diplomatic representative in Paris, Tanaka Fujimaro, while the deputy director was the former chargé d'affaires there, Hara Takashi. Another non-artist ex-student in France, Saionji Kimmochi, was involved, as Minister of Education in 1896, in the establishment of a Western Painting department in the Tokyo Art School, with Kuroda as its first head. The existence of personal links with France was shown by the inclusion of works by Theodore Rousseau and Degas in the second exhibition which the Meiji Art Society held in Tokyo, in 1890; and in its fifth exhibition not only Degas but other French Impressionists were represented, through the cooperation of Hayashi Tadamesa.[182]

Exactly what the painters who trained in France gained from their experiences there can hardly be pinned down precisely, but it has been suggested that the emphasis which some of them placed on individual freedom and equality owed something to their period of study abroad, and that this was a significant factor in their founding, in May 1896, of the White Horse Society, which under Kuroda's leadership rejected the bureaucratic formalism of the Meiji Art Society.[183] Kuroda himself clearly implied that his own work had benefited, albeit intangibly, from his time in Paris when he more than once insisted that most Japanese paintings in the Western style were worthless because the artists did not understand the culture which lay behind the style.[184] If he gained in that important respect, however, he may also have suffered, at least briefly, in another, for he was the first artist to come under public censure for his painting of a female nude.[185] Since the portrayal was far from pornographic, the suspicion can hardly be avoided that it was at least in part his association with a foreign country (at a time when Boissonade's draft Civil Code was being criticized for embodying anti-foreign ideas) which encouraged the attack on Kuroda's work.

The impact of Western art on Japanese painting in the late nineteenth century is not of a nature to be assessed exactly. It is, for example, unclear to what extent the decline of the Japanese woodblock print was due to Western influence; and although Western art undoubtedly opened up new ways of visual expression, there might conceivably have been creative new developments even without its stimulus. Similar difficulties arise with regard to the assessment of the Japanese impact on French art. Scholars who have focused on *Japonisme* naturally tend to emphasize this as a cause of stylistic change more than those writers who see French painting in a primarily European perspective. At one extreme there is an implication that it was Japanese art which opened the eyes of the painters who changed their styles most radically; on the other, it is assumed that French art was already changing and that Japanese influence was limited to creating awareness of some techniques which might be exploited.[186] A further complication is added by the fact that the Japanese artists who provided the greatest inspiration – Hokusai and Hiroshige – may have been found particularly attractive partly because they had incorporated in their work ideas of perspective earlier imported into Japan from the West.

Despite differences of interpretation there is a fairly solid consensus that Japanese art did have a significant impact on French art at a time when French artists, or artists based in France, were playing a leading role in revitalizing Western art and expanding its possibilities. Even allowing for other factors, such as the example of Courbet's rejection of classical and historical subjects, the attraction (for some painters) of Italian, Dutch or Spanish masters of earlier generations or, more importantly, the effects of photography, there are various stylistic grounds on which a case for a meaningful Japanese influence remains strong. It is difficult to list them in order of importance, for the ever-expanding supply of Japanese art meant that the nature of that influence did not remain constant; in particular, the early dominance of Hokusai (and to a lesser extent Hiroshige) gave way to a much broader awareness. More importantly, different French artists were not always struck by the same features in Japanese art. Indeed, such was the variety of the stimuli that the suggestion has been made that it is more appropriate to speak of *Japonismes* than a single *Japonisme*.[187]

One of the earliest attempts to define the nature of Japanese influence was made by Edmond de Goncourt in 1884, when he wrote in his journal that 'when I said that *Japonisme* was in the process of revolutionising the vision of the European peoples I meant that *Japonisme* brought to Europe a new sense of colour, a new decorative system, and, if you like, a poetic imagination in the invention of the *objet d'art*, which never existed even in the most perfect medieval or Renaissance pieces'.[188] A more detached, but hardly less positive, view was expressed by a French art historian, Henri Focillon, in 1921: 'Japanese graphic art electrified Western artists, the would-be renewers of the art of painting, by its sheer modernism: by which I mean its interest in contemporary life, its charm, its audacity, its play of line, its expression of animated, overflowing life, of the instant that comes and is gone; through its fresh colour tones, unburdened and unfalsified by any trace of a shadow; and finally through its modelling, hinted at but never represented'.[189]

Most art historians would not dissent from this assessment, especially the observations about line and colour, but they would not regard the list as complete. Other factors which are cited are the 'two-dimensional flatness' of Japanese prints (although this hardly applies to the later woodblock artists); the asymmetric composition of pictures; exaggerated perspective which draws attention to the foreground; the willingness to adopt viewpoints (from above, for instance) other than the conventional level head-on one; the deliberate depiction of only part of an object by having the edge of a picture apparently cut through it, in order to get away from the idea of artificial composition and create an impression of spontaneity; the willingness to give free rein to fantasy, especially in the portrayal of landscape, while at other times showing close observation in the depiction of birds and other creatures; and the use of simplification to convey the essence of an object. The appearance of motifs which figure prominently in prints, such as bridges and fans, is also noted by art historians, particularly where Japanese influence on Monet is concerned; while the use of colour to express emotion is seen as being of especial relevance to van Gogh. In the case of Degas, a particular debt to Hokusai with regard to drawing women in unerotic everyday activities has been discerned; and his obsession with washerwomen and other women of low status is thought to have been encouraged by the example of Japanese print artists' similar concern with the common life of the 'floating world' of Edo. Not only Degas, however, but most French painters who, because of their interest in experimentation, were not accepted by the art establishment, were probably drawn to the *Ukiyo-e* school partly because of its essentially unaristocratic character. Above all, though, the feature of the Japanese prints which made the deepest impression was the feeling for nature which they so clearly expressed and which seems to have inspired some of the French impressionists to try to capture life and landscape in a new way.

One, or more often a number, of the above characteristics are widely held to have directly or indirectly inspired most innovative French painters from the early 1860s until the end of the century. Japanese influence is generally considered to have been greatest in Manet, Degas and Monet (and, if artists who were in France at important periods of their careers are included, Whistler and van Gogh), but it has also been detected in Pissarro, Gauguin, Cézanne, Seurat, Toulouse-Lautrec and the Nabis (especially Bonnard). Such judgements are essentially based on painting style, but at least in some cases convincing evidence is also provided by the testimony of the artist himself. Monet, for instance (possibly with Hiroshige in mind), acknowledged a debt to Japanese painters when in his later years he said that 'these people taught us to compose in a different way, that is beyond doubt'.[190] Pissarro in 1893 implied that he had, at the very least, received encouragement, when after finding 'the most striking instances of impressionism' in an exhibition of Japanese prints, he wrote that 'these Japanese artists confirm my belief in our vision', adding 'Hiroshige is a marvellous impressionist. Monet, Rodin and I are enthusiastic about the show'.[191]

No painter, however, was more enthusiastic than van Gogh, whose letters are full of his admiration for Japanese print artists and who even moved to Arles in the hope of finding in the south of France a climate, and light, comparable to Japan's. As far as his actual painting was concerned, he openly sought to emulate Japanese style. He informed his brother, Theo, in 1888 that he wanted to make some drawings in the manner of Japanese prints; and when describing the portrayal of his bedroom in October of that year he stressed 'how simple the conception is. The shadows and the cast shadows are left out and it is painted in bright flat tints like the Japanese prints'.[192] Earlier in the same year, he went out of his way to draw attention to Japanese influences which might otherwise have gone undetected in his landscape drawing: 'It doesn't look Japanese, yet it is the most Japanese thing I have done'.[193] So strong did he feel his debt to be that he even wrote: 'All my work is in a way founded on Japanese art'.[194]

Awareness of Japanese art is also evident from references within paintings. These may admittedly reflect not *Japonisme* but a more superficial *Japonaiserie,* as in the case of Whistler's and (in one instance only) Monet's portrayal of a Western woman in Japanese dress. It is possible, however, that when Japanese fans or screens or, especially, prints appear in the background of pictures, they symbolized, in some cases at least, a different approach to art.. That Japanese prints really did hold significance for the new-style artists of the 1860s and after is indicated by the fact that most them showed an avid interest in them. Monet, in particular, built up a huge collection when he was wealthy enough to do so, and they were bought even by such painters as Theodore Rousseau and Millet, who though not noted for succumbing to Japanese influence had gone against convention.[195] For his part, van Gogh was so eager to have prints at hand that he spent money which he could hardly afford on them. The extent of his fascination, and of his belief that there was something vital to be learned from them, is most clearly revealed in the well-known fact that he made copies in oil of three Japanese prints, two of them by Hiroshige.

Other evidence of Japanese influence on French painting can be found in the comments of contemporary critics, some of whom were familiar with the artists. Perhaps the first to make the connection was Émile Zola (the most outspoken champion of Manet) when he suggested in 1866 that it would be interesting to compare the latter's 'simplified painting' in his recent *Le Fifre* with 'the Japanese woodcuts which resemble it by their strange elegance and their magnificent patches [of colour]'. In 1875 Philippe Burty noted the influence of prints on Whistler, but it was Ernest Chesneau who, in 1878, first claimed that many painters – among them. Whistler, Manet, Monet and Degas – had succeeded in assimilating, rather than merely imitating, different characteristics of Japanese art.[197] In doing so, he was pointing to the reason why Japanese influence was difficult to detect and also why it was so significant.

Contemporaries had far less difficulty in perceiving Japanese influence on the decorative arts. Even before the 1867 Exposition Burty had referred in his *Chef-d'oeuvre des arts industriels* (1866) to the fact that porcelain and objects made from bronze and iron had already been affected, and in 1868 he noted that Japanese inventiveness of approach and unusual design had made Japanese cloisonné enamels more artistic than the Chinese and had attracted the attention of leading French artists in the field.[198] The examples of Japanese decorative art at the 1867 Exposition further stimulated French interest, and in 1869, porcelain, sculpture, cloisonné enamel, and various forms of metalwork were shown in the Oriental section of the exhibition of modern decorative work at the *Union centrale des Beaux-Arts appliqués à l'"Industrie.*[199] By 1873 Chesneau was able to write that Japanese art had invaded the shelves of large department stores and that ceramics, jewelry, fabrics and wallpaper were being influenced by Japanese design;[200] and the 1878 Exposition gave further impulsion to this tendency.

It was not only the Japanese decorative arts which proved influential. In their study of '*Japonisme* and French Decorative Arts' Eidelberg and Johnston state that 'albums of *ukiyo-e* prints were of prime significance in providing a decorative vocabulary for French designers'; and they go so far as to assert that the implications of the discovery of this material were as important for the decorative as for the fine arts.[201] As they (like others) point out, the first notable example of Japanese influence – the tea service created by Felix Bracquemond for the firm of Eugène Rousseau in 1866–7 – was more or less copied from the Hokusai illustrations which had appeared in the book of designs by Beaumont and Collinot. From 1868 onwards, ceramic factories and independent ceramists commonly followed Bracquemond's example; while French jewelry and metalwork firms, notably Barbedienne and Christofle, also imitated Japanese products and took designs from prints. Lucien Falize, who extended the use of the cloisonné technique to jewelry, publicly admitted that he himself had made many copies from print albums,even though he argued that French artists should find inspiration in Japanese art rather than imitate it mechanically. He did, nevertheless, recognize that much was owed to Japan; and significantly, in the light of Japanese influence on French painting, he singled out for special note the respect for nature which Japanese art had helped to renew.

Falize's warning against the slavish following of Japanese designs was echoed by others concerned about what Eidelberg and Johnston describe as 'a mania of *Japonisme*'; but the latter observe that, despite such advice, 'an outright imitation of Japanese models predominated through the 1880s, and only gradually waned in the following decade'.[203] Although furniture and wallpaper were much less touched by this fashion, the textile industry in general, and silk in particular, made use of Japanese motifs. Jewellers did so even more, and there was also an element of borrowing from Japan in that under the leadership of Lalique, they came to place less emphasis on precious stones for their own sake and more on colour harmony and craftsmanship on a small scale. Decorative glass was also significantly affected through designers such as Gallé and Dammouse, and the particularly strong inspiration which stemmed from the 'graceful, wavy movement of Japanese lines' carried over into the *Art Nouveau* movement in the 1890s. Eidelberg and Johnston conclude that 'by the end of the 1890s not only could the effects of *Japonisme* in its many forms be seen everywhere in the French decorative arts, but also the decorative arts had become a major form of expression'.[204]

JAPONISME AND FRENCH IMAGES OF JAPAN

The reputation which Japanese art gained in Europe and America might have been expected to improve Japan's general image by counteracting, to some extent at least, the idea that it was backward in comparison with the advanced nations of the West. It has been argued, by Elise Evett, however, that this was not the case. In her view Japanese art was interpreted in such a way as to confirm preconceived ideas. The absence of perspective in most Japanese painting was attributed to ignorance or to a defective style of suggesting space, and this, together with an apparent indifference towards the accurate representation of human form and the supposed lack of a sense of ideal beauty, encouraged the idea that the Japanese remained essentially primitive . Even the feeling for nature which Japanese art revealed was explained in the same way. This did not mean that Japanese closeness to nature was necessarily condemned, or even criticized, for to many it had the appeal of a lost state of nature, and in Evett's words, 'Westerners could admire and even envy the apparent simplicity and purity of the primitive state of being'. She nevertheless insists that their admiration was contingent upon an unshakable assumption of the ultimate superiority of Western civilization.[205] It was the interpretation of Japanese art, she maintains (ignoring Schwartz's attribution of a rather similar effect to Pierre Loti's very popular *Madame Chrysanthème* of 1887), that kept this notion of Japan's primitivism alive.[206]

In support of this argument Evett cites a number of writers, among them Duchesne de Bellecourt, Paul Dalloz, Teodor de Wysewa, Michel Revon, and Georges Bousquet. She justifies her emphasis on the racist nature of the Western – and particularly the French – view of Japan by noting that the supposedly 'infantile' aspects which also characterized Impressionism were not taken as evidence that the Impressionists were limited to the mental capacity of primitive man, whereas 'this notion. . .was applied to the Japanese who were thought of as being restricted in both perceptual and mental capacity to a primitive or childlike level of awareness'.[207] Moreover, because the Japanese were seen as essentially different, their attempt to adopt Western techniques, especially in art, was seen as both futile – since no true synthesis between Western and Japanese artistic notions was possible – and undesirable – since any such attempt would dissolve the imagined purity of the Japanese tradition.[208]

It is hard not to feel that Evett has overstated her case, and her book itself contains evidence which can be deployed against her thesis. For instance, she quotes Ary Renan (the son of Ernest Renan) as writing that 'the Japanese is a sweet child' but does not observe that this is qualified later by a reference to his 'intelligent eyes';[209] and she also fails to note that five years earlier Renan had pointed out that the Japanese artist varied his imitations of nature infinitely and had consistently invented new artistic forms.[210] She further shows that there were critics who appraised Japan without adding disparaging reservations, one example being Ernest Chesneau, who is quoted as writing, as early as 1868, that 'in everything which comes from this artistic people, one finds again this same perfection and this same freedom of taste, unrivalled ingenuity and fecundity of invention'.[211] It is arguable, too, that some of her evidence is distinctly ambiguous. She takes Louis Gonse's statement that the Japanese were 'the most artistic people that have existed, along with the Greeks' as indicating that they were still in the early stages of development;[212] but in view of the esteem in which ancient Greece was held by the classically-educated élites in Europe, it seems hardly likely that such a connotation was intended.

In assessing national images it is important not to make too much of untypical comments, but equally there is a need to avoid oversimplified generalisation. In the case of the influence of Japanese art on French perceptions, it is arguable that further distinctions need to be made. Watanabe Toshio has pointed out that the comments on Japanese art by the chronicler of Perry's 1854 expedition are much less favourable than those made later in the report by an American academic who had been asked to examine the artistic qualities of the works brought back by the expedition.[213] A rather similar difference may have existed between, on the one hand, Frenchmen who had lived in, or visited, Japan but lacked a specialized knowledge of art, and, on the other, French art critics and artists. Both of these categories figure prominently in publications about Japanese art, but the tone of the former tended to be more dismissive and less appreciative than that of the latter. As illustrations of this point one might set Duchesne de Bellecourt's disparaging comment that 'European art has nothing to learn from Japanese painting'[214] against van Gogh's observation that 'the most ordinary prints, coloured in flat tones, seem admirable to me for the same reasons as Rubens and Veronese. I know perfectly well that they are not primitive art'.[215] Japanese artists were also praised in terms which hardly fit Evett's thesis by Albert Jacquemart, the author of a history of porcelain, who in 1873 wrote that in China the artist was always subjected to the school and to the constraints of religious dogma, whereas in Japan he dominated his subject and was freer in his interpretation of it. However oversimplified this view may have been, it led Jacquemart to the conclusion that 'in Japan there is no trace of school; everything is governed by individualism'.[216]

Whatever reservations may be felt, however, about the idea that the interpretation of Japanese art reinforced the perception of Japan as primitive or backward, the fact that disparaging or condescending attitudes were frequently expressed can hardly be denied. Nor should it be forgotten that although in retrospect Japanese art, especially the woodblock print, can be seen to have played a key role in the emergence of new styles, modern art was a minority taste in France well into the twentieth century.[217] Thus a widespread appreciation of the skills of Japanese craftsmen could coexist with a lack of awareness that Japanese art was having a more profound impact. Even if such an awareness had existed, it would probably have been more than counteracted by the knowledge that Japan was still employing foreign advisers. Nor would the quaint or idyllic images of Tokugawa Japan which woodblock prints made familiar have encouraged realisation that, in part with the help of Frenchmen, the country was being effectively transformed. Only with the Japanese military victories against China in 1894–5 and Russia in 1904–5 were most Frenchmen to take Japan seriously.

CONCLUSIONS

THE CHARACTERISTIC which marked French policy towards Japan in the nineteenth century most strikingly was its predominantly negative quality. Even when France took the positive step of entering into relations with Japan in the 1850s, it did so in the wake of the United States and in the shadow of Britain; and when, nearly four decades later, it joined in the Triple Intervention to deprive Japan of its gains in the Sino-Japanese war of 1894–5, it did so not because it wished to act decisively but because it felt obliged to support Russia. In the intervening years the Quai d'Orsay's main concern was the limited one of preserving the advantages that had been so easily obtained in 1858. Ostensibly these advantages were primarily commercial, and French trade did, in fact, attain respectable proportions. It cannot be said, however, that the French government showed particular enthusiasm for extending its scope, and neither French traders in Japan nor French chambers of commerce exerted any significant influence on French policy. Their views were consulted only rarely, and then mostly as a formality. More consideration was paid to the interests of the ship-building and silk industries, but in terms of overall policy their influence remained marginal.

If any consideration was likely to stir France to positive action it was the urge to increase French prestige, an aim which was generally linked with the desire to expand French influence (although occasionally, as in 1889, when prestige dictated the exclusion from French military establishments of Japanese officers, notwithstanding the fact that such a move would eliminate a recognized source of influence, the two conflicted

296

with each other). It was arguably prestige even more than commerce which brought France to Japan in the first place, and much of the French contribution to Japanese modernization, especially in the military sphere, stemmed from the belief that it would confirm France as a power of the first order and make its achievements respected throughout the East. On a more political level, considerations of prestige inclined France to be intransigent over treaty revision. Even prestige, however, had its limitations. The propagation of the French language was generally admitted to be the main foundation for the admiration of French culture, yet the cause of expansion of French education in Japan never attracted from the Quai d'Orsay a sum larger than 4,000 francs, and most years received much less.

The negative quality that marked French diplomacy was not unique to France. None of the European powers either mounted a sustained campaign to exploit Japan's weakness by extorting new privileges or seriously attempted to secure it as a satellite or ally before the end of the century. It might, indeed, be argued that France came nearer (albeit briefly) to pursuing both of these alternative lines of positive policy than any other Power. Jules Berthemy certainly inclined towards the former when he pressed for the opening to trade of the whole of Japan in 1873–4. More significantly, Léon Roches, in seeking, in the 1860s, to change Japan and make it dependent on the country he served, harboured ambitions unmatched by any other foreign representative in modern Japanese history before General MacArthur.

In both these cases, the initiative belonged to the French minister in Tokyo rather than to his superiors in Paris. Positive action of this sort was rarely promoted by the Quai d'Orsay and when an important political initiative did originate with the foreign minister (as in the case of the decision to seek Japanese collaboration against China in December 1884, or Drouyn de Lhuys's offer in 1864 of French help to the Bakufu in opening the Shimonoseki Straits) the French minister in Tokyo's distaste for the idea considerably weakened whatever chance of success it may have had.

These facts invite a comparison of the respective parts played in French policy by the Quai d'Orsay and the French diplomats who served in Japan. One must first recognize that it is impossible to distinguish within the Quai d'Orsay itself between the foreign minister and his permanent, or near-permanent, senior officials. Few of the dispatches sent from the Quai d'Orsay to the Tokyo legation, and few of the regrettably rare marginal comments on reports from French representatives in Japan, bear any clear mark of their real authorship. Since, however, most French foreign ministers were in office for too short a time to gain much knowledge of so distant a country as Japan, and since in only one or two instances was there any discernible shift in policy following a ministerial changeover, it would not seem unreasonable to assume that Japanese affairs were mostly dealt with by the Political or Commercial Directors or their subordinates.

As French diplomats in Japan also succeeded each other at fairly frequent intervals, it might be imagined that they too would be easily controlled by the Quai d'Orsay officials. For a number of reasons, this was not always so. To begin with, the only thing that the Quai d'Orsay seems to have impressed upon its agents was that they must avoid all complications which might lead France into costly military operations or friction with Britain. This, however, was far from being a complete guide for diplomats faced with a variety of new questions arising out of changing circumstances. The distance separating Paris from Tokyo meant that French representatives frequently had to make difficult decisions. If they waited to receive a reply to a dispatch, it took nearly four months, and until the early 1870s telegrams did not make a great deal of difference, since the lines did not extend east beyond Ceylon. Even thereafter they were seldom employed, presumably for reasons of expense.

If distance impeded communication, it also presented diplomats with opportunities. Roches certainly owed much of his freedom of manoeuvre to Japan's remoteness, and if, after the Quai d'Orsay had come to suspect how deeply he had involved France in Japanese politics, a closer rein was kept on him, his successors still had room to act independently in some areas. Differences of personality and approach on the part of diplomats could thus have some influence on French policy. One of the areas in which they did so was the pursuit of influence. The extent to which Japan would turn to the West for help in modernization and the opportunities which this would create could not, for a long time, be fully appreciated in France. Even less could they be anticipated. Not surprisingly, therefore, although the Quai d'Orsay always favoured the acquisition of influence in general, it lacked detailed knowledge of how best to seek it and never gave French diplomats clear guidelines in this regard.

From the time of the Franco-Chinese War, however, it began to be regarded as important that France should have its nationals employed in Japan. This was not only, as hitherto, for reasons of prestige but also so that France should be in a position to influence Japan by having Frenchmen in key positions. By then, however, Japan was dispensing with most of its foreign experts and acquiring relatively few new ones. In these circumstances, the Quai d'Orsay was largely dependent on the legacy of earlier French representatives. As it happened, the majority of these (even though not as pro-Japanese or as sensitive to the idea of France's civilizing mission as Roches, and perhaps Turenne) had been prepared to facilitate or encourage the employment of French lawyers, soldiers, and technicians. If more of them had been shaped in the Berthemy mould, however, the outcome would have been very different.

French representatives also had a discernible influence on the course of revision of the 'unequal treaties', the perennial theme of diplomacy throughout the first three decades of the Meiji period. Their direct knowledge of Japanese conditions compelled Paris to pay considerable attention to their views, and when negotiations were held in Tokyo, they had a tactical advantage in that the Quai d'Orsay was not in a good position to question their reasons for seeking or rejecting cooperation with other Powers. Generally, they tended to hinder the work of revision, and it is worth asking why this was so.

One factor may have been that with very few exceptions the diplomats who served as minister or chargé d'affaires in Japan were men whose careers had mostly been spent outside Western Europe. They were not accustomed to treat the officials with whom they dealt on terms of real equality, and thus they did not adjust well to Japanese circumstances. Japan's attempts to recover full sovereignty, in particular, aroused extraordinary hostility among French diplomats, whose early reports often complained bitterly of Japanese vanity and ambition. The fact that the one French minister who remained in Japan for a longer period showed unmistakable signs of mellowing in his attitude towards the Japanese suggests that French policy may have been affected by the brevity of most French representatives' period of service.

If the high rate of turnover of French diplomats in Tokyo – eight between 1868 and 1883 – meant that the character of French policy was liable to change as a result of the different personalities of French representatives, their transient nature tended to weaken the force of any more positive recommendations which they sent to Paris, especially if these seemed to the Quai d'Orsay to threaten its policy of avoidance of complications. A number of cases of such recommendations being ignored can be cited, among them Thouvenel's rejection of Duchesne de Bellecourt's advice not to allow the postponement of the opening of Hyogo, Osaka, and Edo in 1860, and Decazes' disinclination to adopt the strong line advocated by Berthemy when the latter wished to force the Meiji government to open Japan fully in 1874. A rather different example was Hanotaux's decision, in disregard of Harmand's warnings of the effect that this would have on relations with Japan, to join Russia and Germany in the Triple Intervention. It was then a matter of the minister in Tokyo favouring a policy of restraint and the French government choosing to engage in a policy of thinly veiled intimidation.

In the light of such evidence, there can be little doubt that in the last resort the Quai d'Orsay maintained its control over policy. This meant that whenever there was a conflict, or possible conflict, between French interests in Japan and European considerations (which usually meant the need to keep on good terms with Britain), the former were invariably subordinated to the latter. Even when the major decision-making role was allowed to slip into Roches' hands, the Quai d'Orsay managed to retrieve the situation before it was too late. The one important exception – when the wishes of the Tokyo legation effectively prevailed over those of Paris – was Sienkiewicz's undermining of Jules Ferry's pursuit of a military agreement with Japan in December 1884. Even if the minister in Tokyo had followed the instructions he received from Paris, however, the Meiji leaders would still probably not have countenanced Ferry's proposal, so the outcome would almost certainly not have been different.

With the major exception of Roches' guidance of the Bakufu, France made little direct effort to acquire influence in Japan, and it did not seek to pursue the same end indirectly through economic or financial penetration. Nor did it, at least until the 1890s, show much interest in Japanese foreign policy, except when it reluctantly and desultorily pursued a military agreement during the Franco-Chinese War of 1883–5. Even in this latter case France did not succeed in drawing Japan into the desired military conflict with China. This is not to say, however, that French policy was without influence on Japan's development. There can be no doubt that the French experts who came to Japan contributed appreciably to the consolidation of the Meiji government and to the establishment of a legal system suitable to a modern society. It needs to be noted, too, that the most important French contributions to Japanese modernization depended heavily on French diplomatic concern with prestige and influence.

In some respects, though, French influence on Japan was less welcome. The most notable example was French obstruction of Japanese attempts to secure treaty revision. A number of reasons for the French attitude were suggested by Frederick Marshall, the political adviser to the Japanese legation in Paris, in a perceptive memorandum in 1883. As he saw it,

> When the question of revising the Japanese treaties first came before Europe, France took up an attitude of indifference towards Japan. The Ministry of Foreign Affairs expressed, repeatedly, during several years, in private conversations, the opinion that France had nothing to care about in Japan, and that though she would probably, in the end, act as other European nations might act in the matter, she would take no initiative therein, and would hold to the present treaty as long as she possibly could. France gave several reasons for this attitude. She said, in substance, that her position in Europe was delicate and difficult, that her whole thoughts were absorbed by that position, that her trade with Japan was small and her political interest there null, that she would create difficulties with her European neighbours by assuming an active position in the Japanese revision, and that she wished to trouble herself as little as possible about that revision.[1]

A study of the Quai d'Orsay archives confirms the truth of Marshall's allegations. The French government's preoccupation with Europe prevented the Quai d'Orsay from paying serious attention to the problems of the new Japan. Nor, in the two decades after the Meiji Restoration, did it have, with the possible exception of Turenne, any representative in Tokyo who had either an instinctive understanding of Japanese potentialities or sufficient time to see that the changes taking place were not so superficial as they seemed. Before 1890, certainly, no French diplomat ever showed an awareness that Japan might become a very considerable Power, despite the fact that France was even more involved than Germany in Japan's military modernization and had also been one of the main models in the Meiji leaders' construction of a strong centralized state.

Yet France, more than any other Power, perhaps, would have benefited from, and might have achieved, an entente with Japan. The sense of inferiority which it felt particularly strongly in East Asia because of its military and naval weakness there (compared with Britain's) might have been alleviated by collaboration with the rising state, and the position of both France and Japan with regard to China would have been strengthened. Between the two countries there were no basic conflicts of interest, and because Japan was not an important French market, France's policy was not inhibited, as Britain's to some extent was, by the pressures of an influential trading community. As far as Japan was concerned, a tie based on common interests and an acknowledgement of political equality would, if France could have accepted it, have brought material and psychological advantages.

It may be thought that the idea of a close relationship between France and Japan is an anachronistic one, which was inconceivable at the time. To dismiss it on such grounds, however, is not only to ignore the Anglo-Japanese alliance of 1902 but also to disregard the aims and achievements (however ephemeral they may have proved) of Léon Roches. Many of Roches' successors were men of ability, but to be a successful diplomat in Japan something more was needed.[2] When Sienkiewicz wrote in January 1894 that 'in Europe there is too great a tendency not to take Japan seriously',[3] he was also passing judgement on his own failure, and that of his predecessors, to see beyond their preconceived ideas, appreciate the colossal difficulties which Japan faced in attempting to modernize, and understand that the Japanese response to the West in the nineteenth century was qualitatively different from that of other non-Western countries. The main conclusion that emerges from a study of French policy towards Japan in the nineteenth century is that a great opportunity was lost through lack of imagination.

NOTES

CHAPTER 1

1. Most of what follows in this section is based on J. F. Cady, *The Roots of French Imperialism in Eastern Asia* (New York 1954); H. I. Priestley, *France Overseas Through the Old Regime,* (New York 1939); and H. Blet, *Histoire de la Colonisation Française,* 2 vols, (Paris 1946).
2. Priestley, *op.cit.,* p. 92.
3. On this episode, see Cady, *op.cit.,* pp. 12–14.
4. On this unsuccessful French expedition, see R. Ristelhueber, 'Un diplomate belliqueux déclare la guerre à la Corée (en 1866)', *Revue d'Histoire Diplomatique,* 1958, No. 2, pp. 111–117.
5. *Op.cit.,* p. 2.
6. A. L. Dunham, *The Industrial Revolution in France, 1815–1848* (New York 1955), p. 387.
7. S. B. Clough, *France: a History of National Economics, 1789–1939* (New York 1939), p. 173.
8. The documents in question are contained in the archives of the French Foreign Ministry at the Quai d'Orsay. Most are to be found in the series Correspondance Politique Chine (hereafter referred to as C.P.Chine); but there are also a number of important dispatches and communications in two series devoted to Japan, the Correspondance Politique Japon (hereafter C.P.Japon), and the Mémoires et Documents Japon (hereafter M.D.Japon). Several of the documents in the first of these series are quoted at length by Cordier, 'Le Premier Traité de la France avec le Japon', *T'oung Pao,* XIII, 1912, pp. 209–290.
9. For some idea of missionary feeling at this time, see A. Launay, *Histoire Générale de la Société des Missions Étrangères,* Vol.III, (Paris 1894), p. 201 ff.
10. For full details of this and other missionary activity preparatory to the opening of Japan, see F. Marnas, *La 'Réligion de Jésus' (Yaso Jakyo) Resuscitée au Japon,* Vol. I, (Paris-Lyon 1896), *passim.*
11. These instructions, dated 16 May 1857, are in both C.P.Japon, I (as a first draft) and C.P.Chine, XXI. They are unsigned.
12. C.P.Chine, XV, 6 March 1854.
13. C.P.Japon, I, 16 May 1857.
14. The renunciation was not quite total. In August 1858, before he left Shanghai for Japan, Gros heard, incorrectly, that the Americans had secured a treaty which opened Japan to Christian missionaries and contained an undertaking to abandon the persecution of Japanese Christians; and this led him to state that he would 'seek,

if possible, to introduce a more favourable clause for the religion which we protect in these distant countries than those which are to be found in the treaties already signed'. C.P.Chine, XXV, 26 August 1858, Gros to Walewski. His account of the negotiations, however, gives no indication that he made any such attempt. Even after this, though, there were some lingering hopes. In the instructions later given to the first French representative in Japan, Duchesne de Bellecourt, it was anticipated that despite the limitations placed upon them, missionaires would still succeed in penetrating to the interior, in which case France could not abandon the right of protecting them. C.P.Japon, I, 8 June 1859, Walewski to Bellecourt.

15. M.D.Japon, I, May 1857, Faugère to Walewski. The Quai d'Orsay's receptiveness to Delprat's advice was possibly no unconnected with the fact that it had itself earlier expressed some reservations about the timing of a demand for missionary rights when it informed Bourboulon that 'the most delicate point in this matter is without doubt that of religion and we do not have to make conjectures about the stubborn fear with which the Japanese Government will seek to exclude any attempt at Christian proselytism in its domains. We assuredly do not, at the commencement of our relations with this country, have to make a frontal attack on this intolerance which formerly manifested itself in pitiless persecutions'. C.P.Chine, XV, 8 June 1854.

16. There can be no doubt that it was Delprat who was referred to. He was the only Frenchman at the time who had lived in Japan. His position and experiences at Nagasaki from 1845 to 1849 as a trader who had bought trading rights from the Dutch, are referred to in a memorandum which he wrote for the Quai d'Orsay in November 1854. M.D.Japon, I, p. 26.

17. *Ibid.*

18. 'Le Japon et le Commerce Européen', *Revue des Deux Mondes* (October 1856), p. 640.

19. C.P.Japon, I, 10 June 1854; *Ibid.*, 18 June 1855, *Ibid.*, 21 October, 1857.

20. Articles expressing this viewpoint were ridiculed by Delprat, *op.cit.,* p. 634.

21. *Ibid.,* p. 635.

22. In 1846. See footnote 30.

23. For his letter to the Nagasaki *bugyo* (officials) and his report to the Navy Ministry, see Cordier, *op.cit.,* pp. 228–31.

24. On this point, see W. G. Beasley, *Great Britain and the Opening of Japan, 1834–1858,* (London 1951), pp. 129 –130, 145 –147.

25. *Ibid,* p. 645.

26. Delprat did refer (*Ibid.* p. 638) to the desirability of Japanese ports being opened in order to provide a haven for French whalers during storms, but this can hardly be regarded as an important motive. He felt that France would find it comparatively easy to secure a treaty from the Japan because 'the admiration they have for military glory has made the name of Napoleon popular amongst them'. (*Ibid.* p. 645). Support for this latter claim can be found in P. Humbertclaude, 'La France à l'heure hollandaise', in R. Sieffert (ed.), *Le Japon et la France: Images d'une Découverte* (Paris , 1974).

27. C.P.Japon, I, 16 May 1857.

28. E. Fraissinet, *Le Japon,* Vol.II (Paris, 1853), pp. 4–5. Colbert's involvement is briefly discussed in Étiemble, 'Le Japon des jésuites et des philosophes', in Sieffert, *op. cit.*

29. M. Medzini, 'Léon Roches in Japan' in *Papers on Japan,* vol.2 (Harvard, 1963), p. 184. Medzini is here quoting W. E. Griffis, *Corea, the Hermit Nation* (New York, 1911), but Griffis derived his information on this point from C. Dallet, *Histoire de l'Église de Corée* (Paris, 1874) and in repeating Dallet's account he made a slight but significant alteration. What Dallet wrote was that Cécille 'also had the intention of concluding commercial treaties with the kingdoms neighbouring China, especially

with Korea'. *Ibid.,* p. 257. Japan is not specifically mentioned. For the Orleanist Government to have contemplated an isolated attempt to secure a treaty with Japan would have been quite out of character.

30. There has been some uncertainty over the date of the first visit by French warships to Japan. Most authorities give it as July 1846, but Cady states that it was November 1846, Fraissinet 1847, and G. B. Sansom, *A History of Japan 1615–1867* (London, 1954), 1848. There can be little doubt that the first visit was 29–31 July 1846. It is just possible that there may have been another visit in one of the following years. See also Shinohara Hiroshi, *Rikugun Sosetsu Shi,* (Tokyo, 1983), pp. 41–56.

31. Delprat, *op. cit.,* p. 645.

32. Y. Takekoshi, *Economic Aspects of the History of the Civilisation of Japan,* vol.3 (London, 1930), pp. 277–279, says that Satsuma received from the Bakufu secret permission to trade with the French. Sansom, *op.cit.,* p. 229, alleges that Satsuma arranged through the Ryukyus one transaction, a purchase of arms and machinery. No such transaction is mentioned in Quai d'Orsay records or by contemporary writers, such as Delprat or Fraissinet. Nor is there any reference to it in a report of August 1856 on 'Commerce avec le littoral Japonaise et les Iles Liou Tchiou', by an agent of the Ministry of Agriculture, Commerce and Public Works, A. Heurtier, to be found in the *Annales du Commerce Extérieur (Chine et Indo-Chine, 1855–67).*

33. For details of the treaty and the visits of French naval officers to the Ryukyus, see H. Cordier, *Les Français aux Iles Lieou K'ieou,* (Paris, 1911).

34. C.P.Chine, XV, 6 March 1854, Drouyn de Lhuys to Bourboulon.

35. C.P.Chine, XV, 19 May 1854, Bourboulon to Drouyn de Lhuys.

36. C.P.Chine, XV, 6 March 1854, Drouyn de Lhuys to Bourboulon.

37. C.P.Chine, XV, 3 August 1854, Bourboulon to Drouyn de Lhuys.

38. C.P.Chine, XV, 7 October 1854, Drouyn de Lhuys to Bourboulon.

39. C.P.Chine, XV, 3 August 1854, Bourboulon to Drouyn de Lhuys.

40. See C.P.Japon, I, 9 June 1854, Navy Ministry to Quai d'Orsay.

41. See C.P.Japon, I, 16 February 1855, Drouyn de Lhuys to Walewski. (Ambassador in London).

42. On the difficulties encountered by Britain, see Beasley, *op.cit.,* especially Chapters V-VII.

43. C.P.Chine, XXV, 2 August 1858, Gros to Walewski.

44. C.P.Chine, XXI, 16 May 1857.

45. C.P.Chine, XXV, 2 August 1858, Gros to Walewski.

46. There exist two published accounts of Gros' negotiations in Japan by members of the expedition. They are: Ch. de Chassiron, *Notes sur le Japon, la Chine, et l'Inde* (Paris, 1861), and Marquis de Moges, *Souvenirs d'une Ambassade en Chine et au Japon en 1857 et 1858* (Paris, 1860). The latter was translated into English the same year, but the former is more valuable for Japan. The treaty itself is printed by Cordier, 'Le Premier Traité', pp. 278–290, together with Gros' account of the five negotiating sessions.

47. C.P.Chine, XXVI, 6 October 1858, Gros to Walewski.

48. C.P.Japon, I, 16 May 1857.

49. C.P.Chine, XXVI, 6 October 1858, Gros to Walewski.

50. *Ibid.*

51. C.P.Chine, XXIX, 8 January 1859, Walewski to Gros.

52. C.P.Japon, I, 10 June 1854.

53. It is possible that the desire for influence in Japan sprang also from international rivalry in the Pacific between Britain, France, and the United States and Russia. G. Barraclough, in his essay 'Europe and the Wider World in the 19th and 20th Centuries', in A. O. Sarkissian (ed), *Studies in Diplomatic History and Historiography* (London, 1961), points to such an interpretation. Great power

rivalry may have coloured the Quai's attitude to the opening of Japan, but since it was never explicitly mentioned in this context, it is hard to regard it as more than a marginal influence on French policy. If it existed, it was soon forgotten when the Powers discovered that they would have great difficulty in maintaining trade relations with Japan.

54. Quoted by Cordier, 'Le Premier Traité', p. 233.
55. Dubois de Jancigny, *Japon, Indo-Chine, Empire Birman (ou Ava), Siam, Annam (ou Cochinchine) Péninsule Malaise, etc, Ceylan* (Paris, 1850), p. 110.
56. *Ibid.* p. 206.
57. Marquis de Moges, *Recollections of Baron Gros's Embassy to China and Japan in 1857–58,* (London & Glasgow, 1860), p. 355.

CHAPTER 2

1. Bellecourt was the first permanent French representative in Japan. He served there as consul-général from September 1859 to February 1860, when the title chargé d'affaires was conferred on him to raise his standing with the Bakufu. In June 1862 he was made ministre plénipotentiaire. He was succeeded by Léon Roches in April 1864.
2. C.P. Japon, I, 8 June 1859. The drafter of the instructions is unnamed.
3. C.P.Japon, I, 10 September 1859, Bellecourt to Walewski.
4. C.P.Japon, I, 16 September 1859, Bellecourt to Walewski. For what still remains the best explanation of the interaction between foreign diplomats and late Tokugawa politics, see the introduction to W G Beasley, *Select Documents on Japanese Foreign Policy, 1853–68* (London, 1955).
5. C.P.Japon, I, 8 November 1859, Bellecourt to Walewski.
6. C.P.Japon, I, 10 December 1859, Bellecourt to Walewski.
7. C.C.Yeddo, I, 18 September 1859; C.P.Japon, I, 26 December 1859, both Bellecourt to Walewski. C.P.Japon, II, 19 August 1860, Bellecourt to Thouvenel; C.C.Yeddo, II, 10 April 1861, Thouvenel to Bellecourt.
8. C.P.Japon, I, 20 December 1859, Bellecourt to Walewski; C.P.Japon, II, 15 March 1860, Bellecourt to Thouvenel.
9. See C.P.Japon, III, 25 January 1861, Bellecourt to Thouvenel.
10. C.P.Japon, II, 17 September 1860, Bellecourt to Thouvenel.
11. C.P.Japon, III, 26 January 1861, Thouvenel to Bellecourt.
12. C.P.Japon, IV, 12 July 1861, Bellecourt to Thouvenel.
13. C.P.Japon, IV, 8 October, 1861, Thouvenel to Flahault (London).
14. C.P.Japon, I, 28 November 1861, Thouvenel to Bellecourt.
15. C.P.Japon, IV, 10 December 1861, Thouvenel to Bellecourt.
16. C.P. Japon, V, 26 February 1862, Bellecourt to Thouvenel.
17. C.P.Japon, V, 25 April 1862, Thouvenel to Japanese Envoys; C.P.Japon, V, April 1862, Thouvenel to Russell (via Flahault).
18. British Foreign Office Records. F.O. 391 (the Papers of Sir Edmund Hammond), I, 29 May 1862. See also C.P.Japon, V, 22 March 1862.
19. C.P.Japon, V, 27 May 1862, Thouvenel to Flahault. It is worth noting that a few months later the Navy Ministry informed the Quai d'Orsay that for reasons of economy it would no longer maintain a permanent force in Japanese waters. C.P.Japon, VII, 10 September 1862.
20. M.D.Japon, II, Quai d'Orsay memorandum of October 1862.
21. C.P.Japon, VIII, 3 May 1863, Bellecourt to Drouyn de Lhuys.
22. The home governments, even in their most indulgent moods, never allowed themselves any doubts about the validity of their treaties, but from about mid-1861 their representatives began to have strong suspicions that the authority of the

Mikado (Emperor) was potentially greater than that of the shogun, and from 1864 most of them were in no doubt of the advisability of securing the former's assent to the treaties. Surprisingly, in view of his pro-Tokugawa sentiments, the second French minister, Roches, was one of those who shared this feeling. In a dispatch of 23 September 1864 (C.P.Japon, XII, Roches to Drouyn de Lhuys) he stated bluntly that the *Mikado* was the sole legitimate sovereign and the *Taikoun* (shogun) only his deputy, and that all important measures such as the treaties must be sanctioned by the former. Bellecourt, on the other hand, after all his criticisms of Bakufu weakness, wrote just before he left that the *Mikado* would never acquire the strength of the *Taikoun* and that it was unnecessary to treat with him. (C.P.Japon, XI, 19 March 1864, Bellecourt to Drouyn de Lhuys).

23. See, for example, C.P.Japon, IX, 1863, Bellecourt to Drouyn de Lhuys.
24. C.P. Japon, III, 20 May 1861. Bellecourt derived this information (through his interpreter Blekman) from illicit contacts with pro-foreign Japanese and from secret government publications. Unfortunately, he unwittingly omitted the important *han* of Choshu, shortly to play a leading role in national politics.
25. An example of this can be found in a dispatch of 25 June 1862 (C.P.Japon, VI, Bellecourt to Thouvenel) where the growing authority of the Emperor was interpreted solely in terms of an attempt by reactionaries to invalidate the legal basis of the treaties.
26. C.P.Japon, I, 10 September 1859, Bellecourt to Walewski.
27. C.P. Japon, I, 19 September 1859, Bellecourt to Walewski.
28. C.P.Japon, II, 17 September 1860., Bellecourt to Thouvenel.
29. On their dilemma, which they sought to solve by the marriage of the shogun to the Emperor's sister and by the promise to rid Japan of foreigners within ten years, see Beasley, *Select Documents*, pp. 51–54.
30. C.P.Japon, III, 18 April 1861, Bellecourt to Thouvenel.
31. C.P.Japon, VI, 19 June, 22 June 1862, Bellecourt to Drouyn de Lhuys.
32. C.P.Japon, VI, 4 July 1862, Bellecourt to Drouyn de Lhuys.
33. C.P. Japon, VI, 10 August 1862, Bellecourt to Drouyn de Lhuys.
34. C.P. Japon, VII, 28 September 1862, Bellecourt to Drouyn de Lhuys.
35. C.P.Japon, VII, 10 October 1862, Bellecourt to Drouyn de Lhuys.
36. C.P.Japon, VII, 23 December 1862, Bellecourt to Drouyn de Lhuys.
37. C.P. Japon, VIII, 29 January 1863, Bellecourt to Drouyn de Lhuys.
38. C.P.Japon, VIII, 3 May 1863, Bellecourt to Drouyn de Lhuys.
39. *Ibid.*
40. *Ibid.*
41. Ishii Takashi, *Gakusetsu Hihan Meiji Ishin Ron*, (Tokyo, 1964), p. 264.
42. C.P.Japon, VIII, 10 May 1863, Bellecourt to Drouyn de Lhuys.
43. C.P.Japon, VIII, 27 May 1863, Bellecourt to Drouyn de Lhuys.
44. *Op. cit.* p. 265.
45. C.P.Japon, IX, 18 July 1863, Drouyn de Lhuys to Bellecourt.
46. C.P.Japon, X, 18 September 1863.
47. C.P.Japon, X, 8 October 1863, Drouyn de Lhuys to Roches.
48. C.P.Japon, IX, 24 June 1863, Bellecourt to Drouyn de Lhuys.
49. A contrary view may be found in Hattori Shiso, *Kindai Nihon Gaiko Shi*, (Tokyo, 1954), p. 55.
50. C.P.Japon, IX, 30 June 1863, Bellecourt to Drouyn de Lhuys.
51. C.P. Japon, XI, 11 April 1864, Bellecourt to Drouyn de Lhuys
52. C.P. Japon, IX, 30 June 1863, Bellecourt to Drouyn de Lhuys.
53. C.P.Japon, IX, 23 July 1863, Bellecourt to Drouyn de Lhuys.
54. *Ibid.*
55. C.P.Japon, X, 23 October 1863, Bellecourt to Drouyn de Lhuys. The effect of his

foreign minister's warning was apparent to the British chargé d'affaires for on 31 October he noted 'the marked abatement in the energetic action of the French naval and diplomatic agents . . . which Colonel Neale supposes to be the consequences of orders received from home'. This was referred by the Foreign Office to Paris, where Drouyn de Lhuys informed Cowley, the British ambassador, that 'with the view of avoiding hostilities with the Japanese government the greatest caution had been recommended to the French diplomatic and naval authorities in Japan in their dealings with the Japanese Authorities'. F.O.27, 29 January 1864, Cowley to Russell.

56. C.P.Japon, X, 31 October 1863.
57. C.P.Japon, X, 25 November 1863, Bellecourt to Drouyn de Lhuys. There is a useful article on the mission, focusing on its leader, Ikeda Nagaaki, by A.W.Burks, in B. S. Silbermann & H. D. Harootunian (eds.) *Modern Japanese Leadership; Transition and Change,* (Tucson, 1966).
58. C.P.Japon, XI, 10 March 10 !864, Drouyn de Lhuys to Bellecourt.
59. See Ishii, *op. cit.,* pp. 268–9 and Beasley, *Select Documents,* pp. 72–4. Hitotsubashi Keiki became shogun in 1866 and was then known as Tokugawa Keiki or, more commonly, Tokugawa Yoshinobu.
60. The report by the mission's leaders has been translated into English, *Ibid.* pp. 274–82.
61. By M. Medzini, *French Policy in Japan during the Closing Years of the Tokugawa Regime* (Cambridge, Mass., 1971), p. 63.
62. The offer was made on 7 May, in the first of six conferences with the envoys. A procès-verbal of the conferences is included in C.P.Japon, XI, June 1864. Two other documents relating to the mission, one a memorandum drawn up by its adviser, Philip von Siebold, are to be found in M.D. Japon, I. Siebold urged France to support the shogun and he may have influenced Drouyn de Lhuys and possibly even Napoleon III (See Otsuka, *Bakumatsu Gaiko Shi no Kenkyu*), (Tokyo, 1950), p. 288. It is difficult to see, however, how this influence could have been more than marginal, and it is worth noting that some of Siebold's suggestions – opening Kagoshima, Shimonoseki and Niigata, and closing Kanagawa (Yokohama) temporarily, with compensation being paid to foreign merchants – were completely disregarded.
63. The text, together with a number of dispatches, was printed by the French government in *Documents Diplomatiques,* Paris, 1865. It is also in Beasley, *Select Documents,* pp. 273–4.
64. The suggestion that the envoys might buy old but serviceable French warships seems to have first been made by Napoleon III. M.D.Japon, I, May 1864.
65. They had also become convinced that the Bakufu must abandon without delay the dangerous policy of trying to evade the provisions of the Treaties. See Beasley, *Select Documents,* pp. 277–81.
66. C.P.Japon, XII, 26 August 1864, Roches to Drouyn de Lhuys.
67. C.P.Japon, XI, 19 May 1864, Roches to Drouyn de Lhuys.
68. C.P.Japon, XI, 17 May 1864, Roches to Drouyn. At this stage Roches was still receiving advice from Bellecourt, who remained at Yokohama till 28 May .
69. C.P.Japon, XI, 25 May 1864, Roches to Drouyn de Lhuys.
70. C.P.Japon, XII, 10 August 1864, Drouyn de Lhuys to Roches.
71. C.P.Japon, XII, 15 August 1864, Drouyn de Lhuys to Roches.
72. C.P.Japon, XII, 17 August 1864, Roches to Drouyn de Lhuys.
73. These dispatches were passed on to the Quai d'Orsay by a disgruntled navy minister. See C.P.Japon, XII, 26 August 1864; 16 September 1864; 13 October 1864.
74. Roches further justified himself by pointing to the possibility that Britain, by acting alone, might steal a march on France. 'The maintenance of neutrality by France, in a question where Britain was determined to act', he observed, 'would have left the latter totally in control of the direction its policy should take'. This, he feared, might

lead it to seize an important position in the Inland Sea area and secure special advantages there by dealing directly with a daimyo. C.P.Japon, XII, 17 August 1864, Roches to Drouyn de Lhuys.

75. F.O.46, XVL, No. 51, 25 August 1864, Alcock to Russell.

76. C.P.Japon, XII, 26 August 1864, Roches to Drouyn de Lhuys. Roches noted that the foreign representatives' plan could now go ahead, and that 'this strike which will, I am convinced, be decisive, will terrify our enemies and encourage our friends'.

77. C.P.Japon, XII, 31 October 1864, Roches to Drouyn de Lhuys.

78. C.P.Japon, XII, 1 October 1864., Drouyn de Lhuys to Roches.

79. C.P.Japon, XI, 10 December 1864, Drouyn de Lhuys to Roches.

80. Hints that Roches aspired to play the foremost role among the foreign representatives can be found in his dispatches even before Alcock's recall, for in late 1864 he began to refer to the latter's 'support' or 'loyalty'. See, for example, C.P.Japon, XII, 17 December 1864, Roches to Drouyn de Lhuys. In this context it may be relevant that in November Roches gave Alcock a memorandum in which he set out his views on the situation in Japan at length. According to the British minister, Roches had sent the document, entitled 'Coup d'oeil sur la Politique Étrangère au Japon de 1858 à 1864' to his own government, but it is not in the French archives. F.O.46, XLVII, No. 89, 14 November 1864, Alcock to Russell.

CHAPTER 3

1. C.P. Japon, XII, 15 October 1864.

2. It has received much attention, beginning in the pre-war period with Honjo Eijiro, whose chapters on Léon Roches and the Bakufu reforms in *Bakumatsu no Shin Seisaku* (Tokyo, 1935) appeared in translation in his *Economic Theory and History of Japan in the Tokugawa Period* (New York, 1943, 1965) and Otsuka Takematsu, whose pioneering work in the French archives in 1929 resulted in an article, 'Fukkoku koshi Léon Roches no Seisaku Kōdo ni tsuite', in *Shigaku Zasshi* XLVI (1935), which was subsequently incorporated in his *Bakumatsu Gaiko-shi no Kenkyu* (Tokyo, 1952). After the war further study was carried out by Ishii Takashi, *Meiji Ishin no Kokusaiteki Kankyo* (Tokyo, 1957; expanded edition, Tokyo 1966); Meron Medzini, *French Policy in Japan during the Closing Years of the Tokugawa Regime* (Cambridge, Mass., 1971); Jean-Pierre Lehmann, 'France and Japan, 1850–1885' (Oxford University, D. Phil. thesis, 1976) and Mark Ericson, 'The Tokugawa Bakufu and Léon Roches' (University of Hawaii, Ph. D. thesis, 1978). One reason for the continuation of differences of view may be that the evidence available on these points is quite limited. Of all the representatives whom France sent to Japan in the 19th century, Roches was by far the most irregular correspondent and the most secretive. Consequently the questions which arise from his activities can in most cases be answered only in the terms of probabilities.

3. Drouyn de Lhuys initially in December was inclined to opt for a new open port rather than the indemnity, but he changed his mind in January after receiving Roches' advice. See C.P. Japon, XII, 31 October 1864, Roches to Drouyn; *Ibid.* 10 December 1864, Drouyn de Lhuys to Roches; C.P. Japon. XIII, 10 January 1865, Drouyn de Lhuys to Roches. Immediately after the foreign minister altered his position, the Navy Ministry communicated its preference for an indemnity too. Its basic argument was that if Shimonoseki was opened as a port, 'to protect commerce it would be indispensable not only to maintain a naval force there but also to disembark troops, which would involve us in considerable expense which we could not face but which the English would not draw back from, considering the value of the position. Now I would not see the English establish themselves in Shimonoseki without lively regret'. M.D. Japon, III, 10 January 1865, Chasseloup-Laubat to

Drouyn de Lhuys. The indemnity question dragged on for years because of the difficulty of repayment. Already by mid-1866, a marginal comment, presumably by Drouyn de Lhuys, on Roches' dispatch of 27 May (C.P. Japon, XIV) indicated that he could no longer understand its complexities.

4. C.P. Japon, XIII, 31 October 1865, Roches to Drouyn de Lhuys.

5. See Beasley, *Select Documents*, p. 82.

6. C.P. Japon, XIV, 26 June 1866, Roches to Drouyn de Lhuys. Note also Roches' earlier claim (C.C.Yédo, IV, 1 December 1865).

7. This conflict resulted from the Bakufu's decision to regain prestige by punishing Choshu for undermining the Tokugawa position in Kyoto. The attempt by Choshu samurai, to regain influence over the Imperial Court by seizing Kyoto in 1864, provided the Bakufu with an excellent pretext for raising an expeditionary force which at the end of 1864 achieved the nominal submission of the Choshu leaders without any real fighting. No sooner was the military pressure removed than civil war broke out in Choshu and power in the domain was seized by radical new leaders who were pledged to the Bakufu's overthrow. It thus became necessary for the Bakufu to undertake a new expedition, but the preparations were not completed until July 1866, by which time Choshu had made a secret alliance with Satsuma. Thanks to the secret import of Western rifles, it was able to resist the Tokugawa attack, which was called off before the end of the year. See A.M.Craig, *Choshu in the Meiji Restoration*, (Cambridge, Mass., 1961) and W.G. Beasley, *The Meiji Restoration*, (Stanford and Oxford, 1972).

8. See C.P. Japon, XIII, 26 June 1865, Roches to Drouyn de Lhuys. Roches' military advice is referred to by Ishii *op. cit.*, pp. 625–6. and by Takahashi Kunitaro, in 'Fukkoku no Nekketsukan Léon Roches', *Rekishi to Jimbutsu*, June 1971, pp. 167–8.

9. See C.P. Japon, XIV, 27 August 1866. Roches had already exerted some restraining influence on Parkes through his home government. His complaint that Parkes was acting rashly by opening direct relations with the daimyo was taken up by the Quai d'Orsay with the Foreign Office, which instructed its representative to act with the utmost prudence. See F.O.46, LXIV, No.82, 7 May 1866, Clarendon to Parkes; F.O.27, MDCXVI., No.588, 4 May 1866, Cowley to Clarendon.

10. C.P. Japon, XIV, 27 August 1866.

11. F.O.46, LXX, No.131, 13 August 1866, Enclosure in Parkes to Stanley. It should be noted that Roches at first urged Itakura Katsukiyo that peace might be restored if some concessions were made to the daimyo, but the *roju* rejected this advice as likely to increase the audacity of the Bakufu's enemies and the hesitation of its friends. C.P. Japon, XIV, 27 August 1866., Roches to Drouyn de Lhuys.

12. This concern is attested to in the reports of Satow, the English interpreter who had close contacts with important daimyo and samurai. In Uwajima, for instance, Satow found 'the intimacy of the French with the Bakufu (Tycoon's government) appeared to be a subject of great suspicion with [the ex-daimyo]. F.O.46, LXXVIII, No.8, 18 January 1867, Parkes to Stanley, Enclosure. See also Beasley, *The Meiji Restoration*, p. 266.

13. C.P. Japon, XIII, 16 January 1865, Roches to Drouyn.

14. C.P. Japon, XIII, 18 March, 1865, Drouyn to Roches.

15. A short account of the dockyard by J.Raoulx, 'Les Français au Japon et La Création de l'Arsénal de Yokosuka', can be found in *La Revue Maritime*, May 1939, pp. 588–635. A more recent treatment in Japanese is to be found in Takahashi Kunitaro, *O-Yatoi Gaikokujin: Gunji*, (Tokyo, 1968), pp. 76–123.

16. C.C.Yédo, IV, 17 October 1865.

17. *Ibid.*; also Ibid., 16 December 1865. See also the detailed examination by Shibata Michio and Shibata Asako, 'Bakumatsu ni okeru, France no Tainichi Seisaku – "France Yushutsunyu Kaisha" no Setsururitsu Keikaku o Megutte', *Shigaku Zasshi*,

LXXVI, August 1967, pp. 46–71. A condensed translation of this article was published in *Revue d'Histoire Moderne et Contemporaine*, XVI, 1969, pp. 173–188, under the title 'Un aspect de la relation franco-japonaise à la fin de l'époque de Tokugawa. Le projet de fondation d'une compagnie commerciale'.

18. C.P. Japon, XIV, 15 February 1866., Roches to Drouyn de Lhuys.
19. According to a subsequent report by the chief French officer, Captain Chanoine, many Tokugawa troops fled after the first encounter but 'this example was not followed by the troops taught and trained by the officers of the French mission in Yédo'. M.D.Japon, I, April 1869. The first, and later, military missions have been studied in detail by E. Presseisen, *Before Aggression*, (Tucson, 1965), and by Shinohara Hiroshi, *Rikugun Sosetsu Shi*, (Tokyo, 1983). There is a more recent account of the first mission by J-P. Lehmann, 'The French Military Mission to Japan, 1866–1868, and Bakumatsu Politics, in P. Lowe (ed.), *Proceedings of the British Association for Japanese Studies*, vol. I, part I, 1976. Chanoine later produced an account based mainly on contemporary letters by French officers, *Documents pour servir à l'histoire des relations entre la France et le Japon* (Paris, 1907).
20. Detailed accounts in Japanese of the reforms can be found in Honjo Eijiro, *Bakumatsu no Shin-seisaku*, pp. 188–199, and in Ishii, *Zotei Meiji Ishin no Kokusaiteki Kankyo*, (Tokyo, 1966). In English they are discussed most fully in C. Totman, *The Collapse of the Tokugawa Bakfufu, 1862–68*, (Honolulu, 1980), *passim*.
21. Some Marxist historians even devised the term 'Tokugawa comprador absolutism' to indicate the nature of the regime in its final stages. See Ishii Takashi, *Gakusetsu Hihan Meiji Ishin Ron*, (Tokyo, 1961), pp. 276–277.
22. C.P. Japon, XV, 1 March 1867
23. *Ibid*. 28 November 1867., Roches to Moustier.
24. *Ibid*. 10 April 1867, Roches to Moustier.
25. Ishii Takashi, *Meiji Ishin no Butai-ura*, p. 165.
26. Enclosed in C.P. Japan, XVI, 31 October, 1866. Roches to de la Valette. Though extremely appreciative, this language was not as effusive as that used in a letter sent to Roches in the name of the previous shogun earlier that year: 'But I would be unjust and ungrateful if I did not say that these happy changes are, in large measure, due to your Representative, Léon Roches, who has shown to us everything true, sincere and benevolent in his heart. I have unlimited confidence in him, and I consider, in the future, making him my intimate adviser on all foreign affairs'. M.D. Japon, I. It is dated Keio 1.12.29. (14 February 1866) . Yoshinobu's other letters can be found in C.P. Japon. XIV. 12 October 1866, Roches to de la Valette; *Ibid*. XV, 12 July 1867; 10 August 1867; 26 November 1867, Roches to Moustier.
27. C.C.Yédo, IV, February, 1867. There is no indication of who the author of this assessment for the *Direction Politique* was, but it was obviously based on a memorandum written by Mermet de Cachon (M.D. Japon, I, 18 February 1867). The passage quoted uses Cachon's words almost exactly.
28. See C.C.Yédo, IV, 14 October 186; C.P. Japon, XIV, 28 September 1866, both Roches to Drouyn de Lhuys; C.P. Japon, XIV, 12 and 31 October 1866, Roches to de la Valette. Some military equipment had already been purchased in Europe by the mission led by Shibata Takenaka. See Mark Ericson 'The Bakufu Looks Abroad: the 1865 Mission to France', *Monumenta Nipponica*, XXXIV, No. 4, 1979, pp. 383–407.
29. See C.P. Japon, XIV, 28 September 1866, Roches to Drouyn de Lhuys; XV, 1 March 1867 Roches to Moustier
30. The linkage between the two projects is discussed by Shibata, M. & A., *op. cit.* pp. 63–71.
31. Ishii, *Meiji Ishin no Butai-ura*, pp. 70–171.

32. C.P. Japon, XV, 18 May 1867, Moustier to Roches.
33. Ishii, *Meiji Ishin no Butai-ura,* pp. 10–12.
34. There is no direct evidence, however, for the view, which both Ishii and Inoue Kiyoshi hold, that Britain supported the powerful daimyo in order to prevent a revolution 'from below' in Japan. The numerous exhortations to the *roju* by various British representatives to encourage merchants and foster the growth of a 'middle class' might conceivably be interpreted as indirect support for a Marxist interpretation but can better be seen as indications of the view that Japan would serve itself and Britain best if it could evolve quickly from feudalism and seek to emulate the West.
35. F.O.46, LXIX, No.123, 24 July 1866, Parkes to Clarendon.
36. F.O.46, LXXVIII, No.29, 28 February 1867, Parkes to Stanley.
37. F.O.46, LXXVIII, No.1, 16 January 1867. His enthusiasm faded somewhat at the end of 1867 when the Bakufu failed to find the murderers of some sailors from *HMS Icarus.*
38. F.O.391, XIV, 6 May 1867.
39. See eg. F.O.46, LXIX, No.123, 24 July 1866, Parkes to Clarendon.
40. See Medzini, 'Léon Roches in Japan, 1864–1868', p. 183, where he maintains that by the 1864 Paris Convention, France 'cut herself loose from the policy she had pursued since 1859. The new 'line' was entrusted to her new envoy in Japan – Léon Roches'. Ishii, *Meiji Ishin no Kokusaiteki Kankyo,* p. 615, also sees the appointment of Roches as marking a reversal of French policy. Roches' own dispatches make no reference to any instruction to pursue a new line. When he did refer to his instructions soon after his arrival, he noted that they enjoined him to be conciliatory and moderate, but to require the 'religious observation of the treaties'. C.P. Japon, XI, 25 May 1864, Roches to Drouyn de Lhuys. In the same dispatch he also revealed, significantly, that, before joining in a common action with his diplomatic colleagues, he had re-read the instructions sent to his predecessor.
41. It is not possible to prove that Drouyn de Lhuys was bluffing when he told Ikeda that France would offer the shogunate aid if the latter attempted to re-establish its domination over the elements which were causing it and the treaty powers difficulties, or when he inserted in the Convention the clause providing for French military assistance in opening the Shimonoseki Straits; but the fact that no discussions appear to have taken place within the Quai d'Orsay or with the Navy Ministry would indicate (even without the evidence of his later condemnation of Roches' decision to participate in the actual Shimonoseki Expedition) that the foreign minister was adopting a strong stance in order to impress Ikeda – and through him the Bakufu – with the seriousness of Western concern. That Drouyn de Lhuys was fully capable of dissembling to the Japanese can be seen from his reply to the envoys' request to know whether France would have made the same demands (for making Yokohama, Nagasaki and Hakodate free ports, for example) if the Western mission had not been sent. According to the Quai d'Orsay record, 'the Minister responded affirmatively and gave them to understand that probably, indeed, France, supported by its allies, would first have sent forces to require the opening of all the ports mentioned in the 1858 Treaty, and that it is only in consideration of the friendly démarche which Japan has made by sending an Embassy to Paris that the French Government agrees to show itself less exacting'. C.P. Japon, XI, Procès-verbal of the six meetings held between 7 May and 20 June 1864.
42. See Chapter II.
43. Roches originally came from Grenoble. He was well acquainted with E.Duseigneur, a leading silk merchant in Lyons. See C.C.Yédo, III, 1 September 1864, Roches to Drouyn de Lhuys.

44. See e.g. C.C.Yédo, I, 3 October 1861, Bellecourt to Thouvenel.
45. C.P. Japon, VII, 10 October 1862, Bellecourt to Thouvenel.
46. See F.O.46, LV, 23 June 1865, Winchester to Russell.
47. It should be noted, though, that Bellecourt remained too suspicious of Japanese ultimate intentions to help the Bakufu to acquire the most up-to-date weapons. See C.P. Japon, VII, 10 October 1862, in which Bellecourt reported to Thouvenel an enquiry about artillery innovation and added: 'Evidently the Japanese seek arms and when they see themselves sufficiently provided, they will doubtless seek enemies'. By contrast, one of Roches earliest pro-Bakufu actions was to arrange for the purchase of sixteen rifled cannons in 1865.
48. The impression given by Kurimoto in his memoirs is that certain Bakufu leaders were eager to take advantage of his unusual friendship. Kurimoto Sebei (ed.) *Kurimoto Joun Iko* (Tokyo 1943), pp. 108–109.
49. He was willing, by 1865, to claim a likeness between the Japanese character and that of his own country and in 1866 he went so far as to assert that 'the character of the Japanese distinguishes them essentially from other Oriental peoples, so it is necessary to be towards them good with dignity, severe with justice; one can often appeal to their sense of honour and to their pride. Accustomed as they are to encountering among themselves, even among the lowest classes, the most exquisite politeness, rudeness alienates them; just as they are exasperated by bad treatment, so they are sensible of any consideration shown to them'. C.P. Japon, XIII, 10 January 1865; 15 February 1866. Roches to Drouyn de Lhuys.
50. That Roches felt the need to play down the extent of his influence is indicated in several of his own dispatches and was specifically stated by Mermet de Cachon in a memorandum written for the Quai d'Orsay on 18 February 1867: 'M. Roches in order not to awaken jealousy has had to efface himself and even to lessen his role'. M.D.I.
51. F.O.46, LXXXII, 14 November 1867. Private. With this report Parkes enclosed copies of four letters written to Roches, including two from Coullet and one from Flury Hérard which are extraordinarily revealing. Exactly why Roches showed them to him is not certain, though it may have been intended to prove to him that Comte de Montblanc's military mission to Satsuma did not have official backing. In the light of Coullet's first letter, of 9 August 1867, Parkes' statement that his company had proved an utter failure seems slightly exaggerated. Though Coullet admitted that the public subscription for it had failed, he added that 'there is nothing lost. We are going to restart this business as we did in the beginning . . . the capital, more restricted to begin with, will be found by the immediate adherents of the group of founders, and I hope that we will have a delay but not a heavier setback'. As far as large-scale operations were concerned, however, Parkes' remark seems true enough, for Coullet also wrote: 'You already know that at this moment there can be no question of a Japanese loan'.
52. It is possible that he advised the Oriental Bank not to cooperate with the shogun's government. Such a lack of response by the bank on the spot would certainly have had a discouraging effect on French investors. Whether the loan ever really had much chance is doubtful. With regard to Egyptian securities, a French banker wrote in 1861 that French capitalists 'do not like to risk their funds in little known enterprises', and 'consider, rightly or wrongly, that the countries of the Orient offer little in the way of guarantees'. (D.Landes, *Bankers and Pashas,* London. 1958. p. 105.) In 1867, the collapse of the Crédit Mobilier had made investors even more cautious. In such circumstances the Bakufu loan could have been a serious proposition only if the shogun had been known to possess the unqualified support of both the French and British governments. The Shibatas argue, in the light of their examination of the French financial world in the 1860s, that the loan would have had a much better chance of success than the trading company.

53. If he did so, he was mistaken since according to Roches, the Bakufu subsequently sent Kurimoto to Paris 'to concede to an international company the exploitation of the forests and mines of the great island of Yézo [Hokkaido]'. C.P. Japon, XV, 12 July 1867, Roches to Moustier.

54. This intention became known in France. Oliphant was put off by Lord Stanley and, contrary to what Ishii states in *Zotei Meiji Ishin no Kokusaiteki Kankyo*, pp. 680–81, the only question concerning Japan that was asked by him in Parliament was an innocuous one, concerning the stationing of European troops at Yokohama. (See *Hansard's Parliamentary Debates*, third series, CLXXXVI, 4 April 1867. p. 1107). Nine days later, however, the 14 February edition of the *Japan Times*, which contained a stronger attack on Roches, arrived, and this convinced the Foreign Office that Oliphant's original question could not be ignored. See M.D., III, 18 April 1867, Cowley to Moustier.

55. *Ibid.* Cowley's note spoke of the *Japan Times* imputing to Roches 'a course of proceeding of which it is certain the Imperial Government would not approve'.

56. C.P. Japon, XV, 18 May 1867, Moustier to Roches.

57. See M.D.Japon, I, May 1867. unsigned memorandum; M.D. Japon, I, 9 January 1869 unsigned memorandum. Also Otsuka *op. cit.*, p. 310.

58. Montblanc, after his failure to be accepted as adviser by the Ikeda mission, developed contacts with Satsuma samurai in Europe from 1865, and wrote pamphlets, raised loans and bought arms on Satsuma's account. His outmanoeuvring of Tanabe, which may have been partly due to a failure to appreciate that the word 'gouvernement' (which Montblanc claimed for Satsuma) carried an implication of sovereignty and partly to his being plied with alcohol, is described by Takahashi Kunitaro, 'Baku, Satsu Parii de Hibana-su', *Rekishi Yomihon*, XV, 6, (June 1970), pp. 114–126. See also Willy Vande Walle, 'Le Comte des Cantons Charles de Montblanc – Agent for the Lord of Satsuma', in I. Neary (ed.) *Leaders and Leadership in Japan,* (Richmond, 1996), pp. 44–45. Flury Hérard surprisingly (since he had been appointed Japanese consul-general in France, Japan's first permanent diplomatic representative abroad) did not attend the unfortunate meeting between Tanabe, Montblanc and de Lesseps, and, no less surprisingly, later claimed credit for keeping a low profile and not responding to the provocative newspaper articles. (See his letter of 10 August 1867 to Roches in F.O.46, LXXXII, 14 November 1867, Parkes to Hammond). Although Flury Hérard's inactivity appears reprehensible, the damage done was not quite so bad as had been implied, for Tokugawa Akitake was given an honoured place at several official ceremonies and his reception at the Tuileries on 28 April by Napoleon III (when the emperor 'expressed to the young prince his satisfaction at seeing the brother of a sovereign with whom his Government held the most friendly relations') was prominently reported in *Le Moniteur Universel* the next day. Moreover, the French foreign minister did not (unlike the British Foreign Secretary in 1866) respond favourably to a request in February to meet with a Satsuma representative, and according to Alexander von Siebold, who assisted the Bakufu mission as translator throughout its stay, the separate Satsuma representation at the exposition was not permanent, as 'the whole Japanese collection was afterwards united under the Japanese national flag'. F.O.46, LXXXVI, 11 December 1867. Mermet de Cachon, Roches' translator, who had returned to France on the heels of Tokugawa Mimbu's mission, was disappointed in his hope of becoming the young prince's tutor and adviser. He suddenly turned against the Bakufu and attacked its authority both in the press and in a mémoire addressed to the Quai d'Orsay. (See M.D.Japon, I, 9 May 1867). The latter may have been extremely significant for it referred to an imminent crisis in Japan and was written only nine days before Moustier rapped Roches' knuckles. Mermet de Cachon's rejection by Mukoyama and the other leaders of the mission was

apparently due to his religious status. See Otsuka. *op. cit.* p. 304, and Siebold's report of 18 April 1867 to Lord Stanley, in F.O.46, LXXXV.

59. In reporting this result (which it had not anticipated in late June and mid-July) *The Economist* of 3 August 1867 explained it entirely in terms of the current financial climate.
60. F.O.27, MDCLXI, Cowley to Stanley.
61. C.P. Japon. XV, 18 May 1867, Moustier to Roches.
62. See, for example, Ishii, *Zotei Meiji Ishin no Kokusai-teki Kankyo*, pp. 702–704, and Otsuka, *op. cit.,* pp. 290–291.
63. M.D. Japon, I, 18 May 1867. It included the following: 'The Minister will doubtless judge it useful to have the department write to our agent by the next mail, which leaves on the 10th, communicating to him these complaints, and inviting him to furnish explanations which can be sent, in due course to the British government'.
64. See eg. F.O.46, LIII, 28 February 1865, Winchester to Hammond and Russell (private); *Ibid.* 9 March 1865; *Ibid.*, LV, 23 June, 1865, Winchester to Russell; Also F.O.391, XIV, 16 March 1867; *Ibid.*, 19 September 1868, Parkes to Hammond. Lest it be thought that statements like this were designed to conceal the Quai d'Orsay's Machiavellian plans, it should be added that Roches' successor, who would presumably have been informed on such a point, stated, in speaking of his predecessor: 'He has carried out here only his "personal policy"'. C.P. Japon, XVI, 22 August 1869, Outrey to Moustier.
65. C.P. Japon, XIV, 15 May 1866, Drouyn de Lhuys to Roches.
66. C.P. Japon, XIII, 17 June 1865. Drouyn de Lhuys to Roches. See also *Ibid.*, 19 December 1865, when Drouyn de Lhuys commented on Roches' renewed request: 'I do not believe it to be good to hand back what is due to us. To accustom these governments to not consider their commitments to us as serious seems to me to be a bad practice'.
67. Roches' four years are covered by only five volumes of *Correspondance Politique* and two of *Correspondance Commerciale,* all of average length or under, compared with ten and two respectively for the slightly shorter period of Bellecourt.
68. For a brief assessment of Roches' role in the Maghrib, see J-P. Lehmann, 'Léon Roches – Diplomat Extraordinary in the Bakumatsu Era', *Modern Asian Studies,* XIV, 2, (1980), pp. 275–83. Roches left his own two-volume account of his earlier experiences, *Trente-deux and a travers l"Islam,* (Paris, 1884–5). He continued for many years to correspond with the Algerian leader, Abd al-Qadir, and he is reputed to have written other letters in Arabic for the purpose of confidentiality.
69. C.P. Japon, XIV, 17 November 1866, Roches to Moustier. The speech is quoted in full in Tanaka Sadao, *Les Débuts de l'Étude du Français au Japon,* (Tokyo, 1983), pp. 113–118.
70. M.D.Japon, I. The memorandum is undated but was clearly written early in 1866.
71. See F.O.391, XIV, 6 May 1867. Parkes to Hammond.
72. On this subject and Roches' contribution to French trade generally, see Chapter VIII.
73. This is not to suggest that the French government would ever have gone so far as to intervene during the civil war in favour of the Tokugawa and it is doubtful whether any help short of direct military and naval aid (which in any case would probably have been refused) could have preserved the Bakufu, though strong moral support by the French government might conceivably have boosted Bakufu morale.
74. It might even be argued that when Moustier repudiated Roches' policy, he imagined that he was merely taking precautions against the possibility of any such policy developing. After complimenting Roches for his zeal in securing commercial advantages for France, Moustier added that 'It is today a matter of not compromising them, which would not fail to happen if, by too marked an involvement in the internal affairs of the country and by engaging in its struggles, we

came one day to find ourselves faced by a hostile party in power, disposed to hold us to account for the support we had given to its adversaries'. That Moustier was not deciding policy personally is indicated by the fact that the recommendation to warn Roches was drawn up by an official at the Quai d'Orsay.

75. C.P. Japon, XV, 13 July 1867, Roches to Moustier.

76. There is a detailed treatment of the Urakami problem in 1867 by Fujii Sadabumi, 'Urakami Kyoto Mondai o meguru Nichi-Futsu Kankei', in Kaikoku Hyakunen Kinen Meiji Bunka Shi Jogyokai (ed.), *Kaikoku Hyakumen Kinen Meiji Bunka Shi Ronshu* (Tokyo, 1953), pp. 73–123.

77. See C.P. Japon, XV, 8 August 1867, Roches to Moustier.

78. The missionary writer, Léon Pagès, reflected this when, reviewing the course of the persecution in *Les Missions Catholiques,* V, 3 January 1873, he wrote of ' the connivance of M. Léon Roches, the French minister. It was natural that he should do thus, because M. Léon Roches, born Catholic, abjured the faith of his baptism, and became a Moslem in Algiers'.

79. See C.P. Japon, XV, 15 October 1867, Roches to Moustier.

80. C.P. Japon, XV, 28 November 1867, Roches to Moustier. Yoshinobu's gamble of returning his shogunal powers to the Emperor in the hope of salvaging a substantial part of Tokugawa authority was described by Roches as 'a démarche which is not without grandeur and which I hope will be without danger for the future of his authority'. The dispatch, however, was marked by various sceptical marginal comments, as well as an exclamation mark at the point where Roches had written that 'the prestige of the Taikoun has increased'.

81. C.P. Japon, XVI, 10 January 1868. In this dispatch Roches informed Moustier that he had promised Yoshinobu that 'while any meddling in the purely internal affairs of Japan would be avoided, he would not find France's moral support lacking'.

82. The suggestion is made by Yanaga, *Japan Since Perry,* New York, 1949. p. 46.

83. The nature of Roches' and Chanoine's encouragement of Yoshinobu in early 1868 is discussed in detail by Shinohara, *op. cit.,* pp. 199–213, and by Takahashi, *op. cit.,* pp. 166–9. Their main source is the memoirs of Katsu Awa, who had just been appointed military director of the Tokugawa forces and who resisted very strong pressure from Chanoine, but they also cite a 1907 recollection by a mission member, Descharmes, in which the latter stated that the whole mission urged a strong stand with the help of Aizu domain. It should be noted, however, that a contemporary letter from Descharmes dated 8 February 1868, referring to an Edo Castle conference involving the French mission as well as Bakufu leaders two days earlier (immediately after Yoshinobu's return from Osaka) gives an impression of greater French detachment. See the anonymous article, 'Le lieutenant Descharmes: extraits de lettres inédites', in R. Sieffert (ed.), *Le Japon et la France: Images d'une Découverte,* (Paris, 1974), p. 71.

84. See M.D.Japon, I, 1 April 1868, Ohier to Marine; copy sent from the Navy Ministry to the Quai d'Orsay. Ohier noted in his letter that 'Our situation in Japan has become difficult following a revolution long foreseen by everyone and in the consequences of which our minister did not wish to believe: it has destroyed in a day the preponderant, not to say absolute, influence of M. Roches'.

85. See C.P. Japon, XVI, 17 February 1868, Roches to Moustier. Also F.O.46, XCI, No.35, 15 February 1868, Parkes to Stanley.

86. See F.O.391, XIV, 11 March 1868, Parkes to Hammond. Also C.P. Japon, XVI, 11 March 1868. Roches to Moustier.

87. The crossing of a column of Bizen samurai by a French soldier at Hyogo prompted a display of aggressiveness on their part against foreigners. There was no loss of life, however. See F.O.46, XCI, No.22, 13 February 1868, Parkes to Derby, for a full description of the incident.

88. See C.P. Japon, XVI, 11 March 1868; *Ibid*, 19 March 1868. Roches to Moustier.
89. C.P. Japon, XVI, 2 March 1868, Roches to Moustier.
90. Roches explained to Moustier that he did not wish to leave to Parkes 'the honour of first seeing the divine Sovereign of Japan alone'. C.P. Japon, XVI, 19 March 1868.

CHAPTER 4

1. Satsuma and Choshu, together with Tosa and Hizen, dominated the lower ranks of the new government and it was widely suspected that they would attempt to create a new Bakufu. A detailed account of constitutional arrangements during the first years of the Meiji era can be found in R. A. Wilson, *The Genesis of the Meiji Government, 1868-1871* (Berkeley, 1957). For a broader view, see W. G.. Beasley, *The Meiji Restoration*.

2. The main threat to these – the Japanese attempt to revise the 'unequal' treaties – affected all the Western powers. The process of treaty revision, which is generally considered the chief aim of Japanese foreign policy, lasted well over 20 years, acquiring almost a separate diplomatic existence of its own. France's role in this is treated in Chapter VI.

3. Frenchmen in Japan were very conscious of this. With pardonable exaggeration *L'Echo du Japon* claimed in 1883 that whereas Britain ordered its representatives 'at all costs to defend English interests and make them supreme', instructions to French diplomats 'invariably begin and end with this supreme recommendation: Above all, don't embarrass us!' *L'Echo du Japon*, weekly edition, 2 June 1883. A very similar lament had been voiced four years earlier by Captain Dubousquet to Colonel Chanoine: 'Alas! The Quai d'Orsay is less than ever aware of our interests in these countries. All the instructions repeat and resemble themselves: "March in step with the English".' 'The Cabinet in London seems to prefer this'. Chanoine, *op. cit.,* p. 144.

4. Commenting on the current pro-German tendencies in Japan, which it attributed to the efforts of German diplomats, *L'Echo du Japon* of 26 October 1883 observed that 'unfortunately one cannot say as much of our ministers; regarding themselves as just passing through here, they have generally taken very little trouble'.

5. Even Outrey asked to be moved after a little more than a year; see the letter of August 3, 1869, from a French merchant who claimed that: 'M. Outrey actively wants to return and has already asked the government to send him a successor'. *Moniteur des Soies*, 2 October 1869. The Quai refused to give him another post, so he stayed in Japan. See C.P.Japon, XIX, 9 September 1869. Auvergne-Lauraguais to Outrey.

6. It might be objected that France could never have had much of an impact owing to the differences of national character, political background and social institutions between the two countries. No doubt France was less close to Japan than, say, Germany was in many ways, but there were several aspects of French civilisation, in particular its highly centralised administrative structure which possessed considerable attraction for Japan. In addition, French Far Eastern policy did not obviously conflict with Japanese interests. It seems reasonable, therefore, to suggest that French influence on Japan might have been greater especially in view of France's contribution to the economic development of southern and eastern Europe and the Middle East in the preceding half century.

7. Some details of Outrey's career in Egypt can be found in Landes, *Bankers and Pashas, passim.*

8. C.P.Japon, XVI, 12 August 1868, Outrey to Moustier.

9. C.P.Japon, XVI, 30 September 1868. Outrey to Moustier.

10. The approach by the Meiji government through the Governor of Yokohama was reported in C.P.Japon, XVII, 18 December 1868, Outrey to La Valette. It was

indicated that the rebels would be given land in Hokkaido if they surrendered. Outrey rejected any idea of treating with disobedient officers, so it is hardly surprising that in February he failed to support the appeal of the Hokkaido rebels for a Franco-British mediation. See M.D.Japon, III, undated letter from Brunet to Chanoine. Also Outrey's report in C.P.Japon, XVIII, 10 February 1869. A possible opening for mediation for which Outrey showed even less enthusiasm had earlier been prepared by Commandant du Petit Thouars in July 1868. See M.D.Japon, I, 25 July 1868, Captain Challié to Navy Ministry, copy sent by Navy Ministry to Quai d'Orsay.

11. Two and a half million francs' worth of these goods had not reached the Bakufu and were held by Customs. C.P.Japon, XVII, 7 October 1868, Outrey to Moustier.

12. *Ibid.* The reason for the Meiji government's haste was that the Bakufu had pledged the Yokosuka dockyards as security for payment of its order. There is no indication, however, that France was eager to take advantage of Japanese financial straits or even thought of possession of Yokosuka as a serious possibility. Except for this mention in Outrey's October 7 dispatch, after the matter was already solved, the mortgage of Yokosuka does not figure in the correspondence between Paris and Tokyo. For Parkes' views, see F.O.391, XIV, 19 September 1868, Parkes to Hammond.

13. C.P.Japon, XVIII, 14 January 1869, Outrey to Moustier.

14. See C.P.Japon, XVII, 10 October 1868, Outrey to Moustier.

15. See C.P.Japon, XVIII, 10 February 1869, Outrey to La Valette. France's acceptance that the civil war was over amounted to full recognition of the Meiji government.

16. C.P.Japon, XVIII, 10 May 10 1869, Outrey to La Valette.

17. See a document entitled Historique de la Conduite de M. Brunet, drawn up for the Quai d'Orsay by the Ministry of War on 11 October 1869. M.D.Japon, III. Brunet had come to Japan as a 28 year-old lieutenant. In Chanoine's absence he had acted as second-in-command of the mission.

18. *Ibid.* Brunet had offered his resignation to Outrey soon after the latter's arrival, intending to join the Tokugawa forces who were still opposing the Meiji government. See Takahashi Kunitaro, 'Jules Brunet, Français qui combattit à Goryokaku', *Acta Asiatica*, XVII, (1969), p. 65.

19. M.D.Japon, III, 11 October 1869. Three other officers attempted to resign and follow Brunet, but were dissuaded by Chanoine. Three more NCOs, however, did succeed in joining him and eventually Brunet had nine Frenchmen assisting him. They were not the only foreigners involved in the civil war. According to a report by Outrey to Moustier (C.P.Japon, XVII, 13 November 1868) there were between sixty and eighty others, mostly English and American adventurers, at the time of the siege of Wakamatsu.

20. C.P.Japon, XVII, 16 December 1868, Outrey to Moustier. Japanese sources attribute a more prominent role to the Tokugawa commander, Enomoto Takeaki. See Takahashi Kunitaro, *op. cit.*, pp. 71–2.

21. See F.O.391, XIV, 13 November 13 1868, Parkes to Hammond.

22. See M.D.Japon, III, 9 July 1869, War Ministry to Quai d'Orsay. See C.P.Japon, XVIII, 8 May 1869, Outrey to La Valette.

24. See C.P.Japon, XIX, 1 August 1869. *Ibid.* 4 September 1869, Outrey to La Valette. Outrey resisted these strongly. 'It would be accepting an impossible position to capitulate and the insolence of the Japanese would have no limits', he wrote in his 4 September dispatch.

25. M.D.Japon, I, April, 1869, Chanoine to Marshal Niel.

26. See M.D.Japon, III, Brunet to Chanoine, first letter (The letters are undated, but appear to have been written in March).

27. *Ibid.* Brunet added in his second letter that the commander (Petit Thouars) of the French warship, the *Dupleix,* had gone to survey 'the forts and fortlets which under

my direction are being constructed on all sides; I leave you to appreciate his stupefaction in recognising positively that I have made it impossible to land on the six main points of my islands where this is a danger'. He claimed also to have established a foundry, an arsenal and a workshop, and he confidently predicted that 'either we will not be attacked and then we will continue to perfect our position while awaiting in our island the political changes which will compel our recall to Yedo; or we will be attacked, and in that case the Mikado's Government will make the British happy by ruining itself, to their advantage, a little more'.

28. *Ibid.,* (first letter)
29. *Ibid.,* Brunet's assumption that the Meiji government would not survive was clearly expressed in his first letter to Chanoine: 'The leading figures among my Japanese chiefs believe, like me, in an imminent upheaval on the main island; by its excessively ambitious pretensions, Satsuma is isolating itself more and more from the other domains'.
30. M.D.Japon, III, 22 June 1869.
31. M.D.Japon, III, April, 1869. Though anonymous, this memorandum evidently emanated from within the Quai d'Orsay.
32. *Ibid.*
33. Brunet was punished by being suspended from active service. M.D.Japon, III, 25 October 1869, War Ministry to Quai d'Orsay. This suspension was lifted to allow him to fight in the Franco-Prussian War. The Japanese government withdrew its complaint against him in 1873, and he eventually reached the rank of general. See Chanoine, *Documents pour servir à l'histoire des Relations entre la France et le Japon.* (Paris, 1907) p .83.
34. See Outrey's letter to Saint-Vallier. C.P.Japon, XVI, 22 August 1868.
35. See *Les Missions Catholiques,* I, 17 July 1868.
36. See C.P.Japon, XVII, 10 September 1868, Outrey to Moustier. The Meiji government's policy on Christianity, and the thinking about religion which underlay this, is discussed by John Breen in 'Beyond the Prohibition: Christianity in Restoration Japan', in John Breen and Mark Williams (eds.), *Japan and Christianity* (London, 1996).
37. C.P.Japon, 7 July 1868, Outrey to Moustier.
38. M.D.Japon, I, 30 July 1868, Challié to Navy Ministry.
39. The Meiji government's policy towards Christians was probably affected also by shifts of influence within the government itself, and the period of severest repression did coincide with a temporary weakening of the reforming centralisers' position during 1870.
40. See C.P.Japon, XVI, 27 May 1868, Roches to Moustier. Also M.D.Japon, I, 30 July, 1868, Challié to Marine.
41. C.P.Japon, XVII, 14 September 1868, Moustier to Outrey.
42. C.P.Japon, XVII, 10 September 1868, Outrey to Moustier.
43. C.P.Japon, XVII, 10 September 1868, Outrey to Moustier.
44. See C.P.Japon, XVII, 12 November 1868, Outrey to Moustier.
45. C.P.Japon, XVIII, 12 January 1869. Outrey to Moustier.
46. C.P.Japon, XVIII, 12 January 1869, Outrey to Moustier.
47. C.P.Japon, XVIII, 11 May 1869, Outrey to La Valette. Outrey's reluctance to be more forceful was criticised by Léon Pagès in *Les Missions Catholiques,* 14 February 1873. However, the contemporary comments by missionaries in Japan were more favourable to him, or at least more understanding of his delicate position. See *Les Missions Catholiques,* 16 October 1868 and 29 April, 1870.
48. C.P.Japon, XIX, 22 January 1870, Outrey to Auvergne Lauraguais.
49. *Ibid.*
50. C.P.Japon, XIX, 21 February 1870, Outrey to Auvergne Lauraguais.

51. The letter is dated 20 February 1870 and is in C.P.Japon, XIX. The writer asserted that 'we were wrong not to show more energy, and our Governments would be committing a mistake, which could have the gravest consequences, if they did not insist on the repatriation of all the Christians deported from Urakami and on a certain freedom being accorded to Christian worship in the interior of the country'. He concluded by stating that Outrey favoured a combined démarche too.
52. C.P.Japon, XX, 7 May 1870.
53. In April he accepted the Japanese rejection of a moderately-toned collective note without demur. C.P.Japon, XX, 12 April 1870, Outrey to Daru.
54. C.P.Japon, XX, 11 May 1870, Outrey to Daru. For a discussion of Japanese motives, see Chapter IX.
55. C.P.Japon, XX, 4 June 1870, Outrey to Daru.
56. *Ibid.*
57. C.P.Japon, XX, 4 July 1870. Outrey to Daru.
58. See C.P.Japon, XXI, 18 January 1872 and 9 February 1872, Turenne to Rémusat.
59. C.P.Japon, XXI, 1 April 1872, Turenne to Rémusat.
60. C.P.Japon, XXI, 28 August 1872, Turenne to Rémusat.
61. C.P.Japon, XXI, 20 December 1872.
62. See *Les Missions Catholiques.* 20 December, 1872.
63. C.P.Japon, XXI, 20 December 1872.
64. Hanabusa Nagamichi, *Meiji Gaikoshi*, (Tokyo, 1960), p. 9.
65. See M.D.Japon, II, *Compte-rendu* of the meeting of January 24, 1873.
66. *Ibid.*
67. C.P.Japon, XXI, 23 December 1872, Turenne to Rémusat.
68. C.P.Japon, XXII, 20 January 1873, Turenne to Rémusat.
69. C.P.Japon, XXII, 15 February 1873, Turenne to Rémusat.
70. C.P.Japon, XXII, 24 February 1873, Turenne to Rémusat; C.P.Japon, XXIII, 22 September 1873., Berthemy to Broglie.
71. The signatories wanted 'guarantees analogous to those which were given by the Chinese government in the treaty of Tientsin'. M.D.Japon, II, 25 March 1873.
72. C.P.Japon, XXIII, 7 August 1873., Broglie to Berthemy. The government which Broglie had done much to create in May contained an influential legitimist element, and it had already taken several steps which, in Seignobos' words, 'announced that the legitimists counted on divine help to overcome "the Revolution"'. See Seignobos, *Le Déclin de l'Empire et l'Etablissement de la 3e République,* vol.7 of E. Lavisse, (ed.) *Histoire de France Contemporaine,* (Paris. 1921), pp. 364-5.
73. C.P.Japon, XXIII, 22 September 1873, Berthemy to Broglie. A pencilled comment says: 'This dispatch is a little cold for the missionaries'.
74. C.P.Japon, XXIII, 15 October 1873, Berthemy to Broglie. Apart from the tendency of diplomats of other countries to regard Catholic missionary activities in Japan and China as an embarrassment or even an eventual danger, Berthemy attributed their lack of sympathy to their belief that Western pressure on behalf of the missionaries would seriously weaken the Meiji government.
75. Decazes was, in fact, more opposed than most Orleanists to the legitimist cause and his entry into the *Conseil des Ministres* in November 1873 marked a break with the extreme right. See Seignobos, *op.cit.,* pp. 377–8.
76. C.P.Japon, XXIII, 1 December 1873, Decazes to Berthemy. Not only did Decazes state that he could not associate himself completely with his predecessors' views, he also echoed Berthemy's sentiments in declaring that 'we must be the first to take care that the freedom which we claim for the exercise of the Christian religion does not become the cause of, or pretext for, an explosion of religious passions which would at the same time compromise the very interests for which we are solicitous'.
77. For the 1880s episode, see Chapter VII.

78. An account of the question from the Japanese side (which focuses on its early stages)can be found in Hora Tomio, 'Bakumatsu Ishin ni okeru Ei-Futsu Guntai no Yokohmama-chuton', in Meiji Shiryo Kenkyu Renrakukai (ed), *Meiji Seiken no Kakuritsu Katei*, (Tokyo, 1956).
79. In May 1863, the Bakufu sent Colonel Neale a letter which appeared to accept the occupation. *Ibid.* pp. 189–190. Eventually it even provided barrack areas.
80. C.P.Japon, XIX, 2 October 1869, Outrey to Auvergne-Lauraguais. The two Powers' positions were not completely equal in practice. At the end of the Bakumatsu period there were 800 British troops to 300 French.
81. See C.P.Japon, XX, 24 December 1870, Outrey to Favre.
82. C.P.Japon, XXI, 8 April 1871, Navy Ministry to Quai d'Orsay.
83. C.P.Japon, XXI. 1 July 1871, Outrey to Favre.
84. C.P.Japon, XXI, 21 September 1871.
85. C.P.Japon, XXI, 6 December 1872., Turenne to Rémusat.
86. See C.P.Japon, XXI, 23 December 1872, Turenne to Rémusat.
87. C.P.Japon, XXII, 30 January 1873.
88. M.D.Japon, II., *Compte-rendu* of conference between Rémusat and Iwakura, 24 January 1873.
89. See C.P.Japon, XXIII, 26 June 1873., Broglie to Berthemy.
90. C.P.Japon, XXIII, 1 December 1873, Berthemy to Decazes.
91. C.P.Japon, XXIV, 7 February 1874, Berthemy to Decazes.
92. C.P.Japon, XXV, 21 January 1875, Lord Lyons to Decazes.
93. Before the troops left, Iwakura significantly secured Berthemy's permission to publish their correspondence to show that 'the foreign Powers no longer cast doubt on the stability of the actual Government'. C.P.Japon, XXV, 15 February 1875, Berthemy to Decazes.
94. For all Townsend Harris's moral encouragement it is doubtful whether America would have been willing or able to supply the Bakufu with the means of removing the obstacles to centralised power, while the reaction of the British and French ministers to requests for information about Western military technology had been uniformly unfavourable.
95. French contributions to Japanese modernisation are discussed more fully in Chapter IX.
96. C.P.Japon, XXVI, 21 November 1878, Geofroy to Waddington.
97. See C.P.Japon, XXXIV, 8 May 1889, Sienkiewicz to Spuller.
98. C.P.Japon, XXI, 4 March 1872, Turenne to Rémusat.
99. C.P.Japon, XXI, 25 September, 1872; 21 November 1872; XXII, 22 March1873. Turenne to Rémusat.
100. C.P.Japon, XXII, 20 January 1873, Turenne to Rémusat; XXII, 11 April 1873, Rémusat to Turenne.
101. See also C.P.Japon, XX, 1 August 1870, Outrey to Gramont.
102. Although the Quai d'Orsay never refused a Meiji government request and from 1875 showed a great deal of concern for the continuation of the military mission and French supervision at Yokosuka, it always left the initiative to Tokyo, presumably thinking that new opportunities for French advisers could only be detected and evaluated by their representative on the spot.
103. The first, and most notable, expression of this belief occurred during the Franco-Chinese dispute of 1883–5. See Chapter V.
104. C.P.Japon, XXII, 9 July 1873, Berthemy to Broglie.
105. The second of these factors is stressed by D. E. Westney, *Imitation and Innovation: The Transfer of Western Organisational Patterns to Meiji Japan* (Cambridge, Mass, and London, 1997), p. 22.
106. C.P.Japon, XVI, 9 July 1868, Outrey to Moustier.

107. C.P.Japon, XVI, 22 August 1868, Outrey to Saint-Vallier. In September he claimed that, with the exception of Parkes, 'all other Representatives have a very mediocre opinion of the new government and do not believe in its stability'.*Ibid.,* 12 September 1868.

108. C.P.Japon, XVII, 28 September 1868, Outrey to Moustier. Two weeks later he dismissed the *Seitaisho,* a quasi – constitutional document the publication of which marked a shift in the balance of power within the Meiji government as 'apparently intended much more to impose on public opinion in Europe than to lay the foundations of a serious Government'. *Ibid.,* 14 October 1868, Outrey to La Valette.

109. C.P.Japon, XVIII, 12 April 1869, Outrey to La Valette.

110. C.P.Japon, XVIII, 11 May 1869., Outrey to La Valette. In October he was specific in identifying one of the major obstacles to change: 'Satsuma, which had given the example of abnegation, does not seem at all disposed to be taken at its word. Quite the contrary, its efforts are in the direction of organising its own military forces, and contracts with the Comte de Montblanc for five thousand chassepot rifles and two field batteries are the undeniable proof of this'. *Ibid.,* XIX, 2 October 1869.

111. See C.P.Japon, XIX, 1 August 1869, Outrey to La Valette.

112. C.C.Yédo, VI, 15 March 1870, Outrey to Daru. See also C.P.Japon, XI, 20 January 1870. Outrey to Auvergne-Lauraguais. The Quai d'Orsay did not feel the same way. A pencilled comment on Outrey's March dispatch reads: 'It is regrettable that French industry has found itself completely uninvolved in this enterprise'. The result was a cryptic instruction to renew his efforts to secure such a contract if the opportunity arose again. C.C.Yédo, VI, 25 August 1870, Auvergne-Lauraguais to Outrey.

113. C.P.Japon, XX, 4 June 1870, Outrey to Daru. The recognition that Japan's transformation might prove permanent came after Iwakura had entertained Outrey at a formal dinner. Iwakura's language had convinced him, he wrote, that this influential leader 'takes account of the fidelity of our policy, and that he has come to understand that having no reservations we could be a great support in the reformist course of which he is one of the principal promoters'. *Ibid.*

114. When, in August 1871, the Meiji government took its most important step towards eradicating feudalism and thus weakening potential opposition – by replacing domains with centrally controlled prefectures – the full significance of this action was not perceived by Outrey.

115. C.P.Japon, XXI, 24 March 1872, Turenne to Rémusat. In another dispatch he made some interesting observations on the increase of French influence in Japan and the attitudes of the French and Japanese governments to it, ending: 'Now that [the Japanese government] is aware that our foreign policy is a policy of expectation, it gives freer rein to its feelings of sympathy towards us. If this observation is correct, our role will become that of adviser to the Japanese government. We could not be unhappy with this'. C.P.Japon, XXI, 25 September 1872., Turenne to Rémusat.

116. Turenne may have been influenced by Dubousquet, who had recently moved from the French legation to Japanese government service, but his basic approach seems to have derived from his experience as an aide to Roches, even though he never referred to his former chief in his dispatches.

117. Towards the end of his stay, Turenne reported a conversation with Okuma Shigenobu, 'one of the most influential *Sangi*' (Councillors), in which the latter spoke of 'the desire of the Japanese government to procure in France complete materials for a new railway line'. This led the chargé d'affaires to conclude that 'our great metallurgical enterprises, everything gives me room to think, by this means are going to find find new openings in Japan, of a real importance for the sale of their products'. C.P.Japon, XXII, 17 March 1873, Turenne to Rémusat. Turenne

made it clear that he believed that Okuma's feeler would have been impossible had not Franco-Japanese relations reached such a high point. His success in Japan, however, does not seem to have been particularly appreciated by later foreign ministers. After subsequent appointments to Athens and the Holy See, he was sent in 1877 to Rio de Janeiro, having been promoted to Secretary, First Class, at the by no means early age of 35. In December 1878, his career temporarily came to a halt when he was retired, a victim, presumably, of the Republican triumph of 1877. He re-entered the service as Consul, First Class, in 1884, but was still on the same rank ten years later, when his post was Budapest. Only in 1899 did he achieve the rank of Minister. See the *Annuaire Diplomatique et Consulaire*.

118. C.P.Japon, XXII, 9 July 1873, Berthemy to Broglie. This verdict seemed harsh even to Broglie, who was much less liberal than Rémusat had been. Nevertheless, although he pointed out that 'it is impossible to assess the progress made in these last years', he did nothing to ensure continuity of policy by limiting Berthemy's freedom of action. C.P.Japon, XXIII, 15 October1873, Broglie to Berthemy.

119. C.P.Japon, XXII, 12 July 1873., Berthemy to Broglie.

120. Berthemy was even willing to see the end of the military mission. He urged Decazes to recall it to France, together with the French personnel in Yokosuka, in the event of war breaking out between Japan and China over the Taiwan expedition. See C.P.Japon, XXIV, 8 September 1874. His recommendation aroused the wrath of Colonel Munier, the mission's leader, who, writing to ask his predecessor, Colonel Chanoine, to plead the mission's cause in Paris, referred to Berthemy in contemptuous terms: 'This blind and deaf diplomat, who has pretensions to play a role, does not see that the British and Germans are there, on the alert, awaiting our departure in order to take our place'. Chanoine, *op. cit.*, p. 110. Unlike its representative, the Quai d'Orsay was not prepared to abandon sources of prestige which France already possessed and a telegram was sent instructing the mission to withdraw temporarily to a French ship for the duration of any conflict. C.P.Japon, XXIV. 30 October 1874, Decazes to Berthemy. A dispatch of the same date spoke of 'the foresight which recommends us not to disorganise, unless absolutely necessary, the important military instruction establishment which we have founded in Japan'. *Ibid.*

121. C.P.Japon, XXIV, 10 February 1874, Berthemy to Decazes. He had earlier delivered the judgement that 'as not all peoples have the same temperament, it is dangerous to submit them indiscriminately to the same political regime, and the word liberty can in Japan very well mean licence and anarchy'. *Ibid.*, CXXIII, 22 October 1873, Berthemy to Decazes.

122. C.P.Japon, XXIV, 10 February 1874, Berthemy to Decazes.

123. *Ibid.* It is worth noting that Berthemy had been on fairly good terms with Soejima, and had continued to discuss affairs with him after his resignation. He did maintain earlier that 'the relative liberalism of Soejima is not entirely unconnected with his fall', but this referred more to his attitude towards treaty revision than internal politics. C.P.Japon, XXIII, 9 November 1873, Berthemy to Broglie.

124. C.C.Yédo, VI, 3 April 1874, Berthemy to Decazes.

125. See C.P.Japon, XXV, 4 January 1875, Berthemy to Decazes.

126. C.P.Japon, XXV, 15 August 1876, St. Quentin to Decazes.

127. C.P.Japon, XXV, 5 September 1876, St. Quentin to Decazes.

128. C.P.Japon, XXVI, 6 October 1877, Geofroy to Decazes. About the Satsuma rebellion itself Geofroy had little to say, but in this he was typical of most French ministers, who evidently did not conceive it as part of their task, once order had been established, to report on Japanese politics in detail until the 1890s. St. Quentin, however, did report on the military course of the rebellion, at first suggesting that the government troops were inferior in number but not in

'armament, discipline, and the quality of the officers who command them', but subsequently changing tack by conceding that the government's conscript forces, 'recruited for several years from among the lower classes who have always had a traditional fear of the Samurai or men with swords, do not stand up to their attacks' and that the government had had to use its own samurai forces as much as possible. C.P.Japon, XXVI, 25 February 1877, 25 March 1897, St. Quentin to Decazes.

129. C.P.Japon, XXVI, 11 August 1878, Geofroy to Waddington. He was perceptive enough to realise the importance of the family system and claimed that 'As long as they have not legislated on this fundamental point, one cannot but maintain that their work is superficial and precarious'.

130. C.P.Japon, XXVI, 19 May 1878, Geofroy to Waddington.

131. He had already been in Japan for over a year before he became chargé d'affaires in February 1879, and had three years' experience in China, from 1871 to 1874.

132. C.P.Japon, XXVII, 12 March 1879, Balloy to Waddington.

133. C.P.Japon, XXVII, 25 July 1879, Balloy to Waddington.

134. C.P.Japon, XXVII, 27 June 1879, Balloy to Waddington.

135. C.P.Japon, XXVII, 12 November 1880, Balloy to Barthélemy St. Hilaire.

136. *Ibid.*, 14 September 1880, Balloy to Freycinet.

137. C.P.Japon, XXVII, 12 November 1880, Balloy to Barthélemy St. Hilaire.

138. See C.P.Japon, XXVII, 5 August 1880, Balloy to Freycinet. His successor Roquette was much more fair-minded. After a scrupulous examination of the codes he admitted that the only reasonable objection concerned the quality and experience of the Japanese judges. C.P.Japon, XXVIII, 29 July 1881, Roquette to Barthélemy St. Hilaire.

139. C.P.Japon, XXVII, 8 February 1880., Balloy to Freycinet.

140. C.P.Japon, XXVIII, 19 July 1882, Tricou to Freycinet.

141. C.P.Japon, XXVII, 12 November 1880, Balloy to Barthélemy St.. Hilaire.

142. C.P.Japon, XXVIII, 19 July 1883, Tricou to Freycinet.

143. C.P.Japon, XXVIII, 15 July 1882, Tricou to Challemel-Lacour. Tricou's first dispatch, a month before, had referred to the 'infantile vanity' of the Japanese. C.P.Japon, XXVIII, 16 June 1882.

144. See C.P.Japon, XXVII, 11 December 1880, Roquette to Barthélemy St. Hilaire.

CHAPTER 5

1. Japanese perceptions of their position in the world are described in a masterly fashion by Oka Yoshitake in his article 'Kokumin Dokuritsu to Kokka Risei' in Ito Totono et al., *Kindai Nihon Shiso Shi Koza*), VIII, (Tokyo, 1960). The article has been translated in M. Mayo (ed.), *The Emergence of Imperial Japan* (Boston, 1970).

2. C.P.Japon, XX, 22 August 1870, Outrey to Gramont. It should be added that the murder of the French consul and others at Tientsin in June was still very fresh in the mind of Europeans and that France's naval strength in Japanese waters was temporarily weaker than Germany's.

3. F.O.46, CXXVII, 5 September 1870, Parkes to Granville.

4. See *Ibid.*

5. See C.P.Japon, XX, 30 September 1870, Outrey to Auvergne-Lauraguais. Outrey claimed that the first regulations included some articles which were contrary to the treaties.

6. *Ibid.*

7. Von Brandt's willingness to accept the changes of September 22 is difficult to explain. His memoirs refer to the neutrality question only in general terms of the need for European solidarity. See M. von Brandt, *Dreiunddreissig Jahre in Ost-Asien,* 3 vols., (Leipzig., 1901), vol. II, pp. 288-291. It seems most likely that at the

time of the September agreement the Prussian minister still had no reason to suspect that the French might change their attitude on the desirability of allowing trade to continue freely. This is roughly the view expressed by Parkes in FO.46, CXXVII, 22 October 1870, Parkes to Granville.

8. See Hanabusa Nagamichi, *Meiji Gaiko-shi*, (Tokyo, 1960), p. 18.

9. See C.P.Japon, XX, 15 October 1870, Outrey to Favre. See C.P.Japon, XX, 28 October 1870, Outrey to Favre. Also FO.46, CXXVII, 15 October, 1870, Parkes to Hammond, (Private).

10. Hanabusa, *op. cit.*, p. 18.

11. The treaty was never ratified and the presence of the missionaries had ended in the 1850s, however. See Cordier, *Les Français aux Iles Lieou-Kieou*, Paris, 1911.

12. See C.P.Japon, XXI, 16 October 1872, Turenne to Rémusat.

13. That Germany was suspected of having designs on the Ryukyus was implied by a later French representative, when he reported that von Brandt had urged Iwakura Tomomi to give the islands their independence. C.P.Japon, XXXVIII, 28 July 1881, Roquette to Barthélemy St. Hilaire. French concern about German expansion was stated explicitly regarding Taiwan in 1874. Berthemy reported to the Quai that he was less opposed to the Taiwanese Expedition than his colleagues, because he felt that it would either reawaken China's interest in Taiwan or leave Japan in control, and in either case there was much less chance of an incident occurring which could give Germany any excuse for seizing the island. C.P.Japon, XXIV, 22 May 1874, Berthemy to Decazes.

14. C.P.Japon, XXIV, 30 June 1874, Berthemy to Decazes.

15. See e.g. Decazes' reply, in which, while accepting Berthemy's general conclusions, he held that the danger to Western interests would be greater if China defeated Japan than vice-versa. C.P.Japon, XXIV, 27 August 1874.

16. A recent view of this dispute which plays down Saigo's belligerence is P. Duus, *The Abacus and the Sword*, (Berkeley, Los Angeles & London, 1995).

17. Soejima was extraordinarily frank in his discussions both before and after his resignation. See especially the reports by Parkes in FO.46, CLXVII, No 62, 18 August 1873, and FO.46, CLXVIII, No.91, 3 November 1873, Parkes to Granville.

18. The missionaries' case was presented the following year by Charles Dallet, *Histoire de L'Eglise de Corée*, 2 vols., (Paris, 1874).

19. It should also be noted that Korea had always been regarded as the concern of the French legation in China rather than Japan.

20. C.P.Japon. XXV, 11 March 1876, St. Quentin to Decazes.

21. See C.P.Japon, XXVI, 29 April 1878; *Ibid.* 18 May 1878. Both Geofroy to Waddington.

22. See C.P.Japon, XXVI, 2 December 1878. *Ibid.* December 17, 1868. Geofroy to Waddington. In a letter to Colonel Chanoine, dated 12 April 1879, the ex-member of the first French military mission and long-time adviser to the Japanese government, Captain Dubousquet, wrote that Iwakura had 'clearly declared to the Minister, M. de Geofroy, that the Government of Japan was ready, if France and Britain desired, to recommend to Korea the opening of a port or two, proof that the opening, even apparent, of Korea to the European powers is considered the most effective and practical obstacle to the plans of the Great Neighbour [i.e. Russia]. Chanoine, *op. cit.*, p. 142. On Japanese policy, see H.Conroy, *The Japanese Seizure of Korea, 1866–1910.* (Philadelphia, 1960).

23. C.P.Japon, 9 April 1879, Balloy to Waddington.

24. C.P.Japon. XXVII, 18 May 1879, Waddington to Balloy; *Ibid.*, 19 November 1879, Balloy to Waddington. Balloy did not object to the opening of Korea, but thought it should be done by means of a joint naval demonstration by the Western powers, excluding Russia, which he suspected of harbouring designs of domination. See

C.P.Japon, XXVII, 7 October 1880, Balloy to Barthélemy St. Hilaire. In April 1881 the foreign minister expressed exactly the traditional French attitude, when he emphasised that 'we must also apply ourselves to pushing forward and to profiting from the advantages which will be acquired by the other Powers in these circumstances', but at the same time warned that they should have no thought of 'associating us with any exclusive action, neither taking alone, nor with another power, a pronounced attitude which would risk involving us in difficulties in the Far East and in rivalry with certain European Cabinets'. C.P.Japon, XXVIII, 15 April 1881, Barthélemy St. Hilaire to Roquette.

25. See C.P.Japon, XXIX, 13 June 1883, Viel-Castel to Challemel-Lacour. The establishment of treaty relations between the Western powers and Korea in the early 1880s has been studied in depth by M. Deuchler, *Confucian Gentlemen and Barbarian Envoys: The Opening of Korea, 1875–1885*, (Seattle, 1977).

26. See Hanabusa, *op.cit.* pp. 30–31.

27. See C.P.Japon, XXVI, 2 December 1878, Geofroy to Bourée.

28. C.P.Japon, XXVI, 18 November 1878, Geofroy to Waddington.

29. Japan's offer was conditional on China conceding to her most-favoured-nation rights. Hanabusa, *op.cit.*, p. 32; See also Ohata Tokushiro, *Nihon Gaiko Seisaku no Shiteki Tenkai*, (Tokyo, 1983) and Sato Saburo, *Kindai Nitchu Kosho Shi no Kenkyu*, (Tokyo, 1984).

30. C.P.Japon, XXVIII, 12 October 1881, Roquette to Barthélemy St. Hilaire.

31. C.P.Japon, XXVIII, 16 October 1882, Tricou to Duclerc.

32. The historian who has devoted most attention to the possibility of Franco-Japanese cooperation and has made some use of Quai d'Orsay records (although his interest lies on the Japanese side more than the French) is Ho Takushu (P'eng Tse-chou). He has published the following relevant articles: 'Shin-Futsu Senso no Taikan Seisaku', *Shirin*, XLIII (May 1960); 'Fuerii Naikaku to Nihon', *Shirin*, XLV, (May 1962); 'Chosen Mondai o meguru Jiyuto to Furansu', *Rekishigaku Kenkyu*, CCLXV, (June 1962); 'Fukkoku Koshi no de mita Jiyuto', *Shirin*, XLVIII (March 1965); and 'Koshin Jihen o meguru Inoue Gaimukyo to Furansu Koshi to no Kosho', *Rekishigaku Kenkyu*, CCLXXXII, (November, 1963). French diplomatic records have also been consulted by Nose Kazunori, 'Koshin Seiken no Kenkyu (1): Shin-Futsu Senso to Nihon Gaiko', *Chosen Gakuho*, LXXXII, (January 1977).

33. A good many Japanese diplomatic documents pertaining to relations with France are to be found in the volumes for 1883, 1884 and 1885 in the official Japanese Foreign Office series, *Nihon Gaiko Bunsho* (Japanese Diplomatic Documents). More, however, are to be found in a 3-volume unpublished collection in typescript in the Japanese Foreign Ministry archives. The collection is entitled *Tongking ni kansuru Shin-Futsu Senso* (The Sino-French War over Tongking) and will be referred to hereafter as *Shin-Futsu Senso*. Unfortunately, some of the documents are known only from the brief description of their contents at the beginning of each volume (apparently because they were destroyed by fire before the compilation was completed). In addition, the Foreign Ministry archives also contain four relevant volumes of copies of telegrams (hereafter *Denshin sha-o* (outgoing) and *Denshin sha-rai* (incoming). They too, however, are incomplete, covering only parts of 1883 and 1885 and containing nothing for 1884.

34. 'On the heels of the military reconquest of Chinese Turkestan . . . [China] launched a gigantic political and diplomatic offensive aimed at restoring her dwindling or dormant prestige and influence in Tonkin, Annam, Burma, Tibet, Korea and Manchuria'. A. Malozemoff, *Russian Far Eastern Policy, 1881–1904*, Berkeley, 1958, p. 20.

35. For a detailed study of the origins of the Franco-Chinese Dispute, see B.L.Evans, 'The Attitudes and Policies of Great Britain and China toward French Expansion in

Cochin-China, Cambodia, Annam and Tongking, 1858–83', Ph.D. thesis, University of London, 1961.

36. For details of the war and the various negotiations that were carried on before its outbreak and during its course, see T.F.Power, *Jules Ferry and the Renaissance of French Imperialism,* (New York, 1944) and L. M. Chere, *The Diplomacy of the Sino-French War (1882–1885): Global Complications of an Undeclared War* (Notre Dame, Indiana, 1988). Chinese policy-making is treated in L. Eastman, *Thrones and Mandarins: China's Search for a Policy during the Sino-French Controversy, 1880–1885,* (Cambridge, Mass., 1967).

37. See, e.g. *Shin-Futsu Senso,* I, No. 63, 18 July 1883, foreign minister Inoue to minister in China, Enomoto.

38. The most detailed, and still to a large extent the standard, account of Japanese policy towards Korea in the second half of the nineteenth century is Tabohashi Kiyoshi, *Kindai Nissen Kankei no Kenkyu,* 2 vols, (Tokyo, 1940). In English the examination by Hilary Conroy, *The Japanese Seizure of Korea, 1868–1910,* (Philadelphia, 1960), has been supplemented by a number of scholars, notably Deuchler, *op. cit.*; Kim Key-Kiuk, *The Last Phase of the East Asian World Order: Korea, Japan, and the Chinese Empire, 1860–1882,* (Berkeley and Los Angeles, 1980); and, less convincingly, Seung Kwon Synn, *The Russian-Japanese Rivalry over Korea, 1876–1904,* (Seoul, 1981). Among the studies which focus on the early 1880s, Harold F. Cook, *Korea's 1884 Incident,* (Seoul, 1972); Yur-bok Lee, *West Goes East: Paul George von Mollendorf and Great Power Imperialism in Late Yi Korea,* (Honolulu, 1988), and Kajima Morinosuke, *Nihon Gaiko Shi,* iii, (Tokyo, 1976), are particularly relevant.

39. Among the inner group of Japanese policy makers there were discernible differences between the Court noble and senior minister Iwakura Tomomi, who advocated a policy of complete non-interference in Korea until his death in 1883, Ito Hirobumi, the most influential political leader after 1881, who favoured active support of Korean independence, and Inoue Kaoru, who was more sceptical than his Choshu colleague about the strength and reliability of the pro-Japanese elements in Korea and more hesitant about seeking to extend Japanese influence there. See Inoue Kaoru Ko Denki Hensankai, *Segai Inoue Ko Den,* iii, (Tokyo, 1934), pp. 492–3; Tabohashi, *op. cit.,* pp. 904–907; and Ichikawa Masaaki's supplementary commentary to the second volume of his 7-volume collection of documents on Japanese-Korean relations, *Nikkan Gaiko Shiryo,* (Tokyo, 1979). Others may have been more hawkish. At the time of the incident in Seoul in July 1882, when Korean soldiers attacked the Japanese legation, Yamagata Aritomo, an important military figure, and Kuroda Kiyotaka, the strong man of Satsuma, advocated military measures, such as the occupation of Korean port or islands. See Ichikawa, *op. cit.,* p. 2, and Kawamura Kazuo, *Kindai Nitchu Kankei Shi no Shomondai,* (Tokyo, 1983), p. 40.

40. See Chanoine, *op. cit.,* especially pp. 191–94.

41. For an account of the Sino-Japanese conflict which focuses particularly on these Chinese irregular forces, see Henry McAleavy, *Black Flags in Vietnam,* (London, 1968).

42. C.P.Japon, XXIX. 13 June 1883. Viel-Castel to Challemel-Lacour.

43. *Ibid.* See also *Ibid.,* 30 May 1883; 6 June 1883. Both Viel-Castel to Challemel-Lacour. It should be noted that *L'Echo du Japon* of 2 June 1883 partly shared Viel-Castel's feelings. After suggesting that 'The Japanese hope, perhaps, to profit from a war between France and China . . . to settle definitively the question of the Ryukyus and to revenge themselves for the Chinese intervention in Korea', it commented that 'depending on how things turn out, France may perhaps have in Japan a precious ally'.

44. C.P.Japon, XXIX, Viel-Castel to Challemel-Lacour, 3 July 1883. That Viel-Castel's judgement was unreliable is further indicated by his renewed belief in Japanese willingness to cooperate in September: 'A sympathetic current between the Court of

Tokyo and the French Government would thus seem to exist at this moment to the highest degree, and it would appear that it could easily breach the boundary which separates it from a proper entente'. *Ibid.*, 4 September 1883. There is no support for this suggestion in Japanese records.

45. C.P.Japon, XXIX, 27 April 1883, Challemel-Lacour to Tricou.

46. *Ibid.*

47. *Ibid.* The new French attitude to China was not concealed. Marshall subsequently reported that 'on 27 April France altered her tone. The Political Director informed Marshall that the position had changed, that France was determined to occupy Tonkin and maintain her protectorate, and that he expected that China will really fight'. *Shin-Futsu Senso*, I, enclosure in Hachisuka to Inoue, 22 June 1883. This statement was clearly meant to encourage Japan to adopt a hard line towards China, and was in marked contrast to the dismissive remark made by the same official to Marshall at the time of the recall of the French minister in China, Bourée, in March: 'Pray do not take it as an encouragment for yourselves'. Enclosure in Hachisuka to Inoue, 23 March 1883, in *Nihon Gaiko Bunsho*, XVI, (Tokyo, 1951), p. 460.

48. C.P.Japon, XXIX, 27 April 1883.

49. *Ibid.*, 6 July 1883.

50. *Ibid.*, Challemel-Lacour was almost certainly unaware (and his ignorance may have been shared by Viel-Castel) that the Frenchman with the greatest influence in government circles, the legal adviser Gustave-Emile Boissonade, was already at this time an advocate of an alliance between Japan, China and Korea. See, for example, the report by his colleague, Inoue Kowashi, to Ito Hirobumi, dated 9 November 1882 in Ito Hirobumi Kankei Bunsho Kenkyukai (ed.), *Ito Hirobumi Kankei Bunsho*, (Documents relating to Ito Hirobumi), I, (Tokyo, 1973), pp. 334–5.

51. C.P.Japon, XXIX, 23 August 1883, Viel-Castel to Challemel-Lacour.

52. C.P.Japon, XXIX, 7 November 1883, Sienkiewicz to Challemel-Lacour.

53. See the Japanese foreign ministry's historical survey of the treaty revision negotiations: Gaimusho Chosa-bu, *Joyaku Kaisei Kankei Dai Nihon Gaiko Bunsho*, VI, (Tokyo, 1950), p. 202.

54. *Nihon Gaiko Bunsho*, XVI, pp. 34–5. The French foreign minister prefaced his invitation by drawing the Japanese representative's attention to their two countries' common interest in resisting China's 'excessive and exaggerated claims'.

55. See *Ibid.*, pp. 36–97.

56. *Joyaku Kaisei Kankei Dai Nihon Gaiko Bunsho*, II, (Tokyo, 1942), p. 302.

57. *Shin Futsu Senso*, I, enclosure in Hachisuka to Inoue, 22 June 1883.

58. Even in 1884 negotiations took place between March and May, when a convention was actually signed in Tientsin between Li Hung-chang and a French naval officer, Commandant Fournier. In June, however, the belief that China had violated this agreement led the French to resort to undeclared war, although talks continued sporadically in Europe.

59. C.P.Japon, XXIX, 13 June 1883, Viel-Castel to Challemel-Lacour.

60. *Nihon Gaiko Bunsho*, XVI, pp. 587–91. Viel-Castel did not report to Paris what he had said.

61. C.P.Chine, LXI, 19 June 1883, Tricou to Ferry. This was neither the first nor the last time that he expressed such an opinion. According to a report by the British minister to Japan, Sir Harry Parkes, his French counterpart had, in February, following a dinner at the foreign minister's residence, asked three Satsuma military leaders who were fellow guests 'why they did not send 20, 000 men to China as with such a force they could easily take Peking and if Japan were to undertake an operation of this nature, she would be supported by French action in Tongking'. Both Parkes and Inoue affected to regard this as a bad jest at the time but Inoue expressed concern that it 'might excite the minds of its hearers'. F.O.46, CCIIIC, 17 February 1883, Parkes to Granville.

62. See, for example, his urging of the advantages of an alliance upon the Japanese minister in Peking, as reported by the latter. 22 October 1883, Enomoto to Inoue, in Ichikawa Masaaki (ed.), *Nikkan Gaiko Shiryo*, III, (Tokyo, 1979), pp. 467–71. The French consul in Shanghai, Galy, was even more active in advocating cooperation. See eg. *Shin-Futsu Senso*, I, 31 July 1883, Shinagawa (Japanese consul-general in Shanghai) to Inoue, and *ibid.*, II, 7 February 1884, Higashi (Japanese consul at Chefoo) to Ito Hirobumi.

63. See eg, *Shin-Futsu Senso*, I, 3 July 1883, Shinagawa to vice-minister Yoshida and telegrams from Shinagawa to Inoue, dated 4 and 5 July in *Denshin sha-o*, 1883.

64. See Nose, *op. cit.* One way of doing so was seen to be an international guarantee of Korea's independence. See eg. Viel-Castel's comment that Japan might seek French support for 'a plan which at present preoccupies it and which would consist of having the neutrality of the Korean Peninsula proclaim along the same lines as that of Belgium'. C.P.Japon, XXIX, 13 June 1883, Viel-Castel to Challemel-Lacour.

65. See *Shin-Futsu Senso*, where the summary of a now lost dispatch from Inoue to Enomoto, dated 2 February 1883, states that it was an instruction to link up with French policy in order to reject the Chinese suzerainty strategy, since Japan's urgent duty was to consolidate Korea's independence. Enomoto himself was to express a similar concern to Sienkiewicz the following year: '"We cannot at any price', Admiral Enomoto said to me quite recently, 'permit any power to establish its dominion in Korea: it is a matter of our security"'. C.P.Japon, XXX, 27 June 1884, Sienkiewicz to Ferry.

66. C.P.Japon, XXIX, 23 August, 1883, Viel-Castel to Challemel-Lacour. That Inoue was expressing a genuine concern is suggested by the urgency with which he advocated the purchase of warships in this period. A telegram sent by him to a Japanese official in London on 6 January 1883 explicitly stated: 'We are in a hurry to purchase the vessels in view of China's attitude'. *Denshin sha-o*, 1883. Referring to this period one military historian has stated that 'as regards the strategy of continental field operations, which were anticipated in a war with China, the Japanese were painfully aware of their deficiencies, not only in organization, but still more in numbers'. Fujiwara Akira, *Gunji Shi*, (Tokyo, 1961), p. 43.

67. The question of Japanese neutrality posed some difficulties in 1884. France hoped at first to use Nagasaki as a naval base, but the Japanese government had no intention of responding favourably to such a request. Although the French navy was permitted to purchase coal and provisions in Japanese ports, even this privilege was threatened when the Chinese government notified the Japanese government on 30 August 1884 that China was at war with France and demanded Japan's strict neutrality. Inoue reserved Japan's position. See C.P.Japon, XXIX, 3 January 1884, Sienkiewicz to Ferry; *Ibid.*, XXX, 30 August 1884, Sienkiewicz to Ferry; 1 September 1884; 2 September 1884; 6 September 1884; 13 September 1884; 4 October 1884; 31 August 1884, Billot to Sienkiewicz; 23 October 1884, Hachisuka to Ferry; 30 October 1884, Ferry to Hachisuka.

68. *Nihon Gaiko Bunsho*, XVI, pp. 474–5, 26 April, 1883, Enomoto to Inoue.

69. *Denshin sha-o*, 9 May 1883. In this telegram Inoue also referred to a previous request to have 'something published in French newspapers concerning Corea because I wished to impress upon the mind of Frenchmen some idea of Corean independence'. That his objectives were always strictly limited is evident also from a telegram of 12 March 1883, when he informed a Japanese diplomat that 'We do not take any step against China, but I presume Li may be offended with us, nevertheless no truth in rumour'. *Ibid.* Further evidence of Inoue's change of diplomatic tactics is found in Marshall's report of 6 September 1883 (cited in Note 45) in which, referring to April, he wrote that 'In the meantime, however, the Japanese Government had altered its views and no longer desired to associate itself with France against China'. The

telegram from Ito Hirobumi has not survived, but the autobiography of Aoki Shuzo, a fellow native of Choshu whom Ito visited in Berlin in 1883 on 10 May, reveals that Ito's views were not, at this time, in harmony with Inoue's. Aoki recorded Ito as stating that 'I am very much opposed to rejecting the French proposal. We should accept it with open arms and attack China in alliance with France (*Kinzen sono gi o ire, dokoku to domei shite shinkoku o kogekisubeshi*). Why has Inoue not agreed to the minister's proposal? I am very dissatisfied with him for not discussing this with me quickly'. Cited by Nose, *op. cit.*, p. 148. Ito's sentiments here are consistent with those he had expressed in a letter to Inoue of 27 April 1883, although he had then stressed the unlikelihood of cooperation with France: 'Although France is bound to take further measures in Tongking, it will be very difficult to link this with the Korean incident. The French are intent on independent action. Therefore it can be surmised that even now we will be unable to get them to march in step with us at all'. *Ito Hirobumi Shokan*, I, in the *Inoue Kaoru Kankei Bunsho* held in the *Kensei Shiryo Shitsu* in the Japanese Diet Library.

70. Even Tricou abandoned his enthusiastic attitude after returning to Japan in late 1883 on his way home to France. According to Commandant Fournier, 'while passing through Japan Our Minister ascertained, and I myself have been able to ascertain, that there had been an evident movement in the court of Tokyo's attitude. Far from seeking as hitherto a rapprochement with France, it appears today to wish to disengage itself from a commitment which could become embarrassing'. C.P.Japon, LXIII, 6 December 1883, Fournier to Rear-Admiral Meyer (enclosure in Sienkiewicz to Ferry).

71. C.P.Japon, XXIX, 8 January 1884, Ferry to Sienkiewicz. This attitude did not change even when two months later the director of political affairs at the Quai d'Orsay was asked by the counsellor of the Japanese Legation whether 'France would be disposed to join in a collective démarche, instigated by Japan, to make representations to China on the subject of the ill-defined rights which it claims over Korea, Taiwan, Annam'. Billot's response was that 'such a démarche would be judged inopportune'. C.P.Japon, XXX, 19 March 1884, note by Billot, approved by Challemel-Lacour. There is no evidence in the Japanese records that Marshall's approach was authorized by Tokyo.

72. One of his earliest dispatches referred to the overtures which Viel-Castel had made in August and concluded: 'The result has hardly been favourable; we have granted Japan very important concessions in the question of treaty revision and we have obtain in return only evidence of the fear which the Chinese Empire inspires in the Mikado's Ministers. I have, furthermore, ascertained since my arrival at Yokohama that rumours were circulating of offers of alliances made by us but declined by the Japanese'. As if this were not enough, French exploits in Tongking had not, in his view, been adequately appreciated in Japan, for which fact he was inclined to lay some of the blame at the door of the Japanese officers who had been given permission to observe French operations and who, he suggested, 'would sometimes, in their reports, have indulged in certain criticisms which, without being intentionally disobliging, could only serve to maintain the government in the reserved attitude which it has adopted'. C.P.Japon, XXIX, 7 November 1883, Sienkiewicz to Challemel-Lacour.

73. *Ibid.* He even went on to consider the conditions of a Franco-Japanese agreement: 'Supposing there were, in fact, a rupture between France and China, we could be led to offer a defensive and offensive alliance to Japan, which would probably, finding itself guaranteed by us, cease to fear the consequences of a struggle with the Chinese Empire. But then we would have to supply Japan with ships to transport its troops and, more particularly, with money. It would only be at this price that it would be possible to obtain Japan's cooperation'.

74. See note 62. The 22 October report by Enomoto of Tricou and Galy's urging of an alliance shows that many points were discussed. Tricou was willing to hold out the possibility of a more permanent alliance, as well as assistance with treaty revision; and he again expressed the view that 20, 000 Japanese soldiers could rout the entire Chinese army, provided that France lent naval support. But as Enomoto commented, Tricou's language was vague and his answers to direct questions about the precise nature of the help which might be expected from France were evasive. Neither the Comte de Semallé, who took over as chargé d'affaires in China in October, nor the next minister, Jules Patenôtre, was so inclined to make overtures to Japanese diplomats.

75. *Shin-Futsu Senso,* III, 31 August 1884, Aoki to Inoue. Unfortunately the full dispatch from Aoki is missing, and all that survives is the following summary: 'The French ambassador in Germany states that a Japanese-French understanding concerning China should be achieved, that France will take an important island (Hainan must be meant), that France should act as it wishes in Taiwan, and that neither country should impede the other'. However, there is no reference to such a report in the correspondence between the Quai d'Orsay and the French embassy in Berlin. No details of Inoue's response survive, but vice-minister Yoshida later informed the British minister that the Japanese government had rejected the approach. F.O.46, CCCXVIII, 24 December 1884, Plunkett to Granville.

76. Chanoine, *op. cit.,* p. 193.

77. *Ibid.*

78. Miura Goro, *Kanju Shogun Kaikoroku,* (Tokyo, 1925), pp. 143–63.

79. Details of the mediation attempt can be found in *Shin-Futsu Senso,* III, Nos. 298, 300, 303 and 304. The last of these includes an undated telegram from Inoue to Enomoto which reveals some exasperation at what he perceived to be Chinese intransigence: 'In view of the stupidity of the Chinese Government I agree to let the matter alone'.

80. C.P. Japon, XXX, 15 December 1884. On the same day Ferry also sent a telegram to the French ambassador in London, seeking further information on events in Korea. In it he stated: 'I have no need to lay stress on the interest we have in the addition to China's current difficulties of the encumbrance of a conflict with Japan'. *Documents Diplomatiques Français 1871–1914,* 1st series, V, p. 514.

81. Ho Takushu, 'Fuerii Naikaku to Nihon', *Shirin,* XLV, (May 1962), p. 62. Because of the lack of direct telegraphic communication with Korea, however, it is very doubtful whether news of the credits could have reached Seoul by 4 December.

82. C.P.Japon, XXVIII, 2 December 1882, Tricou to Duclerc. *Ibid.,* XXX, 24 March 1884, 7 June 1884, Sienkiewicz to Ferry. The later approaches were made by Kim Ok-Kiun and So Chae-p'il who, influenced by Japan's employment of French military instructors, wanted France's help in the formation of a Korean army. In his dispatch of 24 March, Sienkiewicz wrote in surprisingly enthusiastic terms that 'the idea of being called to organize the army of a country which until recent times has been under China's influence I find seductive'.

83. C.P. Japon, XXX, 24 July 1884, Ferry to Sienkiewicz.

84. C.P.Japon, XXX, 15 and 27 September 1884, Sienkiewicz to Ferry.

85. The relationship of these two ex-samurai from Tosa with the Choshu leaders within the government, particularly Ito Hirobumi, was ambivalent, and although they made a point of stressing that their views differed from the government's, Sienkiewicz was inclined to regard them as the latter's unofficial emissaries.

86. This is also the conclusion of Ho Takushu in 'Chosen Mondai o meguru Jiyuto to Furansu', in *Rekishigaku Kenkyu, CCLXV,* (June 1962).

87. It is widely held that Takezoe and the Korean radicals were encouraged to take action by their awareness of China's difficulties with France. See, eg, Tanaka

Naokichi and Kim Chong-nyong (ed.), *Nikkan Gaiko Shiryo Shusei*, III, (Tokyo, 1962), p. 480 and Lee, *op. cit.*, pp. 71–2.

90. C.P.Japon, XXX, 4 December 1884, Sienkiewicz to Ferry. Goto also declared that he had been informed by a Japanese journalist in Seoul (presumably the *Jiyuto* activist, Inoue Kakugoro) that he had been told by Takezoe that 'The Japanese Government is resolved to make war on China. It will begin by involving itself in Korea's internal affairs, and if China protests, it will respond with cannon fire. Japan will, besides, supply Korea with all the money it will need'. Sienkiewicz gave little credence to these statements, however, since he believed that there had been a rapprochement between Goto and the Meiji government, and that Goto was seeking to divert France from intervening in Korean affairs itself.

91. The instructions sent to Takezoe are printed in Tanaka and Kim, *op. cit.*, p. 3, and are partly translated in H. F. Cook, *op. cit.*, p. 215. Cook argues on the basis of circumstantial evidence that it reached Takezoe on 3 or 4 December, but that he ignored it. *ibid.*, pp. 215–16.

92. It needs to be emphasised that no alliance was formed because Ho Takushu, in 'Shin-Futsu Senso ni okeru Nihon no Taikan Seisaku', *Shirin*, XLIII, No.3, May 1960, p. 124, states that Inoue 'raised Japan's international position by cooperating with capitalist France'. Power is even more misleading, albeit in a different direction, when he asserts that Ferry 'rejected a Japanese proposal for joint action against China' in December 1884. Power, *op. cit.*, p. 185.

93. *The Times*, 6 February 1885. Some of *The Times*' correspondent's other comments also deserve attention, since they seem to derive from well-placed informants, possibly including the foreign minister himself. On 5 January he stated that 'the maintenance of China and internal reform and consolidation in Japan are seen to be necessary to preserve the balance of power in the Far East. Count Inouyé, the ablest statesman of Japan, holds these views. He keeps his gaze fixed on the north; but popular clamour, stimulated by foreign influences, may overcome him'. And on 17 January he reported that 'At one time the Japanese Government was inclined to yield to the French overtures for an alliance, but the danger passed away. The unsatisfactory financial condition of Japan was taken into account, with the danger of her being left to finish the war with China, and the certainty in that event of Russian action'. The strength of public support for military action is difficult to gauge because of the censorship imposed by the government on the Japanese press. See Sienkiewicz's comments in his dispatches to Ferry of 18 December 1884 (C.P.Japon, XXX) and 13 January 1885 (C.P.Japon, XXXI). Despite the existence of a government pressure, however, a number of Japanese historians have found evidence of widespread agitation for war against China by political party activists and ex-samurai. Hirota Masaki, 'Taigaku Seisaku to Datsu-a Ishiki ', in Rekishigaku Kenkyukai and Nihon Shi Kenkyukai, (ed.) *Koza Nihon Shi*, VII, (Tokyo, 1995), p. 326, states that bellicose patriotic groups were formed in three major cities and 24 of Japan's 46 prefectures, and that there were demonstrations calling for war in Tokyo and Osaka in January 1885. The papers of Inoue Kaoru are cited in Inoue Mitsusada and Kodama Kota (ed.), *Nihon Rekishi Taikei*, IV, (Tokyo, 1987), p. 603, to show that Inukai Tsuyoshi, Ozaki Yukio and other activists petitioned Ito for war against China on 24 December 1884. See also Inoue Kiyoshi, *Joyaku Kaisei* (Treaty Revision) (Tokyo, 1955), pp. 99–103.

94. This had already been suggested in 1883 by Viel-Castel, C.P.Japon, XXIX, 23 August 1883, Viel-Castel to Challemel-Lacour. In the aftermath of the failed coup Plunkett claimed that Russia had warned Japan not to attack Korea. F.0.46, CCXXVII, 19 January 1885, Plunkett to Granville. It was alleged by Miura to Sienkiewicz that certain (unspecified) Powers 'were forbidding the Government of the Mikado to intervene in the Franco-Chinese dispute', and that 'these same

Powers would use every means to prevent Japan from uniting with France'. C.P. Japon, XXXI, 5 February 1885, Sienkiewicz to Ferry. *The Times* of 13 January 1885 warned that 'A hostile intervention of Japan in Corea would almost certainly be followed by a fresh outbreak of revolutionary violence, and this might easily furnish Russia with the opportunity she has long been seeking'.

95. By late February Plunkett had sufficiently revised his opinion to inform the British minister in China that if Ito's forthcoming negotiations with Li Hung-chang should fail, 'war seems inevitable; I expect both France and Russia would support Japan'. Telegram to Parkes, enclosed in F.O.46, CCCXXVIII, 26 February 1885, Plunkett to Granville. It is worth noting that French relations with Germany were unusually good at this time. A.J.P. Taylor, *The Struggle for Mastery in Europe, 1848–1918* (Oxford, 1954), p. 296, states that Bismarck was 'playing genuinely for agreement with France' in later 1884.

96. The possibility of establishing a financial relationship with France, the second-largest exporter of capital, may have held a considerable attraction for those Japanese leaders who were interested in raising a foreign loan to extend the railway system. Among those who advocated such a loan were the Choshu diplomat, Aoki Shuzo, and the Satsuma leader, Kuroda Kiyotaka. For their views see *Denshin sharai*, 24 June 1885; 3 July 1885.

97. Enclosure in C.P.Japon, XXIX, 3 January 1884, Sienkiewicz to Ferry. That he held similar opinions in December 1884 is evident from his comment about the dispute over Korea that 'it is a matter here of a quarrel between yellows, and yellows do not like to involve whites in their quarrels'. *Ibid.*, XXX, 28 December 1884, Sienkiewicz to Ferry. It is tempting to suggest that the greater willingness of Tricou to contemplate cooperation with Japan was not entirely unconnected with the fact that he had a Japanese mistress, who accompanied him to China. See the Comte de Semallé, *Quatre Ans à Pekin*, (Paris, 1933), p. 142.

98. C.P.Japon, XXXI, 11 March 1885, Sienkiewicz to Ferry. This opinion was not shared by Captain Bougouin. His advice to Sienkiewicz was that 'an entente between France and Japan would secure for both these countries very great advantages and would assure them of success', although he believed that Japan would need French naval support. *Ibid.*, XXX, 22 December 1884, Sienkiewicz to Ferry.

99. F.O.46, CCCXVII, 24 December 1884. That Yoshida was not being disingenuous is supported by the fact that he did provide Plunkett with information about Patenôtre's offer and about earlier French overtures and also by the absence of any references in surviving Japanese diplomatic records to any approach by Sienkiewicz.

100. C.P.Japon, XXX, 18 December 1884, Sienkiewicz to Ferry. Sienkiewicz added that 'for a mind as lively and alert as M. Ino-ouye's, this slight indication, which involves no commitment, is sufficient'.

101. Sienkiewicz's own account does not mention any meeting with Inoue until the 18th. C.P.Japon, XXX, 18 December 1884. This lack of urgency contrasts strikingly with the eagerness of at least some of his diplomatic colleagues, for Inoue states in a letter to Ito of 16 December that 'This morning several diplomatic representatives came one by one and asked about the Korean situation, which was very troublesome'. *Ito Hirobumi Kankei Bunsho*, I, p. 188.

102. C.P.Japon, XXX, 18 December 1884, Sienkiewicz to Ferry,

103. Ferry's hopes would also have been lowered by a telegram from Patenôtre of 17 December in which the French minister in China recorded a visit by the Japanese consul in Shanghai, Ando Taro, and concluded: 'I was led to believe that, despite your recent declarations, Tokyo still doubts whether we are resolved on serious action and will consequently hesitate to rely upon us in the Korean question'.

C.P.Chine, LXVI. Another telegram from him on 19 December stated even more clearly that 'we must give up the thought of profiting from the events in Korea'. *Ibid.* Sienkiewicz subsequently sent telegrams which slightly modified the negative impression which he had initially given but still offered no real encouragement. On 19 December he reported: 'Considerable supplies of coal are being established at Nagasaki. A little excitement in the army. Some time will probably pass before the Government takes a decision, and before this decision is known'. This, it may be noted, was less encouraging than the language of the dispatch which he sent on the same day: 'I receive indications of a certain excitement in the army which would be favourable to a policy of action'. *Ibid.*

104. C.P.Chine, LXVI. Patenôtre may have been encouraged to be forthcoming by Ando's declaration that in his view 'this was a unique opportunity for his Government to give to the Korean question a satisfactory solution'.

105. That Patenôtre did speak positively to Ando is confirmed by a telegram which the consul sent to Inoue on 19 December 1884. It read: 'With regard to the French minister's proposal of alliance the said minister stated positively that it emanated from the French government. Moreover, he showed me a telegram from M. Ferry dated the 15th of this month, and in that telegram it stated that the French minister in Japan was instructed to enquire closely into the feelings of the Japanese government concerning the Korean incident and to request the Japanese government to ally with France. However, this telegram was vague in tone, and it is not clear what sort of an alliance is sought; and since I do not know Your Excellency's intentions, I did not enter very deeply into this matter. The French minister's discussion also extended to the matter of the national debt, and I will report the details in my next telegram. The French minister relies on your treating the above communication as highly confidential'. Ichikawa Masaaki, *Nikkan Gaiko Shiryo*, III, p. 42.

106. Patenôtre does not mention an offer of French financial help in any of his reports, but Ando is explicit on this point in a follow-up telegram of 20 December to Inoue: 'The French minister stated that if it is really the case that Japan does not have the strength to engage in war with the Chinese government because of financial difficulties, the French government would, as soon as there was an alliance, exert itself on Japan's behalf to raise a public loan in Paris by the most advantageous means'. *Ibid.*, p. 43. There appears to have been a further telegram (now lost) from Ando to vice-minister Yoshida on 23 December. The unpublished summary of its contents in the Japanese Foreign Office compilation reads: 'Patenôtre, taking advantage of the Korean incident, is urging a Japanese-French alliance (Japan and France would mutually assist each other, the former with its army, the latter with its navy, and France would also agree to a low-interest Japanese loan flotation). There is a telegram which is claimed to be a French government instruction ordering that the views of the Japanese government with regard to a Japanese-French alliance be ascertained and that an alliance be urged upon it'. *Shin-Futsu Senso*, III.

107. Plunkett's previously cited report of 24 December conveys what he had gleaned from the Japanese leaders: 'As yet the only bait held out by France to induce Japan to make this alliance appears to be a promise to help her to obtain a large loan in Europe, and something very vague in regard to Formosa. On this point, Mr. Yoshida was not communicative.'

108. C.P.Japon, XXI, 13 January 1885, Sienkiewicz to Ferry.

109. There is, however, evidence of an approach in Paris at this time by an unnamed junior Quai d'Orsay official who urged that it would be extremely profitable if Japan and France engaged in joint discussions. However, an alliance was not specifically mentioned. See *Nihon Gaiko Bunsho*, XVIII, pp. 548–49, 9 January 1885, Hachisuka to Yoshida.

110. Plunkett was often given confidential information by Inoue and Ito, but his reports need to be treated with some caution because the Japanese leaders had a motive for exaggerating the pressure to which they were being subjected by more hawkish elements. If the British minister could be persuaded that Japan was going to be forced to take action against China, the British minister in China, the redoubtable Sir Harry Parkes, might exert his influence to induce China to make concessions. That this did happen to some extent is suggested by the letters which were exchanged between Plunkett and Parkes. See F.O.46, CCCXXVIII, 20 February 1883, 27 February 1883, Plunkett to Granville. The latter contains a letter from Plunkett to Parkes in which Ito is quoted as saying that if he returned from Peking without a satisfactory solution, it would be 'impossible for the Cabinet to resist any longer the pressure of the War Party. Thus Japan would no longer refuse the proposals which France continues to press on her'. That Ito and Inoue really had to take account of the bellicose feeling is given support by a report written by a British official, J. H. Gubbins, several months after the crisis had ended. In it he noted that 'the surrender made to China rankles still in the breast of a large section of Japanese, and inclines, especially, the Army and the Navy to look with disfavour on the two statesmen who had the courage to make the best of the false position into which the indiscretions of the advanced Party had forced this country'. Enclosure in F.O.46, CCCXXX, 23 November 1885, Plunkett to Granville.

111. F.O.46, CCCXXVII, 3 January 1885, 11 January 1885, Plunkett to Granville.

112. F.O.46, CCCXVII, 16 January 1885. Three days later he offered six reasons why there was a strong war party: the belief that Japan needed to strike before China became strong; the wish to free Korea from Chinese domination; the desire to prove Japan's worth and speed treaty revision; expectation of French financial help and French support for treaty revision; the existence of numerous samurai; and the the influence of inexperienced hotheads. F.O.46, CCCXXVII, 19 January 1885.

113. On the decision to send Ito, Plunkett commented: 'My colleagues generally believe that if Counts Inouye and Ito could have had their way, no special mission would yet have been sent to Peking, but their hand has been forced and Count Ito's mission is the last card played to endeavour to secure the game in favour of peace'. *Ibid.,* 11 March 1885. The fact that Saigo accompanied the mission to China led to speculation since, as a native of Satsuma, he was linked with the supposed war party. According to the telegram which Inoue sent to Enomoto on 24 February, Saigo's appointment as adviser was 'in order to quiet excitement on the part of the military men as well as the public'. Tanaka and Kim, *op. cit.,* III, p. 222. That this was the true purpose is confirmed by the memoirs of Makino Nobuaki, a son of Okubo Toshimichi and a junior member of the mission, who concluded that having Saigo share responsibility was intended to deflect the anticipated criticism that Ito's diplomacy was weak-kneed. Makino Nobuaki, *Kaikoroku,* I, (Tokyo, 1948), pp. 146–47. Ito himself was later to claim that 'popular feeling which had been aroused by the unlawful intervention of China in the Korean incident was becoming increasingly aroused, and there were many who advocated war and sought to ensure that my mission would be unsuccessful, and reports even reached the ears of members of the government that they would try to assassinate me'; and that Saigo concluded that it would be better if he were to die rather than Ito. Kawamura Kazuo, *Kindai Nitchu Kankei Shi no Shomondai* (Tokyo, 1983), p. 37. That this may not be the whole story is suggested by the military historian, Joho Yoshio, who states that at Ito's and Inoue's request, Miura Goro, their Choshu counterpart, visited Saigo and persuaded the Satsuma 'hawks' to abandon their belligerent attitude. Joho Yoshio, *Gunmu Kyoku,* (Tokyo, 1979), p. 112. Ito's concern about the state of feeling, not only among political activists and ex-samurai but also within the military and officialdom, is clearly indicated in a letter which he

sent to Inoue Kaoru on 20 January 1885. See Kaneko Kentaro, *Ito Hirobumi Den,* II, (Tokyo, 1943), pp. 399–400.

114. F.O.46, CCCXVII, 24 January 1885, Plunkett to Granville.
115. C.P.Japon, XXI, 5 February 1885, 17 February 1885, both Sienkiewicz to Ferry.
116. *Ibid.,* 1 March 1885. Roesler attempted to induce the French to take the initiative by claiming that 'the Japanese are timid . . . and do not dare to take the first steps'.
117. F.O.46, CCCXXVIII, l March 1885, Plunkett to Granville. Some weeks earlier he had reported that Admiral Kabayama and General Takashima, both of whom had accompanied Inoue to Korea, had gone straight to Shanghai, and he commented: 'This looks suspicious as it is the French Minister there who is negotiating for alliance with Japan'. *Ibid.,* CCCXXVII.
118. *Ibid.,* CCCXXVIII, 11 March 1885, enclosure in Plunkett to Granville.
119. C.P.Japon, XXXI, 8 April 1885, Sienkiewicz to Freycinet. Miura's sincerity in his dealings with Frenchmen is, however, highly questionable.
120. That Li Hung-chang recognized how much China's difficulties would be increased by an alliance between France and Japan can be discerned from his acknowledgement to a French consul that 'it was thanks to the accord recently reached with the French Government that he had been able to arrive so easily at an entente with Japan'. C.P.Chine, LXVII, 18 April 1885, Patenôtre to Freycinet. (A preliminary agreement had been signed with France on 4 April).
121. Power, *op. cit.,* p. 180, observes that 'The real role of Tonkin in French domestic politics was to give an already determined opposition a point vulnerable to attack by patriotic arguments, a course made possible because the campaign in the Far East was going poorly'.
122. This factor should not be regarded as an absolute bar to an alliance, however, for by this time Japan was beginning to be considered a potential ally by Britain in the event of war with Russia. See F.O.45, CCXXVI, 8 June 1885, Granville to Plunkett, in which the foreign secretary wrote; 'I should be glad to have your opinion as to any steps that it might be desirable to take now or hereafter with the view of securing her [Japan's] alliance'.
123. Japanese Foreign Office records provide an illuminating example of Inoue's concern for stability in mid-1885 after the Tientsin Convention had placed Sino-Japanese relations on a more even keel following the Korean incident of December 1884. In an English-language telegram of 30 June 1885 Inoue requested Enomoto to propose to Li Hung-chang a more regular form of Sino-Japanese cooperation to prevent a repetition of such friction. As the Japanese foreign minister put it, 'Chosen's [ie. Korea's] foreign policy has very close bearing to the interests of both Japan and China and if left to herself no one knows what foreign complications might arise which will seriously embarrass them. Therefore I propose that after Li and myself have confidentially consulted and formed her foreign policy Li will undertake to let Corea adopt and enforce the same'. *Denshin sha-o,* 1885. Inoue's proposal was rebuffed by Li Hung-chang because, according to the historian who examined this exchange from the Chinese side, Li feared that such an agreement would drive the Korean king faster into the arms of Russia and would present practical difficulties, especially if Li and Inoue failed to agree. Moreover, the scheme amounted to a virtual Sino-Japanese condominium, with Li having the executive responsibilities. T.F. Tsiang, 'Sino-Japanese Diplomatic Relations, 1870–1894', *The Chinese Social and Political Science Review,* XVII, No 1, April 1935. Inoue's understanding, however, was that Li Hung-chang was unwilling to accept the provision that the Korean king should invariably consult with Li and through him with Inoue because it would give the impression that Japan was dictating policy. Whatever the basic reason may have been, Inoue's comment to Enomoto that Li's response 'shows the utter want of

discerning the great and far-seeing idea which underlies my views' is extremely revealing. *Denshin sha-o,* 13 July 1885.

124. For evidence of this see F.O.46, CCCXVIII, 31 December 1884, in which Plunkett reported to Granville that Japanese ministers 'speak somewhat as if they considered such an alliance with a Western power against an Eastern neighbour were contrary to the rules of the game'. A few months later Inoue observed in a telegram to Enomoto dealing with the Ryukyus: 'Moreover as the European colonial policy is beginning [*sic*] very strong and aggressive in the direction of Asia we do not wish to surrender the islands'. *Denshin sha-o,* 16 May 1885. The same apprehension of European expansionism was often voiced by other Japanese leaders and newspaper editors, and the existence of such a threat was occasionally recognized by Western diplomats.

CHAPTER 6

1. This is an important theme of Inoue Kiyoshi's *Joyaku Kaisei* (Tokyo, 1955). See also H. Conroy, *The Japanese Seizure of Korea,* pp. 216–218.

2. There are very few studies of treaty revision in Western languages, and despite its age and major limitations no work has appeared to replace F. C. Jones, *Extraterritoriality in Japan ,* (New Haven, 1931). Two other older works which contain quite detailed information on British and American treaty revision policy are F. V. Dickins, *The Life of Sir Harry Parkes,* Vol.2, (London, 1894), and P. J. Treat, *Diplomatic Relations Between the United States and Japan, 1853–1895,* 2 vols, (Stanford, 1932). All of these, however, appeared too early to make use of European diplomatic archives. Japanese, but not Western, diplomatic sources have been utilised in two more recent articles relating to aspects of treaty revision: S. T. W. Davis, 'Treaty Revision, National Security and Regional Cooperation: A *Minto* viewpoint', and R. T. Chang, 'The Question of Unilateral Denunciation and the Meiji Government, 1888–92', both in H. Conroy, S. T. W. Davis, and W. Patterson (eds.) *Japan in Transition* (London & Toronto, 1984). Despite its importance the issue has not, for the most part, been treated particularly well in Japanese either. There are only three full-length general studies: Yamamoto Shigeru, *Joyaku Kaisei Shi,* (Tokyo, 1943); Nihon Gakujutsu Shinkokai (ed.), *Joyaku Kaisei Keika Gaiyo,* (Tokyo, 1950); and Kajima Monosuke, *Nihon Gaiko Shi, II: Joyaku Kaisei Mondai* (Tokyo, 1970). An account which focuses on the efforts to end extraterritoriality is Nakamura Kikuo's *Kindai Nihon no Hoteki Keisei,* (Tokyo, 1956). Two major studies focus on the early stages of treaty revision: Shimomura Fujio, *Meiji Shonen Joyaku Kaisei Shi no Kenkyu,* (Tokyo, 1962); and Ishii Takashi, *Meiji Shoki no Kokusai Kankei,* (Tokyo, 1977). The outstanding work is Ino Tentaro's *Joyaku Kaisei Ron no Rekishiteki Tenkai,* (Tokyo, 1976), which focuses on Japanese attitudes and proposals. Most Japanese documents of any importance (except for those which are included in the regular *Nihon Gaiko Bunsho* series) as well as many communications from foreign diplomats, are reproduced in the Japanese Foreign Ministry's four-volume compilation, *Joyaku Kaisei Kankei Nihon Gaiko Bunsho* (Tokyo, 1941-50), hereafter cited as JKKNGB.

3. It should be noted that, unlike Britain, France was not forced to pay a great deal of attention to the views of its nationals in Japan. They were relatively few in numbers and had no organisation of their own. Though their views were occasionally sought by the French minister in Tokyo there is no indication that their opposition to revision was ever taken very much into account by the Quai d'Orsay.

4. The signing of this new Convention, which improved the Bakufu's standing in the eyes of the Western powers, especially Britain, made it difficult for the Meiji government to claim that the treaties had been imposed upon Japan by the threat of force.

5. See Carol Gluck, *Japan's Modern Myths* (Princeton, 1985).
6. See Yamamoto. *op.cit.*, p. 107.
7. The encouragement given by Secretary of State Fish to the Iwakura mission during its visit to Washington in 1872, and the resulting confusion, are brought out in an article by M. J. Mayo, 'A Catechism of Western Diplomacy: the Japanese and Hamilton Fish, 1872', *Journal of Asian Studies*. May 1967.
8. C.C.Yédo, V, 15 March 1869, Outrey to La Valette.
9. C.P.Japon, XXI, 11 July, 1871., Outrey to Favre.
10. C.P.Japon, XXI, 21 September 1871, Rémusat to Marine.
11. C.P.Japon, XXI, 7 May 1872. Rémusat gave as a reason that the Japanese Ministers 'have shown the intention of claiming, as one of the attributes of territorial sovereignty, a greater judicial authority'.
12. C .P.Japon. XXI. 17 July 1872. In a later memorandum Outrey (in Paris) argued that the jurisdiction question should be solved by means of a gradual transition (C.P.Japon, XXI, 17 December 1872) and Turenne's comments showed that by the end of his stay in Japan he had moved a little nearer to the Japanese position. By April 1873, he was prepared to give Japan some encouragement by permitting Japanese magistrates to deal with a limited range of offences committed by foreigners.
13. M.D.Japon, II, 24 January 1873. *Compte-rendu* of conference between Rémusat and Iwakura. Rémusat prefaced his remarks by saying that France was satisfied with the treaties at present.
14. C.C.Yédo, VI, 20 July 1873, Broglie to Berthemy. Apart from the lowering of tariffs the general view was that the status quo should be maintained.
15. The clearest evidence of this is an anonymous letter, dated 1 March, in the *Moniteur des Soies*, of 17 April 1875. Berthemy, it was reported, had himself stated at a recent dinner that 'his mission was fulfilled'. The writer's comment was: 'Now, as it is seen and known by all the world that our envoy had no other mission than dealing with revision, and that he was chosen expressly for that delicate task because of his tact and skill, it is permissible to suppose that he has failed, like his English colleague, since he announced that his mission has ended, while things remain the same'.
16. Roches had frequently warned against free access on the grounds that it would lead to an over-intensive rearing of silkworms which while bringing quick profits would impair the quality of the stock in the long run. His views were echoed by the Lyons Chamber of Commerce in 1868. See C.C.Yédo, V, 6 August 1868, Outrey to Gramont. Outrey, too, in his memorandum of 17 December 1872, (M.D.Japon, II) was opposed to the opening of the whole country, though he did hope that a passport system would be established which would allow merchants to visit the commercial centres.
17. See C.P.Japon, XXII, 27 March 1873, Turenne to Rémusat; *Ibid.* 12 May 1873, Turenne to Rémusat; C.P.Japon, XXIII, 17 August 1873, Berthemy to Broglie.
18. C.P.Japon, XXII, 27 July 1873, Berthemy to Broglie.
19. C.P.Japon, XXIII, 12 August 1873, Berthemy to Broglie.
20. C.P.Japon, XXIII, 12 October 1873, Berthemy to Broglie. The foreign representatives had, on 27 September, sent a draft set of regulations relating to access to the interior, the main features of which were their acceptance that foreigners outside the treaty ports should be subject to local regulations and their insistence that offenders should be handed over to and judged by their own consul. The Japanese failure to reply at once was presumably due partly to the dispute over Korean policy which led to Soejima's resignation on 22 October, but the main cause was probably their embarrassment over the position in which Soejima's conciliatory attitude had placed them. To allow access to the interior would open the way not only to awkward incidents between Japanese and foreigners but also to foreign economic penetration,

and although in theory foreigners would still not be able to own property outside the treaty ports, Japan would have very little left to hold out in the future as an incentive for complete treaty revision when that aim was made possible by the establishment of a reliable modern legal system.

21. C.P.Japon, XXIII, 9 November 1873, Berthemy to Broglie. The foreign representatives appeared to have been indignant that Terashima had declared that 'the government was not prepared to take a decision on the question which it had taken up, that it considered the situation resulting for it from the treaties as more disadvantageous from the point of view of jurisdiction than that of other non-Christian states . . .' According to Berthemy's report they drew upon their personal experience of countries mentioned by the foreign minister to refute him, whereupon 'very embarrassed by the result of his argument, Terashima considered himself obliged to seek refuge in an almost complete silence'.

22. C.P.Japon, XXIII, 20 November 1873, Berthemy to Broglie.

23. C.P.Japon, XXIII, 7 December 1873, Berthemy to Broglie. The indemnity actually was paid off in 1874.

24. C.P.Japon, XXIII, 28 December 1873, Berthemy to Broglie.

25. C.P.Japon, XXIV, 19 January 1874, Berthemy to Decazes.

26. C.P.Japon, XXIV, 8 July 1874. Berthemy to Decazes.

27. Chanoine, *op. cit.*, p. 108.

28. C.P.Japon, XXIV, 8 July 1874, Berthemy to Decazes.

29. *Ibid.* Just as in his interview with Terashima, Berthemy warned Iwakura that the Powers were liable to abandon their moderate and friendly attitude.

30. A dispatch of 16 July 1874 (C.P.Japon, XXIV) from Decazes had spoken in fairly critical terms of Japanese obstructionism and was quoted by Berthemy to Terashima. On 30 September 1874 (C.P.Japon, XXIV) Decazes wrote again, approving Berthemy for his line of action and, surprisingly, his moderation, and stating that he had recommended collective action to the other Cabinets. However, the lack of reference to this move in the Foreign Office's correspondence with Parkes, and in the correspondence between the Foreign Office and the British Embassy in Paris, indicates that the Berthemy line was not pursued with any vigour, if at all. The same 30 September dispatch actually states, in fact, that stronger pressure would not only have failed to secure the opening of the interior but would have offended the Japanese ministers.

31. See F.O. 46, CLXXXI, No.157, 21 August 1874, Parkes to Derby, and the Foreign Office comment on it.

32. C.P.Japon, 18 August 1874, Berthemy to Decazes.

33. Berthemy admitted this in a dispatch of 6 December 1874. (C.P.Japon, XXIV). The Quai d'Orsay's failure to exert itself in his support is probably attributable to the Japanese concession of 13 July, Japan's successful conclusion of the Formosa expedition, the French desire to maintain a military mission in Japan and habitual caution.

34. The three phases into which this account of treaty revision is divided do not refer primarily to the treaty revision process in general but to the French approach. Broadly speaking, France no longer sought after 1875 to take the initiative in treaty revision, since it was realised than any change in the system would have to be a compromise favouring Japan. Until the later 1880s, therefore, France mostly opposed all efforts to alter the situation. This attitude then changed when Japan's increasing strength convinced French policy-makers that fundamental treaty revision was inevitable and that France should make the best bargain it could, before its treaty was denounced unilaterally.

35. For the background to the Japanese resumption of negotiations, see Shimomura Fujio, 'Joyaku Kaisei', pp. 73–75, in Konishi Shiro (ed.), *Kindai Shakai*, (Tokyo,

1954). By this time there were also some demands for protectionism from the young but very vocal Japanese press.

36. C.P.Japon, XXVI, 16 October 1877, Geofroy to Decazes. Geofroy's last sentence reads curiously in the light of the subsequent failure of the United States-Japan treaty to make any real impact on the course of treaty revision but it does reveal the continuing French fear of isolation, which meant that Japan need not worry overmuch about a French refusal to acquiesce in any new treaty which had won general agreement. It may be worth adding that about this time Geofroy was becoming concerned about France's diminishing prestige in Japan. (See C.P.Japon, XXVI, 28 January 1878, Geofroy to Waddington).

37. C.C.Tokyo, I, 10 February 1878.

38. C.P.Japon, XXVI, 4 April 1878, Waddington to Geofroy.

39. See C.C.Tokyo, I, 20 September 1878. Waddington to Geofroy.

40. M.D.Japon, II, 26 June 1879.

41. Some of the responsibility also rested with the Japanese, who were impatient with any measure of progress which did not promise the abolition of extraterritoriality. Terashima's replacement by Inoue in September 1879 was largely the result of this dissatisfaction. See Hanabusa, *Meiji Gaiko Shi.* p. 65.

42. C.P.Japon, XXVI, 15 December 1878, Geofroy to Waddington.

43. C.P.Japon, XXVII, 25 July 1879, Balloy to Waddington.

44. C.C.Tokyo. I. December 13, 1879. Balloy's language to Inoue on this occasion is not without interest: 'do not lose sight of the fact that the more you appear to be liberal towards us the more quickly you will achieve your purpose, which is to recover the integrity of your rights. In examining the affair from a narrow and petty point of view, as is unhappily too often the case, you do not encourage us to make concessions'.

45. C.C.Tokyo, I *bis,* 21 July 1880, Balloy to Freycinet.

46. For his vigorous and outspoken approach to Kennedy, the British chargé d'affaires, see F.O.46, CCLXVIII, No.123, 13 July 1880, Kennedy to Granville.

47. C.P.Japon, XXVII, 15 September 1879; *Ibid.* 22 April 1880. Balloy also took the unusual step for a French diplomat of seeking the opinion on treaty revision of French traders in Yokohama. See *L'Echo du Japon,* 12 December 1879. Clearly this was with the intention of gaining support for his opposition to the Japanese proposals. Normally little heed was paid to the views of merchants. See *L'Echo du Japon*'s complaint in its edition of 25 November 1881.

48. C.C.Tokyo, I *bis,* 11 June 1880, Freycinet to Balloy.

49. C.C.Tokyo, I *bis,* 24 November 1880, Barthélemy St. Hilaire to Balloy. Formal rejection, however, was only conveyed to Inoue in December, 1881. See C.P.Japon, XXVIII, 8 December, 1881, Roquette to Gambetta. Inoue's proposals had gone beyond what he suggested in early 1880. Owing partly to pressure from public and colleagues, and partly to the completion of a new penal code and a code of criminal instruction, he decided to extend the scope of treaty revision to extraterritoriality as well as tariffs.

50. C.P.Japon, XXVIII, 29 July 1881, Roquette to Barthélemy St. Hilaire.

51. C.P.Japon, XXVIII, 10 August 1881. See also *Ibid.* 2 March 1881; *Ibid.* 18 March 1881. All Roquette to Barthélemy St. Hilaire.

52. C.P.Japon, XXVIII, 1 July 1881; *Ibid.* 10 August 10, 1881, Roquette to Barthélemy St. Hilaire.

53. C.P.Japon, XXVIII, 10 August 1881, Roquette to Barthélemy St. Hilaire.

54. C.P.Japon, XXVIII, 15 July 1882, Tricou to Freycinet.

55. C.C.Tokyo, II *bis,* 14 August 1882, Tricou to Duclere.

56. Oka, in his previously cited essay, 'Kokuminteki Dokuritsu to Kokka Risei', pp. 14–17, stresses the fact that all sections of opinion in Japan showed a similar

consciousness of Japanese inferiority to foreigners at this time, and a fear of economic or political domination from outside was strong enough in a large number of the government's critics for them to oppose immediate mixed residence in the interior even in exchange for the abolition of extraterritoriality.

57. At the end of 1882 the Quai d'Orsay had itself endorsed Tricou's reservations on these points. C.C.Tokyo, II *bis*, 24 November 1882. It informed Tokyo of its changed attitude in July. C.P. Japon. XXIX. 6 July 1883. Challemel-Lacour to Viel-Castel. See also *JKKNGB*, Vol. II, documents 292–302, pp. 918–969. The latter consist mainly of reports by Hachisuka and Marshall, in one of which it is stated that the change of attitude was only arrived at after the Commercial Department of the Quai d'Orsay was subjected to considerable pressure by the Political Department. *Ibid.* p. 924. Nothing of this dispute is visible in the French archives, unfortunately.

58. Britain had moved further from its late 1870s position than had France up to this point and had, in the 1882 preliminary Revision conferences in Tokyo, collaborated with Germany in the drafting of a tariff project which would have gone some way towards meeting Japanese demands for higher import duties. However, commercial expediency dictated that such concessions should go only so far, and in a circular of 16 April 1882, the British government attempted to secure the prior agreement of the Powers to the proposal that the new treaties should be unlimited in duration. *Ibid.* p. 922.

59. *Joyaku Kaisei Keika Gaiyo*, p. 203. It was claimed at the time by Marshall that the French attitude had stimulated the German action also. *JKKNGB,* II. p. 929. Marshall to Ito. 19 July 1883.

60. *Ibid.* p. 832. Mori to Inoue, via Hanabusa. 13 December 1883.

61. See the dispatch of 7 July 1883, from Challemel Lacour to Comte d'Aunay, French chargé d'affaires in London. 19 July 1883, Marshall to Ito, Enclosure I. *Ibid.* pp. 933–5. From a talk between Marshall and Clavery, the Commercial Director at the Quai d'Orsay, it would seem that the main reason for the swift appearance of second thoughts was the hostility of the Commercial Department, which had immediate control over Revision policy. 5 October 1883, Hachisuka to Inoue. 5 October 1883. Enclosure. *Ibid.* pp. 974–8.

62. *Ibid.*

63. C.C.Tokyo, III, 30 December 1883, Sienkiewicz to Ferry.

64. *Ibid.*

65. Sienkiewicz was not sent full powers to take part in a Revision conference until Inoue agreed. For the various stages of the diplomatic interchanges see C.P.Japon, XXIX, 3 December 1883; C.P.Japon, 3 May 1884; C.C.Tokyo, III, 9 June 1884; *Ibid.* July 11, 1884; *Ibid.* 31 July 1884. *Ibid.* 22 August 1884. C.C.Tokyo, IV, 13 December 1884. *Ibid.* 15 December 1884; *Ibid.* 18 December 1884; *Ibid.* 19 December 1884; *Ibid.* 28 January 1885; *Ibid.* 13 February 1885; *Ibid.* 17 February 1885; *Ibid.* 4 May 1886; *Ibid.* 6 May 1886; *Ibid.* 19 May 1886; *Ibid.* 28 May 1886. See also *JKKNGB,* II, pp. 1027–1073.

66. C.C.Tokyo, IV, 9 June 1886, Sienkiewicz to Freycinet. The declaration was made on 8 June in reply to a question from Sienkiewicz. Since, however, the negotiations broke down in the following year and the old import tariff remained in force, the silk export duty was not removed after all.

67. C.P.Japon, XXX, 31 July 1884., Sienkiewicz to Ferry.

68. For Sienkiewicz's reasoning, see C.C.Tokyo, III, 25 May 1884, Sienkiewicz to Ferry. In reality, a working understanding proved impossible to achieve, but the idea persisted for several years.

69. C.P.Japon, XXXII, 4 August 1886, Sienkiewicz to Freycinet. The Quai d'Orsay expressed identical feelings later the same month. C.C.Tokyo, V, 27 August 1886. Freycinet to Sienkiewicz. It should perhaps be added that no Power could maintain

a completely independent position both because of the difficulties its nationals might face in Japan and because, as Marshall observed in 1883, the European Powers 'have always regarded the revision of the treaties with Japan as a question which concerns them collectively, as an element of the dealings of Europe with Asia'. *JKKNGB*, Vol.II, p. 992.

70. C.P.Japon, XXXII, 28 January 1886; C.C.Tokyo, IV, 30 January 1886. Both Sienkiewicz to Freycinet.

71. See eg. C.P.Japon, XXIX, 9 February 1884, Sienkiewicz to Ferry; C.C.Tokyo, IV, 29 August, 1885, Sienkiewicz to Freycinet.

72. C.C.Tokyo, IV, 16 May 1886, Sienkiewicz to Freycinet. Foreign minister Freycinet telegraphed that Japanese laws could only be made applicable if first approved by the Powers. *Ibid.* 21 May 1886.

73. C.C.Tokyo, IV, 24 June 1886, Sienkiewicz to Freycinet.

74. C.C.Tokyo, IV, 30 June 1886, Sienkiewicz to Freycinet.

75. C.C.Tokyo, V, 28 December 1886, Sienkiewicz to Flourens.

76. C.C.Tokyo, V, 30 January 1887, Sienkiewicz to Flourens.

77. C.C.Tokyo, V, 22 March 1887, Sienkiewicz to Flourens.

78. Inoue had kept his negotiations secret even from Yamada, the minister of justice. See Shimomura, 'Joyaku Kaisei', p. 82. It is generally agreed that the source of the original leakage was Boissonade, who objected to the employment of foreign judges in Japanese courts and the necessity for seeking foreign approval for legal codes which were primarily designed to suit Japan. Although his hostility may have derived from resentment at the idea of his own work being tampered with, he was able to present an argument which was convincing to several members of the government. His memorandum on the subject can be found in Yoshino Sakuzo (ed.), *Meiji Bunka Zenshu* , VI, *Gaiko-hen*, (Tokyo, 1928), pp. 447- 471. It was secretly published and, together with the memorandum of Tani Kanjo, an oligarch from Tosa who resigned from the government over this issue, provided the opposition with useful ammunition against Inoue's proposals. See Inoue Kiyoshi, *Joyaku Kaisei*, pp. 112–117.

79. Most of the leaders of the earlier opposition parties, plus some right-wing nationalists, came together briefly under the nominal leadership of Goto Shojiro in the *Daido Danketsu*. See *Ibid.* pp. 119–138.

80. The first alternative was forcefully propounded in Tani's lengthy memorandum, which he presented to the Emperor on 9 August 9 (and which was translated by the French legation). C.P.Japon, XXXIII, 22 January 1888, Bourgarel to Flourens. The demand for unilateral denunciation was made many times by Japanese newspapers, (Chang, *op. cit.*), but in the late 1880s it was not taken seriously by diplomats. See eg. C.P.Japon, XXX, 1 May 1884, Sienkiewicz to Ferry; also C.C.Tokyo, VI, 12 January 1889, in which Sienkiewicz informed foreign minister Goblet that 'Often, colleagues to whom I expressed, at the time of the [1886–7] conference, my fears for the future, replied to me that the Powers had guns and knew how to use them' .

81. It was stated by Sienkiewicz in 1889 that Ito had been deeply involved in Inoue's resignation just as in that of Okuma later. 'From all these complications that which emerges in the clearest way, is the objective pursued by Count Ito. In 1886, he lent his whole support to the treaty revision plans worked out by Count Inoue. This same support he did not haggle about with Count Okuma. But in the one case as in the other, this support was transformed into an opposition as tenacious as it was disguised, at the precise moment when the serious difficulties which were obstructing the conclusion of new treaties appeared to be disappearing'. C.C.Tokyo, VI, 1 November 1889. Whether Ito's actions were due to fear of being overshadowed by a foreign minister who achieved treaty revision, as Sienkiewicz insinuated, or whether they should be attributed to his sensitivity to the changing mood of public opinion, must remain an open question.

82. C.C.Tokyo, IV, 29 August 1885, Sienkiewicz to Freycinet.
83. On 15 February 1889 Okuma informed Tanaka Fujimaro, the Japanese minister in Paris, that 'except for France the whole outlook is entirely favourable'. *Nihon Gaiko Bunsho*, XXII, p. 33.
84. See Kajima, *op. cit.*, pp. 247–8.
85. C.C.Tokyo, VI, 6 July 1889, Sienkiewicz to Spuller. He added, in what ironically resembled Okuma's earlier complaint, that 'besides the fact that this manner of negotiating wastes an enormous amount of time (each session lasts four or five hours), the idle discussions which thus arise in a stubborn manner are profoundly irritating and make possible at any time some grave incident'.
86. *Nihon Gaiko Bunsho*, XXII, p. 34.
87. Kajima, *op. cit.*, pp. 248–9; cf. C.C.Tokyo, VI, 13 March 1889; 4 May 1889, both Spuller to Sienkiewicz.
88. C.C.Tokyo, VI, 12 January 1889, Sienkiewicz to Goblet.
89. C.C.Tokyo, VI, 23 February 1889, Sienkiewicz to Goblet .
90. C.C.Tokyo, VI, 18 March 1889, Sienkiewicz to Spuller. The Quai d'Orsay had sent a telegram to Sienkiewicz two days earlier stating that 'The cabinet of London expresses to us the desire to know if our views accord with its. We will not be hasty in responding'. *Ibid.*
91. C.C.Tokyo, VI, 4 May 1889, Sienkiewicz to Spuller.
92. C.C.Tokyo, V, 18 May 1889, Sienkiewicz to Spuller.
93. *Ibid.*
94. This was first suggested by Sienkiewicz in March 1889. C.C.Tokyo, VI, 18 March 1889. It was confirmed in June by Spuller, when he instructed his Representative to concern himself 'principally with obtaining an advantageous treaty from the commercial point of view'. *Ibid.* 26 June 1889. It was frequently reiterated in succeeding years.
95. See C.C.Tokyo, VI, 23 February 1889, Sienkiewicz to Goblet; also C.C.Tokyo, IX, 30 March 1894, Casimir-Périer to Sienkiewicz.
96. C.C.Tokyo, VI, 27 July 1889, Spuller to Sienkiewicz.
97. C.C.Tokyo, VI, 21 July 1889, Sienkiewicz to Spuller.
98. C.C.Tokyo, VI, 1 August 1889, Spuller to Sienkiewicz; C.C.Tokyo, VI, 5 August 1889, Sienkiewicz to Spuller.
99. C.C.Tokyo, VI, 22 January 1890, Ribot to Sienkiewicz.
100. C.C.Tokyo, VII, 14 June 1890, Sienkiewicz to Ribot.
101. C.C.Tokyo, VII, 30 July 1890. Sienkiewicz to Ribot.
102. C.C.Tokyo, VI, 7 September 1889, Spuller to Sienkiewicz; *Ibid.*, 6 July 1889, Sienkiewicz to Spuller. The same claim was made later in the review of the history of treaty revision which prefaced Hanotaux's instructions to Harmand in 1894. C.P.Japon, XXXIX, 9 June 1894. See also Kajima, *op. cit.*, pp. 250–51.
103. There were some brief exchanges between Aoki and Sienkiewicz at the start of 1890, between Enomoto and Collin de Plancy in January 1892, and between Mutsu and Sienkiewicz in March 1894. See C.C.Tokyo, VI, 7 March 1890; C.C.Tokyo, VII, 25 March 1890; C.C.Tokyo, VIII, 17 January 1892; C.C.Tokyo, IX, 18 May 1894.
104. C.C.Tokyo, IX, 17 August 1894, Harmand to Hanotaux.
105. *JKKNGB*, IV, p. 718, 7 March 1895, Mutsu to Sone. Sone was Japanese minister in Paris, where the bulk of the arduous negotiations eventually took place. They can be followed in some detail in *Ibid.* pp. 653–818.
106. The Quai d'Orsay believed that it had received a raw deal over the 1893 naval orders. C.P.Japon, XXXIX, 9 June1894, Hanotaux to Harmand.
107. In November 1895, Harmand made known to the foreign and navy ministers that France would consider that it had been badly treated if it did not receive its share of

the coming orders. Until this point, he wrote to Hanotaux, he had hesitated to 'make the Minister himself understand more clearly that I could envisage a certain correlation between the signing of the treaty and the orders for naval material to be given to French industry'. C.C.Tokyo, X, 14 November 1895. The Quai d'Orsay itself raised the question in January 1896 with Sone, who stated that such matters could only be dealt with in Tokyo. In a telegram to Tokyo he observed that 'if French Government be assured of one at least of ship-building orders, I think it would be easy to conclude the treaty; otherwise it is very difficult to come to understanding without making concessions'". *JKKNGB,* IV, p. 758, 15 January 1896, Sone to Saionji.

108. C.P.Japon, XLV, 23 April 1896, Harmand to Hanotaux.
109. C.C.Tokyo, X, 19 June 1896. No further details are given. It seems likely that the orders concerned the cruiser *Azuma,* launched in 1899, or four Normand torpedo-boats completed the same year. These were the only ships purchased from French yards between 1895 and 1904. See F. T. Jane, *The Imperial Navy of Japan,* (London, 1904), pp. 195–6.
110. The text of the new treaty, together with its protocol and tariff schedule, can be found in *JKKNGB,* IV, pp. 790–804. There was no debate in the Chamber of Deputies; in the Senate a postponement motion was defeated by 163 to 78. A report of the debate, in which some Senators complained about the tariff agreement, can be found in *Journal Officiel de la République Française,* 1897, XII, pp. 1479–82.
111. 'It is when it claims to be setting out seriously on the way of progress, when it boasts of an unreservedly liberal policy . . . it is at that moment that one sees it refuse, without avowable reason, to merchants, to manufacturers, to foreign travellers, the authorization to go further than six leagues into the interior'. C.P.Japon, XXII, 27 July 1875, Berthemy to Broglie. Berthemy's indignation was not shared by all French diplomats, but his manner of reasoning was. Only fleetingly did any feeling that advantage had been take of Japan appear, and this feeling was confined to the tariff question.
112. C.P.Japon, XXXIX, 9 June 1894.
113. C.P.Japon, XXIV, 4 January 1874, Berthemy to Decazes.
114. C.C.Tokyo, X, 19 January 1895, Harmand to Hanotaux.
115. C.C.Tokyo, IX, 2 April 1893, Sienkiewicz to Develle.

CHAPTER 7

1. C.P.Japon, XXXI, 19 June 1885, Sienkiewicz to Freycinet.
2. See Chapter V, note 122.
3. C.P.Japon, XXXI, 8 October 1885 and15 November 1885, Sienkiewicz to Freycinet.
4. *Ibid.,* XXXI, 1 March 1886, Sienkiewicz to Freycinet.
5. *Ibid.* A rather more favourable appreciation was forthcoming three years later when the Meiji leaders were acknowledged to have expanded education, developed the country's resources and restored the finances. *Ibid.,* XXXIV, 4 February 1889, Sienkiewicz to Goblet.
6. *Ibid.,* XXXI, 15 August 1885, Sienkiewicz to Freycinet.
7. *Ibid.,* 8 October 1885.
8. *Ibid.,* XXXII, 26 January 1886, Sienkiewicz to Freycinet.
9. *Ibid. ,* XXXIII, 31 March 1888, Bourgarel to Goblet.
10. *Ibid.,* XXXIV, 4 December 1890, Sienkiewicz to Ribot. In his next sentence Sienkiewicz made the interesting suggestion that 'for many years England has worked to bring about this union which Russia seeks to prevent by all the means in its power'.
11. *Ibid.,* XXXV, 25 July 1896, Sienkiewicz to Ribot. Sienkiewicz noted that the

Chinese minister in Tokyo had been active in trying to establish a Sino-Japanese entente, but the French minister thought that such an entente would not be easily achieved.

12. *Ibid.*, 14 October 1891.
13. *Ibid.*, XXXVIII., 27 July 1893, Sienkiewicz to Develle.
14. *Ibid.*, 11 August 1893.
15. *Ibid.*
16. *Ibid.*, XLI, 12 November 1894, Harmand to Hanotaux. The concern expressed here about Japanese spying was to be a regular theme in Harmand's reports, and he more than once expressed his suspicions of Japanese ambitions in or around Indochina.
17. *Ibid.*, XLIII, 3 May 1895, Harmand to Hanotaux.
18. *Ibid.*, XXIV, 10 April 1890, Sienkiewicz to Ribot.
19. *Ibid.*, XXVIII, 3 October 1893, Sienkiewicz to Develle.
20. *Ibid.*, XXXIX., 4 January 1894, Sienkiewicz to Casimir-Périer.
21. *Ibid.* , XXXI, 15 November 1885, Sienkiewicz to Freycinet.
22. *Ibid.* , XXXIV, 4 February 1889, Sienkiewicz to Goblet.
23. *Ibid.*, XXXV, 2 July 1891, Sienkiewicz to Ribot.
24. *Ibid.*
25. *Ibid.*, XXXIV, 20 September 1890, Sienkiewicz to Ribot.
26. *Ibid.*, XXXV, 10 April, 1891, Sienkiewicz to Ribot.
27. *Ibid.*, XXXVIII, 24 March 1893, Sienkiewicz to Develle.
28. *Ibid.*, XXXIX, 3 July, 1894, Dubail to Hanotaux.
29. *Ibid.*, XXXII, 21 May 1886, Freycinet to Sienkiewicz.
30. *Ibid.*, XLI, 30 November 1894, Harmand to Hanotaux.
31. *Ibid.*, XXXIII, 1 April 1887.
32. *Ibid.*, XXXV, 9 February 1892, Collin de Plancy to Ribot.
33. *Ibid.*, 24 February 1892.
34. *Ibid.*, XLIV, 5 August 1895, Enclosure in Harmand to Hanotaux. In the intervening period French feeling fluctuated, reaching a low point in1892 when chargé d'affaires Collin de Plancy lamented that German influence had continued to expand and that the pro-German mood in the army had 'even reached such a point that in certain garrisons the free courses in French which had been instituted are no longer followed, so great is the fear of displeasing superior officers or generals imbued with German ideas'. *Ibid.*, XXXVI, 22 January 1892. The mood of pessimism briefly lifted in August 1894, when Harmand felt able to comment on 'the changes, favourable to our influence, which have recently been produced in the personnel of the Japanese military schools', with the ex-military attaché in France, Colonel Ikeda, replacing a German officer at the Staff College and Prince Kanin becoming a teacher at the Tokyo cavalry school in place of a German-trained officer. *Ibid.*, XL, 23 August, 1894. In contrast to this, a report of June 1895 on the French language by François, a teacher at the Military Academy, contained the depressing information that four or five times as many young military students were opting for German in preference to French. François attributed this to 'the conviction brought back from Europe that the organisation of the German army is superior to that of the French', a conviction which received further support from 'the German-style adjustments made to the work of the French military missions under the inspiration of the German teachers or military counsellors who succeeded them'. *Ibid.*, XLIII, 13 June 1895.
35. *Ibid.*, XXXII, 8 October 1886, Enclosure in Sienkiewicz to Freycinet.
36. *Ibid.* See Presseisen, *Before Aggression*, p. 95.
37. C.P.Japon, XXXIII, 7 July 1887, Bourgarel to Flourens.
38. *Ibid.*, 9 August 1887.
39. *Ibid.*, 6 May 1888. Another, albeit more tangential, reason for favouring Satsuma

was that Matsukata Masayoshi, who hailed from that domain and was Meiji Japan's most renowned Finance Minister, openly acknowledged an intellectual debt to Léon Say, describing himself as the celebrated French economist's pupil and friend. *Ibid.,* XXXV, 9 May 1891, Sienkiewicz to Ribot.

40. *Ibid.,* XLIV, 6 September 1895, Harmand to Hanotaux. Some support for the view that Ito was anti-French may be found in a later dispatch in which Harmand complained that 'of all the Japanese ministers he is the only one who shows towards me a reserve which goes as far as coldness'.. *Ibid.,* XLV, 21 February 1896.

41. *Ibid.,* XLVI, 30 October 1896, Harmand to Hanotaux.

42. *Ibid.,* XXXI, 26 October 1885, Freycinet to Sienkiewicz.

43. *Ibid.,* XXXIV, 8 May 1889, Sienkiewicz to Spuller.

44. *Ibid.,* XXXVI, 25 January 1892, Collin de Plancy to Ribot.

45. *Ibid.,* XLV, 3 April 1896, Harmand to Berthelot.

46. *Ibid.,* XLI, 27 December 1894, Harmand to Hanotaux. It is significant that this, like the previous comment, dates from the mid-1890s, by which time French diplomats were also beginning to pay regular attention to Japanese comments about France. By 1895 they were sending to the Quai d'Orsay a fortnightly review of the Japanese press.

47. Presseisen, *op.cit.,* pp. 59, 133–4 . The post was revived in June 1893, however.

48. C.P.Japon, XXVIII, 4 May 1882., Conte to Freycinet . Conte did, though, warn that strong German tendencies existed in both the army and the government.

49. *Ibid.,* XXIX, 5 February 1883, Tricou to Challemel-Lacour. Presseisen's statement that Tricou received Oyama's communication with extreme reserve (*op. cit.,* p. 97) is presumably based on the French minister's statement that he had 'received this communication with a very discreet courtesy in order neither to give umbrage to my German colleague nor to discourage dispositions from which we may be able, depending on developments, draw some profit'. The impression he gives, however, is clearly misleading.

50. C.P.Japon, XXIX, 30 March 1883, Tricou to Challemel-Lacour.

51. *Ibid.,* 17 July 1883, Viel-Castel to Challemel-Lacour.

52. *Ibid.,* 21 November 1883, Sienkiewicz to Ferry.

53. *Ibid.,* 29 January 1884. Sienkiewicz explained the international rivalry for influence in Japan by suggesting that 'in the conflicts which, at a given moment, will arise in the Far East, Japan is called to play, thanks to the warlike spirit of its population, a conspicuous role'.

54. *Ibid.,* XXX, 17 April 1884, Sienkiewicz to Ferry. Oyama sought to sweeten the pill by saying that he proposed to ask for a French lieutenant-colonel for the Staff College later.

55. *Ibid.* When Oyama returned from Europe the following year, he offered the excuse that the decision to employ a German officer had been taken by the government after he had left on the grounds that 'France being a very rich country can have a very costly military organisation while Germany, a poor country, has a more economical organisation which better accords with the feeble resources of Japan'. However exaggerated the language, it may have reflected the fact that France still to some extent clung to the idea of a professional army even though it had had to to adopt conscription. *Ibid.,* XXXI, 4 February 1885, Sienkiewicz to Ferry.

56. *Ibid.,* XXX, 17 April 1884, Sienkiewicz to Ferry.

57. *Ibid.,* 28 July 1884, Ferry to Sienkiewicz.

58. *Ibid.,* XXXIII, 7 July 1888, Bourgarel to Goblet; 25 September 1888, Sienkiewicz to Goblet.

59. *Ibid.* Berthaut's upgraded role seems to have owed much to the encouragement of Prince Komatsu, the head of the Military Academy, and General Miura, his predecessor in that position. *Ibid.,* XXXII, 8 October 1886, enclosure by Bougouin in Sienkiewicz to Freycinet.

60. *Ibid.*, 1 March 1886.
61. *Ibid.*, XXXIII, 28 June 1888, Bourgarel to Goblet.
62. *Ibid.*, 7 July 1888.
64. *Ibid.*, 13 September 1888, Goblet to Sienkiewicz. Telegram.
65. *Ibid.*, 25 September 1888, Sienkiewicz to Goblet.
66. *Ibid.*, 27 November 1888, Sienkiewicz to Goblet.
67. *Ibid.*, 19 December 1888.
68. *Ibid.*, 15 December 1888; 27 November 1888. That this was a considered view was shown by Sienkiewicz's reiteration of it a month later: 'The Japanese are, moreover, under no illusions as to what this means; they have seen it as nothing but a disguised dismissal'. He clearly felt that the Japanese officers in France would decline to make the 'somewhat humiliating' formal requests to stay which he proposed to the French government. *Ibid..*, 27 December 1888.
69. *Ibid.*, XXXIV, 23 February 1889, the head of the Quai d'Orsay Political Department to Sienkiewicz. Sienkiewicz was also told that, contrary to his advice, Yamagata had been allowed to visit French military establishments: 'It would hardly have been politic to keep at a distance a general for whom, I believe, a very eager welcome is reserved in Germany and Italy'.
70. *Ibid.*, LXIV, 5 August 1895, enclosure by military attaché Lieutenant de Labry in Harmand to Hanotaux. In 1894 Sienkiewicz laid the blame for this on the Japanese military attaché in Paris and absolved himself from all responsibility. *Ibid.*, XXXIX, 2 February 1894, Sienkiewicz to Casimir-Périer. The figures, however, suggest that the damage was done in late 1888 when Sienkiewicz's attitude was rather different.
71. *Ibid.*, XXXIV, 12 February 1890, Sienkiewicz to Spuller. Telegram.
72. *Ibid.*, 24 February 1890, Spuller to Sienkiewicz; *Ibid. ,* 12 June 1890, Ribot to Sienkiewicz.
73. *Ibid.*, XXXV, 2 January 1891, Sienkiewicz to Ribot. Telegram.
74. *Ibid.*, 4 January 1891. It is worth noting that Sienkiewicz went so far as to approach some supposedly friendly members of the newly instituted Diet in the hope that the allocation for the employment of the German military instructor might be eliminated from the budget, but he was informed that this was beyond the Diet's powers.
75. *Ibid.*, 20 March 1891, Ribot to Sienkiewicz.
76. See Presseisen, *op. cit.*, pp. 106–112.
77. See *Les Missions Catholiques,* 30 October 1885; also F. Marnas, *La Religion de Jesus au Japon,* Vol. II, pp. 509–17.
78. C.P.Japon, XXI, 14 September 1885, Sienkiewicz to Freycinet.
79. *Ibid.*
80. *Ibid.*, 20 October, 1885.
81. Ohata Kiyoshi & Ikado Fumio, (eds.), *Japanese Religion in the Meiji Era ,* (Tokyo, 1956). p. 212.
82. See, eg., Sumiya Mikio, 'Tenno-sei no kakuritsu to Kirisutokyo', in Ienaga Saburo (ed.), *Minkenron kara Nashionarizumu e* (Vol. 4 of *Meiji-shi Kenkyu Sosho*) (Tokyo, 1956). In Sumiya's view the Meiji leaders regarded Christianity as 'critical of the foundation on which their power stood'. (p. 212). A similar argument had been advanced by Duchesne de Bellecourt with regard to the previous regime in 1863: 'The principles of Christianity alarm the Japanese upper classes more than anything, because they contain the principles of moral enfranchisement which seem to breach the bases of the feudal society of this country, where the subjection of the masses is justified by a sort of theology which accords a respectable primordial origin only to those who belong to the privileged classes'. Mémoires et Documents. Japon, I., 30 August 1863.

83. C.P.Japon, XXI, 14 September 1885, Sienkiewicz to Freycinet .
84. On the general question of the French religious protectorate, see Pierre Guillen, *L'Expansion 1881–1898* (Paris, 1984) pp. 35–40 and, more particularly, Louis Wei, *Le Saint Siège, la France et la Chine sous le pontificat de Léon XIII* (Schoneck/ Beckenried (Switzerland), 1966), and four articles by Albert Sohier in *Neue Zeitschrift fur Missionswissenschaft*: 'La nonciature pour Pékin en 1866', in XXIV, 2, (1968); 'Mgr. Alphonse Favier et la protection des mission en Chine (1870– 1905)' I and II, in XXV, 1, and XXV, 2., (1969); and 'La diplomatie Belge et la protection des missions en Chine', in XXIII, 4, (1967).
85. Marnas. *op. cit.*, pp. 512–13.
86. C.P.Japon, XXXI, 14 September 1885, Sienkiewicz to Freycinet.
87. *Ibid.*
88. Quoted in Wei, *op. cit.* p. 31.
89. C.P.Japon, XXI, 14 September 1885, Sienkiewicz to Freycinet.
90. *Ibid.*
91. *Ibid.*, 20 November 1885, Freycinet to Sienkiewicz.
92. See Wei, *op. cit.*, p. 63–5.
93. C.P.Japon, XXXII, 12 February, 1886, Freycinet to Sienkiewicz.
94. *Ibid.*, 16 March 1886, Sienkiewicz to Freycinet.
95. *Ibid.*, 25 March 1886.
96. *Ibid.*, 28 March 1886.
97. *Ibid.* , 10 September 1886. On 5 November the Director of the Political Department of the Quai d'Orsay informed Sienkiewicz of developments at the Vatican, and added: 'The importance of this result will not escape you. The traditional role of France is safeguarded, and our efforts have succeeded in preventing a change the consequences of which could have been fatal to the maintenance of our position in the Far East'.
98. *Ibid.*, XXXIII, 27 December 1887, Bourgarel to Flourens.
99. *Ibid.*, 25 October 1888, Sienkiewicz to Goblet.
100. *Ibid.*, XXXIV, 9 February 1889, Goblet to Sienkiewicz.
101. *Ibid.*, 7 September 1889, Spuller to Sienkiewicz.
102. *Ibid.*, 1 December 1889.
103. Correspondance Commerciale. Yedo, III, 22 December 1864, Drouyn de Lhuys to Roches.
104. C.P.Japon, XXVI, 28 January, 1878; 13 January 1879 (both Geofroy to Waddington); XXVIII, 19 May 1882, Conte to Freycinet.
105. *Ibid.*, XXXI., 14 September 1885, Sienkiewicz to Freycinet. He had tried, he wrote, to do this earlier but had found on the part of Osouf's deputy, Midon, 'a narrow mind incapable of understanding the reciprocal services which the missionaries can render on the one hand and the protecting power on the other'.
106. *Ibid.*, XXXII, 17 October 1866, Sienkiewicz to Freycinet.
107. *Ibid.*, XXXIII, 12 April 1887, Sienkiewicz to Flourens.
108. *Ibid.*, XXXIV, 1 December 1889, Sienkiewicz to Spuller.
109. *Ibid.; Ibid.* , XXV, 4 September 1891., Sienkiewicz to Ribot. There was also some teaching of French in non-specialised, higher-level, institutions, such as the Imperial University and the Army Staff College.
110. Arrivet also, according to Sienkiewicz, disregarded the fact that the *École de langue française* had only 33 students in 1891 compared with 140 in 1887, that its subvention from the Japanese government had been eliminated from the budget by the newly established Diet, and that it was only surviving through the aid of the Alliance Française. *Ibid.*
111. *Ibid.* Arrivet criticised the Marianites for occupying themselves with the very young, for not giving them access to a 'liberal career', and for being concerned

primarily with the success of a lucrative business operation rather than the development of the study of French. Sienkiewicz defended them by pointing out that the establishment of their school had cost 250,000 yen (which they would not recoup for a long time), by suggesting that they would send students to the prestigious Higher School, and by emphasising the school's French character even though it also taught English: 'what makes the Marianites' school indeed a French school is that the courses are given in the French language'. By 1891 it had 18 teachers and 86 pupils, of whom 36 were Japanese, 23 European, and 27 of mixed blood (*Ibid.*) and by 1895 the number of pupils had risen to 180 (Marnas, *op. cit.* pp. 552–3). In 1891 a second Marianite school – the *Kaisei gakko* – was set up in Nagasaki. In the same year Ribot granted the Marianites a subvention of 500 francs at Sienkiewicz's request. C.P.Japon, XXXIV, 20 December 1890, Sienkiewicz to Ribot; *Ibid.*, XXXV, 28 February, 1891, Ribot to Sienkiewicz.

112. *Ibid.*, 20 September 1891, Sienkiewicz to Ribot.
113. *Ibid.*, XXXVI, 5 April 1892, Collin de Plancy to Ribot.
114. *Ibid.* , XXXVII, 4 August 1892, Ribot to Collin de Plancy.
115. *Ibid.*, XXXIX, 20 March 1894, Sienkiewicz to Casimir-Périer. *Ibid.*, XXXIX, 23 June 1894, Hanotaux to Harmand.
116. *Ibid.*, XL, 7 September 1894, enclosure in Harmand to Hanotaux. Revon expressed regret that when education minister Enomoto in 1890 had reversed an 1886 decision by his predecessor (Mori Arinori) and had reinstated French in secondary education 'we lacked pupils in the private schools and we were unable to supply to the Higher Schools the contingent of students of French language which we ought to have sent to them'. He argued, however, that there was hope of success in creating French courses in the major Japanese schools because he himself had achieved this 'at the special school of Waseda, the most important of all in practice, because it is the nursery of journalists and politicians'.
117. *Ibid.*, 25 October 1894.
118. *Ibid.*, XLII, 8 March 1895, enclosure in Harmand to Hanotaux.
119. *Ibid.*, Arrivet again criticised the *École de l'Étoile du Matin*, asserting that its teaching of Japanese language, literature and history was not good enough to attract Japanese pupils who wished to proceed to a Higher school and the University. He was no longer able to recommend support, however, for the *École de langue française* which had so declined that it had no more than 10 pupils.
120. *Ibid.*, XLII, 10 May 1895, Hanotaux to Harmand.
121. *Ibid.*, XLV, 10 January 1896, Harmand to Berthelot.
122. Official lack of support might easily be assumed to be due to the fact that the Quai d'Orsay annually underwent pressure from the French Chamber of Deputies to reduce its expenditures, which, leaving aside the extra credits which were generally required, amounted to 14, 228, 500 francs in 1890 and 15, 357, 800 francs in 1898 – with the Tokyo legation accounting for 55, 000 francs. There was indeed a stronger attempt to cut the Quai d'Orsay budget in 1894, but it is doubtful whether this would have been directed against a proposal to increase spending on cultural diplomacy. Pierre Guillen has observed that the motivation of 'affirming the influence of France, notably in the countries which were subject to international rivalries, . . . led the deputies to endow French activities abroad with ever more important credits', and that this part of the budget – which mainly consisted of subventions to educational establishments, hospitals and orphanages, and medical missions – rose more sharply than any other type of expenditure – from 250, 000 francs in 1880 to 800, 000 francs in 1898. Moreover, when the figure was increased by 100, 000 francs in 1898, it was because 'it appeared important to develop the influence of France in a new geographical area, the Far East, by giving subventions to schools and hospitals in China and Japan' (*op. cit.*, pp. 31–2). Tardiness rather

than inability to act would therefore seem to be a more plausible explanation of the limited support given to French studies in Japan in the period before 1898.

123. C.P.Japon, XXXIX, 3 April 1894, Sienkiewicz to Casimir-Périer.
124. *Ibid.*, XLII, 8 March 1895, enclosure in Harmand to Hanotaux.
125. *Ibid.*
126. *Ibid.*, XLV, 10 January 1895, Harmand to Berthelot.
127. *Ibid.*, XLIII, 13 June 1895, enclosure in Harmand to Hanotaux.
128. *Ibid.*
129. See *Ibid.*, XXXIII, 25 October 1888, Sienkiewicz to Goblet.
130. Sienkiewicz had already reported to Spuller on 1 December 1889 that 'recently, in particular, Russia has seemed to attach the greatest value to gaining the friendship and trust of the Japanese', and this passage had been marked in pencil at the Quai d'Orsay. *Ibid.*, XXXIV.
131. *Ibid.*, XXXV, 11 March 1891, Sienkiewicz to Ribot.
132. *Ibid.* XXXIX. 4 January 1894. Sienkiewicz to Ribot. An anonymous Quai d'Orsay 'note for the minister' on the eve of war also states that as France had no important interests in Korea, the initiative should be left to powers more directly concerned. *Ibid.*, XXXIX, 5 July 1894.
133. *Ibid. ,* 29 July 1894, Harmand to Hanotaux.
134. *Documents Diplomatiques Français,* 1st series, XI, p. 216, 10 August 1894, Harmand to Hanotaux. By the winter Harmand was showing a clear desire for the war to continue, explicable partly by the hope that the conquest of Taiwan by Japan would lead to Britain's seizure of a Chinese island, which 'would authorise us immediately, and in the most favourable circumstances that one can imagine, to make good one of the most regrettable omissions of our Indo-China enterprise and guard against one of the greatest dangers which threaten our domination in Tongking. I speak of the island of Hainan'. This passage was marked by the Quai d'Orsay. C.P.Japon, XLI, 30 November 1894, Harmand to Hanotaux.
135. Quoted in G. Lensen, *Balance of Intrigue,* 2 vols., (Tallahassee. 1982), I, p. 204.
136. *Ibid.,* p. 197.
137. *Ibid .,* p. 205.
138. *Ibid.* p. 212–3. See also C.P.Japon, XLII., 29 January 1895, Hanotaux to Harmand, Telegram; *Ibid.,* 1 February 1895, Harmand to Hanotaux. Telegram.
139. *Ibid.,* 22 February 1895.
140. *Documents Diplomatiques Français,* 1st series, XI, pp. 668–70.
141. *Ibid.,* p. 672, Minute on Herbette (Berlin) to Hanotaux.
142. See Lensen, *op. cit.,* pp. 291–2.
143. C.P.Japon, XLII.
144. *Ibid.,* 21 April 1895, Harmand to Hanotaux, Telegram.
145. *Ibid. ,* 20 April 1895, Hanotaux to Harmand. Telegram.
146. *Ibid.,* 23 April 1895, Harmand to Hanotaux. Telegram. At the Quai d'Orsay a question mark was pencilled in against Harmand's last words.
147. Harmand later sent a more detailed report in which one can detect a sense of grievance at Hanotaux's diplomacy: 'I possessed not the slightest indication to guide my conduct and was reduced to purely individual conjectures on the motives of general policy which in this situation guided the government of the Republic'. *Ibid.,* XLIII, 2 May 1895, Harmand to Hanotaux.
148. *Ibid.,* XLII.
149. See the two telegrams sent by Harmand to Hanotaux on 29 April and his further telegram of 30 April. *Ibid.*
150. *Ibid.,* XLIII, 1 May 1895, Harmand to Hanotaux. Telegram.
151. *Ibid. ,* 1 May 1895, Hanotaux to Harmand. Telegram.
152. *Ibid.,* 1 May 1895, Beaumont to Navy Minister. Telegram.

153. *Ibid.*, 3 May 1895. (marked 'réservé').
154. *Ibid.*
155. *Ibid.*, 4 May 1895, Hanotaux to Harmand. Telegram; memorandum from Sone, 5 May 1895.
156. See *Documents Diplomatiques Français*, 1st series, XI, p. 553, 15 March 1895, Hanotaux to Montebello (St. Petersburg); pp. 668–70. 9 April 1895, Hanotaux to Vauvineux (St. Petersburg); Lensen, *op. cit.* p. 297; see also the telegram which was not sent to St. Petersburg on 3 May 1895. C.P.Japon, XLIII.
157. *Ibid.*, 25 May 1895, Hanotaux to Harmand. Telegram.
158. Lensen, *op. cit.* pp. 326–8.
159. *Ibid.*, pp. 331–2.
160. C.P.Japon, XLIII, 14 June 1895, Harmand to Hanotaux.
161. *Ibid.*, 19 July 1895. Telegram.
162. *Ibid.*, XLII, 11 January 1895, Harmand to Hanotaux.
163. *Ibid.*, XLIII, 25 May 1895, Harmand to Hanotaux.
164. *Ibid.*, 13 July 1895.
165. *Ibid.*, XLVI, 25 June 1896, Harmand to Hanotaux.
166. *Ibid.* , XLIII, 13 July 1895, Harmand to Hanotaux.

CHAPTER 8

1. A rare exception is to be found in the official publication *Annales du Commerce Extérieur: Chine et Indochine,* (1855–1867), No. 24, (March 1857), where a report dated 28 July 1855 by A. Heurtier states: 'The information which I have gleaned on the islands of Japan attributes to them a population numerically equal to that of France, and more energetic, more enterprising, more ingenious and more warlike than that of the Celestial Empire. It is supposed to be in possession of great agricultural riches and to be dedicated to a very active internal commerce'.
2. See the report by the Vicomte de la Tour du Pin to Bellecourt, which claimed that 25% should be added to official figures to get something like a true picture. C.C.Yédo, 2 June 1861, Bellecourt to Thouvenel. This was still the case in 1876. C.C.Yédo, VI, 15 July 1876, St. Quentin to Decazes.
3. C.P.Japon, II, 24 March 1860, Bellecourt to Thouvenel.
4. C.P.Japon, II, 15 June 1860, Bellecourt to Thouvenel. To prevent the French 'concession' being lost to France by French speculators who had no intention of trading permanently but only wished to take advantage of the high prices likely to develop, Bellecourt stipulated that Frenchmen could only sell this land to other Frenchmen. *Ibid.* This measure produced much dissatisfaction among French traders and was dropped by Roches in 1865. See C.P.Japon, V, 4 January 1862, Bellecourt to Thouvenel; C.C.Yédo, III, 29 November 1863, Bellecourt to Drouyn; C.C.Yédo, IV, 1 February 1865, Roches to Drouyn. On the treaty ports in general see J. Hoare, *Japan's Treaty Ports and Foreign Settlements: the Uninvited Guests 1858–1899,* (Folkestone, 1994).
5. C.C.Yédo, III, 29 October 1863, Bellecourt to Drouyn de Lhuys.
6. C.C.Yédo, III, 29 November 1863, Bellecourt to Drouyn de Lhuys.
7. C.C.Yédo, III, November 1863. Quai d'Orsay memorandum.
8. According to a *North China Herald* article reprinted in the *Moniteur des Soies* of 31 October 1863, the fact that Japan produced silk only became known about the middle of 1859.
9. C.C.Yédo, I, 24 May 1859; C.P.Japon, I, 8 June 1859.
10. See eg. C.C.Yédo, II, 1 February 1862, Bellecourt to Thouvenel. The import duty of 20% was blamed for the lack of success in selling *articles de Paris.*
11. *Ibid.* This was Bellecourt's estimate and also that given in *Annales du Commerce*

Extérieur: Chine et Indochine. No. 23 (although if customs declarations had been accurate, the figure would have been about 2, 160, 000 francs).

12. C.C.Yédo, II, 14 April 1863, Bellecourt to Drouyn de Lhuys. The official figure for exports was 1, 596, 987 francs, of which 1, 497, 135 francs were due to silk. In addition, a good deal of Japanese raw silk was bought by Frenchmen in London, where over 26 million francs' worth was imported in 1862. *Moniteur des Soies,* 2 January 1864.

13. The estimate was Roches'. C.C.Yédo, III, 1 September, Roches to Drouyn de Lhuys.

14. No figure is found for 1864 either in Roches' correspondence or in *Annales du Commerce Extérieur,* but it was probably smaller, for political reasons. The official figures for 1865 was 7, 967, 000 francs. *Annales du Commerce Extérieur: Chine et Indochine.* No. 45, January 1868. For 1866 the same source placed the total at 9, 885, 000 francs. *Ibid. Faits Commerciaux.* No. 45, June1870. The figures given here relate to goods destined for France (*Commerce spécial*), not just passing through France (*Commerce général*). The latter are usually substantially larger.

15. *Ibid.* Of this total, 11, 914, 000 francs came from raw silk.

16. *Ibid.* No.50. November, 1876 .

17. Another factor was the success of *Messageries Impériales* in diverting an increasing amount of silk destined for the European continent from London to Marseilles. As a result France received direct about 50% more raw silk than was sent to London by 1866–7, a very different proportion from that of earlier years. *Moniteur des Soies,* 12 October 1867.

18. *Annales du Commerce Extérieur: XLIII, Chine et Indo-Chine. Faits Commerciaux.* Nos. 45 & 50. They dropped to 10, 950, 550 francs in 1869 (*Ibid.* No. 48, November 1872), to 3, 083, 260 in 1874 (*Ibid.* No. 50), and in 1876 to only 150, 218 francs (*Ibid.* No. 51, February, 1879). See also *Moniteur des Soies,* 6 March 1869.

19. *Annales du Commerce Extérieur: XLIII, Chine et Indochine. Faits Commerciaux,* Nos. 40 & 45.

20. See C.P.Japon, XVII, 7 October 1868, Outrey to Moustier.

21. Cf. *Moniteur des Soies,* 12 October 1867, which reprinted (from the Marseilles paper, *Sémaphore*) a letter dated June 19, from an unnamed Frenchman at Yokohama in which the following appeared: 'there are, moreover, for French commerce, better opportunities than for that of other nations, because of the similarities of character between Japan and France, and also because of the political sympathies which seem to incline Japan towards France in preference to all other countries'.

22. I have used *Kindai Nihon Shi Jiten* (Dictionary of Modern Japanese History), compiled by the Kyoto Daigaku Bungakubu Kenkyushitsu (Tokyo, 1958).

23. *Annales du Commerce Extérieur, XLIII, Chine et Indo-Chine. Faits Commerciaux.* No.50. The editor of this official publication related the decrease in French trade to the effects of the Franco-Prussian War.

24. A sketch of the rise and decline of the silkworm egg trade can be found in *L'Echo du Japon* of 27 June 1879.

25. See the pamphlet by a French consular official, E. Clavery, *Les Etrangers au Japon et les Japonais à l'Etranger,* (Paris, 1904). The increase of Chinese exports of raw silk to France in this period, it should be added, was much greater. See S. Sugiyama, *Japan's Industrialisation in the World Economy, 1859–1899,* (London, 1988).

26. The value of woollen muslins imported from France rose from 971, 325 piastres (i.e. just under 5 million francs) in 1874 to 2, 393, 157 piastres (i.e. roughly12 million francs) in 1875, when they amounted to nearly 60% of total French imports to Japan. C.C.Yédo, VI, 15 July 1876, St. Quentin to Decazes.

27. These and the following figures are taken from *Nihon Kindai Shi Jiten, p. 386 .* The figures given (unlike those which I have previously cited from *Annales du*

Commerce Extérieur) are those for general commerce, which could be anything from 10% to 100% larger than those for special commerce, although 25% appears to be a rough average. It should be noted that the price level in France fell by about 40% between 1873 and 1896, to rise again by about the same amount between 1896 and 1914. Thus it can be seen that, except during the 1880s, the volume of French exports to Japan remained remarkably constant over the whole forty years.

28. This striking drop can be attributed in part to the effects of the Matsukata deflation, but also to the stagnation in France following the imposition of protective tariffs in 1881. See Y. Guyot, *Le Commerce et Les Commerçants* (Paris, 1909), pp. 357–359.

29. In 1873, for instance, France imported from Japan 20, 290, 256 francs' worth. *Annales du Commerce Extérieur, XLIII, Chine et Indo-Chine . Faits Commerciaux.* No.50, but its total imports amounted to 3, 600, 000, 000 francs (M. Block, *Statistique de la France* (Paris, 1875), Vol. II, pp. 282–294). Both figures relate to special commerce. Even in 1907, when Japanese exports to France had increased considerably, Japan with 83 million francs, figures only sixteenth on the list of countries supplying French imports, whereas China, with 212 million francs (special commerce), came eighth. Guyot, *op.cit.,* p. 380. Although France regularly sold more to Japan than to China, except in 1868 and 1869 this superiority was easily outweighed by the greater value of French imports from China.

30. C.C.Yédo, V, 7 January 1868, Roches to Moustier.

31. See G. Chapman, *The Third Republic of France* (London, 1962), p. 109.

32. C.C.Tokyo, IV, 9 October 1885, Freycinet to Sienkiewicz. Sienkiewicz was informed that the French company mentioned was sending a M. Jehenne to Japan.

33. C.P.Japon, XXXII, 9 July 1886, Sienkiewicz to Freycinet.

34. C.P.Japon, XXXVI, 26 January 1892, Collin de Plancy to Ribot. The fact that there was no greater representation in 1892 than in 1886 is surprising in the light of the request from the *Société Générale* in 1888 for the Quai d'Orsay's 'benevolent interest' in securing the inclusion on the list of possible suppliers, which the Japanese navy was supposed to be drawing up, of a newly established *Syndicat Industriel pour le Tonkin, l'Anname, la Cochinchine et le Japon*. C.C.Tokyo, V, 4 January 1888.

35. *Ibid.* Even this was less embarrassing than the case of the *Unebi*, a ship ordered earlier from France which disappeared without trace somewhere between Singapore and Japan. See C.P.Japon, XXXIII, 22 January 1887, Sienkiewicz to Flourens.

36. This is only hinted at in the correspondence between Paris and Tokyo but a clear admission can be found in a letter of 11 May 1896, from General Descharmes to General Chanoine. According to Descharmes, French companies charged 25% more than Armstrong's and took one or two years longer to build. See Chanoine, *op. cit.,* p. 178. This may not have been true for all categories. The order for the *Unebi* was won by the *Forges et Chantiers de la Mediterranée* partly because its tender was lower than Armstrong's, and partly because the Meiji government was uneasy at becoming dependent on Britain when that country had close ties with China, Japan's most immediate naval rival. Shinohara Hiroshi, *Kaigun Sosetsu Shi*, (Tokyo, 1986), pp. 305–7, 326.

37. See the report of July 10, 1886, by Rear Admiral Rieunier to the Ministry of Marine, which the latter sent to the Quai d'Orsay. C.P.Japon, XXXII, 26 August 1886. Sienkiewicz to Freycinet.

38. C.P.Japon, XXXVI, 26 January 1892, Collin de Plancy to Ribot; also C.P.Japon, XXXV, 5 June 1891, in which Sienkiewicz recommended the award in the following terms: 'I will add that we have that much more interest in making it in that there is a question of a very serious internal loan for the purpose of increasing the forces of the Japanese navy'. Though the Quai d'Orsay rejected the suggestion, the language which it used shows that it saw the problem in the same way: 'there is time to wait until he has given real proof of his feelings towards us'. Sienkiewicz was therefore

354

permitted to inform Kabayama of the possibility. C.P.Japon, XXVI, 17 September 1891, Ribot to Sienkiewicz. Kabayama had already, in 1889, been awarded the Cross of Commander of the Legion of Honour, having previously ordered a torpedo-boat destroyer, the *Chishima*, at a cost of 2 million francs. C.P.Japon, XXXIV, 6 July 1889, Sienkiewicz to Spuller.

39. See Chapter VI for details.
40. Otsuka, *Bakumatsu Gaiko Shi no Kenkyu*, p. 295.
41. *Ibid.* See also Ishii, *Gakusetsu Hihan Meiji Ishin Ron*, pp. 270–271.
42. See F.O.46, LIII, 28 February 1865, Winchester to Hammond (Private). Their suspicions became known to Roches, who chided his colleagues for them, but it is interesting that he neglected to inform Drouyn de Lhuys of the details of this misunderstanding. See C.P.Japon, XIII, 26 April, 1865. Roches to Drouyn.
43. C.C.Yédo, III, 1 September 1864, Roches to Drouyn de Lhuys.
44. C.C.Yédo, III, 9 November 1864, Roches to Drouyn de Lhuys.
45. C.P.Japon, XIII, 16 January 1865. Roches to Drouyn de Lhuys.
46. See F.O.46, LV, No.96, 7 June 1865., Winchester to Russell.
47. C.C.Yédo, IV, 11 September 1865, Roches to Drouyn de Lhuys. Whether or not this gift was provoked by Roches is uncertain. He himself claimed that it was a spontaneous act by the *Bakufu.* On the other hand, it is stated, more credibly, by Duseigneur in the *Moniteur des Soies* of 17 March 1866 that Roches asked for a second consignment at his prompting.
48. Winchester's suspicions appear in his private letter to Hammond of 27 April 1865, in F.O.46, LIV. See also the attack in the *Japan Herald*, which the Quai enclosed with a request to Roches for an explanation in C.C.Yédo, IV, 25 September 1866.
49. The main opponent was a Ulysse Pila, who, having secured silkworm eggs himself after much difficulty, resented government competition, as he regarded it, and was particularly aggrieved that Roches had not paid the 5% export duty. See *Moniteur des Soies*, 7 and 14 January, 1865.
50. *Moniteur des Soies*, 13 January 1865; 17 March 1866.
51. C.C.Yédo, III, 22 December 1864, Drouyn de Lhuys to Roches. The foreign minister's instruction not to intervene further was acknowledged by Roches in C.C.Yédo, I, 11 September 1865.
52. That he did not favour any restrictions may be inferred from his comment on the Bakufu edict of May 1866 which finally permitted silk to be brought direct to Yokohama without any transit duty. 'I consider it superfluous to stress the importance of this measure'. C.P.Japon, XIV, 27 May 1866, Roches to Drouyn de Lhuys.
53. C.C.Yédo, IV, 17 October 1865, Roches to Drouyn de Lhuys.
54. F.O.46, LIII, 28 February 1865. Winchester to Hammond (Private) .
55. *Ibid.*
56. *Ibid.* The *Moniteur des Soies* of 21 July 1866 contains a letter from a Swiss consular official in Japan, Ed. Schnell, who asserted that the Japanese decision to abandon its previous attempts to create a monopoly over the sale of silkworm eggs 'was more particularly the work of M. Léon Roches, this distinguished diplomat, to whom is largely owed the development of the closer relations which in recent years have been established between Japan and the Western powers'.
57. 'The silk merchants of Lyon, who disposed of the great part of their output abroad . . . were natural freetraders'. G. Chapman, *The Third Republic of France,* (London, 1962), p. 145.
58. F.O.46, VL, No.50, 23 August 1864, Alcock to Palmerston, Inclosure 17. (Roches to Prince of Choshu, 21 July 1864.)
59. C.C.Yédo, IV, 1 December 1865, Roches to Drouyn de Lhuys.
60. C.P.Japon, XIV, 24 April 1866, Drouyn de Lhuys to Roches; F.O.46, LXV, No.18, 31 January 1866, Parkes to Clarendon.

NOTES

61. See the minister of agriculture's report to the Emperor in the *Moniteur des Soies* of 22 July 1865.
62. C.C.Yédo, III, 16 October 1864. Roches to Drouyn de Lhuys. Duseigneur's opposition to the free opening of Japan to Europeans dealing in Japanese silkworm eggs is put forward in the *Moniteur des Soies* of 15 June 1867.
63. By F. Jacquemart, in a report for the *Société Impériale d'acclimatation* reprinted in the *Moniteur des Soies*, 18 March 1865. Drouyn de Lhuys was President of the Society.
64. C.C.Yédo, III, 22 December 1864, Drouyn de Lhuys to Roches.
65. *Moniteur des Soies.* 18 July 1863.
66. C.P.Japon, IX, 18 July 1863.
67. C.C.Yédo, II, 21 March 1863.
68. C.C.Yédo, VI, 20 July 1873, Broglie to Berthemy. Roquette requested it to do so again in 1882 (C.C.Yédo, II, 19 January 1882), but there is no record of this having been done. French merchants in Japan were asked for their views in 1879 by Balloy (*L'Echo du Japon*, 12 December 1879) and again in 1894 by Harmand (C.C.Tokyo, IX, 24 September1894, Harmand to Hanotaux) but little, if any, attention seems to have been paid to them. It should be noted, though, that Roches had had discussions with the Lyons chamber of commerce, mainly about the importance of Japanese silkworm eggs, before he went to Japan. *Moniteur des Soies*, 4 January 1865, Letter from E. Duseigneur.
69. C.P.Japon, XXVII, 14 September 1880, Balloy to Freycinet. However, St. Quentin did make a general and indirect response to the issue when he argued that Japan would be unable to reverse its unfavourable balance of trade unless it allowed foreign capital in to exploit the country's mineral resources. C.C. Yédo, VI, 15 July 1876, St. Quentin to Decazes.
70. C.C.Yédo, VI, 11 June 1870, Gramont to Outrey.
71. *Ibid.*, 30 September 1870, Outrey to Favre.
72. C.C.Tokyo, II, 28 October 1881. *Ibid.* 31 October 1881. Barthélemy St. Hilaire to Roquette. *Ibid.* Undated telegram, 3 or 4 November; *Ibid.* 7 November 1881. Both Roquette to Barthélemy St. Hilaire.
73. See Chapter VI.
74. C.C.Tokyo, X, 31 March 1897, Harmand to Hanotaux; *Ibid.* 22 July 1897, Harmand to Hanotaux; C.C.Tokyo, XI, 21 May 1898, Harmand to Hanotaux.
75. C.C.Yédo, III, 1 September 1864. Roches to Drouyn de Lhuys.
76. Enclosure in C.C. Yédo, II, 1 February 1862, Bellecourt to Thouvenel. See also Bourret's letter to the *Moniteur des Soies* of 18 February 1865.
77. *Ibid.*, 11 February 1865.
78. Quoted in *Moniteur des Soies*, 27 January 1866.
79. *Moniteur des Soies,* 8 July 1871. Production of cocoons in France had declined from 26, 000, 000 kilos in 1853 to 7, 500, 000 million kilos in 1856 and 4, 000, 000 kilos in 1865. 1866 saw a brief recovery to 6, 400, 000 kilos, but in 1867 an all-time low was reached with 3, 400, 000 kilos. The decline was then halted, but real recovery did not take place until 1871, when 7, 350, 300 kilos were produced. By the mid 1870s the average figure was a little more than 10, 000, 000 kilos. *Moniteur des Soies*, 24 June 1876.
80. Until overtaken by woollen goods in the mid-1870s it had been France's chief foreign currency earner, being worth between 400 million and 500 million francs annually. Chapman, *op.cit.* p. 145.
81. This was pointed out in a *L'Echo du Japon* article which was reprinted in the *Moniteur des Soies* of 8 July 1871. After deploring the deterioration in the quality of Japanese silk the writer expressed his 'astonishment that the Japanese merchants do not seem to have perceived the danger which they ran by selling, year after year,

356

such huge quantities of their best annual eggs to be sent to Europe. The Japanese eggs have powerfully aided France, Italy and other countries to preserve an industry which otherwise would have been ruined, but to the detriment of the products of this country itself'. The story of the relationship between the Japanese and French silk industries had an unexpected twist in 1876 when the French minister, St. Quentin, received a request from the commissioner for the development of Hokkaido, Kuroda Kiyotaka, for two cartons of French silkworm eggs (white and yellow) in order to discover whether the climate of the northern island suited them. C.C.Yédo, VI, 11 January 1876, St. Quentin to Decazes. Two years later St. Quentin's successor reported that the eggs, which had been subjected to a process devised by Pasteur, had proved successful and that Kuroda wished to know how expensive they were. C.C.Tokyo, I, 20 March 1878, Geofroy to Waddington.

82. Encouragement to set up modern filatures came from foreign traders. See e.g. *Moniteur des Soies*, 17 September 1870. Their introduction and spread provided the foundations for the even greater expansion of silk exports at the end of the century.

83. Although in general Japanese silk producers benefited from a buoyant market and sharply rising prices in the 1860s, prices tended to fluctuate thereafter and those who had over-extended themselves sometimes suffered. See, e.g., *Moniteur des Soies*, 4 November 1871; 8 May 1875, and *L'Echo du Japon*, 27 June 1879. See also an earlier letter in the *Moniteur des Soies* of 21 July 1867 which stated that some Japanese merchants committed suicide in 1866 on account of the over-supply of silkworm eggs.

CHAPTER 9

1. One French historian claimed that French officers 'at the cost of a labour and efforts to which one could not render too much homage, created Japan's first military institutions, formed its officer corps, taught its future victors in great wars what a European army is, how it is organized in peacetime, how it is mobilized in wartime, what tactics and strategy consist of; and in sum their work has lasted despite the modifications which the Japanese have since made to it'. V. de la Mazelière, *Le Japon, Histoire et Civilisation*, V, (Paris, 1910), p. 335.

2. See Chapter IV for details of Brunet's action.

3. Roches' request to Drouyn de Lhuys is in C.P. Japon, XIV, 15 February 1866. It was for nine officers and 26 other ranks and it was envisaged that they would instruct 1000 infantry, 650 artillery and 350 cavalry. The Minister of War, Marshal Randon, initially decided to send only three officers and ten non-commissioned officers on the ground that it was necessary to judge from experience whether the mission would be given sufficient support to carry out the services expected of it. At the Quai d'Orsay's request (following an appeal by Roches) he later agreed to add two more officers. M.D.Japon, I, 28 April 1866, Randon to Drouyn de Lhuys; *Ibid*, 26 October 1866, Randon to Moustier.

4. Captain Chanoine and Lieutenant Dubousquet had served in the French campaign in China in 1860, while Lieutenant Brunet had been involved more recently in the Mexican expedition. The most detailed account of this and the later French missions is Shinohara, *Rikugun Sosetsu Shi*. Shinohara, a journalist, made use of some Japanese sources not consulted by Presseisen in *Before Aggression*, and he also discovered the letters of Lebon, a captain in the second mission. Unfortunately he does not give references.

5. P. de Lapeyrère, *Le Japon Militaire* (Paris, 1883), p. 28. H. Kublin, 'The "Modern" Army of Early Meiji Japan', *Far Eastern Quarterly* (November 1949) gives a figure of 250.

6. In a memorandum written after his return to France, Chanoine wrote that in the fighting in early 1868 'the undisciplined bands of the Tycoon and of his supporters disappeared or defected as soon as fortune seemed to turn against that prince. This

example was not followed by the troop units taught and trained by the officers of the French mission at Yedo. With the exception of a battalion of 400 men who had been sent to the south in December 1867 and who returned in good order to Yedo in February 1868 after having, with the men of Aizu, defended almost alone the government of the Tycoon, the troops had had taken no part in the civil war'. M.D.Japon, I, April 1869.

7. General Lebon, who served in the second mission, placed particular importance on the presence of French-trained officers in the new Meiji forces in what was originally a speech, then an article in the *Revue d'Artillerie*, and finally a pamphlet, *Les Origines de l'Armée Japonaise* (Paris, 1898). Tajima figures prominently in Shinohara's previously cited book.

8. The evidence that Yamagata favoured the Prussian system is too strong to challenge, and the claim by his Choshu contemporary, General Miura Goro, (as recounted by Lebon in his *Souvenirs d'une ambassade extraordinaire au Japon* (Paris, 1913) that Yamagata resisted the German current in 1871 and was a staunch advocate of remaining 'faithful to the French army', is, like some of the statements in Miura's memoirs, unworthy of credence. Nevertheless, Shinohara (*op. cit.*, pp. 304–5) puts forward some plausible reasons for believing that Yamagata did not actively try to impose his own views.

9. Other arguments have been put forward, including the speculative suggestion by Lapeyrère (*op. cit.* p. 42) that Germany's reputation was undermined by its failure to challenge the French navy in Japanese waters in the 1870–71 war. More seriously, both Umetani, in *Meiji Zenki Seiji Shi no Kenkyu,* (Tokyo, 1963), pp. 116–121 and Shinohara, *op. cit.*, hold that France chose them partly because this was expected to achieve an early withdrawal of the French troops stationed in Yokohama. As Presseisen points out, however, (*op. cit.*, p. 39) the absence of any evidence in French records that the Meiji government sought to link these two matters makes this view unconvincing.

10. See Umetani Noboru, *O-Yatoi Gaikokujin: Seiji Hosei,* (Tokyo, 1971) pp. 48–56.

11. Umetani, *Meiji Zenki Seiji Shi no Kenkyu* , pp. 112–115, and Shinohara, *op. cit.,* pp. 319–226.

12. Umetani, *Meiji Zenki Seiji Shi no Kenkyu,* p. 112.

13. Shinohara, *op. cit.*, pp. 324–5.

14. *Ibid.*, pp. 366–7. See also Lapeyrère, *op. cit.*, p. 57.

15. T. R. H. Havens, *Nishi Amane and Modern Japanese Thought,* (Princeton, 1970), pp. 191–3.

16. These details are taken from Shinohara, *op. cit.*, pp. 298–301.

17. See Lebon, *Les Origines de l'Armée Japonaise,* and Shinohara, *op. cit.*, pp. 377–8.

18. Chanoine, *op. cit.*, p. 88.

19. *Ibid.*, p. 3.

20. Shinohara, *op. cit.*, pp. 382–400.

21. Shinohara, *op. cit.*, p. 442, notes that in his autobiography Katsura himself used the terms 'German faction' and 'French faction' and acknowledged his membership of the former. See Chapter VII for French diplomatic views of army factionalism in the 1880s and 1890s.

22. Chanoine, *op. cit.*, p. 157. The letter (to Chanoine) is dated 10 December 1879.

23. M.D.Japon, II, 2 July 1884.

24. See Chapter VII for details.

25. See the lists in *L'Echo du Japon,* 5 and 7 October 1877. The awards ranged from second to sixth class.

26. C.P.Japon, XXII, 22 April 1873; 20 January 1873, both Turenne to Rémusat.

27. C.P.Japon, XXVI, 15 April 1878, Geofroy to Waddington. He attributed the praise to the French officers' dignity in their deportment, their diligence.

28. R. Sieffert (ed.), *Le Japon et la France: Images d'une Découverte*, (Paris, 1974), p. 76; Shinohara, *op. cit.*, p. 371.
29. Lebon, *Les Origines de l'Armée Japonaise*.
30. *L'Echo du Japon*, 30 October 1877.
31. The figures come from a later military attaché's report, enclosed in C.P.Japon, LXIV, 5 August 1895, Harmand to Hanotaux. The peak years were 1887 and 1888, with fifteen and eighteen students respectively. Other military students certainly went to France before 1878, and some of their names can be found in Ishizuki Minoru, *Kindai Nihon no Kaigai Ryugaku Shi* (A History of Modern Japanese Overseas Study), (Tokyo, 1972). Among those who studied at St. Cyr was the later Army Minister and Prime Minister, Terauchi Masatake.
32. Their admiration may sometimes, however, have gone in officially undesirable directions, for as one French writer observed, 'our capital offers excessively dangerous attractions which the slightly frivolous character of Japanese students cannot easily resist'. What particularly prompted this comment was the recall of Prince Kanin after a well publicised (and expensive) affaire with a blond actress. C. Loonen, *Le Japon Moderne*, (Paris, 1894), p. 117.
33. Roches had been asked to provide this naval instruction, but had advised against this so as not to offend British susceptibilities. C.P.Japon, XIV, 27 May 1865, Roches to Drouyn de Lhuys.
34. C.P.Japon, XIII, 10 January 1865, Roches to Drouyn de Lhuys. Roches also noted a further advantage: that a survey of Japan's mineral resources would have to be carried out.
35. Details of Verny's activities in France can be found in M. Ericson, 'The Bakufu Looks Abroad: the 1865 Mission to France', *Monumenta Nipponica*, XXXIV, (No. 4, 1979), pp. 396–8.
36. See Shinohara Hiroshi, *Rikugun Sosetsu Shi*, pp. 90–92, where a complete list of the initial French personnel, together with their previous place of employment, their dates of service in Japan, and their rates of pay, can be found.
37. A French civil engineer was still in charge of the dockyard in 1889. See the *New York Times of* 21 April 1889.
38. Takahashi, *O-Yatoi Gaikokujin: Gunji, Seiji*, pp. 119–20.
39. In his pamphlet, *Les Étrangers au Japon et les Japonais à l'Étranger* (Paris, 1904).
40. *Les Débuts de Étude du Français au Japon*, p. 197.
41. Takahashi, *op. cit.*, p. 105. See also H. Jones, *Live Machines: Hired Foreigners and Meiji Japan*, (Tenterden, Kent, 1980).
42. Takahashi, *op. cit.*, p. 106.
43. C.P.Japon, XIX, 2 October 1868, Outrey to Auvergne Lauraguais.
44. C.P.Japon, XXV, 20 November 1875, St. Quentin to Decazes.
45. *Ibid.* He also extracted a promise that no Frenchman would be replaced by a non-Frenchman.
46. C.P. Japon, XXV, 14 May 1876, St. Quentin to Decazes. Dupont's attached memorandum reinforced the chargé d'affaires' last point when it noted that 'the presence at Yokosuka of this old Director recalled to the Japanese a past régime which they had difficulty in freeing themselves from, and made them uneasy and distrustful'.
47. *Ibid.*
48. C.P.Japon, XXVI, 17 March 1877, Decazes to St. Quentin.
49. C.P.Japon, XXVI, 13 May 1877, Geofroy to Decazes.
50. C.P.Japon, XXVI, 24 July 1877, Geofroy to Decazes.
51. C.P.Japon, XXVI, 21 November 1878, Geofroy to Waddington.
52. See M. Howard, 'The Armed Forces', in F. H. Hinsley (ed.), *The New Cambridge Modern History*, XI, (Cambridge, 1962), pp. 231–3.

53. C.P.Japon, XXXI, 17 September 1885, Sienkiewicz to Freycinet. See also Shinohara Hiroshi, *Kaigun Sosetsu Shi* (Tokyo, 1986), pp. 308—10, for Bertin's earlier career and his contacts with Japanese students (sent by Verny, who rated him highly) from 1877 at Cherbourg.

54. *Ibid.*, pp. 310–11.

55. C.P.Japon, XXXIV, 6 July 1889, Sienkiewicz to Spuller.

56. Shinohara, *Kaigun Sosetsu Shi*, p. 334.

57. *Ibid.*

58. A. J. Watts and B. G. Gordon, *The Imperial Japanese Navy*, (London, 1971), pp. 95, 222–3. One cruiser of lesser size and capability (the *Takao*) had earlier been built to Bertin's design. Another torpedo-boat was built in France for the Japanese navy in the early 1890s, and one more was assembled from parts made in France. *Ibid.*, pp. 94, 224, 227. Around the turn of the century, another cruiser the 9, 307-ton *Azuma*) was built in France and over 20 fast torpedo-boats were ordered from France (though most were assembled in Japan). *Ibid.*, pp. 113, 227–8, 236. See also F. T. Jane, *The Imperial Navy of Japan* (London, 1904).

59. Captain Togari, *Louis -Émile Bertin: Son rôle dans la création de la marine japonaise* (Paris, 1935), p. 19.

60. Watts and Gordon, *op. cit.*, pp. 5, 95.

61. Togari, *op. cit.*, pp. 23–4.

62. C. B. Howe, *The Origins of Japanese Trade Supremacy*, (London, 1996), p. 288.

63. A. Gordon, *The Evolution of Labor Relations in Japan; Heavy Industry, 1853–1955*, (Cambridge, Mass., 1985), p. 18. See also T. C. Smith, *Political Change and Industrial Development in Japan: Government Enterprise, 1868–1880*, (Stanford, 1955), pp. 8–9, and Takahashi, *O-Yatoi Gaikokujin: Gunji*, p. 118, who notes Verny's observation, in his final report, that each year on average 15.4% of the Japanese workers left Yokosuka, three times the turnover role in comparable French establishments.

64. *Ibid.*, p. 123.

65. Saigusa Hirota *et al.*, *Kindai Nihon Sangyo Gijutsu no Seioka* (Tokyo, 1960), p. 61.

66. *Ibid.*, pp. 277–361. It should be noted that these figure cannot be regarded as absolutely accurate. On the one hand some names must have been missed, while on the other a degree of double counting was almost inevitable because the rendering of Western names into *katakana* (the Japanese syllabary) was not consistent.

67. Information about Brunat can be found in Saigusa *et al.*, *op. cit.*, especially pp. 146–8; 'Paul Brunat et les filatures' (no author named) in Sieffert, *op. cit.*;T. C. . Smith, *op. cit.*, pp. 59–60; and H. Jones, *op. cit.*, p. 20.

68. Dubousquet seems to have been involved as an intermediary on behalf of Ito Hirobumi, Okuma Shigenobu and Shibusawa Eiichi. Saigusa *et al.*, *op. cit.*, pp. 141–3, 146–7 See also the *Moniteur des Soies*, (17 September 1870) which noted that the hiring of Dubousquet was warmly welcomed by the French community in Japan, because he was expected to purchase the necessary equipment in France and also because his selection was seen as conteracting the preponderant British influence.

69. 'Paul Brunat et les filatures', in Sieffert, *op. cit.*, p. 106.

70. *Ibid.* see also T. C. Smith, *op. cit.*, p. 59.

71. H. Jones, *op. cit.*, p. 20.

72. This account of Coignet's career in Japan is taken from Saigusa *et al.*, *op. cit.*, pp. 20–22, 38–40.

73. Another French mining engineer worthy of note for preparing the way for the modernising of the Besshi copper mine for the Sumitomo company and for establishing a training school during his relatively short period there from March 1873 to November 1874 was Louis Laroque. *Ibid.*, pp. 54–5.

74. This paragraph is based on *ibid.*, pp. 177, 208–9.

75. See E. P. Conant, 'The French Connection; Émile Guimet's Mission to Japan, a Cultural Context for *Japonisme*', in H. Conroy *et al., Japan in Transition*, (London and Toronto, 1984), pp. 129–30.
76. Quoted in Umetani Noboru, *O-Yatoi Gaikokujin: Seiij, Hosei* (Foreign Employees: Politics and Law), (Tokyo, 1971), p. 103.
77. D. E. Westney, *Imitation and Innovation: The Transfer of Western Organizational Patterns to Meiji Japan*, (Cambridge, Mass., and London, 1987), p. 90.
78. *Ibid.*, p. 60. Other innovations included the recruitment of police administrators from leading university graduates, the use of police boxes in cities, and one-man residential posts in rural areas. *Ibid.*, p. 34.
79. *Ibid.*, p. 21.
80. *Ibid*, pp. 42–3. See also the references to reports on the French police system in 1873–4 by Inoue Kowashi and Dubousquet in Umetani, *O-Yatoi Gaikokujin: Seiji, Hosei*, pp. 90–2, 108; Westney, *op. cit.*, p. 41.
82. *Ibid.*, p. 43.
83. See Chapter IV.
84. This paragraph is taken from the chapter on Gambet-Gross in Umetani, *O-Yatoi Gaikokujin: Seiji, Hosei*. See also the report of the funeral oration for Gambet-Gross by a French associate, Boissonade, in *L'Echo du Japon* of 25 November 1881. Since Umetani does not mention it, it may not have been known to the Meiji government that Gambet-Gross had previously been condemned in his absence to ten years' suspension for abuse of trust. (He was later acquitted by the court of assizes at Aix). C.P.Japon, XXV, 15 August 1876, St. Quentin to Decazes. In the same dispatch St. Quentin states that it was Boissonade who persuaded the Japanese government to hire Gambet-Gross.
85. C.P.Japon, XXI, 4 March 1872; 18 June 1872, Turenne to Rémusat. Japanese interest in French governmental administration did not end in the 1870s. In 1881 the Ministry of Public Works (Kobusho) requested detailed information about its French counterpart. C.C.Tokyo, II, 7 December 1881, Roquette to Gambetta.
86. Nagai Michio, 'Westernization and Japanization: The Early Meiji Transformation of Education', in D. H. Shively (ed.), *Tradition and Modernization in Japanese Culture*, (Princeton, 1971), p. 57.
87. D. H. Shively, 'The Japanization of the Middle Meiji', in *Ibid.*, p. 81.
88. This is also suggested by I. Hall in *Mori Arinori*, (Cambridge, Mass, 1973), p. 466. That French influence whether for good or ill, should not be underestimated is indicated by Hall's assertion that 'if Japanese education both before and after [Mori's period as Education Minister from from 1885 to 1889] had to be classified in terms of taxonomical affinity for one particular foreign model, the decision would have to be in favour of France'. *Ibid.*, p. 462.
89. Eto's French orientation remained strong, judging from the opening of a request for information about the French police system which he addressed to the French chargé d'affaires in 1873: 'You are not unaware that I am at this moment occupied in instituting civil laws here in Japan on the model of the Napoleonic code, with the help of M. Bousquet. I have at the same time formed the plan of a judicial organization borrowed from France'. C.P.Japon, XXII, 20 January 1873, Turenne to Rémusat.
90. Umetani, *O-Yatoi Gaikokujin: Seiji, Hosei*, pp. 133–4.
91. Shinohara, *Rikugun Sosetsu Shi*, p. 335.
92. Umetani, *O-Yatoi Gaikokujin: Seiji, Hosei*, pp. 137–8.
93. The best account in English of Boissonade is J-P. Lehmann, 'Nature, Custom and Legal Codification: Boissonade's Introduction of Western Law to Japan', in G. Daniels (ed.) *Proceedings of the British Association for Japanese Studies*, IV, 1979, Part 1, pp. 33–72.

94. Takahashi Kunitaro, 'Boissonade et le droit japonais moderne', in Sieffert, *op. cit.*, p. 108, states this explicitly, but does not give a source.
95. On p. 565 of the 1873 volume.
96. Umetani, *O-Yatoi Gaikokujin: Seiji, Hosei*, pp. 137–47.
97. *Ibid.*, p. 143.
98. The latter point is emphasised by H. Oda, *Japanese Law*, (London, Dublin, Edinburgh, 1992), pp. 136–7.
99. See Toyama Shigeki, 'Minpoten Ronso no Seijiteki Kosatsu' in *Minkenron kara Nashionarizuamu*, vol. IV of Meiji Shiryo Kenkyu Renrakukai (ed.), *Meiji Shi Kenkyu Sosho*, (Tokyo, 1956).
100. G-E. Boissonade, 'Les Nouveaux Codes Japonais: Réponse au manifest de Léistes et aux Objections de la Diète', *Revue Française du Japon*, 1892, No. 8, pp. 229–276.
101. C.P.Japon, XXVIII, 29 July 1881, Roquette to Barthèlemy St. Hilaire.
102. *Ibid.*
103. *Ibid.*
104. *Ibid.* See also the very favourable review of the original project by J. Lefort, 'La Réforme du Droit Pénal au Japon', *Revue de Droit international et de Legislation Comparée*, XII, (1880). Roquette's predecessor, Balloy, had predictably been much more critical of the revised Codes, stating that Boissonade's work had 'lost a great part of its value'. C.P.Japon, XXVII, 5 August 1880, Balloy to Freycinet.
105. See Ishii Takashi, *Meiji Shoki no Nihon to To-Ajia* (Tokyo, 1982), p. 101.
106. *Ibid*, pp. 315–6.
107. See Watanabe Ikujiro, *Kinsei Nihon Gaiko Shi* (Tokyo, 1938). pp. 137–8.
108. *Ibid.*
109. These words were attributed to Boissonade in a farewell speech by a long-time associate, Inoue Kowashi. The speech is quoted by Umetani, *O-Yatoi Gaikokujin: Seiji, Hosei*, pp. 148–9.
110. C.P.Japon, XXXIV, 8 May 1889, Sienkiewicz to Spuller. Despite his awareness that Boissonade had been, and was still, a thorn in France's flesh, the French minister was disposed to emphasise the other side of this. It showed, as he saw it, a conscience which German and British employees of the Meiji government had not demonstrated.
111. The (Japanese) text of his memorandum is to be found in Meiji Bunka Kenkyukai (ed.), *Meiji Bunka Zenshu, XVI, Gaiko-hen*), pp. 452 64.
112. Boissonade's credentials, and Okubo's and Ito's involvement, were reported in *L'Echo du Japon* of 10 January 1876.
113. *L'Echo du Japon*, 19 January 1876 (where the whole of the first lecture is printed).
114. *L'Echo du Japon*, 25 November 1881.
115. Tanaka Sadao, *op. cit.*, pp. 10–11.
116. *Ibid.*, pp. 11–12, 34.
117. The information about Murakami comes from *ibid.*, pp. 21–4. Unusually, there is an account of Murokami's career in a French diplomatic report. C.P. Japon, XXXIV, 24 January 1890, Sienkiewicz to Spuller.
118. On Irie, see Tanake *op. cit.*, pp. 127–41.
119. This estimate appears in a detailed article on the French language in Japan in *L'Echo du Japon* of 17 February 1882.
120. Information about the school can be found in Shinohara, *Rikugun Sosetsu Shi*, pp. 104–113, and Tanaka, *op. cit.*, pp. 105–19;
121. C.P.Japon, XIII, 18 March 1865; 4 April 1865; C.P.Japon, XIV, 5 February 1866, Roches to Drouyn de Lhuys.
122. Tanaka, *op. cit.*, p. 119.
123. *Ibid.*, pp. 203–4. It was reopened in 1872.
124. *Ibid.*, p. 149.

125. See Shigehisa Tokutaro, *O-Yatoi Gaikokujin: Kyoiku, Shukyo* (Tokyo, 1968), pp. 117–21.
126. Shinohara, *Rikugun Sosetsu Shi,* pp. 285–90.
127. Of the fourteen Frenchmen employed by this ministry, a majority were probably language teachers. See the list in Umetani, *O-Yatoi Gaikokujin: Seiji, Hosei,* pp. 255–7.
128. B. K. Marshall, *Learning to be Modern,* (Boulder, San Francisco, Oxford, 1994), p. 36.
129. See the chapter on Dury in Shigehisa, *op. cit.,* especially pp. 130–3.
130. Tanaka, *op. cit.,* pp. 26, 122–5.
131. Nakae's life is discussed in R. J. Lifton, Kato Shuichi and M. Reich, *Six Lives, Six Deaths,* (New Haven and London, 1979).
132. *Ibid.,* p. 135. A similar view is expressed by Haga Toru, 'Les études françaises au Japon', in Sieffert, *op. cit.*
133. See Mitani Taichiro, 'Hara Takashi', in Kamishima Jiro (ed.), *Kenryoku no Shiso,* (Tokyo, 1965), pp. 169–70.
134. C.P.Japon, 13 January 1879, Geofroy to Waddington. The low figures for schools which taught French may have been misleading, for according to *L'Echo du Japon* of 17 February 1882, there were as many as 170 students learning French at one school, probably the *Tokyo Gaikokugo Gakko,* quite apart from Nakae's school.
135. *L'Echo du Japon,* 7 January 1881, 17 March 1881, 6 January 1882.
136. The latter figure was reported by Sienkiewicz at the time. C.P.Japon, XXXIII, Sienkiewicz to Flourens. In 1891, however, he gave the former figure. C.P. Japon, XXXV, 4 September 1891, Sienkiewiz to Ribot. The leading figure in setting up the school, as Sienkiewicz saw it, was the education vice-minister, Tsuji Shinji, with whom he had close relations.
137. For a further discussion of French education in Japan in the late 1880s and 1890s, see Chapter VII.
138. Ishizuki Minoru, *Kindai Nihon no Kaigai Ryugaku Shi,* pp. 301–9.
139. Tanaka, *op. cit.,* pp. 140–1.
140. Ishizuki, *op. cit.,* p. 205.
141. Conant, *op. cit.,* pp. 133–4.
142. D. Roden, *Schooldays in Imperial Japan,* (Berkeley, 1980), pp. 53–4. Kinoshita criticised France, however, for being excessively concerned with theory.
143. An article in the magazine *L'Art* (XIV, 1878) on the exposition by the well-known critic, Philippe Burty, described Maeda as 'a subtle, discreet, active, patient, tenacious young man'. Quoted in E. G. Holt (ed.), *The Expanding World of Art, 1874–1902,* (New Haven and London, 1988), p. 40.
144. Lifton *et al., op. cit.,* pp. 132–5.
145. W. L. Schwartz, *The Imaginative Interpretation of the Far East in Modern French Literature,* (Paris, 1925), pp. 51–2.
146. C.P.Japon, XXIII, 30 November 1873, Berthemy to Decazes.
147. Tanaka, *op. cit.,* pp. 70–101. The Bakufu apparently possessed 3600 titles, of which 2325 were preserved after 1868 at Shizuoka. Of the latter, 241 were in French, although some of these were translations from other languages, Dickens being the most common author.
148. P. Humbertclaude, 'La France à l'heure hollandaise', in Sieffert, *op. cit.,* pp. 26–33.
149. C.P.Japon, XLII, 8 March 1895. Enclosure in Harmand to Hanotaux.
150. Haga Toru, 'Les premières traductions', in Sieffert, *op. cit.,* p. 100.
151. Ito Hirobumi, 'Some Reminiscences of the Grant of a New Constitution', in S. Okuma (ed.), *Fifty Years of New Japan,* I, (London, 1910).
152. J. Pittau, *Political Thought in Early Meiji Japan, 1868- -1889,* (Cambridge, Mass., 1967), p. 112. Okawada Tsunetada has made a close examination of Nakae's

translation/adaptation: 'Chomin-Rouseau', in Nihon Seiji Gakkai (ed.), *Nempo Seijigaku 1975; Nihon ni okeru Sei-o Seiji Shiso* (Tokyo, 1976).

153. Schwartz, *op. cit., passim.* Among the reflections of French literary interests in Japan which Schwartz found after exhaustive research, the most notable may have been Judith Gautier's 1885 *Poèmes de la Libellule* (Poems from the Land of the Dragonfly) in which she rendered into rhyming stanzas 85 Japanese classical poems which Saionji Kimmochi had translated into French prose. The 1875 novel (*L'Usurpateur*) and the 1888 and 1890 plays (*La Marchande des Sourires* and *Princesses d'Amour*), all of which were set in feudal Japan, attracted more attention, however. The first French play with a cast of Japanese characters was Ernest d'Hervilly's 1874 *La Belle Sainara.* Saint-Saens tried his hand at an opera with a Japanese element, *La Princesse Jaune* in 1872, but this was unsuccessful, unlike the 1876 comic opera, *Kosiki*, with music by Lecoq and a libretto by Busnach and Liorat, which ran for 76 nights. *Ibid.*, pp. 52, 54, 87–9, .

154. This is the judgement of a French scholar, Bernard Frank, in 'Les Études Japonaises', *Le Journal Asiatique*, (1973), p. 255.

155. R. Sieffert, 'Léon de Rosny et le Congrès des Orientalistes', in Sieffert, *op. cit.*

156. The congress is also discussed in Conant, *op. cit.*, pp. 119–21.

157. A large body of writing now exists on the Japanese impact on Western art, and there is an excellent guide to most of the books, articles, catalogues and theses which have appeared in Western European languages: G. P. Weisberg and Y. M. L. Weisberg, *Japonisme; An Annotated Bibliography,* (New York and London, 1990). It lists and summarises 713 items. Several major exhibitions relating to *Japonisme* have also been held.

158. P. Landy, *Rencontres Franco-Japonaises: Catalogue de la collection historique réunie sur les rapports de la France et du Japon du XVIIème siècle au XXème siècle* (Paris & Osaka, 1970), pp. 35–38.

159. See, eg., Weisberg & Weisberg, *op. cit.*, especially p. 81.

160. Among others Watanabe Toshio, 'The Western Image of Japanese Art in the Late Edo Period', *Modern Asian Studies*, XVIII (October, 1984), note 9.

161. The date of de Beaumont and Collinot's publication is normally given as 1859, but G. Lacambre states that it was a continuing series which included Japanese designs only from August 1861. 'Sources du *Japonisme au* XIXe siècle', in *Le Japonisme* (exhibition catalogue, Paris, 1988). Its title is normally stated to be *Recueil de dessins pour l'art et l'industrie,* but Weisberg &Weisberg, *op. cit.*, p. 13, list as *Ornements du Japon. Recueil de dessins pour l'art et l'industrie,* (Paris, 1859).

162. K. Berger, *Japanisme in Western Painting from Whistler to Matisse,* (Cambridge, 1992), pp. 11.

163. Some insight into the Japanese background is offered by Takakura Shinji, 'Pari no Chonmage Taishitachi', and Nagai Goro, 'Nippon Banbaku no Chichi – Shimizu Usaburo', both in *Rekishi Yomihon* (June 1970). Details of the Saga exhibit can be found in A. Cobbing, *Bakumatsu Saga no Taigai Kankei no Kenkyu,* (Saga-shi, 1994), pp. 94–111.

164. P-A Rémy in *L'Illustration.* His article is reprinted under the title 'Exposition universelle de 1867' in Sieffert, *op. cit.*

165. See, eg., J. Dufwa, *Winds from the East,* (Stockholm, 1981), pp. 42–50.

166. *Ibid.*, p. 46. The importance of this article is also stressed by M. Fried, *Manet's Modernism or The Face of Painting in the 1860s,* (Chicago & London, 1994), p. 161.

167. Quoted in Holt, *op. cit.*, pp. 226–7.

168. According to M. Sullivan in *The Meeting of Eastern and Western Art,* (2nd edition, Berkeley, Los Angeles and London, 1989), p. 222, Renoir 'felt that a people had no right to appropriate an art that belonged to another race. The Japanese cult disgusted him, as it did Degas, and he remarked once to Veuillard

that "perhaps it's having seen so much japonaiserie that has given me this horror of Japanese art'".

169. Berger, *op. cit.*, pp. 88–90.
170. For the fullest account of Guimet, see Conant, *op. cit.* She states (p. 139) with regard to the transfer of the museum, that 'one of the men who helped to insure that the project succeeded as planned was Léon Roches'.
171. Philippe Burty in *L'Art*, quoted in Holt, *op. cit.*, p. 39.
172. See, eg., the lengthy review by P. Mantz in *Le Temps,* 26 April 1883.
173. Uyeno Naoteru, *Japanese Arts and Crafts in the Meiji Era,* (Tokyo, 1958), pp. 23–4.
174. Schwartz, *op. cit.*, p. 101.
175. Lacambre, *op. cit.*, p. 32. Weisberg & Weisberg, *op. cit.*, p. 87, referring to a book on the company by Hida Toyojiro, gives the more likely date of 1873 for its founding.
176. See the scathing report in the *New York Times* of 17 September 1882, which claimed that 'the Japanese received a tremendous stimulus to produce their own works in a quantity to which they were neither accustomed nor for which they were in any way prepared', adding that 'they had to contend, moreover, with the skillful forgers of native work on the banks of the Seine'. It concluded that 'the influence of the Western 'demand has been for the time being nearly fatal to Japanese art'.
177. Schwartz, *op. cit.*, pp. 101–2.
178. It is worthy of note, however, that the *Bibliothèque Nationale* had possessed volume six of Hokusai's *Manga* since 1843, prints by Koryusai since 1848, and fourteen more volumes since 1863. See *Le Japonisme*, p. 76. Moreover, Jules Ferry had, as minister for education and the fine arts, tried from 1882 to 1885 to arrange an exchange of works of art which would provide France with paintings from the Momoyama and early Edo periods and allow the establishment of a Japanese section in the Louvre. See Conant, *op. cit.*, p. 138; C.P. Japon, XXIX, 4 August 1883, Viel-Castel to Challemel-Lacour; *Ibid.,* XXX, 20 August 1884, Ferry to Sienkiewicz. Ferry's interest in Japanese art was unusual, however, and there was probably less government interest in this area than both Conant and Weisberg suggest. The only other example involved a proposal, conveyed by Boissonade, for Japanese workers to study the ceramic processes at Sèvres. On condition that this allowed Sèvres to study the processes of oriental ceramics, the French government encouraged the proposal but the Meiji government abandoned it. See C.C.Yedo, VI, 30 April 1975, Decazes to Berthemy; *Ibid.,* 15 August 1875, St. Quentin to Decazes.
179. Yoshida Mitsukuni *et al.* (eds.), *The Hybrid Culture,* (Hiroshima, 1984), p. 88.
180. Quoted in Holt, *op. cit.*, p. 100.
181. Kuroda studied with Raphael Collin and painted in what has been described as an 'essentially bland impressionistic style'. J. M. Rosenfield, 'Western-Style Painting in the Early Meiji Period and its Critics', in Shively, *op. cit.*, p. 165.
182. *Ibid.,* pp. 33–46.
183. *Ibid.,* p. 49.
184. D. Keene, 'The Sino-Japanese War of 1894–95 and its Cultural Effects in Japan', in Shively, *op. cit.*, p. 165.
185. *Ibid.*
186. For an example of the former view, one might cite Berger, who writes of the 'liberating, fostering role' of *Japonisme* and asserts that 'it can only have been the nature of the Japanese artistic principles involved – with something to offer both to 'late' Impressionism and to the innovatory styles that followed – that caused such momentous consequences to spring from such small beginnings'. At the other extreme, Kenneth Clark omitted any reference to Japanese painting in his *Landscape into Art,* (Harmondsworth, 1956).

187. By Berger, *op. cit.*, p. 4.
188. *Ibid.*, p. 1.
189. *Ibid.*, p. 22.
190. Dufwa, *op. cit.*, p. 190.
191. Sullivan, op. cit., p. 215; R. Needham, 'Japanese Influence on French Painting, 1854–1910', in *Japonisme. Japanese Influence on French Art*, (Cleveland Museum of Art catalogue, Cleveland, 1975), pp. 118–9.
192. Sullivan, *op. cit.*, p. 232; R. de Leeuw (ed.), *The letters of Vincent van Gogh*, (London, 1996), p. 418.
193. Sullivan, *op. cit.*, p. 232.
194. Sir N. Pevsner, 'Art and Architecture', *The New Cambridge Modern History*, XI, (Cambridge, etc., 1962), p. 168.
195. Rousseau supposedly repainted *Le Village* in 1863 in such a way that 'all but the fixed forms of the mere configurations became Japanese through the style (*le mode*) of colouring', but when it received a highly critical response at the next Salon, he restored the old version'. Berger, *op. cit.*, p. 17.
196. Dufwa, *op. cit.*, p. 76.
197. In an article on the 1878 Exposition in the *Gazette des Beaux-Arts*, (September 1878). See the summary in Weisberg & Weisberg, *op. cit.*, pp. 173–4.
198. *Ibid., op. cit.*, pp. 21–3.
199. *Ibid.*, pp. 148–50. Representatives from the Sèvres and Limoges ceramics factories spent much time at the exhibition.
200. *Ibid.*, p. 160.
201. M. Eidelberg & W. R. Johnston, *'Japonisme* and French Decorative Arts', in *Japonisme. Japanese Influence on French Art*, p. 142.
202. Weisberg & Weisberg, *op. cit.*, p. 183.
203. Eidelberg & Johnston, *op. cit.*, pp. 144, 148.
204. *Ibid.*, p. 153.
205. E. Evett, *The Critical Reception of Japanese Art in Late Nineteenth Century Europe*, (Michigan, 1982), pp. xiii–xv.
206. *Ibid.*, p. 59.
207. *Ibid.*, p. 39.
208. *Ibid.*, p. 100.
209. *Ibid.*, p. 43.
210. In *L'Art Japonais*, (Paris, 1884). See Weisberg & Weisberg, *op. cit.*, p. 47.
211. Evett, *op. cit.*, p. 69.
212. *Ibid.*, p. 79.
213. Watanabe, *op. cit.*
214. Quoted in Evett, *op. cit.*, p. 5.
215. De Leeuw, *op. cit.*, p. 407.
216. 'Les Bronzes japonais au Palais de l'industrie', *Gazette des Beaux-Arts*. See Weisberg & Weisberg, *op. cit.*, p. 159.
217. See the chapter on 'Fashion and Beauty' in T. Zeldin, *France 1848–1945: Taste and Corruption*, (Oxford, etc., 1980), especially pp. 104–5.

CONCLUSIONS

1. JKKNGB, II, p. 962, 13 September 1883, enclosure in Hachisuka to Inoue.
2. The criticism (in a private letter of 10 October 1881 to F.V.Dickins) by the British diplomat and scholar, Ernest Satow, of his own minister's approach has a certain relevance here: 'We have I think made a great mistake in pursuing an unfriendly, harsh policy towards the [Japanese] government, the knowledge of which has come to the ears of the common people and has caused them to look on foreigners in

general, and Sir Harry Parkes in particular, as their enemy. . . . He would do excellently in Peking. But here he is the square in the round hole, the Japanese require a diplomatist of the Talleyrand type who would smooth them down and attain his ends at the same time, everyone knows that argument is not persuasion'. Quoted by G. Daniels, *Sir Harry Parkes: British Representative in Japan, 1858–83* (Richmond, 1996).

3. C.P.Japon, XXXIX, 4 January 1894, Sienkiewicz to Casimir-Périer.

ABBREVIATIONS

C.P.Japon.   Correspondance Politique. Japon.
C.P.Chine.   Correspondance Politique. Chine.
C.P. Allemagne.   Correspondance Politique. Allemagne.
M.D.Japon.   Mémoires et Documents. Japon.
C.C.Yédo.   Correspondance Commerciale. Yédo.
C.C.Tokyo.   Correspondance Commerciale. Tokyo.
Shin-Futsu Senso.   Tongking ni Kansuru Shin-Futsu Senso.
F.O.46.   Foreign Office General Correspondence. Japan.
F.O.27.   Foreign Office General Correspondence. France.
F.O.17.   Foreign Office General Correspondence. China.
F.O.391.   The Hammond Papers.
JKKNGB   Joyaku Kaisei Kankei Nihon Gaiko Bunsho.

GLOSSARY

Bakufu.	Literally 'tent government'. The Tokugawa administration.
Bakumatsu.	The final years of Tokugawa rule, c. 1853–1868.
Bugyo.	Bakufu officials
Choshu.	A major domain in western Honshu, with Shimonoseki as its chief port.
Daimyo.	Lords who held fiefs valued at 10,000 koku (4.96 bushels) of rice per year or above. Divided into two main categories, *fudai* and *tozama*, the former being the descendants of men who had served Ieyasu, the founder of the Tokugawa dynasty before thedecisive battle of Sekigahara in 1600, the latter being descendants of his allies or his opponents.
Fukoku Kyohei.	Literally 'rich country, strong army'. A slogan which expressed the key aim of the Meiji leaders.
Han.	Domain ruled by a daimyo. The main political unit in the Tokugawa period.
Hanbatsu Seifu.	Literally 'government by *han* cliques'. A term used by the opposition to suggest that the Meiji government was dominated by men from the *han* of Satsuma and Choshu.
Hatamoto.	Tokugawa vassals with fiefs valued at less than 10,000 koku per year.
Kobu-Gattai.	Literally 'unity of Court and *Bakufu*. It referred to the idea of Bakufu political reform based on consultation and power-sharing with the leading *han* in the 1860s.
Mikado.	A title widely used by foreigners to denote the Emperor.
Roju.	The senior Bakufu council, consisting usually of 4 or 5 of the more powerful *fudai daimyo*.
Sakoku.	Literally 'closed country'. Referred to the Tokugawa policy of seclusion from the outside world.
Samurai.	Members of the warrior class which before its abolition in the1870s comprised about 5% of the population.
Satsuma.	A major domain located in the south-western island of Kyushu.
Shogun.	Hereditary ruler of the Tokugawa Bakufu, whose powers to control national affairs were delegated to him, in theory, by the Emperor.
Sonno-Joi.	Literally 'Honour the Emperor – Expel the Barbarian'. A slogan which after 1858 became an effective banner of the opponents of the Bakufu.
Taikoun.	In English generally 'tycoon'. The title, deriving from *Taikun* (great ruler) by which foreigners generally referred to the Shogun.
Tosa.	An important domain located in the southern island of Shikoku.

Appendix A

FRENCH REPRESENTATIVES
IN JAPAN, 1859–94

Duchesne de Bellecourt June 1859 – April 1864. Previously a member of Baron Gros' mission to China. Not listed in the *Dictionnaire Diplomatique*. Later Consul-General, Batavia.

Léon Roches April 1864 -June 1868. Born 1809. Previous service in North Africa and Trieste.

Ange-Maxime Outrey June 1868–October 1871. Born 1822. Previous service in Damascus, Beirut and Alexandria.

Paul de Turenne d'Avnac Chargé d'affaires, October 1871–June 1873. Born 1842. Previous service in Japan, the Quai d'Orsay (*Direction Politique*), and Washington.

Jules Berthemy June 1873–April 1875. Previously Minister in Peking and Washington.

Ange-Guillaume Ouvré de Saint-Quentin Chargé d'affaires, April 1875–May 1877. Born 1828. Previous service on Pyrennees Commission, in Stuttgart, Tangiers and Lima.

Francis-Henri-Louis de Geofroy May 1877–March 1879. Born 1822. Previous service in Washington, Athens, Madrid, the Quai d'Orsay and Peking.

Marie-René-Davy de Chavigné de Balloy Chargé d'affaires, March 1879–December 1880. Born 1845. Previous service in Brussels, Berlin, Peking and Teheran.

Guillaume de Roquette December 1880–March 1882. Born 1837. Previous service in London, Tangiers, Peking and Berne.

Arthur Tricou June 1882–May 1883. Born 1837. Previous service in Beirut, Constantinople, Cairo and Teheran.

Ulric de Viel-Castel Chargé d'affaires, May 1883–October 1883. Previous service in Madrid and St. Petersburg.

Joseph-Adam Sienkiewicz October 1883–May 1894. (On leave May 1887–September 1888 and November 1891–February 1893). Born 1836. Previous service in Smyrna, Panama, Hong Kong, Malta, Beirut and Cairo.

Ernest-Adrien Bourgarel Chargé d'affaires, May 1887–September 1888. Born 1850. Previous service in Peking, the Quai d'Orsay, Berne, Santiago and Rome.

Victor-Joseph Collin de Plancy Chargé d'affaires, November 1891–February 1893. Born 1853. Previous service in Peking, Shanghai and Seoul.

Pierre-Georges Dubail Chargé d'affaires, June–July 1894. Born 1845. Previous service in Santiago, Peking, Chefou, the Quai d'Orsay, Rome, Quebec, Amsterdam and Shanghai.

François-Jules Harmand July 1894–1905. Born 1845. Previous service in Bangkok, Tongking, Calcutta and Santiago.

Appendix B

FRENCH FOREIGN MINISTERS, 1854–96

Minister	Date of Appointment
Drouyn de Lhuys	July, 1852
Walewski	May 8, 1855
Baroche	January 5, 1860 (Interim)
Thouvenel	January 24, 1860
Drouyn de Lhuys	October 15, 1862
la Valette	September 1, 1866 (Interim)
Moustier	October 2, 1866
la Valette	December 17, 1868
d'Auvergne Lauraguais	July 17, 1869
Daru	January 2, 1870
Ollivier	April 14, 1870. (Interim)
Gramont	May 15, 1870
d'Auvergne Lauraguais	August 10, 1870
Favre	September 4, 1870
Rémusat	August 2, 1871
Broglie	May 26, 1873
Decazes	November 26, 1873
Banneville	November 23, 1877
Waddington	December 13, 1877
Freycinet	December 27, 1879
Barthélemy Saint-Hilaire	September 23, 1880
Gambetta	November 14, 1881
Freycinet	January 30, 1882
Duclerc	August 7, 1882
Fallières	January 29, 1883. (Interim)
Challemel-Lacour	February 21, 1883
Ferry	June 16, 1883–July 1, 1883 (Interim)
"	Sept. 16, 1883 -Sept. 29, 1883 (Interim)
"	Nov. 8, 1883–Nov 20, 1883 (Interim)
"	November 20, 1883
Freycinet	April 6, 1885
Flourens	December 11, 1886
Goblet	April 3, 1889
Spuller	February 22, 1889

Minister	Date of Appointment
Ribot	March 17, 1890
Develle	January 11, 1892
Casimir-Périer	December 3, 1893
Hanotaux	May 30, 1894

BIBLIOGRAPHY

I. PRIMARY SOURCES

A. UNPUBLISHED

1. French
Archives of the Ministère des Affaires Étrangères at the Quai d'Orsay
Correspondance Politique, Japon, Volumes I–XLVI. These volumes, averaging about 700 pages in length, cover the years 1854–1896. Their content is highly political, presumably because French ministers interested themselves less in commercial and other matters than their British counterparts. The arrangement of the volumes is straightforwardly chronological, with Quai d'Orsay dispatches (in draft) being interspersed with those from the French representative in Japan. In the earlier volumes it is common to find duplicates of dispatches from the Correspondance Commerciale series. Besides the correspondence between Paris and Tokyo, relevant dispatches to and from the French ambassador in London are also included, as are a considerable number of inter-ministerial communications, though these become rare in later years.

Correspondance Commerciale, Yédo (Yeddo), Volumes I–VI, (1859–1876).
Correspondance Commerciale, Tokyo, Volumes I–XI, (1877–1899). These two series, which are really one, contain, as well as the occasional political dispatch, the correspondence between the Commerical Department of the Quai d'Orsay and the legation in Japan on matters of general commercial interest. They are very patchy in places (one volume covering the whole of the period 1870–1877, for instance) but they do provide the bulk of the material relating to the later stages of treaty revision.

Mémoires et Documents, Japon, Volumes I–III. These three volumes, which cover the years 1854–70, 1871–84 and 1864–73 respectively, are of considerable importance. They contain most of the memoranda, either official or unofficial, which influenced (or failed to influence) French policy, particularly in the 1850s and 1860s, and thus provide valuable insights into Quai d'Orsay decision-making. They also include documents which, because of their length, irregular form, or unusual source, were not inserted in the Correspondance Politique. Into these categories fall Brunet's letters, the translation of a Japanese historical claim to sovereignty over the Ryukyus, the account of the 1873 interview between Rémusat and Iwakura, and a number of documents relating to the terms of employment of the military missions.

Correspondance Politique, Chine. This series is an essential supplement to the series on Japan for the 1850s and for the Franco-Chinese dispute of 1883–5.

373

Mémoires et Documents, Chine. Though there is more material in this series than the comparable one for Japan, it reveals nothing about the efforts of Patenôtre to secure agreement with Japan in 1884.

Correspondance Politique, Allemagne. This series was used only to investigate the suggestion in the Japanese records that a French attempt to secure an entente was made in 1884 through the Japanese Minister in Berlin.

2. Japanese
(a) Archives of the Japanese Foreign Ministry (Gaimusho)
Tongking ni Kansuru Shin-Futsu Senso (The Sino-French War Over Tongking), 3 volumes. This undated typewritten series comprises a substantial selection, running to about 2, 000 pages in all, of the correspondence between the Japanese Foreign Office (*Gaimusho*) and its agents, both ministerial and consular, in China, Korea and Europe. Unfortunately, not all of the 371 dispatches listed in the index are present, presumably because there was a gap between its compilation and that of the volumes themselves. A separate series dealing with reports of a Franco-Japanese alliance is referred to in the index, and it seems likely that the missing dispatches were placed in this instead, only to be destroyed by fire later, like the original dispatches.

Denshinsha-o (Copies of Telegrams – outgoing), (1883, 1885), 2 volumes.
Denshinsha-rai (Copies of Telegrams – incoming, (1883, 1885), 2 volumes. These four surviving volumes of copies of telegrams provide a valuable guide to foreign minister Inoue's main preoccupations at this time. The Japanese government used telegrams much more extensively than did the Western powers and English was the language normally employed.

(b) Material kept at the Diet Library. Constitutional History Records Room (Kenseishiryoshitsu)
Ito Hirobumi Kankei Shiryo (Records Relating to Ito Hirobumi). Series 624, *Ito Hirobumi Ke Bunsho* (Ito Hirobumi Family Documents), *Inoue Kaoru Shokan* (letters from Inoue Kaoru), 5 vols.

Inoue Kaoru Kankei Bunsho (Records Relating to Inoue Kaoru). Series 657, *Aoki Shuzo Shokan* (letters from Aoki Shuzo), 3 vols.; Series 661, *Inoue Hirobumi Shokan*, (letters from Ito Hirobumi), 4 vols.

These three series were the only ones at the Diet Library which yielded any information regarding the Japanese attitude towards the Franco-Chinese War. Other series looked at contained letters from Inoue to Yamagata, Goto to Ito, and Kuroda to Inoue.

3. British
Foreign Office Records kept at the Public Record Office
F.O.46. This series contains the general correspondence with the British minister in Japan. It was used extensively to supplement the *Correspondance Politique. Japon* for the 1860s, and also for the 1870s and 1880s in several cases where the policies of Britain and France were marked either by cooperation or discord.

F.O.17. This correspondence with the British minister in China was consulted for background to French diplomacy in China and Chinese attitudes in 1884.

F.O.27. This series, which contains the correspondence between the Foreign Office and the British ambassador in Paris, was consulted for details of British approaches to France and for reports on French policy towards Japan.
F.O.391. (The Hammond Papers). Volume I consists of letters between the Permanent Under-Secretary of State for Foreign Affairs and Alcock. Volume XIV consists of letters

from Parkes during 1866–68 and presents a clear picture of the latter's attitude to Roches.

B. Published

Annales du Commerce Extérieur. This series consists mainly of reports to the Ministry of Agriculture, Commerce and Public Works, plus fairly detailed official statistics. Japan is covered in the volumes entitled *Chine* and *Indochine.*

Beasley, W. G. *Select Documents on Japanese Foreign Policy, 1853–68,* (London, 1955). Contains some French documents, but is most valuable for its long introduction.

Billot, A. *L'Affaire du Tonkin,* (Paris, 1888). By the Political Director at the Quai d'Orsay, but does not refer to France's interest in Japanese assistance in 1883–5.

Boissonade, G. N. '*Saiban-ken no Joyaku So-an ni Kansuru Iken*' (Opinion on the Treaty proposal concerning jurisdiction), in Meiji Bunka Kenkyukai (ed.), *Meiji Bunka Zenshu,* (Collection of Materials illustrating various aspects of the Meiji Period), Volume VI, (Tokyo, 1928).

—— 'Les Nouveaux Codes Japonais: Réponse au Manifeste des Légistes et aux Objections de la Diète', *Revue Française du Japon'*, No.8, 30 September 1892.

—— *Projet de Code de Procédure Criminelle pour l'Empire du Japon,* (Tokyo, 1882).

Bousquet, G. *Le Japon de nos Jours,* 2 volumes, (Paris, 1877).

Brandt, M. von. *Dreiunddreissig Jahre in Ost-Asien,* 3 volumes, (Leipzig, 1901). Though it contains some details of diplomacy, this is basically a general review of events in the Far East.

Chanoine, Général. *Documents pour servir à l 'Histoire des Relations entre la France et le Japon,* (Paris, 1907). A collection of letters to the leader of the first military mission by several members of the second, notably Descharmes, and byDubousquet.

Chassiron, C. de. *Notes sur le Japon, la Chine et l'Inde,* (Paris, 1861). Contains the fullest published description of Gros' negotiations in 1858.

Delprat, J . C. 'Le Japon et le Commerce Européen', *Revue des Deux Mondes,* October 1856. An important article written by a merchant who influenced French policy before the French treaty with Japan was signed.

Gaimusho, *Nihon Gaiko Bunsho* (Japanese Diplomatic Documents), (Tokyo, 1933–50). The main official Japanese series, which devotes a large volume to each year.

—— *Joyaku Kaisei Kankei Nihon Gaiko Bunsho* (Japanese Diplomatic Documents relating to Treaty Revision), 4 volumes, (Tokyo, 1941–50). These volumes provide an extremely comprehensive coverage of the Treaty Revision negotiations.

Gérard, A. *Memoires d'Auguste Gérard,* (Paris, 1928). This book by Harmand's successor provides an interesting comparision between French policy in the twentieth century and that of the period covered by this book.

Hansard. *Parliamentary Debates,* Third Series, Volume CLXXXVI, (1867).

Hara, Takashi (Kei). *Hara Takashi Nikki* (The Hara Takashi Diary), 10 volumes. (Tokyo, 1950–1). The first volume of this famous source for Japanese political history contains some references to Hara's work as consul at Tientsin during the Franco-Chinese War.

Ichikawa, Masaaki (ed.). *Nikkan Gaiko Shiryo* (Documents relating to Japanese-Korean Diplomatic Relations), 7 volumes, (Tokyo, 1979). Essentially a reprint of the compilation by Tanaka Naokichi.

Ito Hirobumi Kankei Bunsho Kenkyukai (ed) *Ito Hirobumi Kankei Bunsho* (Documents Relating to Ito Hirobumi), I, (Tokyo, 1973).

Jancigny, Dubois de. *Japon, Indo-Chine, Empire Birman (ou Ava) Siam, Annam (ou Cochinchine), Peninsule Malaise, etc.,* Ceylan, (Paris, 1850). An illuminating expression of an important aspect of French feeling about the Far East.

—— *Journal Officiel de la République Française.* Contains an account of the previous day's debates in the National Assembly.

Kurimoto, Sebei (ed.) *Kurimoto Joun Iko* (The Posthumous Memoirs of Kurimoto). (Tokyo, 1943). The recollections of a Bakufu official who was one of the chief architects of the special relationship with France and who became an outstanding jouralist after the Restoration.

Lebon, G. *Les Origines de l'Armée Japonaise*, (Paris, 1898). Colonel (later General) Lebon's memories of the work of the second military mission. They appeared originally in the *Revue d'Artillerie*.

—— *Souvenirs d'une ambassade extraordinaire au Japon* (Paris, 1913).

Lensen, G. (ed.) *The D'Anethan Dispatches from Japan, 1894–1910* (Tokyo, 1967).

Makino, Nobuaki *Kaikoroku* (Memoirs), Volume I, (Tokyo, 1948). Interesting comment on Ito's mission to China, of which the author was a member.

Meiji Bunka Kenkyukai (ed.) *Meiji Bunka Zenshu, XVI, Gaiko-hen* (Collected Documents on Meiji Culture, XVI, Diplomacy).

Ministère des Affaires Étrangères, France. *Documents Diplomatiques,* Volumes V, VI, (Paris, 1865–6). This general series contains a few extracts from Roches' dispatches, edited for public consumption.

—— *Documents Diplomatiques Français, 1871–1914*, (Paris, 36 vols., 1929 *et seq.*) This series has nothing on Japan before 1894, except a footnote in the 1884 volume. Its coverage of the Tokyo side of the Sino-Japanese War is very far from complete.

Miura, Goro. *Kanju Shogun Kaikoroku.* (A General's Memoirs). (Tokyo, 1925). An important, but not entirely reliable, source for the French approaches to Japan in mid-1884.

Moges, Marquis de. *Recollections of Baron Gros's Embassy to China and Japan in 1857–58,* (London & Glasgow, 1860), p. 355, a translation of *Souvenirs d'une Ambassade en Chine et au Japon en 1857 et 1858.* (Paris, 1860). By a member of Gros' mission, but very sketchy on Japan.

Montblanc, C de. *Le Japon tel qu'il est,* (Paris, 1867). An anti-Tokugawa pamphlet.

Roches, L. *Trente-deux ans à travers l'Islam,* 2 volumes. (Paris, 1884–5). Roches' life-story up to the age of 40, told in flamboyant style. Provides valuable insights into his character. His sophisticated views about Arab students and French education are particularly worthy of note.

Roussin, A. *Une Campagne sur les Cotes du Japon.* (Paris, 1866). An account of the Shimonoseki expedition by a participant.

Satow, E. M. *A Diplomat in Japan.* (London, 1921). A very important source, but one which has led Japanese historians to see a greater difference between Parkes' and Roches' policies than actually existed.

Semallé, Comte de. *Quatre Ans à Péking.* (Paris, 1933). Observations and gossip by a diplomat who served as chargé d'affaires in China between the departure of Tricou and the arrival of Patenôtre in 1884. He has nothing to say about French approaches to Japan.

Tanaka, Naokichi (ed.) *Nikkan Gaiko Shiryo Shusei,* (Collection of Materials relating to Japanese-Korean Diplomatic Relations), 7 volumes, (Tokyo, 1962). Contains some documents not to be found in the *Gaimusho* archives, including an important telegram to Inoue about French overtures in December, 1884.

3. Newspapers and Periodicals

L'Echo du Japan. This was the only French newspaper that had any success in Japan. It was published in Yokohama from 1870 to 1885 and a considerable number of copies are to be found at the *Bibliothèque Nationale.* These, however, are copies of the weekly mail edition, and though almost complete for the period 1880–85, are few for the preceding five years, and entirely lacking for the period 1870–75. A more complete collection exists in the *Meiji Shimbun Zasshi Bunko* in Tokyo University, and has the advantage of being composed of copies of the daily edition. This collection too, however, contains nothing for the first five years. As a newspaper *L'Echo du Japon* was not of much stature, but its coverage of the silk trade was extremely good, and it has provided a certain amount of useful information to supplement the relatively thin French diplomatic records.

Le Temps. This influential newspaper, which was closely connected with the French metallurgical industry, was consulted in the hope of discovering whether there was any public interest in the idea of a Franco-Japanese entente in 1883–5. It proved to reflect the official neglect of Japan in containing no serious article on that country.

Annales de la Propogation de la Foi. Published annually in Lyons, this contains some useful material on early missionary efforts to enter Japan.

The Economist. The Foreign Correspondence of this journal in 1866 and 1867 contains details of the formation and failure of Coullet's trading company.

L'Economiste Française. Has occasional articles on the progress of Japan from the late 1870s, but contains virtually nothing on French interests in Japan before the Meiji Restoration.

Les Missions Catholiques. A Lyons weekly, which is an important source for the Urakami persecution and the later advance of Catholicism. It first appeared in 1868.
Moniteur des Soies. Another Lyons weekly, of even greater importance. It first appeared in 1862 and soon became a forum for the vigorous expression of differing viewpoints about the French silk industry by leading merchants and experts. Contains much information about Japan in the 1860s and 1870s.

Revue Militaire de l'Étranger. Between 1878 and 1885 occasional articles on the Japanese army appear in this semi-official review but they are chiefly statistical and contain no revelations.

II. SECONDARY SOURCES

Akita, G. *The Foundations of Constitutional Government in Modern Japan, 1868–1900,* (Cambridge, Mass., 1967).
Allen, G. C. & Donnithorne, A. *Western Enterprise in Far Eastern Economic Development.* (London, 1951).
Barraclough, G. 'Europe and the Wider World in the Nineteenth and Twentieth Centuries', in Sarkissian A.O.(ed). *Studies in Diplomatic History and Historiography.* (London, 1961)
Beasley, W. G. *Great Britain and the Opening of Japan,* (London, 1951).
—— *The Meiji Restoration,* (Stanford & Oxford, 1972).
—— *The Modern History of Japan,* (London, 1963).
—— *Japan Encounters the Barbarian,* (New York & London, 1995).
Berger, K. *Japonisme in Western Painting,* (Cambridge, 1992).
Blet, H. *Histoire de la Colonisation Française,* 3 volumes, (Paris, 1946)
Block, M. *Statistique de la France,* 2 volumes, (Paris, 1875).
Borton, H. *Japan's Modern Century,* (New York, 1955).
Breen, J. 'Beyond the Prohibition: Christianity in Restoration Japan', in Breen, J. & Williams, M. (eds). *Japan and Christianity,* (London, 1996).
Brown, D.M. *Nationalism in Japan,* (Berkeley, 1955).
Burks, A. *The Modernizers: Overseas Students, Foreign Employees and Meiji Japan,* (Boulder & London, 1985).
Cady, J. F. *The Roots of French Imperialism in Eastern Asia,* (New York, 1954).
Caille, J. *Une Mission de Léon Roches à Rabat en 1845,* (Casablanca, 1947).
Cameron, R. E. *France and the Economic Development. of Europe,* (Princeton, 1961).

Carroll, E. N. *French Public Opinion and Foreign Affairs*, (New York, 1931).

Chapman, G. *The Third Republic of France: The First Phase, 1871–94*, (London, 1962).

Chastenet, J. *La République des Républicains, 1879–1893*, (Paris, 1954).

Clavery, E. *Les Étrangers au Japon et les Japonais à l'Étranger*, (Paris. 1904).

Clough, S. B. *France: A History of National Economics, 1789–1939*, (New York, 1939).

Cobbing, A. *Bakumatsu Saga no Taigai Kankei no Kenkyu* (A Study of the Foreign Relations of Saga in the Bakumatsu Period), (Saga-shi, 1990).

Conant, E. P. 'The French Connection; Émile Guimet's Mission to Japan, a Cultural Context for *Japonisme*', in Conroy. H. *et al.*, *Japan in Transition*, (London and Toronto, 1984).

Conroy, H. *The Japanese Seizure of Korea, 1868–1910*, (Philadelphia, 1960).

Conroy, H. *et al.*, *Japan in Transition*, (London & Toronto, 1984).

Cook, H. F. *Korea's 1884 Incident*, (Seoul, 1972).

Cordier, H. *Les Français aux IIes Lieou K'ieou*, (Paris, 1911).

—— 'Le Premier Traité de la France avec le Japon', *T'oung Pao*, XIII, (1911).

Craig, A. M. *Choshu in the Meiji Restoration*, (Cambridge, Mass., 1961).

Dallet, C. *Histoire de l'Église de Corée*, 2 volumes, (Paris, 1874).

Daniels, G. *Sir Harry Parkes: British Representative in Japan, 1865–83*, (Richmond, 1996).

Deuchler, M. *Confucian Gentlemen and Barbarian Envoys: The Opening of Korea, 1875–1885*, (Seattle, 1977).

Dickins, F. V. *Life of Sir Harry Parkes*, Volume 2. (London, 1894).

Dufwa, J. *Winds from the East*, (Stockholm, 1981).

Duke, F. B. *Les Relations entre la France et la Thailande au XIXe Siècle*, (Bangkok, 1962).

Dunham, A. L. *The Industrial Revolution in France, 1815–48*, (New York, 1955).

Duus, P. *The Abacus and the Sword*, (Berkeley, Los Angeles & London, 1995).

Eastman, L. *Thrones and Mandarins: China's Search for a Policy during the Sino-French Controversy, 1880–1885*, (Cambridge, Mass., 1967).

Ericson, M. 'The Bakufu Looks Abroad: the 1865 Mission to France', *Monumenta Nipponica*, XXXIV, (no. 4, 1979).

—— 'The Tokugawa Bakufu and Léon Roches', (University of Hawaii, Ph. D. thesis, 1978).

Evans, B. L. 'The Attitudes and Policies of Great Britiain and China Toward French Expansion in Cochin China, Cambodia, Annam and Tongking, 1858–83', (University of London, Ph.D. thesis, 1961).

Evett, E. *The Critical Reception of Japanese Art in Late Nineteenth Century Europe*, (Michigan, 1982).

Fraissinet, E. *Le Japon*, 2 volumes, (Paris, 1853).

Frank, B. 'Les Études Japonaises', *Le Journal Asiatique*, (1973).

Fried, M. *Manet's Modernism or The Face of Painting in the 1860s*, (Chicago & London, 1994).

Fujii, Sadabumi 'Urakami Kyoto Mondai o Meguru Nichi-Futsu Kankei', (Japanese-French Relations over the problem of the Urakami Christians) in Kaikoku Hyakunen Kinen Meiji Bunka Shi Jogyokai (ed.), *Kaikoku Hyakunen Kinen Meiji Bunka Shi Ronshu* (Essays in Meiji History to Commemorate the Centenary of the Opening of the Country), (Tokyo, 1953).

Fujiwara Akira. *Gunji Shi*, (A History of the Army), (Tokyo, 1961).

Gluck, C. *Japan's Modern Myths*, (Princeton, 1985).

Gordon, A. *The Evolution of Labor Relations in Japan: Heavy Industry, 1853–1955*, (Cambridge, Mass., 1985).

Grierson, Captain. J.M. *The Armed Strength of Japan*, (London, 1886).

Griffis, W. R. *Corea, The Hermit Kingdom*, (7th edition, London, 1905).

Gubbins, J. H. *The Making of Modern Japan,* (London, 1922).

Guillen, P. *L'Expansion, 1881–1898,* (Paris, 1984).

Guyot, Y. *Le Commerce et les Commerçants.,* (Paris, 1909).

Haga, Toru 'Les études françaises au Japon', in Sieffert, R. (ed.), *Le Japon et la France: Images d'une Découverte,* (Paris, 1974).

—— 'Les premières traductions', in Sieffert, R., *Ibid.*

Hanabusa, Nagamichi *Meiji Gaiko Shi* (A Diplomatic History of the Meiji Period), (Tokyo, 1960).

Hattori, Shiso *Kindai Nihon Gaiko Shi,* (A Diplomatic History of Modern Japan), (Tokyo, 1954).

Havens, T. R. H. *Nishi Amane and Modern Japanese Thought,* (Princeton, 1970).

Hirota, Masaki 'Taigai Seisaku to Datsu-a Ishiki' (Foreign Policy and the Separation from Asia Consciousness) Rekishigaku Kenkyukai & Nihon Shi Kenkyukai (eds.), *Koza Nihon Shi,* VII, (Tokyo, 1995).

Ho, Takushu *'Fuerii Naikaku to Nihon',* (The Ferry Cabinet and Japan), *Shirin,* XLV, (May 1962).

—— *'Chosen Mondai o Meguru Jiyuo to Furansu',* (The Jiyuto, France and the Korean Problem), *Rekishigaku Kenkyu,* No. 265, (June 1962).

—— *'Fukkoku Koshi no de mita Jiyuto',* (The Jiyuto seen through the Eyes of the French Minister), *Shirin,* XLVIII, (March 1965).

—— 'Koshin Jihen o meguru Inoue Gaimukyo to Furansu Koshi to no Kosho', (The Negotiations Between Foreign Minister Inoue and the French Minister over the 1884 Seoul Incident), *Rekishigaku Kenkyu,* CCLXXXII, (November 1963).

—— Shin-Futsu Senso ni okeru Nihon no Taikan Seisaku' (Japan's Korean Policy during the Franco-Chinese War). *Shirin,* XLVIII, (May1960).

Hoare, J. *Japan'sTreaty Ports and Foreign Settlements: the Uninvited Guests 1858–1899,* (Folkestone, 1994).

Holt, E. G. (ed.) *The Expanding World of Art, 1874–1902,* (New Haven & London, 1988).

Honjo, Eijiro *Bakumatsu no Shin Seisaku,* (The New Policies of the *Bakumatsu* period), (Tokyo, 1935).

Hora, Tomio 'Bakumatsu Ishin ni okeru Ei-Futsu Guntai no Yokohama – chuton' (The Occupation of Yokohama by British and French Forces in the Bakumatsu and Restoration Period) in Meiji Shiryo Kenkyu Renrakukai (ed.), *Meiji Seiken no Kakuritsu Katei* (The Consolidation-process of the Meiji Government), (Tokyo, 1956).

Howe, C. B. *The Origins of Japanese Trade Supremacy,* (London, 1996).

Howard, M. 'The Armed Forces' in F. H. Hinsley (ed.), *The New Cambridge Modern History,* XI, (Cambridge, 1962).

Hozumi, N. *Lectures on the New Japanese Civil Code as Material or the Study of Comparative Jurisprudence.* Revised edition, (Tokyo, Osaka, Kyoto, 1912).

Humbertclaude, P. 'La France à l'heure hollandaise', in Sieffert, R. (ed.), *Le Japon et la France: Images d'une Découverte,* (Paris, 1974).

Ike, N. *The Beginning of Political Democracy in Japan,* (Baltimore, 1950).

Ino, Tentaro *Joyaku Kaisei Ron no Rekishiteki Tenkai* (The Historical Development of the Treaty Revision Issue), (Tokyo, 1976).

Inoue Kaoru Ko Denki Hensankai. *Segai Inoue Ko Den* (The Life of Marquis Inoue), 5 volumes, (Tokyo, 1934).

Inoue, Kiyoshi. *Joyaku Kaisei* (Treaty Revision), (Tokyo, 1955).

Inoue, Mitsusada & Kodama, Kota (eds.). *Nihon Rekishi Taikei* (Main Lines of Japanese History), IV, (Tokyo, 1987).

Ishii, Takashi. *Meiji Ishin no Kokusaiteki Kankyo* (The Meiji Restoration in its International Perspective), (Tokyo, 1957).

—— *Meiji Shoki no Kokusai Kankei* (International Relations in the Early Meiji Period), (Tokyo, 1977).

—— *Meiji Shoki no Nihon to To-Ajia* (Early Meiji Japan and East Asia), (Tokyo, 1982).

—— *Meiji Ishin no Butai-ura* (Behind the Scenes in the Meiji Restoration), (Tokyo, 1960).

—— *Gakusetsu Hihan Meiji Ishin Ron* (The Meiji Restoration: A Critical Discussion of Scholarly Interpretations), (Tokyo, 1961).

—— *Zotei Meiji Ishin no Kokusaiteki Kankyo* (The Meiji Restoration in its International Perspective, enlarged edition), (Tokyo, 1966).

Ishizuki, Minoru. *Kindai Nihon no Kaigai Ryugaku Shi* (A History of Modern Japanese Overseas Study), (Tokyo, 1972).

Itagaki, Taisuke. *Jiyuto-shi* (History of the *Jiyuto*) 3 volumes, (Tokyo, 1958).

Ito, Hirobumi. 'Some Reminiscences of the Grant of a New Constitution', in S. Okuma (ed.) *Fifty Years of New Japan*, I, (London, 1910)

Iwata, M. *Okubo Toshimichi*, (Berkeley, 1964).

Jane, F. T. *The Imperial Navy of Japan*, (London, 1904).

Jansen, M. B. *Sakamoto Ryoma and the Meiji Restoration*, (Princeton, 1961).

—— *The Japanese and Sun Yat-sen,* (Cambridge, Mass., 1954).

Joho, Yoshio *Gunmu Kyoku* (The Military Affairs Bureau), (Tokyo, 1979).

Jones, F. C. *Extraterritoriality in Japan*, (New Haven, 1931).

Jones, H. *Live Machines: Hired Foreigners and Meiji Japan,* (Tenterden, Kent, 1980).

Joseph, P. *Foreign Diplomacy in China, 1894–1900,* (London, 1928).

Kajima, Morinosuke. *Nihon Gaiko Shi,* II, *Joyaku Kaisei Mondai* (Japanese Diplomatic History. II. The Treaty Revision Question), (Tokyo, 1970).

Kaneko, Kentaro. *Ito Hirobumi Den,* II, (Tokyo, 1943).

Kawamura, Kazuo *Kindai Nitchu Kankei Shi no Shomondai* (Problems in the History of Modern Japanese-Chinese Relations, (Tokyo, 1983).

Keene, D. 'The Sino-Japanese War of 1894–95 and its Cultural Effects in Japan', in Shively, D. H. (ed), *Tradition and Modernization in Japanese Culture,* (Princeton, 1971).

Kennedy, M. D. *The Military Side of Japanese Life.*, (London, 1924).

Kim, Key-Kiuk *The Last Phase of the East Asian World Order: Korea, Japan, and the Chinese Empire, 1860–1882,* (Berkeley & Los Angeles, 1980).

Kishimoto, H. *Japanese Religion in the Meiji Era,* (Tokyo, 1956).

Kiernan, E. W. G. *British Diplomacy in China, 1880–85,* (Cambridge, 1939).

Kublin, H. 'The "Modern" Army of Early Modern Japan', *Far Eastern Quarterly,* (November, 1949).

Landes, D. S. *Bankers and Pashas,* (London, 1958).

Landy, P. *Rencontres Franco-Japonaises: Catalogue de la collection historique réunie sur les rapports de la France et du Japon du XVIIème siècle au XXème siécle,* (Paris & Osaka, 1970).

Langer, W.L. *The Diplomacy of Imperialism.* (New York, 1951).

Lapéyrère, P. de. *Le Japon Militaire,* (Paris, 1883).

Latourette, K. S. *Christianity in a Revolurionary Age, Volume III, The Nineteenth Century Outside Europe,* (New York, 1959).

Launay, A. *Histoire Générale de la Société des Missions Etrangères,* III, (Paris, 1894).

Lee, Yur-bok *West Goes East: Paul George von Mollendorf and Great Power Imperialism in Late Yi Korea,* (Honolulu, 1988).

Lefort, J. 'La Réforme de Droit Pénal au Japon'. *Revue de Droit International et de Législatiøn Comparée,* XIII, 1880.

Lehmann, J-P. 'France and Japan, 1850–1885'. (Oxford University, D. Phil. thesis, 1976).

—— 'The French Military Mission to Japan, 1866–1868, and Bakumatsu Politics', in

Lowe, P. (ed.), *Proceedings of the British Association for Japanese Studies'*, Vol. 1, Part 1, (1976).

—— 'Léon Roches – Diplomat Extraordinary in the Bakumatsu Era', in *Modern Asian Studies,* XIV, No. 2, (1980).

—— Nature, Custom and Legal Codification: Boissonade's Introduction of Western Law to Japan', in G. Daniels (ed.) *Proceedings of the British Association for Japanese Studies,* IV, (1979), Part 1.

Lensen, G. *Balance of Intrigue,* 2 vols, (Tallahassee, 1982).

Levy, R., Lacam, G. & Roth A. *French Interests and Policies in the Far East,* (New York, 1941).

Lifton, R. J. *et al. Six Lives, Six Deaths,* (New Haven, London, 1979).

Lockwood, W. W. *The Economic Development of Japan,* (Princeton, 1955).

Loonen, C. *Le Japon Moderne,* (Paris, 1894).

Lowe, P (ed.) *Proceedings of the British Association for Japanese Studies,* Vol.I, part I. (1976).

Malozemoff, A. *Russian Far Eastern Policy, 1881–1904,* (Berkeley, 1958).

Marnas, F. *La Religion de Jésus (Yaso Ya-kyo) Ressuscité au Japon,* 2 volumes, (Paris, Lyon, 1896).

Mayo, M. J. 'A Catechism of Western Diplomacy: The Japanese and Hamilton Fish, 1872', *Journal of Asian Studies,* (May 1967).

Mayo, M. J. (ed.) *The Emergence of Imperial Japan,* (Boston, 1970).

Marshall, B. K. *Learning to be Modern,* (Boulder, San Francisco, Oxford, 1994).

Martin, B. *Japan and Germany in the Modern World,* (Providence & Oxford, 1995).

Matsuda, Kiyoshi. 'Furansu kara mita Bummei Kaika' (Progress and Enlightenment as seen from France) in Hayashiya Saburo (ed.), *Bummei Kaika no Kenkyu* (Studies of Progress and Enlightenment), (Tokyo 1979).

Matsushita, Yoshio. *Meiji no Guntai* (The Meiji Armed Forces), (Tokyo, 1960).

Mazelière, V. de la. *Le Japon, Histoire et Civliisation,* V, (Paris, 1910).

McAleavy, H. *Black Flags in Vietnam,* (London, 1968).

McLaren, W.W. *A Political History of Japan, 1868–1912,* (London, 1916)

McMaster, J. 'British Trade and Traders in Japan, 1859–69', (University ofLondon Ph.D. thesis, 1962).

Medzini, M. *French Policy in Japan during the Closing Years of the Tokugawa Regime,* (Cambridge, Mass., 1971).

—— 'Léon Roches in Japan, 1864–68', *Papers on Japan,* Volume II. (Harvard, 1963).

Mitani, Taichiro. 'Hara Takashi', in Kamishima Jiro (ed.), *Kenryoku no Shiso* (The Mentality of Power), (Tokyo, 1965).

Nagai, Goro. 'Nippon Banbaku no Chichi – Shimizu Usaburo' (Shimizu Usaburo – Father of Japan's Universal Expositions), *Rekishi Yomihon,* (June 1970).

Nagai, Michio. 'Westernization and Japanization: The Early Meiji Transformation of Education', in Shively D. H. (ed.). *Tradition and Modernization in Japanese Culture,* (Princeton, 1971).

Nakamura, Kikuo. *Kindai Nihon no Hoteki Keisei* (The Legal Shaping of Modern Japan), (Tokyo, 1956).

Nezu, Masashi. '1864-nen no Parii Kyoyaku o meguru Furansu Daini Teisei to Tokugawa Bakufu to no Kosho' (The Negotiations between the Second Empire and the Tokugawa Bakufu surrounding the 1864 Paris Convention), *Rekishigaku Kenkyu,* No.210 (1956).

—— 'Bakumatsu no Furansu Gaiko Bunsho kara mita Furansu no Tai-Nichi Hosaku' (French Policy towards Japan as seen through French Diplomatic Documents of the *Bakumatsu* Period), *Shigaku Zasshi,* XIX, 1960.

Nihon Gakujutsu Shinkokai. (ed) Joyaku Kaisei Keika Gaiyo (General Outline of the Course of Treaty Revision), (Tokyo, 1950).

Nitobe, Inazo (ed). *Western Influences in Modern Japan.* (Chicago, 931).

Noda, Y. *Introduction au Droit Japonais,* (Paris, 1961).

Norman, E. H. *Japan's Emergence as a Modern State,* (New York, 1940)

Nose, Kazunori. 'Koshin Seiken no Kenkyu (1): Shin-Futsu Senso to Nihon Gaiko' (Studies of the 1884 Seoul Incident (1): the Sino-French War), *Chosen Gakuho,* LXXXII, (January 1977).

Oda, H. *Japanese Law,* (London, Dublin, Edinburgh, 1992).

Ohata, K & Ikado, F. *Japanese Religion in the Meiji Era,* (Tokyo, 1956).

Ohata, Tokushiro. *Nihon Gaiko Seisaku no Shiteki Tenkai* (The Historical Development of Japanese Foreign Policy), (Tokyo, 1983).

Oka, Yoshitake. *Kindai Nihon no Keisei* (The Shaping of Modern Japan), (Tokyo, 1947).

—— 'Kokuminteki Kokuritsu to Kokka Risei' (National Independence and Raison d'État), in Ito, Totono *et al.Kindai Nihon Shiso-Shi Koza* (Lectures on Modern Japanese Intellectual History), VIII – *Sekai no Naka no Nihon* (Japan in the World) (Tokyo, 1960).

Okawada, Tsunetada. 'Chomin-Rousseau', in Nihon Seiji Gakkai (ed.), *Nempo Seijigaku 1975: Nihon ni okeru Sei-o Seiji Shiso* (Political Science Annual 1975; Western European Political Thought in Japan), (Tokyo, 1976).

Otsuka, Takematsu. *Bakumatsu Gaiko Shi no Kenkyu.* (Studies in *Bakumatsu* Diplomatic History). (Tokyo, 1952).

—— 'Fukkoku Koshi Leon Roches no seisaku kodo ni tsuite' (Concerning the policy and actions of French Minister Léon Roches), *Shigaku Zasshi,* XLVI, 1935.

Pagès, L. *Le Japon et ses derniers Traités avec les Puissances Européennes,* (Paris, 1859).

Perez, L. G. 'Revision of the Unequal Treaties and Abolition of Extraterritoriality', in Hardacre, H. (ed), *New Directions in the Study of Meiji Japan,* (Leiden, New York, Cologne, 1997).

Pittau, J. *Political Thought in Early Meiji Japan, 1868–1889,* (Cambridge, Mass., 1967).

Porch, D. *The March to the Marne: the French Army, 1871–1914,* (Cambridge, 1981).

Power, T. F. *Jules Ferry and the Renaissance of French Imperialism,* (New York, 1944).

Presseisen, E. L. *Before Aggression,* (Tucson, 1965).

Priestley, H. J. *France Overseas: A Study of Modern Imperialism,* (New York, London, 1938).

—— *France Overseas through the Old Regime,* (New York, London, 1939).

Raoulx, J. 'Les Français au Japon et la Création de l'Arsénal de Yokosuka', *La Revue Maritime.* (May 1939).

Ray, J. *Le Japon,* (Paris, 1941).

Ristelhueber, R. 'Un diplomate belliquex déclare la guerre à la Corée (en 1866)', *Revue d'Histoire Diplomatique,* (1958). No.2.

Ralston, D. B. *Importing the European Army: The Introduction of European Military Techniques and Institutions into the Extra-European World,* (Chicago & London, 1990).

Renouvin, P. *Histoire de Relations Internationales,* VI, (Paris, 1955).

Roden, D. *Schooldays in Imperial Japan,* (Berkeley, 1980).

Rosenfield, J. M. 'Western-Style Painting in the Early Meiji Period and its Critics', in Shively, D. H. (ed.), *Tradition and Modernization in Japanese Culture,* (Princeton, 1971).

Saigusa, Hiroto *et al. Kindai Nihon Sangyo Gijutsu no Seioka.* (The Westernisation of Industrial Technology in Modern Japan), (Tokyo, 1960).

Sansom, Sir G. B. *The Western World and Japan,* (London, 1950).

—— *A History of Japan, 1615–1867,* (London., 1964).

Sato, Saburo. *Kindai Nitchu Kosho Shi no Kenkyu* (A Historical Study of Modern Japanese – Chinese Negotiations), (Tokyo, 1984).

Schuman, F. L. *War and Diplomacy in the French Republic,* (Paris, 1931).

Scalapino, R. A. *Democracy and the Party Movement in Prewar Japan,* (Berkeley, 1953).

Seignobos, C. *Le Déclin de l'Empire et l'Établissement de la 3e République,* vol. VII of E. Lavisse (ed), *Histoire de France Contemporaine,* (Paris, 1921).

Seung, Kwon Synn. *The Russian-Japanese Rivalry Over Korea, 1876–1904,* (Seoul 1981).

Shibata, Michio & Shibata, Asako. 'Bakumatsu ni okeru France no Tainichi Seisaku – "France Yushutsunyu Kaisha" no Setsuritsu Keikaku o Megutte' (French Policy Towards Japan in the Bakumatsu Period – on the Plan for the Establishment of the French Export and Import Company), *Shigaku Zasshi,* LXXVI, (August 1967).

Shigehisa, Tokutaro. *O-Yatoi Gaikokujin: Kyoiku, Shukyo* (Hired Foreigners: Education, Religion), (Tokyo, 1968).

Shimomura, Fujio. 'Joyaku Kaisei' (Treaty Revision) in Konishi Shiro (ed). *Kindai Shakai* (Modern Society), (Tokyo, 1954).

—— *Meiji Shonen Joyaku Kaisei Shi no Kenkyu* (A Study of Treaty History in the Early Years of Meiji, (Tokyo, 1962).

—— *Meiji Ishin no Gaiko* (The Diplomacy of the Meiji Restoration), (Tokyo, 1948).

Shinohara, Hiroshi. *Kaigun Sosetsu Shi* (A History of the Establishment of the Navy), (Tokyo, 1986).

—— *Rikugun Sosetsu Shi* (A History of the Establishment of the Army), (Tokyo, 1983).

Shively, D. H. 'The Japanization of the Middle Meiji', in Shively D. H. (ed.), *Tradition and Modernization in Japanese Culture,* (Princeton, 1971).

Sieffert, R. *'Le Japon et la France: Images d'une Découverte,* (Paris, 1974).

—— 'Léon de Rosny et le Congrès des Orientalistes' in Sieffert, *Ibid.*

Silberman, B. S. & Harootunian, H. D. (eds.) *Modern Japanese Leadership: Transition and Change,* (Tucson, 1966).

Sims, R.L. *A Political History of Modern Japan, 1868–1952,* (Delhi, 1991)

—— 'Japan's Rejection of Alliance with France during the Franco-Chinese Dispute of 1883–1885', *Journal of Asian History,* XXIX, No. 2, (1995).

—— 'The "Progress of Japan", as seen by French Diplomats in the First Half of the Meiji Period', *Proceedings of the Japan Society of London,* (1978)

Smith, T. C. *Political Change and Industrial Develpment in Japan, 1868–1880,* (Stanford, 1955).

Sohier, A. 'La diplomatie Belge et la protection des missions en Chine,' *Neue Zeitschrift fur Missionswissenschaft,* XXII, 4 (1967);

—— 'La nonciature pour Pékin en 1866', *Ibid.,* XXIV, 2, (1968);

—— 'Mgr. Alphonse Favier et la protection des missions en Chine (1870–1905), I & II, *Ibid.,* XXV, 1 & XXV, 2 (1969).

Sugiyama, S. *Japan's Industrialisation in the World Economy, 1859–1899,* (London, 1988).

Sullivan, M. *The Meeting of Eastern and Western Art,* (2nd edition, Berkeley, Los Angeles & London, 1989).

Sumiya, Mikio. 'Tenno-sei no Kakuritsu to Kirisuto-kyo' (Christianity and the Establishment of the Emperor-system) in Ienaga Saburo (ed.), *Minkenron kara Nashionarizumu e* (From People's Rights to Nationalism), Vol. IV of Meiji Shiryo Kenkyu Renrakukai (ed.), *Meiji Shi Kenkyu Sosho*), (Tokyo, 1956).

Takahashi, Kunitaro. 'Baku, Satsu Pari de Hibana-su' (The Bakufu and Satsuma Strike Sparks in Paris), *Rekishi Yomihon,* XV, 6, (June 1970).

—— 'Boissonade et le droit japonais moderne', in Sieffert, *op. cit.*

—— Fukokku no Nekketsukan Léon Roches' (France's Hot-Blooded Léon Roches) in *Rekishi to Jimbutsu,* (June 1971).

—— 'Jules Brunet, Français qui combattit à Goryokaku', *Acta Asiatica,* XVII, (1969).

—— *O-Yatoi Gaikokujin: Gunji* (Hired Foreigners: the Military), (Tokyo, 1968).

Takakura, Shinji. 'Pari no Chonmage Taishitachi', (The Ambassadors in Traditional Hair-style in Paris), *Rekishi Yomihon,* (June 1970).

Takekoshi, Y. *Economic Aspects of the History of the Civilsation of Japan,* 3 vols., (London, 1930).

Takeuchi, T. *War and Diplomacy in the Japanese Empire,* (London, 1936).

Tanaka, S. *Les Débuts de l'Étude du Français au Japon,* (Tokyo, 1983).

Taylor, A. J. P. *The Struggle for Mastery in Europe,* (Oxford, 1954).

Togari, Captain. *Louis-Émile Bertin,* (Paris, 1935).

Totman, C. *The Collapse of the Tokugawa Bakufu,* (Honolulu, 1980).

Toyama, Shigeki. *'Mimpo-ten Ronso no Seijiteki Kosatsu'* (A Political Consideration of the Dispute over the Civil Code), *Minkenron kara Nashionarizumu e,* (Tokyo, 1956).

Treat, P. J. *Diplomatic Relations between the United States and Japan, 1853–1895,* 2 vols., (Stanford, 1932).

Tsiang, T. F. 'Sino-Japanese Diplomatic Relations, 1870–1894', *The Chinese Social and Political Science Review,* XVII, No. 1, (April 1935).

Umetani, Noboru *Meiji Zenki Seiji Shi no Kenkyu,* (Studies in Early Meiji Political History), (Tokyo, 1963).

—— *O-Yatoi Gaikokujin* (Hired Foreigners), (Tokyo, 1965).

—— *O-Yatoi Gaikokujin: Seiji, Hosei* (Hired Foreigners: Politics. Law), (Tokyo, 1971).

Uyeno, N. (ed.) *Japanese Arts and Crafts in the Meiji Era,* (Tokyo, 1958).

Vande Walle, W. 'Le Comte des Cantons Charles de Montblanc – Agent for the Lord of Satsuma), in I. Neary (ed.)*Leaders and Leadership in Japan,* (Richmond, 1996).

Villaret, E.de. *Dai Nippon,* (Paris, 1889).

Watanabe, Ikujiro. *Kinsei Nihon Gaiko Shi* (Modern Japanese Diplomatic History), (Tokyo, 1938).

Watanabe, Toshio. 'The Western Image of Japanese Art in the Late Edo Period', *Modern Asian Studies,* XVIII (October 1984).

Watts, A. J. & Gordon, B. G. *The Imperial Japanese Navy,* (London, 1971).

Wellesley, F. A. *The Paris Embassy during the Second Empire,* (London, 1928).

Wei, L. *Le Saint-Siège, la France et la Chine sous le pontificat de Léon XIII,* (Schoneck/Beckenried, Switzerland, 1966).

Westney, D. E. *Imitation and Innovation: The Transfer of Western Organisational Patterns to Meiji Japan,* (Cambridge, Mass., & London, 1987).

Wilson, R. A. *The Genesis of the Meiji Government, 1868–71,* (Berkeley, 1957).

Yamamoto, Shigeru. *Joyaku Kaisei Shi* (A History of Treaty Revision), (Tokyo, 1943).

Yanaga, C. *Japan Since Perry,* (New York, 1949).

Yoshida, Mitsukuni. *The Hybrid Culture,* (Hiroshima, 1984).

Zeldin, T. *France 1848–1945: Taste and Corruption,* (Oxford, 1980).

III. BIBLIOGRAPHIES AND REFERENCE WORKS

Académie Diplomatique International, *Dictionnaire Diplomatique* Volume V, (no date). This volume contains many biographies of diplomats, but except for Roches no French diplomat who served in Japan receives more attention than a list of posts held.

Annuaire Diplomatique de l'Empire Française, (Paris, 1858–70.)

Annuaire Diplomatique de la République Française, (Paris, 1871–7)

Annuaire Diplomatique et Consulaire de la République Francaise, (Paris, 1879–). This publication, the nearest French equivalent to the British Foreign Office List, is of somewhat uneven quality. In its early years it gives no more than the rank and existing post of diplomats, but from 1879 it includes a list of previous posts. Through it one can also follow the organisational changes at the Quai d'Orsay.

Balteau, J. *Dictionnaire de Biographie Française*, (Paris, 1933).

Borton, H. *et al. A Selected List of Books and Articles on Japan*, (Cambridge, Mass., 1954).

Cordier, H. *Bibliotheca Japonica*, (Paris, 1912).

Kokusai Bunka Shinkokai. *A Classified List of Books in Western Languages relating to Japan*, (Tokyo, 1965).

Kokusai News Jiten Shuppan Iinkai, Mainichi Communications (ed.) *Gaikoku Shimbun ni Miru Nihon* (Japan Seen by Foreign Newspapers), vol. I (1852–1873); vol. 2 (1874–1895) (Tokyo, 1990).

Kyoto Daigaku Bungakubu Kenkyushitsu (ed.) *Nihon Kindai-shi Jiten* (A Dictionary of Modern Japanese History), (Tokyo, 1960). Has a 600-page biographical section.

Martens, E. *Nouveau Recueil Général des Traités*, Volume XVI, second part, (Gottingue, 1860). Contains the first French treaty with Japan. Second series, Volume XXV, (Leipzig, 1900). Contains the revised treaty of 1896.

Nachod, O. *Bibliographie von Japan, 1906–26*, (Leipzig, 1928).

Okubo, Toshiaki (ed.) *Nihon Shigaku Nyumon* (Introduction to the Study of Japanese History), (Tokyo, 1965). A survey of Japanese scholarship in each field and period.

Unesco Bunka Kenkyu Centre. *Shiryo O-Yatoi Gaikokujin* (Historical Materials relating to Hired Foreigners), (Tokyo, 1975).

Weisberg, G. & Y.M.L. *Japonisme: An Annotated Bibliography,* (New York & London, 1990).

—— Summarises the contents of over seven hundred books, theses, articles, and review articles, mainly in English, French and German.

Wenckstern, Fr. von. *A Bibliography of the Japanese Empire*, Volume I, (Leiden, 1895); Volume II. (Tokyo, 1907). A comprehensive list of books and articles on Japan in Western languages.

INDEX

Abel-Rémusat, 279
Acollas, Émile, 275–6
Akashi, 85
Alcock, Sir Rutherford, 25–6, 29, 32, 43–5, 47, 49, 57–8, 310n
Alliance Française, 349n
Ando Nobumasa, 33
Ando Tarō, 137, 334–5n
Annam, French involvement in, 6, 10, 119f
Anthologie Japonaise, 279
Aoki Shūzō, 129, 173, 332n, 334n
Army Ministry, Japanese, 239, 243, 271
Army Staff College, 189–91, 349n
Arrivet, 206–7, 349n
Art Nouveau, 285
Aston, W. G., 279
Astruc, Zacharie, 282
Austria, 22
Aventures de Télémaque, 277
Azuma, 360n

Bakufu: relations with foreign countries, 5, 31–3, 46, 58, 61; political position of, 23–4, 36–7, 39, 41, 46, 48; special relationship with France, 48f, 225–8, 245, 270, 301, 311n; reforms, 54–6, 65–6, 236, 312n; foreign loan plan, 56, 62–4, 70
Balloy, Marie – René – Davy de Chavigné de, 106–8, 117, 159–60, 163, 341n, 356n, 362n
Bansho Shirabesho, 270
Barbedienne, 292
Barlandier, 226
Barthélemy St. Hilaire, 327n
Baudelaire, 281
Beaumont, A. de, 281, 292, 364n
Bellecourt, Duchesne de, 24f, 59–61, 95, 108, 220, 230, 282, 293, 295, 300, 307n, 308n, 314n, 348n, 352n

Berger, K., 365n
Berthaut, 185, 191–3, 195, 243, 347n
Berthemy, Jules, 92–3, 99–100, 103–5, 114–16, 152–6, 175, 200, 274, 297, 299–300, 321n, 324n, 326n, 339–40n, 345n
Bertin, Louis-Émile, 97, 187, 225, 249–52, 360n
Besshi copper mine, 360n
Bibliothèque Nationale, 365n
Bing, S., 283–5
Bizen incident, 71, 317n
Blekman, 31, 308n
Boissonade de Fontarabie, Gustave-Émile, 3, 97, 146, 187–8, 206, 208, 261–9, 273, 287, 329n, 343n, 361–2n, 365n
Bonnard, 289
Bougouin, Captain, 124, 140, 186, 188, 190–1, 194, 242, 334n
Bourboulon, 14f
Bourgarel, Ernest-Julien, 179, 186–7, 191–3, 203
Bourret, F., 232
Bousquet, Georges, 257, 261, 279, 293, 361n
Bowring, Sir John, 15–6
Bracquemond, Félix, 281, 291
Brandt, Max von, 88, 100, 111–3, 152, 154, 325n
Britain and treaty revision, 144–5, 162, 165, 342n
British policy towards Japan, 26, 28, 30, 43–4, 49–51, 57–9, 177
Broglie, Duc de, 91–2, 95, 321n, 324n
Brunat, Paul, 253–4, 360n
Brunet, Jules, 78–82, 236, 242, 319–20n, 357n
Buddhists, Japanese, 69, 83–4, 197, 200, 276
Burty, Philippe, 280, 284, 291, 363n

Cady, J.F., 7
Campenon, General, 130–1, 191
Camus, Lieutenant, 27, 40
Capuchins, 6
Caron, Francois, 14
Catholicism, French support for, 6, 10, 85–93, 276; see also French religious protectorate
Cazeneuve, 78
Cécille, Admiral, 9, 13, 15, 305n
Cernuschi, Henri, 283
Cézanne, 289
Challemel-Lacour, 123–6, 329n
Challié, Captain, 83–4
Chamberlain, B. H., 279
chambers of commerce, 151, 230–1, 296
Chanoine, Charles, 79–82, 154, 237, 241, 243, 257, 312n, 317n, 357n
Chapdelaine, Father, 7, 17
Chef-d'oeuvre des arts industriels, 291
Chesneau, Ernest, 282, 291, 294
Chishima, 251, 355n
Chōshū, 27, 43–6, 51, 54, 58–60, 73, 101, 186–7, 190, 195, 229, 238, 240, 242, 271, 311n, 318n, 332n
Christianity, 69, 83–4, 87, 320n, 348n; see also Catholicism; Urakami Christians; French missionaries; French religious protectorate
Christofle, 292
Civil Code, 262–4, 275, 287
cloisonné, 291
Code of Civil Procedure, 262
Code of Criminal Procedure, 262
Coetlogon, 82
Coignet, François, 254–5, 360n
Colbert, 7, 14
Collin, Raphael, 365n
Collin de Plancy, Victor-Joseph, 188, 206–7, 224, 346n
Collinot, E., 281, 292
Commercial Convention (1866), 50, 147, 160, 229, 338n
Compagnie des Forges et Chantiers, 224
Compagnie des Indes, 7
Comptoire d'Escompte, 8
Conant, Ellen, 365n
Congress of Orientalists (1873), 280
Conte, 189, 205
Cook, H. F., 333n

Coullet, Jacques, 53, 56, 68, 221, 314n
coup d'état of 1868, 70
Courant, Maurice, 279
Courbet, Admiral, 132, 140
Cowley, Lord, 63–4, 309n
Crimean War, 13, 16
Criminal Code, 262

Dajōkan, 238, 264
Dammouse, 292
Davidov, 197
Decazes, Duc de, 92, 248, 300, 321n, 340n
decorative arts, Japanese influence on French, 291–3
Degas, 286, 289, 364n
Delprat, Charles, 11–14, 305n
Descharmes, 130, 142, 154, 240, 243–4, 317n, 354n
Deshima, 26
Diet, Japanese, 183–4, 348–9n
Drouyn de Lhuys, 38, 40–6, 49, 60 -1, 64–8, 227, 229–30, 297, 309n, 310n, 313n, 356n
Dubail, Pierre-Georges, 184
Dubois de Jancigny, 21–2
Dubousquet, Albert, 238–40, 242, 318n, 323n, 326n, 357n, 360–1n
Dumas, Alexandre, 277
Dunham, Arthur, 7
Dupont, 247–9, 359n
Duranty, Édouard, 282
Duret, Théodore, 283
Dury, Léon, 271–2, 275
Duseigneur, Edmond, 229, 232, 313n, 355–6n
Dutch East India Company, 281

École des Beaux Arts, 280, 285
École de l' Étoile du Matin, see Marianites
École de langue française, 206–7, 349–50n
École des Langues Orientales, 279
École du droit francais, 205
École Supérieure de Guerre, 185, 194
Edo (Yedo, Yeddo), 18, 27–8, 30–1, 34, 39, 42, 68
Education Ministry, Japanese, 271–2, 274, 283

Eidelberg, M., 292–3
Élémens de la Grammaire Japonaise, 279
Elgin, Lord, 1, 17
Emperor (Kōmei), 32, 35–7, 308n
Enomoto Takeaki, 128, 173, 319n, 330n, 350n
Etō Shimpei, 98, 115, 258, 260–1, 361n
European solidarity in Japan, 26, 36, 44, 49, 112, 325–6n, 343n
Evett, Elise, 293–5

Falize, Lucien, 292
Fénélon, 277
Fenollosa, Ernest, 286
Ferry, Jules, 120, 126, 131–3, 135–6, 140–2, 300, 332n, 365n
First Higher School, Tokyo, 206, 208, 274–5
Flury Hérard, 68, 314–5n
Focillon, Henri, 288
Forcade, Bishop, 9
foreign employees in Japan, 252–3, 363n
Foreign Ministry (Gaimushō), 271
Formosa, see Taiwan
Fornier-Duplan, Captain, 9, 13
Franco-Prussian War, effects of, 75, 90, 94, 99, 111, 146, 353n; Japanese neutrality during, 111–13
François, 209–210, 346n
French activities in East Asia, 6f, 110, 113, 115, 327n
French assessments of Japanese military power 145, 179, 181–182
French diplomats, character of, 3, 66–7, 74, 98–9, 102–9, 298f, 318n
French East India Company, 7
French education, influence of, 259–60
French education and language in Japan, 204f, 242, 269f, 297, 346n, 349–50n, 363n
French industry and Japan, 323n, 345n; see also modernisation; warships
French interest in entente with Japan, 119f, 161, 331–3n, 335n
French interest in Japanese art, 244, 280f, 364–6n
French law, influence of, 260–6, 361–2n; see also Boissonade; modernisation

French local government, influence of, 259
French military missions to Japan, 53, 78, 88, 96, 102, 105, 169, 189–95, 236–44, 312n, 322n, 324n, 346n, 357n
French missionaries, 7–12, 20, 69, 83, 85–6, 89–93, 113, 116, 198, 200, 204–5, 276, 304n, 305n, 320–1n, 326n; see also French religious protectorate
French National Assembly, 90, 132, 174, 345n, 350n
French naval assistance to Japan, 52, 71, 318n; see Verny; Bertin
French naval power, 10, 16, 19, 36, 62, 94, 112, 302, 307n
French police system, influence of, 256–9, 361n
French policy towards Japan, general character of, 3, 19, 59–60, 74–5, 110–11, 115, 296f, 318n
French policy towards Korea, 7, 115–17, 211, 351n
French relations with Britain, 15–16, 28, 44, 49–51, 59–60, 63–4, 68, 76, 78, 88, 92, 94, 162, 172, 213, 298, 316n, 344n
French relations with China, 7 10, 119f, 330n
French relations with Russia, 146, 210, 212–18, 296
French religious protectorate, 93, 196f, 349n
French Revolution, 7, 67, 277
French trade: with China, 7, 17, 223, 353–4n; with Japan, 12, 24, 75, 145, 158, 219–34, 296, 302, 306n, 352–7n
French views of the Japanese economy, 107, 356n
French views of the Japanese political situation, 31f, 104, 107, 171, 182–4
French views of Japan and the Japanese, 11–12, 35, 100, 102, 104–8, 135, 170–1, 178f, 278f, 293–5, 314n, 334n, 345n, 347n, 352n
Freycinet, 184, 200
fudai daimyō, 35
fukoku kyōhei, 74
Fukuoka Kōtei, 273
Fukuzawa Yukichi, 257, 278–9

Furansu -jihan, 270
Futsugakusha , 272
Futsugo Meiyō, 270

Gaikokugo Gakkō, 272
Gallé, 292
Gambet-Gross, Prosper, 258, 269, 361n
Gauguin, 289
Gautier, Judith, 276, 364n
Genrō-in, 264, 268, 272
Geofroy, Francis-Henri-Louis de, 105–6, 116–18, 157–60, 205, 244, 248–9, 273, 324–5n
Germany and treaty revision, 146, 157, 162–3, 165
German influence on Japan, 100, 185–7, 189–92, 195, 205, 208–9, 262–3, 318n, 346–7n
Getsuyōkai, 186
Goncourt brothers, 281–2, 284–5, 288
Gonse, Louis, 284, 294
Gotō islands, 82, 86
Gotō, Shōjirō, 133–4, 333n, 343n
Gros, Baron, 9–11, 17–20, 269, 304n
Granville, Lord, 95, 177, 337n
Gubbins, J. H., 279, 336n
Guérin, Rear-Admiral, 15, 21
Guimet, Émile, 283–4, 365n

Hachisuka, Mochiaki, 125–6, 128–9, 163
Hainan, 351n
Hakodate, 18, 21, 42, 62, 81, 271, 313n
Hall, I., 361n
Hammond, Edmund, 30, 59, 62
Hanotaux, 175, 207, 213–16, 300, 344n, 351n
Hara Takashi (Kei), 131, 273, 286
Harmand, François-Jules, 173–5, 181, 185, 187– 8, 207, 209, 211–18, 300, 344n, 346– 7n, 351n, 356n
Harris, Townsend, 1, 26–27, 35, 61, 322n
Hashidate, 251
hatamoto, 55
Hayashi Tadamasa, 284, 286
Heigakuryō, 271
Heurtier, Auguste, 20
Heusken, 27
Hiroshige, 287–291

Hizen, 101
Hō Takushu, 333n
Hokkaidō (Yézo), 79–81, 270, 315n, 319n, 357n
Hokusai, 281, 285, 287–9, 365n
Holland, 22, 24, 26, 44, 49, 61, 78
Home Ministry, (*Naimushō*) , 259, 271
House of Commons, 63, 315n
Hyōgo, opening of, 18, 29–30, 49

Ii Naosuke, 23, 31
Ikeda, Colonel, 346n
Ikeda (Nagaaki) mission, 41–43, 45, 65, 309n
Ikuno mines, 246, 254
Imperial Court, 33, 41, 49, 73
Imperial University (Tokyo), 206–9, 271–6, 349n
Inoue Kakugorō, 333n
Inoue Kaoru, 109, 117, 121, 125–8, 131, 134, 137, 139–40, 142, 163f, 179, 190, 196, 203, 267–8, 328–34n, 336–8n, 341n, 343n
Inoue Kowashi, 267–8, 271, 361n
Inukai Tsuyoshi (Ki), 333n
Irie Bunrō, 270
Ishii Takashi, 2, 37, 55
Ishizuki Minoru, 274
Italy, 78, 152–3, 157, 223
Itagaki Taisuke, 115, 133
Itakura Katsukiyo, 311n
Itō Hirobumi, 128, 133–4, 139–40, 160, 174, 184, 187, 190, 196, 256, 268, 277, 328n, 330n, 332n, 336n, 343n, 347n, 360n
Itō Yukio, 251–252
Itsukushima, 251
Iwakura mission, 90–1, 95, 150–1, 153
Iwakura Tomomi, 78, 87, 90–1, 95, 102, 114–15, 121, 149–51, 153, 159, 195, 267, 278, 322–3n, 326n, 328n, 339n

Jacquemart, Albert, 295
Jacquemart, F., 356n
Japan Herald, 183, 355n
Japan Times, 63, 315n
Japan and South East Asia, 180–1, 211
Japanese arms purchases, 56, 217, 311–12n, 314–5n
Japanese attitudes towards foreigners,

25, 74, 83, 88, 93, 102, 196, 278, 325n, 338n, 341n, 347n
Japanese diplomatic missions, 29, 38, 40–3, 45, 279, 309n, 312–313n
Japanese policy towards Korea, 106, 115–17, 121, 128, 131f, 179–80, 266–7, 326n, 328n, 330n
Japanese prints, 281f
Japanese relations with China, 113–14, 118, 127–8, 132f, 179–81, 266–7, 326n, 328n, 330n
Japanese spying, French suspicions of, 181, 346n
Japanese students in France, 55, 191, 194–5, 244–5, 261, 274f, 348n, 359n
Japonaiserie, 290
Japonisme, 4, 280, 285, 287–8, 290–2, 365n
Jaurès, Admiral, 38, 44, 245
Jiyūtō, 133
Johnston, W. R., 292–3
Jourdan, Captain, 240–1
Justice Ministry, Japanese, 257, 261–2, 264, 272

Kabayama, Sukenori, 225, 250, 337n, 355n
Kaisei Gakkō, 271, 350n
Kaiseijo, 270
Kanagawa, see Yokohama
Kanin, Prince, 185, 194, 245, 346n, 359n
Katsu Awa, 317n
Katsura Tarō, 195, 242, 271, 358n
Kawaji Toshiyoshi, 257–8
Kawamura Sumiyoshi, 249
Keishi-chō, 256–259
Kido Takayoshi (Kōin), 74, 115
Kim Ok-kiun, 131, 133, 332n
Kinoshita Hiroji, 275, 363n
Kiritsu Kōshō Kaisha, 285
kōbugattai, 37
Kokumin, 217
Komatsu, Prince, 186, 194, 347n
Komatsu Tatewaki, 83, 85,
Kōryūsai, 365n
Kosiki, 364n
Kōunkan, 271
Kurimoto Joun, 6, 257, 270, 278, 314–15n
Kuroda Kiyotaka, 140, 173, 186–7, 328n, 334n, 357n

Kuroda Seiki, 286–7, 365n
Kyoto, 33–5, 37, 39, 41, 73, 255, 272

L'Écho du Japon, 139, 259, 269, 318n, 328n, 356n
L'Étendard, 282
L'Usurpateur, 364n
La Belle Sainara, 364n
La Civilisation Japonaise, 280
La Marchande des Sourires, 364n
La Princesse Jaune, 364n
La Vie de Jésus, 276
Labry, Lieutenant de, 186
Lacambre, G., 364n
Laguerre, Admiral, 16
Lalique, 292
Lapeyrère, P., 358n
Laroque, Louis, 360n
Lebon, Captain, 261, 357–8n
Le Creusot, 251
Le Japon Artistique, 285
Le Japon de Nos Jours, 261, 279
Le Poer Trench, P., 212
Li Hung-Chang, 131, 199, 337n
Limoges, 366n
Longford, J. H., 279
Loti, Pierre, 293
Louis-Philippe, 7, 9, 21
Louvre, 285, 365n
Lyons, 226, 255, 283, 355–6n

Madame Chrysanthème, 293
Maeda Masana, 275, 284, 363n
Manet, 289, 291
Manga, 365n
Marianites, 205–6, 228, 233, 349–50n
Marie-Antoinette, 280
Marquerie, Lieutenant-Colonel, 239–40
Marshall, Frederick, 123, 126, 128, 301–2, 329n
Matsukata Masayoshi, 107, 128, 187, 347n
Matsushima, 251
Meckel, Major, 192, 195, 226, 243
Medzini, Meron, 2, 313n
Meihōryō 261
Meiji Art Society, 286–7
Meiji emperor, 5, 71–3, 76, 80, 84, 183, 194, 196–8, 202, 243, 266, 308n

Meiji government: 71–4, 80, 82f, 320n; and Japanese foreign policy, 3, 110f
Meiji Hōritsu Gakkō, 262
Meiji Restoration, causes of, 1; French views of, 100–2; Western neutrality during, 76–78, 319n
Mermet de Cachon, Eugène – Emmanuel, 31, 34, 52, 62, 64, 269–71, 312n, 314n
Messageries Impériales, 220, 226, 353n
Midon, 349n
Military Academy (*Shikan Gakkō*), 192, 209, 241, 243, 274
Military Affairs Ministry (*Hyōbushō*), 238, 240
Millet, 290
Ministry of Agriculture, Commerce and Public Works, 12, 20, 53, 231, 233
Ministry of the Interior, 98, 258–9
Ministry of War, 65, 80, 236, 239
Mitsui, 284
Mitsukuri Rinshō, 261
Miura Gorō, 130–131, 139, 186, 333n, 336–7n, 347n, 358n
modernization, French contributions to Japanese, 4, 74, 96–100, 102, 104, 234, 236f 298–9, 301–302, 357n
Moges, Marquis de, 22
Monet, 289–291
Moniteur des Soies, 227, 230, 232–3, 254
Montblanc, Comte des Cantons de, 64, 72, 83, 238, 314–15n, 323n
Montebello, Comte de, 76, 87
Montesquieu, 277
Motoki Shōzaemon, 270
Mount Fuji, 67
Moustier, Marquis de, 57, 63–5, 67–8, 72, 85, 316n
Munier, Lieutenant-Colonel, 240–2, 324n
Murakami Eishun, 270, 272, 362n
Muther, Richard, 286
Mutsu Munemitsu, 173
Musée Guimet, 283

Nabis, the, 289
Nagai Michio, 260
Nagasaki, 11–12, 18, 35, 42, 51, 69, 220, 229, 270–2, 281, 313n, 330n, 335n; see also Urakami incident

Nakae Chōmin, 272–3, 275, 277
Napoléon I, 276, 305n
Napoléon III, 6, 8, 19–20, 309n , 315n
Navy Ministry: French, 15–17, 20, 45, 95, 97, 310n, 313n; Japanese, 97, 224, 271
Neale, Colonel, 30, 35–7, 39
New York Times, 365n
Nihon Shoki, 279
Niigata, 18, 27, 30
Nippon, 217–18
Nishi Amane, 239
northern daimyō, 76–8
Numa Morikazu, 257

Ogasawara Nagamichi, 39
Oka Yoshitake, 325n, 341n
Ohier, Admiral, 70, 317n
Okakura, Kakuzō, 286
Ōkubo Toshimichi, 74, 106, 115, 195, 256, 259, 266, 268–9, 279
Ōkuma Shigenobu, 74, 168–70, 173, 203, 323n, 343n, 360n
Oliphant, Laurence, 63, 315n
Ōmura Masujirō, 237–8
Oriental Bank, 77, 314n
Osaka, 18, 29–30, 34, 42, 49–50, 237, 333n,
Osouf, Mgr., 188, 196, 199, 205
Ōtsuka Takematsu, 2
Outrey, Ange-Maxime, 75f, 94f, 111f, 149, 231, 247, 318–21n, 323n, 339n
Ōyama Iwao, 129–30, 189–92, 194, 347n
Ozaki Yukio, 333n

Paris Convention (1864), 42–3, 45–6, 313n
Paris Exposition: of 1867, 57, 64, 114, 254, 282, 285, 291; of 1878, 275, 284–5, 291; of 1889, 285; of 1900, 280, 285
Parkes, Sir Harry, 32, 47, 49–51, 57–8, 62, 71, 75, 89, 94–5, 111, 140, 152, 155–6, 229, 311n, 329n, 336n, 367n
Pasteur, Louis, 233, 357n
Patenôtre, Jules, 131, 137, 142, 332n, 334–5n
pébrine, 223, 233–4
Pelegrin, Henri, 255

Petit-Thouars, Commandant du, 319n
Petitjean, Bishop Bernard , 271
People's Rights movement, 144, 166, 198, 275, 277
Perry, Commodore, 1, 13, 15–16, 20, 294
Pigneau de Béhaine, 6
Pila, Ulysse, 355n
Pissarro, 289–290
Plunkett, Sir Francis, 134–5, 138–40, 164, 166, 197, 334–7n
Poèmes de la Libellule, 276, 364n
Pompadour, Madame de, 280
Pope Leo XIII, 196–7, 199–203, 210
Power, T. F., 333n
Projet de Code de Procédure Criminelle pour L'Empire du Japon, 265
porcelain, 280, 291
Presseisen, Ernst, 347n, 357–8n
Princesses d'Amour, 364n
Promenades Japonaises, 284
Promenades Japonaises – Tokyo – Nikko, 284
Prussia, 22, 61, 78, 100, 111–12
Pruyn, Robert, 35, 61
Public Works Ministry, Japanese, 271, 361n

Quai d'Orsay (French Foreign Ministry): policy of 2, 10, 38, 57, 65–6, 75, 99, 116, 126, 161, 210, 297f, 342n

Randon, Marshal, 357n
Recueil de dessins pour l'art et l'industrie, 364n
Régamey, Felix, 284
Rémi Schmidt, 232
Rémusat, Comte de, 90–1, 95, 149–51, 339n
Renan, Ary, 294
Renan, Ernest, 276
Renoir, Auguste, 283
Revon, Michel, 207, 209, 276, 293
Revue des Deux Mondes, 11–12, 279, 282
Revue Française du Japon, 206–8, 263
Ribot, 194–195, 207
Richardson (Namamugi) incident, 27, 35
Richemont, Comte de, 90–91

Rigault de Genouilly, Admiral, 17
Roches, Léon, 2–3, 32; 43f, 81–5, 96, 99, 223, 226–30, 236–7, 245–6, 270, 272, 297, 299, 301–2, 308–14n, 317n, 339n, 352n, 355–7n, 359n, 365n; personal policy of, 2, 65, 300, 316n; repudiation of, 57f, 315–17n; and the Meiji Restoration, 68f, 318n
Rodin, 290
Roesler, Hermann, 140, 337n
rōjū, 33, 44, 48, 51, 311n
Roquette, Guillaume de, 109, 118, 160–1, 231, 264–6, 325n, 356n
Rosny, Léon de, 279
Rousseau, Jean-Jacques, 277
Rousseau, Eugène, 292
Rousseau, Théodore, 286, 290, 366n
Russell, Lord, 30
Russia: activities in East Asia, 13, 22, 61, 134, 171, 210–11; and treaty revision, 146, 157; attitude towards Japan, 351n; French attitudes towards, 117, 187;
Ryūchikai, 284
Ryūkyū islands, 9, 13, 15, 113–14, 118, 127, 269, 306n, 326n, 328n, 337n

Saigō Takamori, 87, 105–106, 115, 257, 326n
Saigō Tsugumichi, 114, 139, 174, 186, 250,
257, 336n
Saibikan, 271
Saigusa Hiroto, 252–253
Saint-Saens, 364n
Saionji Kimmochi, 271, 275, 278, 286, 364n
Sakai incident, 72
Samejima Hisanobu, 158, 261
samurai: xenophobic, 23, 27, 33–4, 71–2, 94, 333n; reforming, 5, 58, 73–74, 101; discontent, 91
Sango Benran, 270
sankin kōtai, 54
Satow, Ernest, 31, 58, 311n, 366n
Satsuma, 27, 34–5, 37, 41, 51, 54, 58–9, 63–4, 72–3, 81, 83, 86, 88, 96, 101, 105, 114, 139, 186–7, 238, 240, 254, 282, 306n, 311n, 315n, 318n, 320n, 323–4n, 329n, 336n, 346–7n

Savatier, Dr., 247
Sawa Nobuyoshi, 87
Say, Léon, 347n
Schnell, Ed., 355n
Schwartz, W. L., 293, 364n
Sei-in, 268
Seitaisho, 323
Semallé, Comte de, 332n
Seurat, 289
Sèvres, 365–6n
Shibata, Asako and Michio, 314n
Shibata (Takenaka) misssion, 279, 312n
Shibusawa, Eiichi, 360n
Shimonoseki Expedition, 43–6, 48–9, 60, 67, 226
Shimonoseki Indemnity, 46, 49, 66, 78, 153–4
Shimonoseki Intervention (Triple Intervention), 212–17, 296, 300
Shinohara, Hiroshi, 357–8n
Shizuoka, 363n
shogun, see Bakufu; Tokugawa Yoshinobu
Sichel, Philippe, 283
Siebold, Alexander von, 31, 315n
Siebold, Philip von, 281, 309n
Sienkiewicz, Joseph-Adam, 124, 127, 129, 131, 133, 135–8, 140, 142, 162f, 188, 190f, 250, 267, 300, 302, 331–4n, 343n, 345n, 347–51n, 354n, 362n
silk, French interest in Japanese, 12, 48, 60, 75, 98, 163–4, 175, 220–1, 226, 229–34, 296, 339n, 352–3n, 355–7n
Sino-Japanese War (1894–5), 210–12, 244, 251–2, 295–6
Soejima Taneomi, 89, 104, 115, 152, 324n, 326n, 339n
Société des Études Japonaises, Chinoises, Tartares, Indo-chinoises, 279, 283
Société des Forges et Chantiers de la Méditerranée, 174, 354n
Société des Missions Étrangères, 6, 9, 199
Société du Jing-lar, 282
Société Française d'Exportation et d'Importation (*Société Franco-Japonaise*), 52, 56–57, 64, 70, 77, 227–8
Société Générale, 53, 77, 354n

Société Japonaise pour la Propagation de la langue française au Japon (*Société de langue française*) 206, 273–4
Sone Arasuke, 271, 344–345n
sonnō jōi, see samurai
south-western *han*, 58–9, 66, 69, 81; fears of Tokugawa revival, 51
Spuller, 344n
St. Cyr, 241, 257, 358n
St. Quentin, Ange-Guillaume de, 105–6, 116, 247–8, 324n, 356–7n
Stanley, Lord, 315n
Stirling, Admiral, 13, 16
Sullivan, M., 364n
Syndicat Industriel pour le Tonkin, l'Anname, la Cochinchine et le Japon, 354n

Taikoun, see Bakufu; Tokugawa Yoshinobu
Taiwan (Formosa), 130, 135, 185, 216, 335n, 351n; Japanese expedition to, 114–15, 118, 266, 326n
Tajima Ōshin, 237, 240, 243
Takahashi Kunitarō, 1
Takao, 360n
Takashima Kayuemon, 255
Takehashi Mutiny, 265
Takemoto Masao, 37
Takezoe Shinichirō, 131–4, 332–3n
Tanabe Taichi, 64, 315n
Tanaka Fujimaro, 169, 286
Tanaka Sadao, 246
Tani Kanjō, 186–7, 194, 343n
Tardy de Montravel, Captain, 13
tariffs, 18, 20, 50–1, 145, 147, 157, 173–4, 229, 231, 345n
Tatsuridō, 272
telegraphic comunication, 24, 75
Temps, Le, 188
Terashima (Terajima) Munenori, 87–9, 97, 116, 151, 153–5, 157, 340–1n
Terauchi, Masatake, 359n
Thibaudier, 246–8
Thouvenel, 28–30, 300
Tientsin conventions, 140–1, 177, 179, 329n
Times, The, 333–4n
Titsingh, Isaac, 281

Tokugawa, see Bakufu
Tokugawa Akitake (Mimbu Tayu), 55, 79, 315n
Tokugawa Yoshinobu (Hitotsubashi Keiki), 41, 54, 59, 69–72, 237, 317n
Tomioka silk filature, 98, 234, 253
Tokyo, 333n
Tokyo Art School, 286
Tosa, 72, 101, 240, 272
Toulouse-Lautrec, 289
Toyama school, 241, 243
Tōyō Jiyū Shimbun, 275
tozama daimyō, 54
Treaty of Edo (1858), 1, 5, 18–20, 147–8; motivation for signing, 8f; negotiation of, 18–19; maintenance of, 24f, 38–9
Treaty of Kanagawa (1854), 1, 13, 20
treaty revision, 97, 103, 106, 109, 125, 143f, 267, 299, 337n, 340–1n
Tricou, Arthur, 108–9, 127, 133, 142, 161, 189, 329–30n, 334n, 347n
Tsuji Shinji, 363n
Tsushima, 28
Turenne d'Aynac, Comte de, 67, 90–2, 95, 97, 99, 102–3, 114, 244, 299, 302, 323n, 339n

Ukiyo-e, 289
Umetani Noboru, 358n
'unequal treaties', see treaty revision
Unebi, 251, 354n
United States, 13, 15, 18, 20, 22. 24, 44, 49, 61, 273; and treaty revision, 157–8
Upton, Major-General, 244
Urakami (Christian persecution) incident, 69–70, 82–91, 103, 321n
Utamaro, 285
Uwajima, ex-daimyo of, 85

Van Gogh, 289–91, 295

Verne, Jules, 276
Verny, Lieutenant François-Léonce, 52, 97, 246–50, 271, 359–60n
Vieillard, Captain, 241
Viel-Castel, Ulric de, 122–3, 126–7, 161, 189, 328–31n
Villaret, de, 178, 191–2, 243
Vuillard, 364n

Wa-Futsu Hōritsu Gakkō, 262, 274
Waddington, 158
wakadoshiyori, 55
warships, Japanese purchase of French, 174, 224–5, 250–2, 344–5n, 360n
Waseda, 350
Watanabe Ikujirō, 267
Watanabe Toshio, 294
Watson, Robert, 95
Westney, D. Eleanor, 256–7
Whistler, 289–91
White Horse Society, 287
Winchester, Charles, 49, 226, 228, 355n

Yamada Akiyoshi, 191, 238
Yamagata Aritomo, 173, 190–2, 195, 238, 244, 328n, 348n, 358n
Yokohama, 18–19, 26, 28, 35–36, 39–42, 67, 70, 219–21, 226, 230, 240, 246, 252–3, 255, 269, 271–2, 341n, 355n; French merchants in, 219–20, 227, 341n; withdrawal of foreign troops from, 93f, 103, 149, 322n, 358n
Yokohama Chamber of Commerce, 68
Yokosuka dockyard, 52, 97, 246–9, 251–2, 254, 270–1, 319n, 322n, 359–60n
Yomiuri, 217
Yoshida Kiyonari, 134–5, 334n

Zola, Émile, 282, 291